Swearing

THE LANGUAGE LIBRARY

EDITED BY DAVID CRYSTAL

The Articulate Computer	*Michael McTear*
The Artificial Language Movement	*J. A. Large*
Children's First School Books	*Carolyn D. Baker & Peter Freebody*
Children's Writing and Reading	*Katharine Perera*
A Child's Learning of English	*Paul Fletcher*
Clichés and Coinages	*Walter Redfern*
A Companion to Old and Middle English Studies	*A. C. Partridge*
A Dictionary of Literary Terms and Literary Theory (third edition)	*J. A. Cuddon*
A Dictionary of Linguistics and Phonetics (third edition)	*David Crystal*
The Foreign-Language Barrier	*J. A. Large*
How Conversation Works	*Ronald Wardhaugh*
An Informal History of the German Language	*W. B. Lockwood*
Language and Class in Victorian England	*K. C. Phillips*
The Language of *1984*	*W. F. Bolton*
Language, Society and Identity	*John Edwards*
Languages in Competition	*Ronald Wardhaugh*
Modern Englishes: Pidgins and Creoles	*Loreto Todd*
Non-Standard Language in English Literature	*N. F. Blake*
Oral Cultures Past and Present	*Viv Edwards and Thomas J. Sienkewicz*
Puns	*Walter Redfern*
Rhetoric: The Wit of Persuasion	*Walter Nash*
Seeing Through Language	*Ronald Carter and Walter Nash*
Sense and Sense Development (revised)	*R. A. Waldron*
Shakespeare's English	*W. F. Bolton*
The Study of Dialect	*K. M. Petyt*
Swearing	*Geoffrey Hughes*
Words in Time	*Geoffrey Hughes*
The Writing Systems of the World	*Florian Coulmas*

SWEARING

A Social History of Foul Language, Oaths and Profanity in English

Geoffrey Hughes

BLACKWELL
Oxford UK & Cambridge USA

First published 1991

Basil Blackwell Ltd
108 Cowley Road, Oxford, OX4 1JF, UK

Basil Blackwell, Inc.
3 Cambridge Center
Cambridge, Massachusetts 02142, USA

British Library Cataloguing in Publication Data

A CIP catalogue record for this book is available from the British Library.

Library of Congress Cataloging in Publication Data

Hughes, Geoffrey, 1939–
Swearing : a social history of foul language, oaths, and profanity in English / by Geoffrey Hughes.
p. cm. — (The Language library)
Includes bibliographical references.
ISBN 0-631-16593-2
1. Swearing—History. 2. English language—Social aspects.
3. English language—Slang—History. I. Title. II. Series.
PE3724.S85H8 1991
427—dc20 90-23129
CIP

Typeset in $10\frac{1}{2}$ on $12\frac{1}{2}$ pt Ehrhardt
by Photo·graphics, Honiton, Devon
Printed in Great Britain by
T. J. Press Ltd, Padstow, Cornwall

Contents

Contents

Preface

In his *Worlde of Wordes*, published in 1598, John Florio defined Italian *fottere* as 'to iape, to sard, to fucke, to swive, to occupy,' running through the whole gamut of copulatory registers with typical Renaissance exuberance. A century and a half later, two society ladies brimming with propriety, 'very much commended Dr Johnson for the omission of all naughty words' from his *Dictionary*. 'What! my dears!' the doughty Doctor archly replied, 'then you have been looking for them?' In 1896, Dr J. S. Farmer became involved in a lawsuit when his publishers refused to publish certain obscene words in his dictionary of slang. Today an editor is more likely to incur censure for prissiness or cowardice through omitting words which are widely in use (outside the range of ears polite) but nevertheless regarded as not 'fit to print'.

These anecdotes and observations bring out the perennial ambivalence of attitudes towards foul language. Similarly, although swearing obviously thrives in astonishing profusion in many quarters and is never heard in others, there is also hesitancy over accepting it as a proper topic for public display or serious discussion. There are sound academic reasons for this, for swearing exists in such variegated forms, from the deadliest curse and most serious asseveration down to the flippant ejaculation of annoyance, that often the exact meaning and intention of the form of words lie only with the speaker. The fields are hedged about with all manner of complex pressures, personal, societal, religious, sexual, and other forms of taboo which still seem only imperfectly understood. Origins and practices are alike elusive and imperfectly documented, as tends to happen when tacit understandings are at work. A researcher from a different period may thus easily misinterpret a meaning or a causation entirely. Why, for instance, should the word *donkey* make a curiously sudden appearance in the mid-eighteenth century? Why should *coney* make an equally odd disappearance from the vocabulary? The explanations are similar, involving shifts in the respective semantic fields. *Ass* was acquiring an uncomfortable phonetic proximity to *arse*, just as *coney* was to *cunt*, requiring both terms to be dropped and replaced. An outsider to a culture may be equally non-plussed: what would a newly-arrived visitor to Australia make of the observation 'He's a good bastard'? How do rational explanations cope with the paradox Defoe commented on with exasperation: 'They call the dogs sons of whores, and the men sons of bitches'?

Not the least of the problems facing an historical study of swearing is that of organization. I am reminded of the memorable images used by Barbara Strang in her *History of English* twenty years ago, when she wrote in her Preface of the 'ceaselessly, oceanically, heaving, swelling, flowing, ungraspable mass that historians corset into manageable chunks on to which quasi-scientific labels can be stuck'. This awareness leads to the major question: is it more illuminating to focus on different segments of time and consider developments within each phase, or to trace themes across time? Each mode has its advantages and drawbacks. I have preferred the former approach, chiefly because modes and referents in swearing do not appear to be constant: a topic like 'Sexual Swearing from *Beowulf* to *Who's Afraid of Virginia Woolf*' would have to pass over several of the earlier centuries in tantalized silence, while, conversely, the theme of 'Oaths of Heroic Undertaking' would run dismally dry in modern times. The fascinating convention of ritual insult known as *flyting* has a disjunctive history, flourishing in Viking times, dwindling away in Middle English, reviving as a Scots literary genre in the Renaissance, and then largely petering out in Modern English, although a continuation can be seen in the cognate practice of 'sounding' in black American English.

As Murray put it with his usual incontestable clarity in his Preface to the *OED*, 'No one man's English is *all* English.' This observation becomes highly pertinent to the demotic domain, where a person may have a huge general vocabulary but will usually have highly personal preferences in swearing, drawn from background factors of family, school, class and calling. My own decent bourgeois background meant that the most vehement personal denunciations and expletives heard from my elders and betters (as they were archaically styled) were 'that bloody fool!' or 'the bastard!' and the strongest exclamation of frustration or anger was 'For Christ's sake!' I do not recall hearing the unprintable 'four-letter words' used until I went into national service: at school the word which excited greatest erotic interest was *friction*, since it was defined in the dictionary as 'heat generated by two bodies rubbing together'. Those days are over. Today, in film and television dialogue, as well as in much family discourse, the old taboos are noisily disintegrating, not without resistance or protest. The old censorship of *pas devant les enfants* has been reversed into *pas devant les parents*.

Half a century ago, Robert Graves observed in the opening page of his *Lars Porsena: The Future of Swearing*: 'Of recent years in England there has been a noticeable decline of swearing and foul language . . . .' It is unlikely that he would now take the same view. Both the facts of the resurgence of swearing and the possible social explanations supply the matter for the last part of this study.

It may be asked why I have included the older term *oaths* in addition to *swearing*, which is obviously more current. The choice is not simply that of preference for a philological archaism. *Oaths* still resonates with the formality and seriousness which verbal undertakings have traditionally been regarded, while *swearing* is now common, personal and largely debased. Since this study was partly intended to explore some of the older, highly potent workings of words in society, the more venerable term seemed appropriate.

Clearly, this is a field which Eric Partridge made very much his own. In dedicating this work to him (*in absentia*), I also acknowledge copious assistance from his pioneering efforts in exploring the linguistic underworld. Ashley Montagu's fine study, *The Anatomy of Swearing*, issued some twenty years ago, has also proved a valuable source of historical documentation.

Finally, I owe a great debt of gratitude to Philip Carpenter of Basil Blackwell for his enthusiastic backing of this book right from the inchoate and muddled first draft, and to my Editor, David Crystal, who has always been forthcoming with sound advice and constructive assistance. Andrew McNeillie of Basil Blackwell was most competent and supportive in the final stages of production.

G. H.

Pineslopes, Transvaal

Acknowledgements

The authors and publishers wish to thank the following for permission to use copyright material: Peter Carey, Faber and Faber Limited, and the University of Queensland Press for an extract from *Oscar and Lucinda*; The Estate of Philip Larkin and Faber and Faber Limited for extracts from *High Windows*; Stephen Ullmann and Basil Blackwell Limited for an extract from *Semantics*; A. P. Watt Limited on behalf of The Trustees of the Robert Graves Copyright Trust for extracts from *The Future of Swearing and Improper Language* and from *Difficult Questions, Easy Answers*; David Lodge and William Heinemann Limited for an extract from *Nice Work*.

Sources and Abbreviations

THIS study is, of necessity, heavily dependent on the master-work on semantic change in English, the *Oxford English Dictionary* (*OED*). For economy of reference, a raised 'O' is used (e.g. 1934°) to refer to the main *Dictionary* (1884–1928), which was the collaboration of Murray (pre-eminently), Bradley, Craigie, Onions and Furnivall, 'with the assistance of many scholars and men of science'. A raised 'S' refers to the *OED Supplement* (1972–86), produced by Dr Robert Burchfield and his research team at Oxford. The fourth and last volume, published in 1986, completes what is clearly a worthy sequel to its predecessor, so aptly described by Otto Jespersen as 'that splendid monument of English scholarship'. Although the two sequences were consolidated in 1990 into the Second Edition, I have preferred to keep references to them separate, since apart they record changing policies and attitudes towards swearing, foul language and profanity. This acknowledgement of logophiliac dependence is in no way intended to implicate any Oxford lexicographer in the inferences and conclusions which follow.

Other abbreviations used are:

OE	Old English	used interchangeably
A-S	Anglo-Saxon	
ME	Middle English	
Mn.E	Modern English	
ON	Old Norse	
OF	Old French	
COD	*Concise Oxford Dictionary*	
DSAE	*Dictionary of South African English*	
EDD	*English Dialect Dictionary*	
EETS	*Early English Text Society*	
ODQ	*Oxford Dictionary of Quotations*	
THES	*Times Higher Education Supplement*	
TLS	*Times Literary Supplement*	

To
Eric Partridge
intrepid explorer
of the lexical underworld

I

A Cursory Introduction

The air is full of our cries. But habit is a great deadener.

Samuel Beckett

Oaths are the fossils of piety.

George Santayana

Deceive boys with dice, but men with oaths.

Lysander

'Our family like the word "Budgerigar!" You can really get your tongue round that one.'

informal informant

'*Fuck* originated from a royal injunction at the time of the Plague, when it was very necessary to procreate; it was a code word in which the letters stood for "fornicate under command of the King".'

informal informant

As soon as you deal with it [sex] explicitly, you are forced to choose between the language of the nursery, the gutter and the anatomy class.

C. S. Lewis

'THE English (it must be owned) are rather a foul-mouthed nation,' opined William Hazlitt in 1821.[1] Though this view might be surprising to some, it was not new. Indeed, the nation's time-honoured reputation for swearing reaches back at least to the time of Joan of Arc, when the French termed them 'les Goddems [the goddams]'. Their modern descendants have maintained the tradition by acquiring (from the same quarter) the sobriquet of 'les fuckoffs' (Mort, 1986, p. 77). Between these two points of reference, one thinks of Harry Hotspur enjoining his wife to utter a 'good mouth-filling oath' (as would be befitting a noblewoman), of Queen Elizabeth upholding the practice, of Sir Charles

Sedley's witticism, upon being fined (three centuries ago) the formidable sum of £500, that 'he thought that he was the first man that paid for shitting', and of Robert Graves observing (about half a century ago), that 'Of recent years in England there has been a decline of swearing and foul language' (1936, p. 1).

These observations and notable practitioners remind us of the continuing currency of coarse speech which, though staple to many tongues, has generally been ignored in standard histories of the language, even some of the most recent. The conventional understanding that the levels of discourse should be separated has hardened into an academic practice whereby studies of the 'proper' language (the upper levels) are kept apart from the 'improper' (or lower levels). None of the standard histories of the language has accorded the lower registers or the idioms of obscenity much attention. This is true of both traditional studies, such as those of Jespersen (1905), Baugh (1951), Potter (1963) and Barber (1964), and, less justifiably, of the more recent studies offered under the banner of descriptive linguistics, such as those of Pyles and Algeo (1970), Bloomfield and Newmark (1963) and Leith (1983), which purport to deal with the language 'really' in use, namely the protean varieties of oral usage. The same reticence is found in several excellent linguistic studies of English as an international or world language. These ignore such basic lexical and semantic points of difference as the copious use of *bloody* and *bastard* in Australian English and the use of *motherfucker* and *cocksucker* as a major feature in American English, particularly in black parlance.[2]

For centuries the division of usage into the decent bourgeois standard and the less acceptable lower varieties of slang has been *de rigueur*. The split is notable in the dictionary, where one finds a 'proper' tradition of Bailey (1728), Johnson (1755) and Murray et al. (1884–1928), and a 'canting', slang or underworld tradition (which is actually older) starting in Elizabethan times with works by Harman (1567), Greene (1591) and others, continued by Grose (1785), Farmer and Henley (1890–1904) and Partridge (1937), and is currently showing a resurgence with a variety of works appearing virtually on an annual basis. The title of Francis Grose's exuberantly witty thesaurus, *A Classical Dictionary of the Vulgar Tongue*, highlights for us the semantic shift undergone by *vulgar*. Did he intend the old meaning of the 'common, ordinary or vernacular language used by the majority', or the more class-bound sense of the language used by those 'not reckoned as belonging to good society' or 'lacking in refinement and good taste, uncultured, ill-bred', as the *OED* defines the various categories? The second sense is the more likely, but the persistence of the older meaning reminds us of the robust prevalence of the majoritarian 'vulgar'.

It is a fascinating speculation to consider how far this public separation of registers accords with the facts of private linguistic life. While we can be fairly certain that, say, Jane Austen, George Eliot and Henry James would have maintained roughly the same level of discourse in private life and in their published works, we can be less certain about, say, Charles Dickens, Oscar Wilde and many modern authors. Such observations, though interesting biographically, can (of course) be of only limited general value, since one needs to focus more on conventional mores than on individual cases. At any rate, a convention of linguistic censorship has not always obtained. It seems ironic that a medieval poet, Chaucer, should, in fact, have been one of the few major literary artists who could fearlessly use the whole gamut of the vocabulary without evident reprisal. All the available coarse vocabulary and a stupendous variety of oaths appear in his work. In the North the traditions of flyting kept both strains flourishing until the mid-sixteenth century. But by the time of Shakespeare, thanks to the efforts of the ill-called Master of the Revels in curbing what was styled as Profanity on the Stage, most of the vituperative energies of the tongue had been driven underground. There they have remained until quite recently, emerging only occasionally in spectacularly outrageous flaunters of convention like Rochester, Urquhart and Motteux, Swift and Lawrence. The days when the dandelion could be called the *pissabed*, a heron could be called a *shiterow* and the windhover could be called the *windfucker* have passed away with the exuberant phallic advertisement of the codpiece.

Whatever this Anglo-centric view might suggest, swearing is not universal. According to Montagu, several substantial speech communities, including the American Indians, the Japanese, the Malayans and most Polynesians, do not swear (1973, p. 55). Never the less, in many cultures swearing is fascinating in its protean diversity and poetic creativity, while being simultaneously shocking in its ugliness and cruelty. Whereas Proteus merely changed shape, the same form of an oath or a curse yields many meanings. Swearing draws upon such powerful and incongruous resonators as religion, sex, madness, excretion and nationality, encompassing an extraordinary variety of attitudes, including the violent, the amusing, the shocking, the absurd, the casual and the impossible. Being manifestly not a simple matter, it seems to raise more questions than answers. Why, for example, is swearing not constant in its modes, styles and referents? Why is it that some forms of swearing appear to be universal, while others are more specific to a culture?

Within the English-speaking community, what variants emerge over time on the basis of nationality, class and sex? How is it that the categories of the sacred and the profane become so paradoxically intertwined in oaths? Why is swearing taken more seriously in some periods than others, even being raised at some stages of the culture to a verbal art form? What happens when swearing is driven underground? What is to be deduced from those changes which can be detected over time? These are some of the questions which this book will attempt to answer.

Swearing now encompasses so many disparate forms that some broad distinctions need to be made at the outset. We swear *by*, we swear *that* (something is so), we swear *to* (do something), we swear *at* (somebody or something), and sometimes we swear simply out of exasperation. These different modes might be re-termed by a variety of classical equivalents, asseveration, invocation, imprecation, malediction, blasphemy, profanity and ejaculation, with an admixture of that most complex and unstable category, obscenity. Although we are familiar with all these types now, they have not been constantly present in the past. They represent an agglomeration of various linguistic modes which have evolved over centuries. The crude history of swearing, however named, which this book will unfold in all its strange, violent and comic detail, is that people used mainly to swear *by* or *to*, but now swear mostly *at*.

Although the main framework of the argument will be historical, this introductory chapter will perforce be discursive, surveying various aspects which are integral to the topic. Subsequent chapters will pursue particular themes, tracing their development in given periods of time. Since the main ambit of the argument will be evolutionary, the early chapters will focus more on swearing *by*, while the later will be more concerned with swearing *at*.

As was mentioned previously, swearing shows a curious convergence of the high and the low, the sacred and the profane. From the 'high' dualistic perspective, it is language in its most highly charged state, infused with a religious force recognizable in the remote modes of the spell, the charm and the curse, forms seeking to invoke a higher power to change the world, or support the truthfulness of a claim. At base these varieties are profoundly serious. Although they may sound far-fetched (*drat*, for example, originally meaning 'God rot your bones!' – or any other part of the anatomy), there is always the alarming possibility of the words coming true. However, a major shift has occurred in comparatively recent times in that a quite different emphasis has become dominant. The 'lower' physical faculties of copulation, defecation and urination have come very much to the fore as referents in swearing.

Though they may be deeply wounding, many of these forms of words, such as *bugger off, son of a bitch* and so on deal with literal or practical impossibilities. In this respect they are different in literal potential from the 'high' variety. However, as we shall see, there is a recurring problem of analysis which concerns the degree to which any person (other than the utterer) can know how literally to interpret forms of swearing.

Because 'sacral' notions of language tend to be very powerful at primitive stages of society, taboos have traditionally grown up around offensive usages. Swearing is, in one sense, a violation of these taboos: the 'high' varieties violate the taboo of invoking the name of the deity, while the 'low' are often violations of sexual taboos, especially those concerning incest. Some of the major problems frustrating an attempt at an historical study are consequently the obstacles of suppressed or garbled evidence, found in uncertain etymologies and incomplete semantic histories. Suppression, discussed more fully in subsequent chapters, is a perennial feature. Garbled, mangled or 'minced' oaths are also more common than is generally realized. (*Gorblimey!* is similar to *drat* cited above, being a corruption of *God blind me!*, mainly Cockney in use, dating from *c.*1870[O].)

To modern ears, most oaths are now usually 'demystified' into mere forms of words. Statements are now made under oath only in formal, for instance, legal proceedings, or in such necessary rituals of social and political continuity as taking an oath of allegiance. They form the basic structure of trust on which all society is based, so that every culture has some form of binding oath, as it has some form of verbal taboo. One of the many forms of ritualized reinforcement of an oath is this practice recorded a century ago:

> Among the Nagas of Assam two men will lay hold of a dog or a fowl by head and feet, which is then chopped in two with a single blow of the dao [a tool, half chopper and half sword], this being emblematic of the fate expected to fall the perjurer. Or a man will take hold of the barrel of a gun, a spearhead or a tiger's tooth, and solemnly declare, 'If I do not faithfully perform this my promise, may I fall by this!'[3]

In elucidating the ancient sense of *by* in forms of swearing, the *OED* observes that the word originally 'must have had a local sense "in the presence of", or perhaps "in touch of" some sacred object' though 'to modern apprehension there is apparently no notion of place, but one approaching that of instrumentality or medium'. Invocations of the Almighty, previously so feared and respected, are now generally regarded as 'taking the Lord's name in vain', a phrase which has changed revealingly over the past centuries: its original sense essentially criticized the abuse of the mystical power of the Lord's name; now the kernel of the phrase *in vain* is more suggestive of scepticism about the validity of that power. Corroborating this point are the great numbers of 'self-immolating' oaths and curses, such as *strike me dead! blow me down! shiver me timbers! Gor blimey!* (cited above) and those clearly derived from judicial oaths, such as *so help me!* On this point, the brilliant insight of Vico is pertinent: in his analysis, language evolves through three stages, being originally sacred, then poetic and finally conventional (1948, pp. 306–7). His evolutionary framework of ideas is particularly germane to our theme. It also points up the difficulty of knowing exactly what degree of literalism is being invoked in a particular form of words, without an intimate knowledge of the cultural period concerned.

In the past, when honour and language were more closely interlinked, oaths (or their abrogation) changed the fates of nations. For instance, William of Normandy's claim to the English throne depended initially on no more than his word that Edward the Confessor had formally named him as his successor. When his rival, Harold Godwinson, was shipwrecked and captured on the Normandy coast, William granted him his freedom only upon the exaction of an oath supporting this claim (against Harold's own). However, Harold was subsequently named by Edward the Confessor as his successor, was elected by the English *witenagemot* (Privy Council) and crowned, so that William had to assert his claim by conquest.

Duels have been fought over words carrying only the faintest implication of dishonour. The intensely personal commitment which an oath requires was vividly apparent when Francis I of France abrogated a treaty and declared war on Spain in 1528. Charles V of Spain accused Francis of ungentlemanly behaviour and challenged him to a duel. (It did not take place.) We cannot imagine a similar consequence arising from, for example, Chamberlain challenging Hitler to a duel on the parallel grounds of the Führer's abrogation of their agreement signed at Munich in 1938.

Personal insults can likewise have devastating consequences, belying the naive, childish chant: 'Sticks and stones may break my bones, but words will never hurt me'. One of the more spectacular social instances arose from the visiting card delivered by the Marquess of Queensberry to the Albermarle Club on 18 February 1894 with the words 'To Oscar Wilde posing Somdomite [sic]' (Ellmann, 1988, p. 412). This precipitated the lawsuit and accompanying society scandal which ruined Wilde. Today such a sexual slur would be less likely to incur litigation.

Indeed, a review of a recent biography of Truman Capote began in cavalier fashion: 'Truman Capote was the sort who gives sodomy a bad name.'[4] Never the less, oaths, curses and insults directed at individuals can still have serious repercussions. In modern times, however, cases of *crimen injuria* are more likely to arise from racist slurs than sexual insults.

WORD-MAGIC AND TABOO

Charms, spells and curses (which are treated in more detail in the following chapter) represent survivals of primitive beliefs in word-magic, which tend to become less potent as a society develops. We can see this evolution encapsulated in the semantic history of the word *curse*. Of uncertain origin and unique to English among the European languages, its Old English meaning was 'to damn'; in Middle English the primary sense developed as the ecclesiastical specialization 'to excommunicate or anathematize'. Since then it has steadily diminished in force as a verb, though the noun still has potency. Dr Johnson defined *cursedly* as 'miserably, shamefully', commenting that it was 'a low cant [slang] word'. We can trace the weakened fossilized forms in *curst*, 'perversely cross, contrary', much used of Kate in *The Taming of the Shrew* and *cussed*, the colloquial American variant, recorded from *c.*1848O. An exactly parallel semantic development can be seen in the word *damn*, which has moved from its strictly ecclesiastical 'infernal' sense to one of milder disapproval or exasperation, reflected in the altered forms of *demn* and *dem*, current in the late seventeenth century and facetiously extended by Dickens in *Nicholas Nickleby* to *demnition*. (The American forms *darned, durned* and late eighteenth-century *tarnation* show the same development.) Otto Jespersen noted appositely, 'Thus we have here a whole family of words with an initial *d*, allowing the speaker to begin as if he were going to say the prohibited word, and then turn off into more innocent channels' (1962, p. 229). *Blast* has shown similarly pattern of diminishing force since Elizabethan times. So, in a more limited fashion, has *take*, which had an earlier sense of 'exert a malign influence', still heard in imprecations like 'The Devil take it!' In one of his horrifying curses against Goneril, King Lear uses the term in this sense:

> . . . Strike her young bones,
> You taking airs, with lameness!
> (II. iv. 160–1)

Our modern insensitivity to the language of cursing clearly derives from our becoming inured through exposure to the numerous forms of violent expression found in modern life. Consequently, it is a shock to come across words such as these (penned to an 'agony columnist'): 'Tremble and repent, unholy monstrous woman. You defile the country and young virgins. I curse you in God's name and may you go childless all the rest of your days.'[5]

In several religions, such as Brahmanism, Judaism and Islam, direct reference to the name of God is taboo. In such cultures belief in the sacral power of words is, consequently, more explicit. Montagu, in his major study, *The Anatomy of Swearing*, mentions 'the behavior of certain Arabs who, when cursed, ducked their heads or fell flat on the ground in order to avoid a direct hit' (1973, p. 8).

Stephen Ullmann has reminded us of one consequence of word-magic, namely that 'Linguistic superstitions and prohibitions have left their imprint on many sectors of the vocabulary' (1951, p. 76). He mentions the euphemistic, presumably pacifying, circumlocutions which have been resorted to in earlier stages of the culture in order to avoid direct mention of creatures which exercised a totemic force, such as the weasel and the bear:

> In the Romance languages there are only isolated survivals of *mustela*, the Latin name of the animal [the weasel]. In French it has been replaced by *belette*, a diminutive of *beau, belle*, which literally means 'beautiful little woman'. Elsewhere, the euphemism has worked mainly by change of meaning: the Italians and Portuguese call the weasel 'little lady' (*donnola, doninha*), the Spaniards 'gossip' (*comadreja*), whereas in Denmark it is known as 'beautiful' and 'bride', in Sweden as 'pretty little girl', in Greece and Albania as 'sister-in-law', etc. In English the weasel once had the by-name of *fairy* ... (Ullmann, 1962, p. 206)

In another area of the bestiary, there are propitiatory or ingratiating phrases used for the bear, namely 'honey-eater' and 'honey-pig'. Given the totemistic aura of the animal among the Germanic peoples, it is a possibility that the heroic name *Beowulf*, literally 'bee wolf', might be a coded reference to 'bear'.

Virtually all societies, even the most modern, retain some taboos against swearing. Such prohibitions existed in English for centuries before Captain Cook introduced the word *taboo* from Tongan into English in 1777. In the earlier stages of a culture verbal taboos are greatly intensified, and also very complicated, largely because language in that social setting is highly charged. Malinowski has described the potency of language in non-literate society in these terms: 'The word has power of its own; it is a means of bringing things about ....

Language in its primitive function is to be regarded as a *mode of action* rather than as a countersign of thought' (in Montagu, 1973, p. 8).

Donald F. Thompson showed, in his researches among the Australian aborigines of the Cape York peninsula in northern Queensland, that an elaborate etiquette of swearing existed among the tribes of the area, one based more on social position than content. Thompson found that, except in the presence of certain relatives, 'there is no restriction upon reference to the genitalia or the physiological functions of reproduction, defecation or micturition'. He cites the greeting of a two-year old child at the breast who dropped the nipple to glower at him and exclaim: 'Devil! excrement foul! excrement foul!' (1935, p. 465). The dynamic perception of language is graphically illustrated when a man finds that his words have been overheard by one who stands in a certain social relationship to him. 'He exclaims, "My mouth is foul," and sometimes takes a lighted firebrand and passes it backwards and forwards before his mouth as a purification ritual' (1935, p. 468). We recognize in this behaviour an illuminating counterpart to the severe remedy of literally washing out the 'foul mouth' of an offender with soap and water.

Thompson also found a clear distinction between situations of what he termed 'unorganized' and 'organized' swearing. In the first category, swearing and obscenity fall under no sanction and are 'used by both sexes in quarrels, and as taunts to goad an enemy to fight' (1935, p. 469). This latter practice, fascinatingly, used to exist in the English tradition and will be discussed in subsequent chapters under the convention of *flyting*. Thompson's alternative category (of 'organized' or 'licensed' swearing) is stranger to us, since it involves 'swearing and obscenity that is not only permissible, but obligatory, between those who stand in certain relationships under the classificatory system' (1935, p. 469). Organized swearing has three other remarkable features: it is carried out in public; it is immune from the extreme taboos governing other relationships, and 'it is supposed to induce a state of euphoria: in the words of my informants, to "make everybody happy" ' (1935, p. 469). 'Organized' swearing consists of two distinct types. One is 'obscenity pure and simple, consisting of more or less stereotyped references to the pudenda . . . Certain relatives are also permitted to snatch playfully at one another's genitalia, and even to handle these organs in public.' The other is termed 'bad language, consisting chiefly of references to the anus and to excrement' (1935, p. 469).

Clearly, these quite different attitudes and practices, now lost to us, invite reflection. Swearing in public is now totally unacceptable, as alien to us as the notion of obligatory swearing. While there are still vestiges of the 'relationship taboo', these seem in recent years to have changed from *pas devant les enfants* to *pas devant les parents*. So far as euphoria is concerned, it is now commonly only the swearer who may 'feel better' after an outburst. Commenting on these findings, Montagu reflects upon the 'remarkably humane and intelligent manner in which these so-called primitive peoples have handled a problem that the self-styled civilized peoples of the West have failed both to understand and to control, and have therefore condemned out of hand'. He concludes: 'This form of socialized swearing (which is also found among the Eskimos) constitutes one of the most widely diffused and efficient devices for assisting to preserve the equilibrium of the individual and his society' (1973, p. 13).

Generally speaking, taboos may be categorized as universal or societal. Virtually all societies have, for instance, taboos against direct reference to death: invariably preferred is some euphemism concerning a journey to an unknown destination, such as *pass on, pass away* or the more uplifting variant of the Salvation Army, *promoted to glory*. The common Anglo-Saxon terms for 'to die' were *steorfan*, literally 'to become stiff' (recorded only from *c.*1000[O]), *forðferan, forðgan* and *gewitan*, literally 'to go forth' or 'to depart'. It may not be a coincidence that *die* itself is a Norse borrowing, since the Anglo-Saxon terms might possibly have become too direct: the *OED* observes that 'No instance of the word is known in Old English Literature.' Taboo areas paradoxically encourage the opposite verbal reaction to euphemisms, namely *dysphemisms*, which are startlingly direct and shockingly coarse violations of a taboo: in the field of 'death' one could cite *pushing up daisies, snuff it* and *croak* as gruesomely dysphemic references to the physical act of death, including the death-rattle and subsequent incorporation into the cycle of nature. A great deal of swearing, foul language and profanity is deliberately dysphemic.

Yet there are different degrees of tolerance within the same broad cultural grouping. Perhaps as a reflection of the optimistic, positive and 'progressive' ideology of America, the euphemized vocabulary of death is far more developed in the United States than in Britain. *Mortician* dates from *c.*1895[S], and *casket* is recorded from 1849[S]. Although the latter was stigmatized over a century ago by Hawthorne as 'a vile modern phrase', both are well established in the undertaking trade, which categorizes its clients in the terms of the sentimental cliché *the loved ones*. However, invocations of death also figure largely in transatlantic locutions like *Drop dead!* and, less terminally, in lethal invitations such as *Go jump in the lake, Go and play in the traffic* and so on. As we shall see, taboos against direct reference to sexual matters were far more stringent in America than in Britain until the 1960s, but since then the floodgates have opened.

Societal taboos, therefore, become revealing indicators of evolving social mores, and reflect differing attitudes towards major forces which sustain, alter or threaten life. These can be very diversified or specific, but commonly involve the deity, death, madness, sex, excretion and strangers. As we shall see, these categories acquire quite different emphases at different stages and sectors of the same basic culture. It would seem, for example, that faeces are universally used in oaths and insults, while sex is used in a culture-specific variety of ways, emphasizing, for example, incest in terms like *mother-fucker* in some cultural groupings, adultery in *cornuto* in others, and a polymorphous variety in the application of the terms for the genitalia.

There is also the interestingly exact correlation between degree of taboo in verbal usage and the degree of taboo in actual public exhibition of the referent. The point is graphically made in the following scale:

Action	**Word**
barely acceptable in public	*fart*
	piss
totally unacceptable in public	*shit*
	fuck

This is a rare instance of reactions to language being the same as reactions to referents.

Taboos often reveal divisions within a society, there being different conventions according to class, position, sex and age. In some societies taboo terms may be uttered only by the priestly class (as in such formal cursing as the anathema) while in others they are the sole class prohibited from taboo utterances: it would be most inappropriate for a Western priest to indulge in genital swearing. As the following chapters will show, the relationship between class and swearing in England is fascinatingly complex.

CENSORSHIP, DISGUISE MECHANISMS AND LINGUISTIC FORM

As the previous references to word-magic indicate, taboos generate forms of censorship which may be overt or covert. The latter kind is characterized by a surreptitious erosion of the unacceptable or taboo form, transforming it by means of phonetic disguise into a seemingly innocuous variant. Thus *by golly!* was originally a Negro euphemism for *by God!*, traceable to *c.*1743, when *by goles!* and *gosh* were fulfilling the same function. Examples are set out in figure 1.1. French *bleu*, in various compounds and phrases, such as *sacre bleu*, is the similarly disguised form of *Dieu*, God. The forms are often termed 'minced oaths'. In Judaism, the process has generated both the disguised abbreviation *JWH* (for Yaweh or Jehovah) and the quite alien forms *Adonai* and *Eloim*.

Virtually all swear-words generate disguised variants. The stronger the taboo, the greater the number of evading forms: thus Farmer and Henley cite under the euphemistic heading 'Monosyllable', also 'the female pudendum' or 'cunt' approximately seven hundred synonyms. Polite evasions of *bloody* (a comparatively recent swear-word borrowed about three centuries ago from underworld slang) are, variously, *ruddy*, *blooming* and the truncated *b*, as in 'the *b* thing won't work!' Related abbreviations of *fuck* are the alphabetically symbolic *eff*, *eff off!* and *effing*, which seemed to be the result of an efflorescence during the Second World War: *effing* is recorded from 1944[S]; to *eff and blind* from the previous year. *Adjectival*, older and blander, is recorded from *c.*1910. Dickens, with his sure ear, anticipated the usage in this passage from 1851: 'I won't,' says Bark, 'have no adjective police and adjective strangers in my adjective premises! I won't, by adjective and substantive.'[6] The majority of examples show that the forms are frequently created, interestingly, on either a rhyming basis (as in *ruddy*) or an alliterative one (as in *blooming* or *bleeding*).

Cockney rhyming slang exemplifies a highly developed 'disguise mechanism' in its witty and ingenious coded formulas, such as the familiar *trouble and strife* for *wife* and *apples and pears* for *stairs*. According to Partridge, it is a comparatively recent idiom: 'The beginnings of rhyming slang are obscure,' he writes. 'In colloquialism and slang and cant there are scattered traces of it in the seventeenth and eighteenth centuries, but there existed no body of rhyming slang before about 1840. . . .' (1960, p. 273).

Even today there is dispute over the question of how far rhyming slang has accommodated the two most egregious taboo words in English.

Term	*Date*	*Euphemism*
God	1350s	gog
	1386	cokk
	1569	cod
	1570	Jove
	1598	'sblood
	1598	'slid (God's eyelid)
	1598	'slight
	1599	'snails (God's nails)
	1600	zounds (God's wounds)
	1601	'sbody
	1602	sfoot (God's foot)
	1602	gods bodykins
	1611	gad
	1621	odsbobs
	1650s	gadzooks (God's hooks)
	1672	godsookers
	1673	egad
	1695	od
	1695	odso
	1706	ounds
	1709	odsbodikins (God's little body)
	1728	agad
	1733	ecod
	1734	goles
	1743	gosh
	1743	golly
	1749	odrabbit it
	1760s	gracious
	1820s	ye gods!
	1842	by George
	1842	s'elpe me Bob
	1844	Drat! (God rot!)
	1851	Doggone (God-damn)
	1884	Great Scott
	1900	Good grief
	1909	by Godfrey!

FIGURE 1.1 Euphemisms.

Term	*Date*	*Euphemism*
Jesus	1528	Gis, Jis
	1660	Gemini
	1830s	Jiminy
	1848	Jiminy Crickets
	1857	Gee whillikins
	1895	Gee wiz
	1900	Jeez
	1905	Gee
	1920s	Jeepers
	1922	Jesus wept
	1922	Judas Priest
	1924	Jesus H. Christ
	1934	Jeepers Creepers
Christ	1680	Criminy
	1839	Crickey
	1840s	Cripes
	1897	Jiminy Christmas
	1898	Christmas
	1924	for crying out loud
Lord	1725	Lud
	1765	Lawks!
	1835	Lor!
	1844	Law sakes!
	1861	Law!
	1865	Lor-a-mussy! (Lord have mercy!)
	1870s	Lawdy!
	1898	Lumme! (Lord love me!)
Devil	1690	Deuce
Hell	1839	Sam Hill (US)
	1892	heck
Damn(ed)	1837	darned
	1876	durned
Shit	1847	shucks
	1934	shoot/shute!
	?*	sherbet!

*This usage highlights the problem of sources, since it is common, but unrecorded in *OEDS*, Chapman, Wentworth and Flexner, Green, indeed in any of the standard authorities.

FIGURE 1.1 Euphemisms. Continued

Term	*Date*	*Euphemism*
Fuck	1592	foutre/foutra (from Fr. *foutre*)
	1600s	foot/sfoot (from Fr. *foutre*)
	1753	footer (from Fr. *foutre*)
	1785	footy (from Fr. *foutu*)
	1785	frig/frigging
	1929	effing
	1943	eff and blind
	1950	eff
Pagan Substitutes		
	1570	by Jove
Miscellaneous Polysyllabic Variants		
	1600	Fiddlesticks
	1784	Fiddlededee
	1801	Botheration
	1820s	Thunderation
	1849	Confounded
	1890s	Perdition
Miscellaneous Odd Conjunctions		
	1830	Holy poker! (*EDD*)
	1837	I'm/I'll be jiggered
	1920	Holy smoke!
	1921	Holy Moses
	1942	Holy cow

FIGURE 1.1 Euphemisms. Continued

Some authorities, notably Julian Franklyn in his *Dictionary of Rhyming Slang* (1960, 1975), contend that they are present in the displaced forms *Berkeley* (or *Berkshire*) *Hunt* (=*cunt*) and *Friar Tuck* (=*fuck*, although there would seem to be a Spoonerism at work here as well). Among Cockney habitués, according to this view, there are ingenious abbreviations, and in extreme cases even double codes can be detected. Thus, 'You stupid *berk*!' and 'I don't give a Friar Tuck!' are short-hand versions of the forms just discussed, while the name of the department store C & A has, reputedly, a double significance: 'straight' rhyming (=*gay*) and crudely direct 'Cocksucker and Arsehole'.[7] A different, but more traditional, route to the same destination is via *Elephant and Castle* (=*Arsehole*), often abbreviated to plain *elephant*. In similar fashion, *raspberry tart* (=*fart*) is often abbreviated to plain *raspberry*, commonly accompanied by an onomatopoetic representation which suggests that the original significance has been lost. (Franklyn states that *raspberry tart* had in the nineteenth century meant 'heart', but the later, vulgar sense displaced the earlier.) Figures 1.2 and 6.2 give some idea of the surprising scope of the use of rhyming slang to refer to sexual matters and foreigners in a coded fashion.

However, the authors of *The Muvver Tongue* (1980), Robert Barltrop and Jim Wolveridge, who 'both belong to the Cockney homeland of East London', dispute the genuineness of *berk*, contending that 'Cockneys never used [berk] and it was unheard of before the television comedy series ['Steptoe and Son']' (1980, p. 11). *Berk* is, however, recorded by the *OEDS* as far back as 1936. They also claim that 'There is no Cockney word for homosexuality', pointing out that '*queer* has always meant "ill"' (1980, p. 81). However, Franklyn cites *ginger beer* (=*queer*), often reduced to plain *ginger*, and recorded from 1944. And all authorities agree on *poof*, tracing it via ironic alternative rhyming slang versions, *horse's hoof* and *iron hoof*, often abbreviated to plain *iron. OEDS* records *poof* as far back as *c.*1850–60: 'These monsters in the shape of man, commonly designated Margeries, Pooffs etc.'[S] The older form of the word was often *puff*, which Farmer and Henley record as meaning '"a sodomist" in tramps' slang.'

Place-names figure ingeniously in this category: *Bristol cities* (= *titties*); *Khyber Pass* (= *arse*); *Jodrell Bank* (= *wank*) and *Hampton Wick* (= *prick*). Once again, abbreviations come into play, as in 'Cor, there aren't half some Bristols about!' *Wick*, especially in the set phrase, '*He gets on my wick!*' has been current (though seldom comprehended) since the early part of this century. *Dipping one's wick* is a less obscure reference to coitus. More recently, *flashing his Hampton* [*wick* = *prick*] (for public indecency) gave rise to *flasher*. Originally a police back-formation, this has become very common.[8] Whether used knowingly as witticisms and 'in-group' code-jokes, or uncomprehendingly in general parlance, these forms of rhyming slang reveal the same disguise mechanism at work.

The rhyming principle is also apparent in cruder exclamations of general currency quite lacking in disguise: *hell's bells!*, *fuck a duck!* and – imperfectly – in *shit a brick!* and *stone the crows!* Other deflected or disguised forms are *poppycock*, which originates in crude Low Dutch *pappa kak*, literally 'soft shit'.

The extent to which these 'disguised' forms or 'minced oaths' are consciously contrived is not certain, but one can point to specific examples where some form of censorship acts as a catalyst to create the disguised form. Sterne creates a wonderfully absurd situation in *Tristram*

Long version	*Short version*	*Disguised Term*
All forlorn	Allfor	Horn
Almond rock	Almond	Cock
Alphonse	Alphonse	Ponce
Berkeley/Berkshire Hunt	Berk	Cunt
Bolt the door	Bolt	Whore
Bottle and glass	Bottle	Arse
Braces and bits	Braces	Tits
Brighton pier	Brighton	Queer
Bristol Cities	Bristol	Titties
Cattle truck	Cattle	Fuck
Charley Ronce	Charley	Ponce
Coachman on the box	Coachman	Pox
Cobbler's awls	Cobblers	Balls
Colleen Bawn	Colleen	Horn
Cuddled and kissed	Cuddled	Pissed
Early morn	Early	Horn
Elephant and Castle	Elephant	Arsehole
Feather/Pheasant plucker		Fucker
Fife and drum	Fife	Bum
Fish and shrimp	Fish	Pimp
Friar Tuck		Fuck
Ginger beer	Ginger	Queer
Goose and duck	Goose	Fuck
Grumble and grunt	Grumble	Cunt
Hampton Wick	Hampton	Prick
Hit and miss	Hit	Piss
Horse and trap		Clap/crap
Iron hoof	Iron	Poof
Jane Shore		Whore
Jere[1]		Queer
Joe/Charlie Hunt	Charlie	Cunt
Joe Ronce	Joe	Ponce
Khyber Pass	Khyber	Arse
King Lear	King	Queer
My word	My	Turd
Orchestra stalls	Orchestras	Balls
Pony and trap	Pony	Crap
Richard the Third	Richard	Turd
Russian duck		Fuck
Tickle your fancy		Nancy
Tom tit	Tom	Shit
Uncle Dick		Prick

Note
[1]*Jere* (sometimes misspelt *jeer*) is a seventeenth-century term meaning a turd. In the eighteenth and nineteenth centuries it acquired the sense of the posteriors in showman's slang. The sense of 'homosexual' developed in this century.

FIGURE 1.2 Sexual and anal codes in rhyming slang.

Shandy (Book VII, chapters 20–25) where two bog-bound French nuns have to resort to uttering two unmentionable ejaculations to make their mules pull more strongly and thus extricate them. Sterne plays with the taboo by teasing the reader thus: '. . . a French post-horse would not know what in the world to do, was it not for the two words ****** and ****** in which there is as much sustenance, as if you gave him a peck of corn.' After embarrassed whisperings between the nuns (which the reader cannot overhear) it turns out that the offensive terms are *bouger* and *fouter* (*bugger* and *fucker*). The nuns contrive (with ingenious sophistry) to avoid uttering the taboo terms by splitting them into inoffensive halves, one nun uttering the first syllable, the other the second:

Abbess {bou--- bou--- bou---
Margarita {---ger ---ger ---ger

This artful resource dramatizes extempore in fiction the same process which was in fact taking place within the speech-community over generations or even centuries. (Sterne, naturally, compounds the humour by replicating in print format the 'disguise' that his nuns produce orally, so that the joke is transparent throughout. In the course of the nuns' hilariously embarrassing dilemma, he ironically interjects, with mock politeness: 'The old mule let a f-'.)

A spectacular series of Elizabethan minced oaths (discussed more fully in chapter 5) occurred in response to the Puritan injunctions against Profanity on the Stage. Within a few years the name of God had been so successfully apostrophized that it was barely recognizable in the mangled forms '*sfoot!*' and '*snails!*' and '*zounds!*' for (respectively) 'God's foot!', 'God's nails!' and 'God's wounds!' The truncation effectively blocked understanding of the forms, so that within a few generations *zounds!* was being pronounced '*zaunds!*'

These mutilated and abbreviated alternatives are called upon whenever uttering the word in question would be a breach of decorum, in the view of the speaker. What constitutes a 'breach of decorum' has, of course, both personal and social criteria. In the early nineteenth century some referred to a political extremist as a *r-c-l*; in 1819 Scott observed in a letter that 'Radical is a word in very bad odour here, being used to denote a set of blackguards'[O]. The practice of using asterisks to denote omissions (as in Grose's *c**t*) was established by the early eighteenth century and continued to the early part of this, the abbreviations *f****, *f**k*, *f*ck* then being commonly encountered. Surprisingly, *The Erotic Tongue*, by Lawrence Paros, published in 1988, still uses the device. A laughably extreme example of the ultimate form of censorship, namely total expungement of the offending word, is found in Alexander Pope's edition of Shakespeare. An innocent line in *Julius Caesar* describing the appearance of the conspirators at Brutus's house appears in Pope's text as:

> Their ---- are pluckt about their ears. (II. i. 73)

The excised word, so offensive to Pope's sense of decorum, was *hats*. All these instances show censorship at work in the print format, since all would be unpronounceable orally, especially Pope's. Print-forms often develop into obvious codes, ironically referring to the offending word in fractured form as if it were an open secret. It is interesting, in this context, that the word *blank* should have become a general euphemism; even in 1854 it could be used in this comically opaque fashion: 'I wouldn't give a blank for such a blank blank', and by 1908 people are recorded referring to 'this blankety blank train'.[O] *Bleep*, derived from the radio censorship of offensive material, is recorded in contemporary American reference works (e.g. 'no bleeping good'), but does not appear, interestingly, in either *OEDS* or Green's *Thesaurus* (1988).

Among several curious by-products of collective, and seemingly unconscious censorship, there is the mysterious appearance of the word *donkey* surprisingly late in the day, *c.*1785, first recorded in Grose's slang dictionary. The time-honoured accepted synonym, *ass*, started to fall into disrepute through uncomfortable phonetic proximity to *arse*. Rochester and Swift had already rhymed *asses* with *passes*, and Grose observed: 'a lady who affected to be extremely polite and modest would not say ass because it was indecent.' It has remained displaced by *donkey* as the common term for the animal, even though *ass* and *arse* have since diverged in pronunciation, except in America, where both words are pronounced with the short [a]. Lawrence Paros (1988, p. 90) produces an amusing anonymous nineteenth-century limerick on the point:

> There was a young lady called Glass
> Who had a beautiful ass,
> Not round and pink
> As you might think,
> But gray, and had ears, and ate grass.

Another instance is to be found in the relative absence of the word *cock* in earlier American parlance, and the substitution, variously, of *rooster* (a soporific euphemism which censors out any sexual suggestion), *faucet* for *cock* in the sense of *tap*, and the emasculated form *roach* for *cockroach*. As is made clear in chapter 8, the taboo has now been comprehensively broken.[9]

A major consequence of taboos is that the evidence of what might be termed 'heavy swearing' tends to be suppressed and therefore more easily lost than other kinds of language. Tracing the existence, let alone the development, of what are termed in America 'the Big Six', sometimes Bigsix (*shit*, *piss*, *fart*, *fuck*, *cock* and *cunt*) is often a question of piecing together fragmentary survivals. The first cited instance in the *OEDS* of *cunt* occurs in a London street name with the enticing (or monitory) appellation *Gropecuntlane*, dated 1230. Such public evidence, alongside the ubiquitous *Pissing Alley* and *Shitteborwelane*, a London street name of 1272, suggests that *cunt* must have been a publicly acceptable term. The variant form *queynte* appears in the bawdy tale of Chaucer's Miller and in the risqué memoirs of his Wife of Bath. In a not very courtly episode in the romance of *Sir Tristram* (*c.*1320) we read:

> Hir qeynte abouen hir kne
> Naked þe kniȝtes knewe.

It is a likely speculation that the Norman French title Count was abandoned in England in favour of the Germanic Earl (A-S *eorl*, a nobleman, ON *jarl*, a viceroy) precisely because of the uncomfortable phonetic proximity to *cunt*, which in Middle English could be spelt *counte*. The Earl/Countess conjugation is uniquely anomalous among English titles in that the partners are drawn from different word-stocks. *Swive* was the principal medieval word for 'copulate' and seems to have been acceptable in a great variety of contexts before suffering a mysterious demise towards the end of the last century. Though it first appears in the bawdy 'cherle's tale' of Chaucer's Miller, it never acquired the extraordinary grammatical flexibility of modern *fuck*, but was used with the comparative comfort of modern *bonk*: 'Don't bathe on a full stomach: nor swive', is some advice given in 1440°. It is the more curious, therefore, that *fuck* should be traceable only to 1503, in an instance in the indefatigable Dunbar.

All these words were recorded in the dictionaries of Florio (1598) and Bailey (1721 and 1730). Johnson (1755) and even the irrepressible Grose (1785) showed varying degrees of censorship which the *OED* maintained in finally eschewing *fuck* and *cunt*. It found a place, however, for *windfucker*, *twat* and *bugger*. Even the Third Edition of *Webster* (1961) which outraged many by its adoption of an oral standard of acceptability, did not feel secure enough from protests and boycotts to include the terms; nor, in 1963, did the *Dictionary of American Slang*, edited by Harold Wentworth and Stuart Berg Flexner. It is often claimed that the *Penguin English Dictionary* (1965) was the first standard reference work published in this century to include all the 'four-letter words', a euphemism which itself dates from 1934[S]. In fact this honour (if that is the right term) belongs to Sir William A. Craigie's *Dictionary of the Older Scottish Tongue* (1938–51). It includes the interesting compound *cunt-laird* with the designation 'meaning obscure'. Several standard American works still do not include all. Although the trial which led to the unbanning of *Lady Chatterley's Lover* seemed at the time (1960) to be a watershed, various state mechanisms of censorship have continued to be exercised over broadcasting. These are discussed further in chapter 9 and the Conclusion.

EXPLETIVE IDIOM AND RHYTHM

Formal oaths have rigid formulas of words, as do curses, anathemas and exorcisms. The more 'informal' swearing becomes, the more the language becomes elastic, malleable and flexible. Consequently, idiomatic and grammatical complexity become remarkable features. In some contexts word-choice seems to be almost totally random and variable, while in others it has to be very precise to be effective. For example, it is a curious feature in the taxonomy that of the various forms of excretion and eructation, *shit* should be the most used term (cf. German *scheiss*, French *merde*, Italian *stronzo*, English *turd*). By comparison, *fart* has diminished force, *piss* has little currency (beyond the contemptuous *piss artist* and the unceremonious *piss off!*) while *burp* has none whatever. It would seem that the two dominant factors in making terms in this field highly charged or otherwise are their degree of solidity and their proximity to the genital/anal area. Though the action of spitting at someone is the most concentratedly contemptuous piece of body language possible in many cultures, there is no place, on a verbal level, for *spit*, *burp*, *vomit* or *puke* beyond their figurative uses.

Although flexibility among adjectives is almost random (so that *bloody* can be replaced by *fucking*, *stupid* or *damned*), such interchangeability does not apply to nouns, where there may be a world of difference between alternatives. The interesting exception occurs within formulas; in this context nouns become interchangeable. Thus the emotive kernel of the formula for exasperation, 'For *Christ's* sake!' might, in other company, transform to 'For *pity's* sake!', 'For *shit's* sake!' or even 'For *fuck's* sake!' This series might provoke the obvious (but naive) question 'What do *Christ*, *pity*, *shit* and *fuck* have in common?' The answer, in this context, is, of course, 'Nothing whatever. They are simply terms of high emotional charge which have accreted over time into the formula to the point that they can now be used interchangeably.' Similarly, the formula of surprise, 'Bless me!' has the variants 'Blow me down!', 'Bugger me!' and the interesting fossil 'blimey!' also 'Gor Blimey!', a minced version of 'God blind me!' Both kinds of formula show another common feature, namely indiscriminate variation between sacred and profane, while the second group is of the self-immolating variety.

In contexts without a fixed form of words, the terms of insult have to be far more precise. Imagine the following exchange:

X Rapist!
Y Bastard!
X Child molester!
Y Son of a bitch!
X Plagiarist!
Y Cretin!
X Embezzler!
Y Coward!

Clearly, X's epithets are, technically, more damaging since they stigmatize his enemy in powerfully anti-social terms, but Y's have greater impact, not because they are more critical, but because they have acquired a weight of tradition in the speech community. Similarly, the caustic observation 'Snooks is a penis of the first order, and his sidekick Smithers is a real little nipple' has no impact, since *penis* and *nipple* are not terms of insult, whereas their low register synonyms *prick* and *tit* are emotionally charged terms, the more so when accompanied by *little*. The same applies to *shit* and *turd*, as opposed to *dung*, *ordure* and *excrement*. Here the differing impact of contrasting registers is apparent, since the Anglo-Saxon element of the language provides much more emotional force than does the Norman French or the Latin. *Copulating pandemonium!* conveys none of the emotional charge of the native equivalent *fucking hell!*

It might be useful to bring into play at this point two observations which raise swearing above the level of the prosaic. G. K. Chesterton commented that 'The one stream of poetry which is constantly flowing is slang.' (From *The Defendant* 1901, cited in Partridge's *Slang* (1960), p. 24). Louis MacNeice comes closer to our theme in his poem 'Conversation', (1929). 'Ordinary men,' he writes,

Put up a barrage of common sense to baulk
Intimacy, but by mistake interpolate
Swear-words like roses in their talk.

While it may be objected, quite validly, that most swearing makes no attempt at originality, relying largely or exclusively on established formulas, certain affinities with poetry can be observed. In both fields the language used is highly charged and very metaphorical; extreme, pointed effects are created by alliteration or by playing off different registers of the word-hoard against each other, and rhythm is very important.

The interplay of short and long words is used to accentuate rhythmic effects, to create symmetrical patterns and to put the greatest emphasis on what is usually the most wounding term. A common rhythmic structure is [-/-˘/=], with the major stress [=] falling on the last word, which the pattern requires to be short, as in 'the stupid bitch!', 'that bloody fool!' also found in a formula common in the 1950s, 'You clumsy clot!' (Most of these short words will be discussed and analysed below.) Very often a long adjective is linked to a short noun to achieve both an effective rhythmic patterning and a contrast of register. Though these effects are largely unconscious, they emerge with a regularity which cannot be accidental: 'You parsimonious old shyster!' was just such a resounding combination which I recall being uttered by a lady of normally decorous speech when reprimanding a builder. The contrast of literary *parsimonious*, common *old* and foreign *shyster* was quite devastating. A more contrived, but no less powerful example of contrasting registers is found in the provocative pseudo-rhetorical question asked by one of the 'alternative' papers: 'Isn't Quentin Hogg an unremitting shit?' (*International Times*, 27 October, 1967).

Interesting stress patterns also emerge, whereby the rhythmic structure of the noun (which comes last in many formulas of abuse) seems to modify and predetermine the rhythm of the preceding qualifiers. Thus, for example, the common bisyllabic nouns *bastard*, *bugger*, *fucker* and so on tend to invite adjectives with a similar pattern [-˘] to counterbalance them, e.g. *bloody*, *silly*, *stupid* and so on. The overall pattern then becomes [˘/-˘/=˘] in, for example, 'the silly bugger!' Alternatively a common, simple low register word, such as *old* or *little* acts as a fulcrum, producing a symmetrical pattern and balanced rhythm: [˘/-˘/-/=˘] in, for example, 'the bloody old bastard!'

These last examples accentuate the prevalence of alliteration in swearing formulas. Many of the most used terms in English now start with the letters 'b' and 'f', for reasons which are not easily explained. Could it be that voiced bilabial plosives and fricatives are the most satisfactory phonetic expression of emotional release? Or does the alliterating factor come into play? Is it a survival from flyting? As we shall see in subsequent chapters, alliteration figures largely in medieval swearing, essentially because of the dominance of the alliterative scheme in the poetics of the period.

However, the overriding importance of rhythm is most clearly shown in the way that words are often broken up (or even stuck together) into stress components in order to fit a particular pattern, regardless of dislocations of meaning. Two striking medieval examples emphasize the point in different ways. In this exclamation (from *c.*1330), 'Bisengeme, ihc habbe i-fought Otuwel', the first word is meaningless until we realize that it is a conflation of 'By Saint James'. The staple alliterative metre of medieval poetry also facilitated some memorable conjugations, such as the reference (in the Chester Miracle play *c.*1500) to 'a shitten-arsed shrew'. Modern instances of rhythm dislocating sense are *Not bloody likely!*, *abso-bloody-lutely* and the splendid Australian syncopation *kanga-bloody-roo* [-˘/-˘/=]. This phenomenon is also known as the integrated adjective.

ETYMOLOGIES

The etymologies of taboo terms seem to act as excitants of the imagination. I am sure that I am not the first logophile to have been informed (on several occasions and with complete assurance) that the origin of *bloody* lies in the religious ejaculation *By our lady!*, and even more ingeniously, that the etymology of *fuck* lies alternatively in a police abbreviation 'for unlawful carnal knowledge' or, more eminently, in a royal edict issued at the time of the Plague: 'fornicate under command of the King'. Why precisely procreation should ever become a Royal Command Performance, and why the injunction should be issued in such arcane form are only two of the more obvious objections to such an explanation: Charles II would have been more like to echo Lear's ferocious edict: 'Let copulation thrive!'

These two instances are, of course, classic cases of folk etymology, namely, the plausible but inaccurate explanation of the origin of a word, often accompanied by a tall corroborating story. Few lexicographers, however, have managed entirely to avoid the occasional blunder into folk etymology.[10] Our ignorance about the origins of several of the major swear-words is one aspect of the problem of suppressed or buried evidence. However, an analysis in terms of origin is revealing. It gives the lie to the popular misconception (which is perpetuated even in academic circles) that the 'four-letter words' are exclusively Anglo-Saxon in origin.[11] This generalization turns out to be true only of the main anal terms, as the table below and figure 1.3 show:

Anglo-Saxon	*Norman French*	*Latin/Greek*	*Uncertain*
shit	piss		fuck
turd			crap
arse			bum
(fart)			cunt
			twat

Figure 1.3 illustrates the earliest recorded instances of the four-letter words. The Anglo-Saxon terms can, expectedly, be traced to ancient roots, some with a surprisingly vigorous significance: *shit* turns out to be related to *shoot* while *turd* is a distant relative of legal *tort*, both rooted in the act of twisting (corroborated graphically by Barry McKenzie's observation of 'twice round the porcelain'). The quaint definition of *fart* (not actually recorded in Old English) namely 'to break wind', points us in the direction of the cognate French root *peter*, meaning both 'to fart' and 'to explode', whence English *petard*, a bomb. Without knowledge of these fundamental associations, the following passage from Caxton's *Æsop* (1483–4) might be hard to understand. A lamb in hound's clothing

piss c.1290
shit c.1000
fart c.1250
fuck c.1503
cunt c.1203
turd c.1000
arse c.1000
cock c.1400
tarse c.1000–c.1730
weapon c.1000–c.1370
limb c.1000
yard c.1397–c.1884
tail c.1362
tool c.1552
prick c.1592
penis c.1676

Notes

1 Only *shit, arse* and *turd* can genuinely be termed 'Anglo-Saxon' words on an etymological and historical basis.

2 Nearly all the older words for 'penis' are metaphors of some kind, which makes their semantic history hard to trace. *OED* gave the earliest instance of *cock* as Bailey (1730); *OEDS* extended the sense back to 1618, but (as the discussion indicates) the sense seems to have been current in the fifteenth century.

FIGURE 1.3 Earliest recorded instances of the 'four-letter' words (wearing the pelt of a fierce dog as a disguise, since it has been shorn) is chasing a wolf:

> And thenne the sayd wether ranne after him / And the wulf which supposed that it had ben the dogge shote thryes by the waye for the grete fere that he hadde .... [Later he explains] 'I dyde shyte thre grete toordes.' (1967, pp. 160–1)

Since Caxton was generally inclined to err on the side of bourgeois decorum, this passage suggests that several of the genuine Anglo-Saxon terms seem to have had a fairly broad currency, which extended to insult and invective during the Middle English period. *Cock* is, in many ways, the odd word out in that the sense of 'penis' is a metaphorical extension deriving potentially from two other meanings, namely the gallinacious sense of 'the male farmyard fowl' and the plumbing sense of a 'tap or spout'. The farmyard sense goes back to Anglo-Saxon, the plumbing sense goes back to the late fifteenth century, but the sense of 'penis' is more difficult to trace, precisely because it is metaphorical. The *OED* refers to Bailey's Dictionary (1730–6), Farmer and Henley refer to Shakespeare's *Henry V* (II. i. 56) ('Pistol's cock is up, and flashing fire will follow'), while Partridge (1947) cites this exchange from *The Taming of the Shrew* (II. ii. 225):

> *Katharina* What is your crest? A coxcomb?
> *Petruchio* A combless cock, so Kate will be my hen.

All of these are antedated by a risqué lyric of the early fifteenth century, 'I have a gentle cock'. It describes what sounds like a close relative of Chauntecleer in Chaucer's *Nun's Priest's Tale* for four verses, using terms such as *crystal, coral, azure* etc., and then in the final pair of lines makes a sudden switch to an undoubtedly phallic dénouement:

> And every night he percheth him
> In mine lady's chaumber.

The original Anglo-Saxon terms were *teors*, later *tarse* (the only non-metaphorical term), *wæpen*, later *weapon*, and *lim*, which became *limb*. Of these, only *weapon* has survived, in self-conscious, facetious use, but in earlier times it was neutral and common: a male infant or plant was termed in Anglo-Saxon *wæpened*, 'weaponed' or 'armed'. *Tarse* seems to have a limited currency up to the seventeenth century; after some brief and energetic use by Rochester, for whom it supplied a conveniently cheeky rhyme with *arse*, the word appears to have expired.

Piss, like *fart*, is regarded as 'ultimately echoic' (Partridge, *Origins*). Though the distribution of *fart* is described as 'common Germanic',

A-S *feortan* is a hypothetical form, and the first recorded instance is only *c.*1250. *Piss* was borrowed into English from Old French. The *OED* suggests that *piss* was originally a euphemism, though for what has never been explained. All the words categorized under 'Uncertain' are first recorded after the Anglo-Saxon period; of them only *bum* has been recorded for more than four hundred years.

Cunt is first recorded in ME (*c.*1200), and although there are many ancient cognate Germanic forms, such as Old Norse *kunta*, Old Frisian, MLG, M. Dutch *kunte*, the word is not found at all in Old English.[12] Robert Burchfield, in his 'Outline History of Euphemisms in English' (in *Fair of Speech*, 1985), does not mention *cunt* in the context of Old English at all, and observes that 'The normal term for the female genitalia was *gecyndlic*' (p. 22). The *OEDS* says of the etymology that 'the ulterior relations are uncertain', since scholars are divided about the likely but problematic link with Latin *cunnus*, possibly related to *cuneus*, 'a wedge', which has supplied the Romance relatives *con* (French and Middle French), *conno* (Italian) and so on. As Partridge (1977) observes: 'The presence of the *t* in the Germanic has long puzzled the etymologists.' The French form is recorded from *c.*1200, and although always 'une terme bas' ('a low word'), is more acceptable in literary contexts than its English equivalent.

A similar etymological conundrum concerns the relations between *fuck* (recorded only from Early Modern English) and its Continental semantic partners, French *foutre* and German *ficken*, 'to strike'. Eric Partridge, discussing these matters in his lively etymological dictionary *Origins* (1977), makes much of the relationship between Latin *futuere* (the root of French *foutre*) and Latin *battuere*, to strike. The curious forms *windfucker* (for *windhover*) and Scots *fucksail* (for foresail) suggest yet another potential root in ON *fukja*, 'to drive', in this case 'to be driven by the wind'.[13] Despite the blandly accepting common phrase, 'different strokes for different folks', some might feel that beating, driving and love-making are quite distinct for most people. These are clearly deep metaphorical matters. In English alone we can see (if we want to) the link between the different strokes in the slang terms for sexual intercourse, *bang*, *knock*, and the recently fashionable *bonk*. The metaphors for 'penis' are no less suggestive: *tool*, *prick*, *chopper* and *weapon*, the last of which, as was previously noted, goes right back to Anglo-Saxon.

Crap derives (according to Rosie Boycott) from the name of Thomas Crapper, the inventor of Crapper's Valveless Water Waste Preventor, the euphemism by which the first water closet was sold in Victorian times. (In Elizabethan times, Sir John Harington's facetiously titled *A New Discourse of a Stale Subject Called the Metamorphosis of Ajax* (1596) (= *Discourse on the Jakes*) was a risqué study of the same implement.) Boycott's suggestion, while eminently plausible, is not supported by any of the major reference works. Though it is difficult to distinguish the various senses of 'rubbish' and 'waste' which accumulate around *crap*, they seem to have solidified into the main low sense of 'excrement' by the late eighteenth century, at least fifty years before Crapper was born in 1837. *Twat* is discussed at the opening of chapter 7, on Victorian attitudes. *Bum* is a much older word, recorded from early Middle English, derived from Germanic roots.

It is important, for the purposes of this study, to make two major distinctions. The first is that between the initial appearance of these words as terms of general acceptability, and their first use as terms of insult. There is a most interesting division in this respect between the anal or excretory terms on the one hand and the sexual on the other. This becomes apparent from the dictionary entries under *arse*, *bum*, *fart*, *shit*, *turd* and *piss*, all of which have formulas of the kind 'Not now in decent/polite use', implying a previous acceptability. Johnson included, without embarrassment or caution, such terms as *arse-foot* 'A kind of water fowl', a flower called, incredibly, *arse-smart*, possibly because it grew on dunghills, *pissburnt* meaning 'stained with urine' and the old, vulgar term for the dandelion, namely *pissabed*, so called on account of its diuretic properties.

The second distinction concerns gradations in personal application, what might be called the 'evolution of directness'. There is clearly a difference between, say, the Host in *The Canterbury Tales* exclaiming (quite justifiably) that Chaucer the pilgrim's doggerel tale of Sir Thopas 'is nat worth a toord!' (l.930), and more direct personal applications, such as the challenging insults, 'a fart for your family!' (1685) or 'you bitch!' (1675, in Hobbes' *Odyssey* xviii, l.310).

In the case of sexual terms, this final extension of meaning has taken place only in the past century. In the table below, *bugger* and *bastard* have been included for the sake of comparison. According to the *OEDS*, the first recorded insulting applications of the terms are:

bugger	1719
bastard	1830
fucker	1893
prick	1928
cunt	1929

twat	1929
tit	1947

The equivalent French terms have also become abusive comparatively recently: *con*, in the phrase *vieux con*, for instance, being used of a stupid person for about a century. However, the older excretory terms have remarkable histories in this regard: *fart* goes back to *c.*1450, while *shit* and *turd* are found in flyting contexts from fifty years later. As the terms passed out of polite usage, so there arose contemptuous terms like *fart-catcher* (for a footman) and *fart-sucker* for a toadying parasite later known as an *arse-creeper* in British English and a *brown nose* in American. Similarly, *shit-breech*, recorded from the thirteenth century, was still flourishing as a seventeenth-century epithet of abuse, as in a reference to 'a Scurvy shit-breech Lad' in 1675, while a century later Grose defines *shit-sack* as 'a dastardly fellow: also a non-conformist'. Some of the creative range of the past is shown in figure 1.4, 'The Semantic Field of Shit-words'.

*c.*1202	*shit-breech*	'Randulfus Bla de Scitebroc'
*c.*1250	*shit worde*:	'So herdes [herdsmen] doþ oþer mid schit worde.'
*c.*1386	*shitten*:	'A shiten shepherde and a clene sheepe' (Chaucer).
*c.*1508	*shit* (personal epithet):	'[Thou art] A schit, but wit' (Dunbar).
*c.*1598	*shit-fire*:	'A hot, violent fellow, a shite-fire' (Florio, translating *Cacafuoco*).
*c.*1690	*shitabed*:	'[They] gave them ill language, calling them Tooth-Gapers, Sherks, Shittabeds, Slubber-degullions.'
*c.*1663	*shit* (vb – to abuse):	'Knocking a shiting Porter down . . . backwards into his own Surreverence' (1704).
*c.*1769	*shit-sack*:	'A dastardly fellow' (Grose – 1785).
*c.*1795	*shit house*:	'For the honour of the Scots, we have his [Wallace's] effigy in the shite houses to this very day.'

FIGURE 1.4 The semantic field of shit-words.

Philologists and lexicographers have spent a lot of time tracing the origins of the word 'bloody'. According to a common folk etymology, the word is a corruption of 'by our lady'. This is clearly not logical, in that 'by our lady' would not fit into the adjectival function which 'bloody' so readily does. ('By our lady hell!' would be an odd conjunction.) In fact 'bloody' comes, unsurprisingly, from 'bloody', but has become used in a great variety of emotive or intensive ways. As is often the case with underground or slang usage, the origins are difficult to trace, but most authorities take the sense back to the early eighteenth century. The connection seems to have started with 'bloody drunk', which meant 'fired up and ready for a fight'. However, as the following chapter shows, there is an instance suggesting that Gavin Douglas used the word in this sense in 1513.

In recent years there has been much discussion on the extent of 'the semantic derogation of women' and the question of whether terms of feminine anatomy, such as *cunt* and *tit*, or terms such as *bitch* and *cow*, have greater currency or potency than the equivalent male terms *prick* and *balls*, *pig* and *swine*. This issue is taken up in greater detail in chapter 10, 'Sexuality in Swearing'.

EMOTIVE FORCE AND FLEXIBILITY

As terms become more highly charged, so they acquire greater grammatical flexibility. Thus *fuck* has extended grammatically from being exclusively a verb in late ME to virtually every part of speech, and in American idiom can be used as a personal noun expletive: 'You're cheating, you fuck!' (King, 1986, p. 275). In its most emotive uses, the word ranges from the barely plausible *you fucking bitch!* to the incestuous improbability *mother-fucker*, finally reaching the physical impossibilities of *fuck off!* and *go fuck yourself!* The general phenomenon of flexibility is illustrated in figure 1.5, 'Flexibility in Swearing Terms'.

Within the idiom of swearing, curious varieties of impacted word-groups establish themselves. Consider, for instance, the use of *the hell* in the following idioms:

> 'What *the hell* is going on?'
> 'Who *the hell* does he think he is?'
> 'I've got *the hell* in with the management.'
> '*The hell* he is!' [rebutting some statement].

Clearly one would be hard put to it to explain these usages in terms of traditional grammar or ordinary logic. It is as if there is a syndrome

Categorization

1 personal: 'You ----!'
2 personal by reference: 'The ----!'
3 destinational: '---- off!'
4 cursing: '---- you!'
5 general expletive of anger, annoyance, frustration: '----!'
6 explicit expletive of anger, annoyance, frustration: '---- it!'
7 capacity for adjectival extension: '----ing' or '----y'
8 verbal usage: 'to ---- about'.

Term	*Category*							
	1	2	3	4	5	6	7	8
damn (vb)	o	o	o	*	*	*	o	o
fuck (n + vb)	*(US)	o	*	*	*	*	*	*
cunt (n)	*	*	o	o	o	o	o	o
shit (n + vb)	*	*	o	o	*	o	o	o
fart (n + vb)	*	*	o	o	o	o	o	*
piss (n + vb)	o	o	*	o	o	o	o	o
bugger (n + vb)	*	*	*	*	*	*	*	*
bastard (n)	*	*	o	o	o	o	o	o
arse (n + vb)	*	*	o	o	o	o	o	*
asshole (n)	*	*	o	o	o	o	o	o

Notes

The asterisk denotes usage, while o denotes lack of capacity in a particular category. Clearly, only those terms which can be used as both noun and verb are likely candidates for use in all the modes set out above: the nouns are by definition only eligible for the first two categories. However, it is surprising that *piss*, for instance, should be so limited in range and that *bugger* should be the only term which can be used in all modes. (The use of *fuck* in category 1 is confined to American usage.)

FIGURE 1.5 Flexibility in swearing terms.

whereby, in an emotional context, normal constraints of usage and grammatical function are relaxed, enabling curious idioms to be generated. (One notes that in most of the expressions cited above, *the hell* could be replaced by *the fuck*, and that a similar series of idioms clustered round *the devil* in earlier times.)

The incestuous term *mother-fucker* (recorded from 1956^{S}) is interesting on two counts.[14] The first is that the incestuous relationship is always referred to from an 'Oedipal' rather than an 'Electral' point of view, *father-fucker* not being a term used in any culture. 'Go and have intercourse with your mother!' and its variants is, contrariwise, highly dispersed, being recorded in many European languages (some of which extend the invitation to one's sister), as well as among the Cape York aborigines of Australia (Montagu 1973, p. 17) and in Cameroon pidgin as 'Chuk yu mami!' (Todd, 1984, p. 104). Norman Moss, however, made the observation in his *British/American Dictionary* (1984), that *mother-fucker* is a term 'so obscene as to be beyond the bounds of native British speech'.

Although *mother-fucker* might suggest some sort of universal paradigm for an ultimate insult, there are varying cultural gradations of severity. Thus among American negroes it can be used with familiarity, even with friendliness: 'Hi, you old mother-fucker, where you been?' is heard daily on Forty-Second Street. It is often abbreviated to plain *mother*, as in 'We're going to give those mothers hell when we catch up with them.' Similarly, *bastard*, a severe insult in American and British English, can be used in a congenial fashion in Australian English. In *The Complete Barry McKenzie* it is glossed, paradoxically, as 'a nice person'. Michael Sawtell elucidates this point by noting that 'If we wish to express our contempt for a man, we say "He's a proper bastard", meaning, he is vile. If we wish to praise him, we say: "He's a good bastard", meaning that he is a good fellow' (Hornadge, 1980, pp. 148–9). No such meaning was implied when the term turned out to be the sticking point in the memorable confrontation between the England cricket Captain Mike Gatting and the Pakistani umpire Shakoor Rana, who was quoted as saying: 'Calling me a bastard may be excusable in England, but here people murder someone who calls another man a bastard' (*The Star* (Johannesburg) 11 December 1987, p. 20). Yet Bastard is not unknown as a surname in English: Pepys writes in his Diary (10 May 1660) of a Mr Whore.

The comparative untranslatability of many insults (another aspect of their being culture-bound) can be seen in the great native potency of German *schweinhund*, French *cochon*, Italian *cornuto* and their comparative disuse in other, closely related cultures. *Pig* is, however, recorded by Grose (1785) as an underworld slang term for 'a police officer', and a *cornuto* was borrowed into English in the fifteenth century. It had a fairly racy career in Elizabethan times, when 'adulterine' comedy and open mockery of cuckoldry thrived. In *The Merry Wives of Windsor* there is a comment laden with sexual Schadenfreud to 'The peaking Cornuto her husband' (III. v. 71). The temporary growth of the field to include the verb *cornute* (1597), *cornuted* (1612) and *cornutor* (1675)[O] (at a time when Italy was associated with corruption) reveals the element of fashion in linguistic culture.

The growth of nationalism is reflected in terms which Eric Partridge has discussed under the heading of 'Offensive Nationality', such as *Hun* and *Frog*, while racist sentiments have also found ready expression in opprobrious terms such as *kaffir* and *kike*. Very often the growth of these terms is the consequence of mercantile expansion or military conflict, as is shown in the discussion in chapter 6. It is significant that the most potent forms of modern swearing should be related to group identity rather than individual morality.

SWEARING AND AUTHORITY

The relations between authority and swearing are fascinatingly complex. Whereas Henry VIII, for example, swore freely and exuberantly, as did his daughter Elizabeth, such verbal behaviour has increasingly come to be regarded as inappropriate to those in high office. It is a nice speculation as to when the last publicly shocking oath was uttered by a monarch. Occasional critical – or rather, hypocritical – comments are made in this respect about members of the British Royal Family, notably the Duke of Edinburgh. In 1982 the British press gloatingly publicized Princess Anne's exasperated reaction: 'Naff off!', while in 1989 Prince Charles drew attention to his experience of low standards of English in his office by commenting that 'English is taught so bloody badly.' By and large, it would seem that although royalty has been subjected to a great deal of 'embourgeoisification', it still retains a privilege of linguistic insouciance.

In democratic dispensations the acceptability of swearing in high places is, paradoxically, more problematic, since, from an ideological point of view, the use of demotic language should be welcomed. There is no doubt that presidents who exhibit 'the common touch' by the use of low register language usually find favour. Harry Truman's popularity derived in part from this. His wife commented once that he 'liked to call horse-manure horse-manure', adding that it had taken her a long time to get the President to use this polite version. He commented in 1961: 'I fired [General] MacArthur because he wouldn't respect the authority of the President. I didn't fire him because he was a dumb son of a bitch, although he was . . . .' (Flexner, 1976, p. 233). But there is a fine but important line between straight talk and low talk. Nowhere was this more apparent than in the demise of President Richard Nixon in 1974. The final destroyer of his reputation was the revelation (so fastidiously preserved by himself on the Watergate tapes) that the incumbent of the office of Jefferson and Lincoln spoke like a common gangster.[15] The euphemism 'expletive deleted' led the way to 'president expelled'.

NATIONAL AND REGIONAL DEGREES OF TOLERANCE

Regional differences in the social tolerance of swearing within the English-speaking world are very striking, and form the theme of the last three chapters, especially that of chapter 8, 'Swearing in the New Worlds'. The make-up of the various settler populations is, of course, a key factor in the development of these various English-speaking communities. Although Victorian attitudes of decorum and propriety became strongly entrenched in the linguistic mores in England, such standards did not, however, apply uniformly throughout the Empire, let alone the English-speaking world. While the East Coast of America was to some extent still under the censoring influence of the severe Puritanism and Quakerism of the Pilgrim Fathers, accounts of the American Wild West emphasize the swashbuckling, devil-may-care attitude of diminished morality found in the land-grab and gold-rush, in the frontier brothel and saloon. The transportation of convicts was also an undoubted factor. After the American War of Independence, convicts were no longer sent to America, since penal colonies for 'marinated' felons were set up in Australia, starting in 1803 at Botany Bay. By and large, the traditions of Australian swearing flourished steadily from the beginning, and have continued to be upheld. By contrast, the more bourgeois English colonies set up in New Zealand, Canada and South Africa would appear to have maintained comparative mildness in the matter of oaths. These differences complicate any final assessment on the 'state of swearing and foul language' in the English-speaking world.

NOTES

1 Hazlitt, 1. Table Talk xxii, 'On Criticism' 1821.

2 Examples of works with such omissions include the following: Peter Trudgill and Jean Hannah, *International English* (London: Arnold, 1982); 'English Overseas' in *Oxford English* (Oxford, OUP, 1986) and R. McCrum *et al.*'s *The Story of English* (London, Faber, 1986), which studiously maintains a thoroughly sanitized treatment of the language, presumably because the book was based on the BBC television series. Not even *bloody* is mentioned, though there is a risqué excursion into *jelly-roll* (pp. 220–1).

3 Butler, *Journal of Asiatic Society* (Bengal, 1875, p. 316).

4 *Guardian Weekly*, 11 September 1988, p. 29.

5 *New Statesman and Society*, 2 September 1988, p. 14.

6 *Household Words*, 14 June 1851, pp. 270–1.

7 Leonard R. N. Ashley, 'The Cockney's Horn Book,' in Reinhold Amman (ed.), *The Best of Maledicta* (1988), p. 31.

8 See Barltrop and Wolveridge (1980, p. 82).

9 Jespersen cites as euphemisms for *cock* 'he-biddy – a male fowl. A product of prudery and squeamishness' (Farmer's *Americanisms*) and the even more quaint *roosterswain* (1960, p. 230). Leonard Bloomfield also commented on the point in *Language* (New York, 1933, p. 396). It is interesting that *cockroach* (originally a corruption of Spanish *cucaracha*), was recorded by Captain John Smith in 1624, indicating that *cock* would have been acceptable. In 1821 James Flint 'reported that *rooster* had been substituted for *cock* (the latter having acquired an indelicate anatomical significance),' as Mencken puts it (1936, p. 301). Rawson (1981) has a splendid entry on these euphemisms under *rooster*.

10 A classic example of folk etymology is that of Grose's charmingly imaginative entry on *cur*: 'A cut or curtailed dog. According to the forest laws, a man who had no right to the privilege of the chase, was obliged to cut or law his dog: among other modes of disabling him from disturbing the game, one was by depriving him of his tail: a dog so cut was called a cut or curtailed dog, and by contraction a cur.' Equally fanciful is the explanation that Spanish *gringo* derives from the singing of 'Green Grow the Rushes O' by early British settlers. Philip Howard has an interesting divertissement on the topic in *A Word in Your Ear* (1985), pp. 54–8.

11 The simplistic (but erroneous) equation of 'four-letter' and 'Anglo-Saxon' is surprisingly common, even in educated circles. In his judgement in the matter of *The United States v. One Book Called 'Ulysses'* (1933), Judge Woolsey observed that 'The words which are criticized as dirty are old Saxon words known to almost all men and, I venture, to many women . . . .' On 21 July 1959, a US Federal Judge, Frederick van Pelt Bryan, handed down a decision in favour of *Lady Chatterley's Lover*, referring to 'Four-letter Anglo-Saxon words . . .' (cited in Montagu, 1973, p. 311). 'The English language of sex is curt and Anglo-Saxon,' states Pearsall (1969, p. 368). More recently, Erving Goffmann has written of '. . . words (involving blasphemy and – in English – Anglo-Saxon terms for bodily functions) . . .' (*Forms of Talk* (Oxford, Blackwell, 1981, p. 114).)

12 Eric Partridge notes (in *Origins*) that it is recorded once in OE. In his *Dictionary of Historical Slang* he seems to ignore the Germanic cognates, commenting: 'The -nt, which is difficult to explain, was already present in OE *cunte.*'

13 According to Craigie, *fucksail* ('foresail') acquired the transferred sense of 'a woman's skirt' (unsurprisingly), and was also reduced to plain *fuck*.

14 Though the earliest *OEDS* quotation for *mother-fucker* is dated 1956, Montagu mentions instances as far back as 1917 (1973, p. 313).

15 The *obiter dicta* of President Nixon were, in fact, rather banal, consisting in the main of *crap, bullshit, asshole, I don't give a shit* and the odd idiom *it's just a bunch of crap* (1974, pp. 9, 55, 70, 183 and 75).

2

Unlocking the Word-hoard: the Germanic Heritage

> Language in its primitive function is to be regarded as a *mode of action* rather than as a countersign of thought.
>
> Malinowski

> The man who overreaches his opponent by breaking his oath reveals that he is afraid of his enemy, but despises the god he has invoked.
>
> Lysander

> Blasphemy itself could not survive religion; if anyone doubts that let him try to blaspheme Odin.
>
> G. K. Chesterton

OUR knowledge of the full variety of swearing in past cultures must necessarily be incomplete. This is especially the case in ancient English society, since the dissolution of the monasteries and its attendant reformist zealotry led perforce to the systematic destruction of vast quantities of valuable records and innocent literary texts. The few survivors of this extirpation would have been subjected to a severe ecclesiastical censorship, their main chance for survival being that they were written in a form of language which was becoming increasingly incomprehensible. It is a sobering reflection that if the unique charred and beer-stained manuscript Cotton Vitellius A xv had been destroyed in a fire in 1731, instead of only being charred at the edges, there would now be no record whatsoever of Beowulf the hero, let alone of the stern dignity, courtliness and heroic values which his poem so movingly depicts. That fire, which decimated the treasure-house of the Cotton Library, swallowed up much of the evidence which would have filled out our sketchy knowledge of Anglo-Saxon and Middle English literature, and provided the tacit understandings which are the essence of literary interpretation.

Given this situation of partial ignorance deriving from the accidental survival of texts, it seems both prudent and reasonable to widen the net both thematically and geographically at the outset of this chapter so as to include evidence from cognate Germanic languages and literatures (especially Old Norse) which were not subject to the same interference and censorship which English has suffered. For in those literatures are retained various features which disappeared quite early in English. The surviving texts preserve a variety of ancient forms which can be well understood in terms of the illuminating triple categorization of Vico, who designated the earliest stages of language as being that of gods, superseded first by that of heroes, and finally by that of men (Vico, 1948, pp. 306–7). We find clear survivals of Vico's first two categories in the forms of the spell and the charm, where language becomes a repository of mystic force, a god-like code which man seeks to fathom and control. Socially it is the welder of bonds of almost sacred significance between warriors. The corollary is that those who break oaths or fail to live up to them are subjected to the severest obloquy. The most striking and paradoxical feature of all, however, is that oaths are uttered without appealing to any force above or beyond the speaker's own sense of honour. God is mentioned thirty times in *Beowulf*, but never invoked as a prop and never named in vain. The same is true of *The Battle of Maldon, The Wanderer, The Seafarer* and the whole corpus of secular poetry. Invocations of a religious kind become the dominant driving force of oaths only from Middle English onwards.

These linguistic features corroborate, fascinatingly, the description of the Germanic tribes in the first century AD by the Roman historian Tacitus in his *Germania*. Although one suspects that Tacitus might be 'ennobling the savage' at the expense of contemporary, decadent Rome, his description of the social mores of the Germans has both clarity and detail. Tacitus admires the intense loyalty which existed between the lord and his band of personal followers, termed the *comitatus* in Latin and the *cynn* in Anglo-Saxon (chapter 14). Focussing on a bond of another kind, he observes that 'the German women live in a chastity that is impregnable' and that the Germanic tribes were almost unique among the barbarians in practising monogamy (chapters 18–19). It may be relevant to comment here that the English term for the formalization of marriage, namely *wedding*, derives from A-S *wedd*, meaning a pledge, as does A-S *locc*, the second element of *wedlock* (which thereby becomes something of a tautology).[1] These senses are reinforced by the central statement of the ceremony, 'I *plight* thee my *troth*'. This formula employs two archaic forms, *plight*, derived from A-S *plihtian*, 'to expose to danger', still surviving in 'a sorry plight', and *troth*, which is a doublet of *truth*. The development of these two cognate terms has been highly significant. Whereas *troth* has remained personal, binding, and largely archaic, *truth* has become public, demonstrable by evidence and, in a sense, greater than the individual.

NUMINOUS WORDS: CHARMS, SPELLS AND RUNES

Representing the earliest of Vico's categories are those forms of word-magic termed charms, spells and exorcisms. These are found in great numbers in Anglo-Saxon manuscripts, though only those with reasonably metrical schemes are given prominence in scholarly studies. Some 'are probably among the oldest lines in the English language' (Gordon, 1954, p. 85). A pagan deity is even invoked in a charm for unfruitful land ('Erce, Erce, Erce, mother of earth'), though most of the charm is Christian in its references. Other charms, with quite complex and lengthy incantations, are directed against wens, swarms of bees, convulsive diseases and theft of cattle. A charm for a safe journey contains an illuminating formula which alludes explicitly to the magical power of words: 'I chant a charm of victory, I bear a rod of victory / Word-victory, work-victory' (Gordon, 1954, p. 91).

It is a curious semantic point, however, that both *charm* and *spell* do not acquire their present 'magical' senses until Middle English at the earliest. *Spell* in Old English meant simply 'speech, narrative, discourse'. We have to wait centuries until the *Glossary to Spenser's Shepherds' Calendar* by 'E. K.' (possibly Edward Kirk) in 1579 to be told 'Spell is a kinde of verse or charme, that in eldre tymes they vsed often to say ouer evry thing that they would haue preserved, as the Nightspel for theeves, and the woodspell'. This would suggest a hiatus in the evidence rather than the practice. The earliest recorded survival of the nightspell is the comic instance riddled with ironies in Chaucer's *Miller's Tale*, discussed in the following chapter. There is no recorded medieval instance of the woodspell, to protect travellers from the dangers of the forest. It would appear that from the time of the Renaissance *spell* started to acquire exclusively malignant properties. Though *charm* exists in Old English in the senses of 'noise' or 'blended voices', the earliest recorded instance of the magical sense of 'incantation, enchantment' is the *Cursor Mundi*, *c.*1300. As Arcite lies mortally wounded in the *Knight's Tale*, we are told of the 'leches' that 'Somme hadden salves, and somme hadden charmes' (2712). The word has managed to retain its benevolent sense.

In the cognate Germanic literature we find fuller references to these primitive forms of word-magic. The Old Norse *Elder Edda* embodies the more developed tradition of Icelandic charms, in which there is an inseparable interinvolvement of form and meaning:

> Charms exist intact in Icelandic only in runes – the pre-Christian Germanic form of writing. Runes ('mysteries, secrets') are magic signs whose individual shape or *stafr* (English *stave*) represents an incantation – that is, a charm itself. Runes are not a practical form of writing, but priestly inscription for divination or sortilege. Each rune is associated intrinsically with a particular charm. (Salus and Taylor, 1969, pp. 23–4)

In the *Havamal*, 'The Sayings of the High One', Odin learns charms in runic form, the first being a 'Help' charm based on the runic letter for N, which stands for Norse *Nauthr*, 'need'. 'N-runes seem to have been used especially for delayed child-birth,' according to Salus and Taylor (1969, p. 24). Both runic inscriptions and references to charms are more plentiful in Scandinavia than in the British Isles, for 'magic continued to influence domestic life and thought for centuries after the arrival of the Christian Church' (Salus and Taylor, 1969, p. 23). However, a transcription of an Anglo-Saxon *Runic Poem*, in which each letter of the runic alphabet is explained stanza by stanza, is regarded as older than similar poems in Norwegian and Icelandic.[2]

Runic charms in Old Icelandic poetry have a far greater range of function than their Anglo-Saxon equivalents, which are basically domestic and benevolent. In the Norse tradition, there is even a developed categorizing terminology: the general term, *galdr* (related to A-S *galan*, 'to sing') covers those which, like the Anglo-Saxon equivalents, seek to harness the forces of nature, or suspend them, for benevolent or malign purposes. However, some Norse varieties are used against weapons to render them inoperable, while others (termed *seid* and *ergi*) are closer to sorcery, and can be used for shape-changing as well as to influence behaviour in order to make the recipient ignominious, revolting or amorous. Even resurrection from death can be achieved. In the largely matter-of-fact world of the sagas, magic runes make occasional spectacular entries. The death of the hero of *The Grettis Saga* is contrived by a spell of evil runes cut into a tree stump by a witch and then reddened with her blood. Although Grettir intuitively recognizes the stump as fateful, and seeks to avoid it, it never the less becomes the agent of his death (chapters 79–82). On the other hand, the great Norse skald, Egil Skallagrimsson, saves his own life by the use of runes. A poisoned beer-horn having been given to him, 'Egil graved runes upon it, spread them with blood, and chanted a verse' (chapter 44). The horn splits apart and the poisoned drink runs down into the straw.

Curiously, one of the most dramatic instances of the use of a malign spell in Anglo-Saxon literature is wrought by the monster Grendel. Described as one of the evil tribe of Cain and an enemy of the Lord, he puts a spell on the weapons of his victims, the Scyldings (ll. 801–5). The key verb in the text at this point is, fascinatingly, *forsworen*, literally 'forsworn', indicating that the verb *forswerian* could mean 'to hinder by swearing; to render powerless by incantation; to make useless by magic'. In the provenance of history, a similar spell is dramatically recorded in the *Life of St Wilfrid* after a storm cast the saint and his companions ashore in 666: the chief priest of the South Saxons 'took up his stand in front of the pagans, on a high mound, and like Balaam, attempted to curse the people of God, and bind their hands by means of his magical arts'.[3] Bede also mentions a pertinent anecdote in his *Ecclesiastical History* (Book iv, chapter 22) concerning a prisoner whose bonds miraculously fell from him at intervals. The explanation emerges that his brother, an abbot, believing that he had been killed in battle, sang regular masses for his soul. At each celebration of the mass the bonds were loosed. The captors, not realizing the explanation, asked the prisoner the revealing question of 'whether he knew the releasing rune and had about him the *stafas* (incantations) written out, such as men tell idle tales of'.[4]

More in the realm of wisdom literature than word-magic are the Anglo-Saxon *Gnomic Verses*, which contain a mixture of descriptive and proverbial material, including various endorsements of loyalty, such as 'Faith shall be in an earl, wisdom in a man' (Gordon, 1954, p. 314). Numerous monitory maxims concern the punishment of the faithless man, who is reduced by ostracism to that most feared condition, harped on in so many Anglo-Saxon poems, the miserable state of exile as a solitary wanderer 'unfriended, unblest, with wolves as companions' (Gordon, 1954, p. 314).

THE CONVENTION OF RETICENCE

The epic, heroic and moralizing qualities of the surviving Anglo-Saxon poetry limit the kind of swearing encountered in those texts to asseverations. Oaths are reserved for the serious commitments of the warrior ethic, not for momentary outbursts. When, for example, the doughty Beowulf's sword breaks in the crucial confrontation with the dragon, he responds with philosophical dignity, not with the expletive (muttered, mild or four-letter) typical of his modern equivalent. Expressions of exasperation, where they do occur, are commonly laced with the cool irony endemic to Germanic literature, or with grim understatement. In *Njal's Saga*, when Gunnar, the hero, is under desperate siege in his house, he asks his wife Hallgerth for some locks of her beautiful hair to replace his broken bowstring. When she refuses, he replies laconically, 'To each his own way of earning fame. You shall not be asked again' (chapter 77). As the siege intensifies, the language becomes the more restrained. Perhaps the most memorably taciturn and quintessentially Norse exit-line of the whole literature is uttered at this moment of the saga:

> Thorgrim the Easterner climbed on to the roof. Gunnar caught sight of a red tunic at the window. He lunged out with his halberd and struck Thorgrim in the belly. Thorgrim dropped his shield, lost his footing, and toppled down from the roof. He strode over to where Gizur and the others were sitting.
> Gizur looked up at him and asked, 'Is Gunnar at home?' 'That's for you to find out,' replied Thorgrim. 'But I know that his halberd certainly is.' And with that he fell dead. (chapter 77)

Gnomic commonplaces in Anglo-Saxon verse urge caution before giving vent to feelings or a boast. This instance from *The Wanderer* is an often repeated formula: 'A wise man must be patient, not over-passionate, nor over-hasty of speech . . . A man must bide his time, when he boasts in his speech, until he knows well in his pride whither the thoughts of the mind will turn' (65–72). The poem ends commenting on the extremes of faith and foolhardiness in language: 'Good is he who keps faith; nor shall a man ever show forth too quickly the sorrow of his heart, unless he, the earl, knows how to work its cure bravely' (112–14). This is not, of course, a prohibition against swearing *per se*, but a caution recognizing the vital, indeed sacred, link between words and deeds upheld in such a society. Faith in this bond is seen, for example, when Beowulf undertakes to destroy the marauding monster Grendel. His word is taken, not as a mere statement of intent, but as an article of faith (and, therefore, as grounds for rejoicing) by his hosts, the beleaguered Scyldings, since he retains the hero's special magic ability to transform words into deeds. Beowulf also epitomizes that complex ideal of heroism, a mixture of modesty and ferocity recognizable centuries later in Chaucer's Knight and Malory's Lancelot: lion in battle but lamb in the hall.[5] The final words bestowed on his memory by his people describe him, pointedly, as *manna mildust*, 'the kindest of men'

(l. 3181). It is especially revealing that as he lies dying, Beowulf reflects modestly, not on his superhuman achievements, but on the simple point that he kept faith: 'I did not pick treacherous quarrels, nor have I sworn unjustly any oaths' (ll. 2740–1).

LEGAL CONSTRAINTS ON SWEARING

All the surviving evidence of Anglo-Saxon culture shows a people and a society that took language very seriously. Reading the poetry, we are very aware of the dignified restraint of the language, deriving from an intense respect for the relationship between words and deeds. Although such reticence might be slightly idealized in a literary text, several of the Anglo-Saxon laws corroborate the same essential underlying rigour. Laws are revealing, of course, in that they focus only on those breaches of conventional behaviour which a society regards as unacceptable and punishable. Here is one such instance:

> If anyone in another's house calls a man a perjurer, or shamefully accosts him with insulting words, he is to pay a shilling to him who owns the house, and six shillings to him to whom he spoke that word, and to pay twelve shillings to the king. (Laws of Hlothhere and Eadric, kings of Kent (673–85?), no. 11)

Apart from the hierarchical scale of punishment, what is notable to us is that the verbal offence is sufficient of itself to incur the penalty (which, incidentally, is the same as that for stealing a cup). We should now expect the matter of perjury to be handled by a court, not treated in so summary a fashion.

A revealing constraint from the Laws of Alfred (900) is contained in the injunction: 'Do not ever swear by the heathen gods.' (This comes some three hundred years after Christianity was first brought to England.) The literature shows virtually no instances of such swearing, apart from the pagan invocation in the Anglo-Saxon charm for fertility and the episode in the *Life of Wilfred*, both cited earlier. However, the Scyldings in *Beowulf* show a serious instance of 'back-sliding' by resorting to devil worship when they are unable to counter the marauding raids of Grendel (ll. 175–80). Wulfstan, Archbishop of York at the time of the worst of the Viking depradations, denounced the wholesale breaking of faith in his *Sermo Lupi ad Anglos* (1025): 'Many are forsworn, and grievously perjured, for pledges are broken over and over again' (ll. 87–8).

So far as the validity of oaths is concerned, the laws show a trust in statement under oath which is shaming to our modern cynicism over such matters, where perjury is regarded as only a legal offence. 'He who kills a thief,' runs one of the laws of Ine (688–94), 'may declare with an oath that he slew him as a guilty man . . .'. However, some oaths are weightier than others. The Anglo-Saxon laws show a revealing discrimination in the relationship between the validity of oaths and the status of the swearer. Under the code of Hlothhere and Eadric we find the following distinctions: 'A twelve hundred man's oath stands for six *ceorl's* oaths'. 'If a man of Kent buys property in London, he is to have then two or three honest *ceorls*, or the King's town-reeve, as witness.'

SELF-BINDING OATHS: BOASTS, CHALLENGES AND VOWS

Although reticence is an honoured linguistic mode at this stage of the culture, the verbal responses of the Anglo-Saxons take on an altogether fiercer tone when honour is at stake. The Viking challenge in the preamble to the actual engagement celebrated in *The Battle of Maldon* is met by an English answer loaded with stinging irony:

> Byrhtnoth raised his shield, brandished his slender ashen spear and ground out words; furious and resolute, he gave the messenger answer: 'Do you hear, seafarer, what this people say? They intend to present you with spears for tribute, poisonous points and heirloomed swords, tribute which will profit you naught in the fight.' (42–8)

A word of importance to our theme which is buried in this passage is *answer*, which is today an unremarkable, mundane term. As the example of *forswerian*, just discussed, suggests, the term has greater potency and acquires increasingly serious implications as one goes back in time. This earlier notion of 'answer' is vitally related, in the *Maldon* context and elsewhere, to its etymology, since Anglo-Saxon *andswarian* means literally to 'swear against', to make a formal, legal reply to a charge. Indeed, the dominant early meaning of the word was legal, a sense we are still aware of in the phrases 'to be answerable for something' and 'to answer to a charge'.

The acute sense of verbal honour under discussion is not limited to the noble class. As the *Battle of Maldon* makes very clear, every English man in his station, from Byrhtnoth, who is 'Æðelredes eorl', King Ethelred's earl or viceroy, down the social hierarchy via Aescferth, the hostage from Northumbria, to Dunnere, the humble churl, each is given his moment to make good the English boast to give the Vikings a bloody tribute of weaponry instead of their expected *danegeld*, or protection money. (It is some nobles, in fact, who treacherously flee at a critical phase when Byrhtnoth has fallen and the battle seems lost.) It is then, paradoxically, that the deeper duty of vengeance falls to Byrhtnoth's troop. At this point Aelfwine, a warrior young in years, reminds the English of their obligations of honour: 'Remember the times when often we made speeches at the mead-drinking, when on the bench we made vows, heroes in hall, about hard strife. Now whoever is brave may put it to the test' (212–14).

Aelfwine announces his lineage and proceeds into the battle, rallying the demoralized English. His noble behaviour encapsulates a notably repeated formula in the poem whereby a warrior makes some kind of oath, formalizes his 'taking of a stand' by the raising or brandishing of a weapon, and then proceeds into the battle to make it good. (Stefan Einarsson has examined a number of similar contexts in Old English and Old Norse literature and has found that the Old English *beot* ('oath taking') is older than the Norse equivalent, *heitstrenging*: both terms are discussed below.[6]) In *Maldon* one can see the motif repeated half a dozen times. One of the most memorable instances comes from a warrior called Leofsunu, who also brings out the extreme ignominy of returning home lordless:

> Leofsunu spoke, he raised his linden shield, and answered the warrior thus: 'I promise this that I shall not flee from here one foot's space, but will advance and avenge my dear lord in battle. The steadfast warriors around Sturmere shall not have cause to criticise me, now that my dear lord has fallen, that I should turn my back on the fight and travel lordless home.' (244–52)

The passage endorses entirely the observation on the warrior ethic made by Tacitus in his *Germania* nearly a thousand years previously: 'As for leaving a battle alive after your chief has fallen, *that* means lifelong infamy and shame' (chapter 14).[7] In four lines the *Maldon* poet sets the archetypes of loyalty and cowardice alongside each other: 'Aelfnoth and Wulfmaer both fell there; they gave up their lives alongside their lord. Then those who did not wish to be there turned from the battle . . .' (183–5)

EMPTY VOWS AND OSTRACISM

As might be expected in a society endorsing the ethos of warrior loyalty so strongly, a place of extreme contempt is reserved for oath-breakers. In a bitter commentary on the cowardice of those ('who cared not for the fight'), the *Maldon* poet not only singles them out by name, but brings out the treachery damningly by informing the reader of the fallen Byrhtnoth's generosity to them. He also takes us back in time to a warning spoken by Offa at a prior meeting 'that many who spoke bravely there would fail in the hour of need' (200–1). No doubt such warnings have been reiterated a thousandfold before and since. However, as language has, in Vico's model, changed from being heroic to conventional, so the ignominy attaching to vow-breaking has diminished. Indeed, the undertakings of modern politics are tacitly assumed to be statements of intent (and therefore alterable with circumstance) rather than statements under oath. This point – exemplified in so many modern instances – is illustrated in a nicely cynical comment in a recent cartoon: the billboard reads 'LABOUR BACK-TRACKS ON DEFENCE', while the astonished comment of the bright young social thing is: 'But I thought they did that only when they got elected.'

To return to the vows of heroes, in the previously quoted speech of Aelfwine, the word translated as 'vows', namely *beot*, could also be taken as 'boasts', which (together with *brag* and *vaunt*) now has a pejorative sense, denoting empty claims and vainglorious speech. But, as the slightly archaic phrase *to make good a boast* implies, the more serious sense of a verbal undertaking lies at the root of the word. *Beot*, like much of the heroic vocabulary of Anglo-Saxon, has now passed away. It is derived from a contraction of A-S **bi-hatan*, meaning 'promise'. The root word *hatan* contains an important semantic complex of ideas, since it means 'to call (by name)', 'to be called', 'to command' and 'to promise'. These meanings clearly establish a person's position and obligations within a society from various perspectives. *Boast, brag* and *vaunt* are, however, still with us, having undergone an interestingly parallel decline. *Brag* originally meant 'to bray like a trumpet', just as the earliest noun sense of *boast* was 'loud noise of the voice' or 'outcry'. Wycliffe wrote in 1382: 'Whanne the voyce of the trompe . . . in youre eeris braggith,' and Gavin Douglas gives us a colourful description in his *Æneis* (1513) of the 'terribill brag of brasin [brazen] bludy soundis'. – (His use of *bludy* seems to be a most interesting anticipation of the subsequent emotive sense, which is usually dated far later, to the early eighteenth century.[8]) From these beginnings as a literal 'big noise', both words have sunk to the state of 'empty vessels'.

The most ignominious decline in the field, however, is shown by *yelp*. A-S *gielpan* was a specially heroic term meaning 'to challenge', found in many stirring contexts, and related to *gylp-word*, 'challenging speech' or 'fighting talk', the essential currency of heroes. Before plunging without hope into the battle at Maldon, a man called simply Edward the Tall speaks such *gylp-word*, swearing 'that he would never flee the space of a foot, nor turn his back' (274–6). Beowulf's boast (before retiring at Hrothgar's court) that he will destroy Grendel is similarly termed *gylpword* (675). The canine deterioration seems to date from around 1550, being well exemplified in a comment by George Peele (1593), 'As dogs against the Moone that yelpe in vayne', and in a contemporary complaint about the yelping of a 'rash bethlem brained [mad] hound'. However, as Johnson's most interesting and much later definition (1755) suggests, not all connotations of valour were immediately lost. He defines *yelp* as: 'To bark as a beagle-hound after his prey.' The word moved back into the human provenance for a while, to mean 'complain or whine', as is seen in the contemptuous comment of Hearne in 1706: ' 'Twill make ye Whigg Pamphleteers yelp.' But it has never recovered its previous heroic status.

THE RITUAL INSULTS OF FLYTING

Although reticence is a much-prized virtue within ancient Germanic society, there co-exists with it the quite contrary convention of ritual insult known as *flyting*. The Old English root *flítan* includes the broader senses of 'to contend or strive' and is used, for example, of horse-racing in *Beowulf* and the struggle between David and Goliath. This introduces into flyting the element of a competition or contest. From the earliest times, however, the word had a strong verbal association, meaning 'to chide, wrangle or scold'. It is so used in Bede to cover the sense italicized in this passage: 'Then the evil spirits *made accusations against* him while the good spirits defended him' (*Ecclesiastical History*, III. 19). The Old Norse root, *flyta*, seems initially to be restricted to a heroic ambience. In this brand of flyting, the insults are deliberately provocative, designed, to use another Northern word, to *egg* the opponent into action. Although the language is often gross, even grotesque and astonishingly scatological, there is also a certain element of play. Skill in barbed insult, dexterity in the wounding phrase, is very much a part of heroic language of the North, where the complexity of word-play reaches astonishing proportions in skaldic verse, which was delivered *ex tempore*. It is the verbal equivalent of virtuoso sword-play. The existence of this acceptable convention of insult in such a restrained linguistic régime suggests that it was a species of safety-valve of the kind which has been described among the Australian aborigines and discussed in the first chapter.

In the comparatively uncensored verbal provenance of Old Norse, there seem to have been far more survivals of various forms of set-piece insult than is the case in early English. Such were the *flím* and the *níðvísur,* which specialized in the foulest infamy. In one of the latter category, two early missionaries to Iceland are accused of homosexuality: according to the scandalous calumny, the Bishop (Frithrekr) is said to have given birth to nine children, his assistant (Thorvald) being the father. Thorvald killed two men in retaliation (Einarsson, 1957, p. 47). The great *skald* Egil Skallagrimsson showed total fearlessness in his flyting verses, even to the point of grievously insulting Erik Bloodaxe, the King of Norway, and his Queen Gunnhildr. In his *níð* ('curse') uttered in the King's presence, Egil calls him 'This inheriting traitor [who] disinherits me by betrayal' and later: 'Lawbreaker not lawmaker ... brothers' murderer ... [whose] guilt stems all from Gunnhild' (*Egil's Saga*, chapters 56–7).

Einarsson traces various kinds of verbal contests in Germanic literature:

> In the Eddic poems [calumny and slander in verse] is represented by the quarreling between heroes (or a hero and giantess) in the Helgi lays, and between gods in the *Hárbarðsljóð* (Oðinn against þórr) and *Lokasenna* (Loki against the gods). These heroic boasting matches are old; witness the flyting between Beowulf and Unferð [discussed below]. They live on in the sagas in the form of *mannjafnaðr*, 'man matching,' the most famous example being the verbal contest between the two royal brothers in *Heimskringla*, Sigurðr and Eysteinn, sons of King Magnús berfoettr. (Einarsson, 1957, pp. 38–9)

In his flyting with the gods (*Lokasenna*), Loki singles each out, stanza by stanza, accusing them of cowardice, adultery, incest, homosexuality and (possibly) urolagnia. Their responses show justifiable annoyance at this affront to their dignity. On the other hand, the episode from *Heimskringla* emphasizes more the aspect of play and performance. The retinues of the two young kings Eystein and Sigurd are in a state of wintry depression at a feast because of the quality of their ale. Thereupon Eystein makes this suggestion: 'Let us provide some amusement with the ale; then there will yet be some jollity among the men, for surely, brother Sigurd, they will all think it most fitting if we two start some bantering talk', since, as he explains, 'It has often been an ale custom to match men one against another' (1932, p. 624).

Furthermore, insults by women which would be unthinkable at such an early stage of English linguistic culture are quite common in Old Norse literature. In *Kormak's Saga* Steingerth divorces her husband

Bersi for an apparent homosexual attachment; before decamping, she says that he deserves to be called 'Buttocks Bersi' (chapter 13). Women equally insist that insults be avenged, not waiting for men to champion their cause. The whole action of the *Droplaugarsona Saga* is precipitated by the widow Droplaug's desire for revenge over an insult. Indeed, women's insistence on vengeance or redress by persistent egging is a major motif in saga literature.

Salus and Taylor have an interesting theory relating to the evolution of flyting from charms:

> Charms in Ireland and Wales seem to have degenerated into curses and insults after the arrival of Christianity, and there are comparable curses and insults in the flyting episodes of Old Icelandic heroic poetry, where exchange of words between antagonists before a battle seems to have lost its character of invoking divine assistance in favour of heaping imprecations. (1969, p. 23)

Given these ancient Germanic roots of flyting, there appears to be a considerable hiatus in the practice in English literary history. As has been mentioned, there are vestigial examples of flyting in Anglo-Saxon literature in the prelude to the *Battle of Maldon*, where Viking and Saxon insult each other across the river Blackwater before joining battle, and in an exchange in *Beowulf*, to be considered in a moment. Thereafter there seem to be no instances until the un-heroic trading of insults of the Middle English poem *The Owl and the Nightingale* (*c.*1250), after which the tradition seems to decline, appearing vestigially in the *Morte d'Arthur*, and in Shakespeare's *Romeo and Juliet* and *Julius Caesar*. However, as we shall see in the next chapter, the traditions were sustained and most vigorously revived in the North of Britain (where the Norse influence is strongest), especially in Scotland.

Returning to *Beowulf*, let us briefly consider the problems of interpreting the tenor of speech which can arise in ostensibly simple situations, when one is so far removed from the cultural context of a verbal exchange. A classic instance is that termed by Klaeber 'the Unferth Intermezzo'. The hero, having just arrived at the court of the Scyldings (who are suffering the depredations of the monster Grendel) is being fêted and feasted as a saviour. In the course of this welcoming banquet a character called Unferth, a Scylding of some undefined office who sits in a privileged position at the feet of the Scylding king, Hrothgar, proceeds to insult the hero publicly by casting aspersions on his valour, referring particularly to an allegedly ignominious episode in his youth when he lost a swimming contest. Nobody reprimands Unferth. Nobody seems embarrassed. Nobody intervenes. Beowulf responds in kind. With a mixture of humour and irony he brushes off the insults, remarks that the speaker has drunk well of the beer, clears his own name and blackens that of his accuser, alluding to some treacherous behaviour in Unferth's past.

What does this exchange mean? Is it a piece of flyting, an exchange of ritual insults between champions, or a piece of fooling, or an elaborate exercise in irony? Is it even a curious way of testing a visiting champion's credentials? We do not certainly know, because we are ultimately ignorant of the conventions which apply to this situation. Consequently, the Unferth episode has inevitably attracted a great diversity of modern interpretations.[9] One thing is clear, however: the language is restrained and dignified; inflammatory words like *coward* or *loser* are avoided in favour of euphemistic circumlocutions. This moves the piece away from typical flyting, but makes the insults more sophisticatedly wounding.

XENOPHOBIA

Hatred of strangers appears to be an ingrained feeling which has been verbally impacted for centuries, as chapter 6 will show in greater detail. It arises from a variety of catalysts, of which martial invasion and religious competition are the most prominent. Both factors are strongly at work in the Anglo-Saxon period. In view of the ferocity of the Viking invasions, it is hardly surprising that originally denotative terms describing the invaders soon became highly emotive. The first mentions of Viking incursions in *The Anglo-Saxon Chronicle* (from 787) refer to them neutrally as *Dene*, 'Danes', although this term included Norwegians and Swedes. Over the years the term acquired increasing emotive force. *Wicing*, which is derived alternatively from OE *wic*, 'a settlement' or ON *vik*, 'a creek', is glossed by Aelfric (*c.*955–*c.*1020) as *pirata*, 'pirate'.

The view that the Vikings were pagans was widespread, largely justified, and intensified native feelings of animosity. Wulfstan, Archbishop of York from 1002 to 1023, writes bitterly of thralls who have abandoned their lords and gone over to the Danes as 'leaving Christendom to become pirates' ('of cristendome to wicinge weorðe'). When Byrhtnoth addresses the Viking host in the exchange of flyting in *The Battle of Maldon*, he refers to them contemptuously as *hæðen*, 'the heathen', a term which was first used in *The Anglo-Saxon Chronicle* as far back as the terrifying entry for the year 793:

> In this year terrible portents appeared in Northumbria, and miserably afflicted the inhabitants; these were exceptional flashes of lightning, and fiery dragons were seen flying in the air, and soon followed a great famine, and after that in the same year the harrying of the heathen miserably destroyed God's church in Lindisfarne by rapine and slaughter. (from the *Parker Chronicle*)

This entry, with its alarming portents and their cruel fulfilment, shows the Vikings being cast in the role of demonic forces especially intent, like some monstrous Antichrist, upon the destruction of Christ's kingdom on earth. This view is indelibly recorded in Wulfstan's jeremiad sermons. However, in contexts uncomplicated by fire and the sword, *heaðen* could also be used to mean 'gentile' (as distinct from 'jew'), and is even the word applied to the Good Samaritan. These usages underscore the fairly obvious point that the polarizations of war and religion create their own semantic correlatives.

When the Vikings charge across the river in *Maldon*, the poet refers to them with vehement hatred as *wælwulfas* ('slaughterous wolves') – an appropriate 'kenning' or condensed metaphor which does not contain as great a degree of hyperbole as might now be assumed. Although there has been an attempt in recent years to improve the 'image' of the Vikings, by styling them 'traders, not raiders', the devastating accounts of their marauding incursions in *The Anglo-Saxon Chronicle* attest to the appropriateness of the poet's term. *Maldon* appears to have been the celebration of a final stand, the last refusal to 'buy off' the Vikings; thereafter England slid into a state of supine surrender. Some twenty years after Maldon, in 1012, a Viking host barbarously murdered Ælfheah (later Alphege), Archbishop of Canterbury, who refused any ransom to be paid for him: in the words of the Laud Chronicle, 'they pelted him to death with bones and the heads of cattle.'

A revealing semantic change in the Anglo-Saxon period is to be seen in *wealh*, the term used by the Anglo-Saxon settlers to describe the Celtic inhabitants. (It is the root form of *Wales*, the second element of *Cornwall* and the first element of *walnut*.) Its earlier sense was, simply, 'foreigner', which reflects an ironic reversal of roles as well as the dominance of the invaders. However, as the Celts lost status, so the term started to acquire the sense of 'slave' or 'servant'. Finally, as the term deteriorated to mean 'a shameless person', a variety of disreputable compounds developed, such as *wealh-word*, 'a wanton word', and *wealian*, 'to be impudent, bold or wanton'. Usages often have sexual associations, as in 'he used impudent language [*wealode*] and said that he intended to enjoy his wife during the ?forbidden period.' The details of this deterioration are of interest since they reveal a pattern of stereotypic decline which is paralleled in a great number of similar sociolinguistic circumstances to be discussed more fully in chapter 6.

CONCLUSION

Beowulf epitomizes Germanic heroism in that he signally represents an intense commitment to language and honour. When he faces his horrifying enemies (Grendel mère et fils and the fire-breathing dragon) he is quite alone, with solely his armour, his strength and his courage to sustain him. He does not have the verbal fortification or spiritual assurance of an appeal to the Almighty which his medieval Christian counterpart could claim. Instead, like the heroes of *Maldon*, he swears that he will simply 'trust in his own strength' to defeat the enemy. Some critics have criticized his self-sufficiency in this regard. But for Beowulf there is no certainty of a Lord to appeal to (or for others to take in vain). Yet the poem was written at least three hundred years after St Augustine brought Christianity to England. The idea of this cultural gap, of a christianized poet looking back into the pagan abyss and marvelling at the greatness of man entirely alone, trusting in no more than his own strength and his own sense of honour, was perceptively and movingly recreated by Tolkien, in his wonderful British Academy lecture, 'The Monsters and the Critics' in 1936. Specifically rejecting Chadwick's view that 'Beowulf, for all that he moves in the world of the primitive Heroic Age of the Germans, nevertheless is almost a Christian knight', Tolkien argues for a bleaker magnificence:

> . . . one thing [the poet] knew clearly: those days were heathen – heathen, noble and hopeless. [In the alien universe of] the great earth, ringed with the shoreless sea, beneath the sky's inaccessible roof . . . as in a little circle of light about their halls, men with courage as their stay went forward to that battle with the hostile world and the offspring of the dark which ends for all, even the kings and champions, in defeat. (67)

Perhaps the most moving moment of heroic commitment in the literature of the North comes at the climax of *Njal's Saga*, or, to use the work's honorific title, *The Saga of Burnt Njal*. When the cycle of vengeance leads remorselessly to the burning of Njal's familial homestead, Flosi, the unwilling agent of the blood feud, implores Njal to spare himself. Njal replies:

> 'I will not come out,' said Njal, 'for I am an old man and little able to avenge my sons, and I will not live in shame.'
> Then Flosi said to Bergthora [Njal's wife], 'You come out, Bergthora, for under no circumstances do I wish you to burn.'
> Bergthora replied, 'I was given to Njal in marriage when I was young, and I have promised him that we would share the same fate.' (chapter 129)

In leaving the heroic ethos of ancient Germanic literature, we note its admirable simplicity and unmixed loyalties. When one moves forward to the world of adulterous romance in medieval literature, the whole notion of 'honour' becomes far more complex, and in places disturbing ironies emerge. Lancelot and Tristan are at once heroes and traitors. In Malory's *Morte d'Arthur*, Lancelot knowingly indulges in sophistry when defending Guinevere's honour (impugned by Meliageaunt), asserting: '. . . I say nay playnly, that thys nyght there lay none of thes ten knyghtes wounded with my lady, quene Gwenyver, and that woll I prove with myne hondys [hands] that ye say untrewly in that' (Book xix, chapter 7). Since Lancelot himself has slept with the Queen, his defence is sound, but profoundly cynical. He duly wins the trial by combat and the threat of Meliageaunt is removed. Even more disturbing is the episode of Isolde's trial by ordeal in Gottfried Von Strassburg's *Tristan*. Isolde's wording of her oath of innocence shows a similar legalistic guile: 'That no man in the world had carnal knowledge of me or lay in my arms or beside me but you, always excepting the poor pilgrim [Tristan in disguise] whom, with your own eyes, you saw lying in my arms.' When the climactic moment of the ordeal comes, the author appears to connive blasphemously at the amazing outcome. 'In the name of God she laid hold of the [red-hot] iron, carried it, and was not burned. Thus it was made manifest and confirmed to all the world that Christ in His great virtue is pliant as a windblown sleeve. . . He is at the beck of every heart for honest deeds or fraud. Be it deadly earnest or a game, He is just as you would have him' (1960, pp. 247–8). In comparison with these sentiments, those of the pagan forbears show an enviable innocence, existential courage and lack of duplicity.

NOTES

1 Of the other major European terms, *marriage* is a French importation, and related ultimately (according to Partridge) to Sanskrit *máryas* young man, lover, Greek *meirax*, a youth, a girl and others. *Matrimony*, on the other hand, emphasizes legal maternity, while German *Hochzeit* meaning a 'high time', concentrates on the celebratory aspects.

2 Anderson (1962), pp. 181–2.
3 Eddius, *Life of Wilfrid* (ch. xiii), ed. B. Colgrave, pp. 26–9.
4 See the differing interpretations put upon this episode by R. I. Page (1973), p. 112 and Ralph W. V. Elliott (1959), p. 67.
5 Chaucer's Knight is described, in what seems to us a daringly incongruous simile, as 'meek as a maid' (*Prologue*, 1. 69); Lancelot is similarly eulogized in Sir Ector's threnody in Malory's *Morte d'Arthur* as 'the kindest man that ever put spear in the rest' (Book XXI).
6 Stefan Einarsson, 'Old English *beot* and Old Icelandic *heitstrenging*,' *PMLA*, Vol. XLIX (1934), pp. 975–93.
7 There is an interesting parallel among the Zulu, described by George Thompson in 1827: 'They charge with a single umconto, or spear, and each man must return with it from the field, or bring that of his enemy, otherwise he is sure to be put to death' (*DSAE*).
8 Partridge and the *OED* agree in locating the earliest uses of the 'low colloquial intensive' sense in the eighteenth century, usually in relation to *bloody drunk*.
9 Unferth has been interpreted variously as a Fool, a councillor and a champion.

3

Paynims and Charlatans: Swearing in Middle English

At churche in the charnel cheorles aren yuel to knowe,
Other a knyght fro a knaue other a queyne fro a queene.

Piers Plowman

Christ's blood, these days, is reckoned of little price among the greater part of the people.

John Waldeby, in a sermon

THE great and obvious force behind most medieval swearing was Christianity. Just as Black Magic is a monstrous parody of orthodox religion, so blasphemous utterance is the obverse side of an age of faith. An astounding volume of religious asseveration, ejaculation, blasphemy, anathema and cursing, both personal and institutional, fraudulent and genuine, poured forth in the course of the Middle Ages. The word of God, so signally absent from the older heroic asseverations, was used and abused, elevated, debased and distorted as never before. The sacred was made profane in a way which seems to us utterly paradoxical, particularly when one considers this debasement in relation to the major counter-trend of medieval literature, namely the elevation, glorification, indeed near deification of woman in the 'Petrarchan' convention. Perhaps because that poetic convention was secular in application, it was regarded as a collective fancy. Never the less, the grisly invocation of Christ's body, blood and nails in the agony of the Crucifixion seems as grotesque and bizarre to us now as modern genital, copulatory, excretory and incestuous swearing would have seemed to medievals. Indeed, sexual swearing, now very much *de rigueur*, is hardly apparent, in fact 'non-existent in Chaucer', according to Ralph Elliott (1974, p. 241). But whereas sexual swearing is now taken seriously by some and lightly by others, the religious swearing of the Middle Ages had altogether greater force and impact.

The scale and intensity of religious swearing alters through the period. In the early stages it tends to consist of the mildest invocations of spiritual qualities, such as *by my faith!*, through appeals to the Virgin Mary and the saints, ascending to the godhead in its various serene aspects, as in *by God that sits above!*, but reaching its most potent expressions in the intimate references to the person and sufferings of Christ, already alluded to, as in *by Goddes corpus! Cristes passioun!* and the various gruesomely explicit evocations of the Crucifixion.

Other semantic developments derived from martial competition with rival religions, especially Islam, and that between Christian sects. This is reflected in such words of chauvinist vilification as the older term *heathen*, which was first joined by *paynim* (*pagan*), and later, towards the end of the medieval period, by *infidel*. The energies involved in the eventual destruction or confinement of Islamic expansionism through the various Crusades were subsequently diverted, ironically, to the equally violent splintering and atomization of the Christian faith into sectarian strife. As reformist impulses grew, the monolithic structure and the vocabulary of the Mother Church disintegrated. Consequently, the whole nature of religious utterance changed in quality from being profoundly mystic and arcane, borne by strange tongues, to the articulation of reformist sentiments which were vehemently social and political, spreading as a mighty force through whole nations via the vehicle of the vernaculars. This development forms the theme of the following chapter.

As the period developed, a major shift occurred in the form of an increased incidence of personalized 'swearing at', as against the more impersonal mode of 'swearing by'. This change brings into play a whole variety of new personal referents in swearing, which are entirely secular and which we now take for granted, such as age, stupidity, low status, meanness and uncleanness, conveyed in new emotive uses of words like *old*, *fool*, *churl* and *lousy*. Perhaps the most significant of these categories derives from the semantic change ably described by C. S. Lewis in *Studies in Words* as 'the moralisation of status words' (1960, p. 7). By this process (which seems initially to reflect the difference in status between Norman overlords and Saxon underlings) terms like *knave* and *noble*, which originally denoted only status, came in the course of time to acquire moral overtones dissociated from their original notions of rank. Some, like *gentle*, *liberal*, *frank* and *free* ameliorated, but nearly all the words which underwent deterioration were of Anglo-Saxon origin and had thus denoted low rank for centuries. These included *wretch* (A-S *wræcca*, 'an exile'), *churl* (A-S *ceorl*, 'a man', but on occasions 'a hero' or even 'a prince'), *knave* (A-S *cnapa, cnafa*, 'a male child') and *villein*, (Latin *villanus*, 'a servant at a villa'). All of these had become terms of opprobrium or personal abuse by *c.*1400. They were to be joined in the following centuries by *beggar* and *rascal* ('the rabble of an army; common soldiers or camp-followers; persons of the lowest class'); by *blackguard* ('the lowest menials in a household, who had charge of the pots and pans and other utensils') and by *scullion* ('a domestic servant of the lowest rank').

Emotive language starts to acquire such force that words lose touch with their etymological anchors altogether. When the devil-figure in Chaucer's *Friar's Tale* observes, 'A lowsy jogelour [juggler] kan deceyve thee' (1467), *lousy* is used (for the first recorded time) in an obviously disparaging fashion which is still current today, but the word never the less has a potential literal force, given the prevalence of lice in the Middle Ages. When, however, Lydgate writes (*c.*1430), 'A precious knave that cast nevyr to thryve', *precious* is obviously quite dissociated from its primary sense of 'valuable'. It has, in fact, moved into an oxymoronic relationship with the noun. This is maintained in subsequent uses, such as Shakespeare's 'precious villain!' (*Othello*, V. ii. 233) and the modern idiom 'precious little'. The twin processes of 'emotive intensification' and 'verbicide' or 'weakening' are essential features of the language of oaths.

FLYTING

The ritual insults and swearing-matches of flyting also form an important feature of oaths in the Middle Ages. A relevant text in this category is *The Owl and the Nightingale* (*c.*1250), from which most of the more fulsomely vituperative sections were censored in the early editions. Yet in comparison with the earlier Norse and later Scots examples, the poem is fairly polite, and has an academic or intellectual component which places it more in the tradition of the medieval *débat*. Most of the contest derives from the two birds deriding the unpleasant habits of the other. As the Nightingale has it:

Most foul you are and most unclean:
Your nest shows clearly what I mean,
For there you rear your noisome brood
On filthy putrefying food;
And you know what they do with it:

They foul themselves chin-deep and sit
Amid the muck as if quite blind . . . .
(91–7: all translations by Brian Stone)

Yet the participants are also described as 'psyching' themselves up for battle in the manner of the Germanic heroes and berserks:

The owl held back till evening fell:
Then, as her heart began to swell,
Her breath to catch, her rage to grate,
She felt she could no longer wait,
And straight away exploded. . . .
(41–5)

With some irony, given the context, the Owl claims to show considerable verbal restraint when provoked by the smaller birds:

What profits should I then produce
By routing them with loud abuse
Reviling them with shout and curse
As foul-mouthed shepherds do, or worse?
(283–6)

The text, interestingly, contributes two new phrases for 'strong language', namely *fule worde* ('foul words') and the stronger *shit worde* ('shit words'), of which only the first has remained current. Although the poem has a considerable scatological element, it supplies some interesting glosses in dealing with 'indelicate subjects'. For instance, in the passage where the Owl is making much of the fact that the Nightingale lives by the privy, a variety of euphemisms is used, namely: *seotle* ('settle', 'throne'), *at rum huse* (literally and ironically, 'at the spacious house'), þar men goþ to heore neode ('where people go when it's necessary'), þar men worpeþ heore bihinde ('where people waggle their behinds'). The last instance, incidentally, contains the first recorded use of *behind* as a euphemism, anticipating the *OED* instance by several centuries.

Chaucer's *The Parlement of Foules* (*c.*1382) is also not purely within the flyting genre, since it is predominantly a love-vision. However, as the title implies, the Valentine's Day decision of the tercels, the highest of the eagles, comes to involve the whole avian parliament. Indecision in high places provokes increasingly sharp, impatient and uncourtly reactions as the focus moves down the hierarchical ladder. As in *The Nun's Priest's Tale*, Chaucer makes considerable humorous capital by applying human idioms incongruously to the fowls:

'Wel bourded [joked],' quod the doke [duck], 'by min hat!'
(589)

The goos seyde, 'Al this nys nat worth a flye!'
(501)

In the ensuing altercation, the insults become lower in tone as the debate proceeds: 'Now parde! fol' is followed by the ridiculous 'Ye quek!', so that at one point the tercelet intervenes to upbraid a low comment in these terms:

'Now fy, cherl!' . . . .
Out of the donghil cam that word ful right!'
(596–7)

But worse is to follow in the merlin's outburst against the cuckoo:

'Thow mortherere of the heysoge [hedgesparrow] on the braunche
That brought the forth, thow rewtheless glotoun!
Lyve thow soleyn [alone], wormes corupcioun!'

At this point, when comedy is giving way to serious friction, Nature interposes to call a halt to the proceedings. There is a notable shift in idiom as the debate proceeds. The royal tercel swears simply in terms of personal honour, appealing to nothing outside himself, in the heroic style seen in the previous chapter. The work's principal religious oath is then uttered by a tercel 'of lower kynde':

'I love her bet than ye don, by seint John'
(451)

Thereafter, apart from the sparrowhawk's *parde!*, much of the idiom of abuse is taken from secular, rather than religious references. This stylistic difference is, assuredly, Chaucer's sociolinguistic observation on the oaths of his time.

PENALTIES AND CONDEMNATIONS

Not surprisingly, the efflorescence of swearing induced institutional opposition. This took two basic forms, namely judicial punishment and ecclesiastical denunciation. Both varieties of this punitive response seem to us now to be excessive, if not slightly deranged. Henry I (1068–1135), the son of William the Conqueror, is accredited with the following fines for swearing within the precincts of the royal residence: a duke, 40 shillings; a lord, 20 shillings; a squire, 10 shillings; a yeoman, 3 shillings and 4 pence (half a mark); a page, a whipping (Montagu, 1973,

p. 108). According to John Bromyard, Saint Louis of France (1214–70) decreed that swearers should 'be branded upon the face with a hot iron for a perpetual memorial of their crime, and later on, indeed, ordained that they should be set in a public place in the high stocks . . . similar in form and mode of punishment to that inflicted upon cutpurses in England' (Montagu, 1973, p. 111).

False swearing becomes one of the most commonly (and vehemently) denounced sins of medieval times. In his devotional manual with the quaint but thoroughly English title of the *Ayenbite of Inwit* (the 'Again-Biting of the Inner Wit', or less opaquely, the 'Remorse of Conscience') written *c.*1340, Dan Michel, a brother of the Cloister of Saint Austin at Canterbury, deals with swearing under one of the sins of the tongue, namely lying, observing that 'light' swearing becomes habitual to the point that the practitioners 'can say nothing without swearing'. Such folk, Michel observes, 'hold God in great contempt'. In what seems to us an intemperate, indeed almost hysterical denunciation, but one which became a topos in medieval strictures against swearing, Michel observes: 'In this sin, the Christians are worse than the pagan or infidel', or as he describes them, 'þe sarasyn'. He continues:

> They are worse than the Jews, who crucified Christ, but did not break any one of his bones. But these mince him smaller than men do swine in a butchery. These people do not even respect Our Lady, but are villainously destructive of her and of the saints to the point that it is a wonder that Christendom suffers it. (Folio 19a, p. 64)

He uses an equally violent image under the heading of blasphemy, when he denounces swearers as being 'like mad hounds that bite and know not their lord' (folio 20b, p. 70).

Such severe condemnations based on the literal interpretation of religious swearing are to be repeated time and again, over the centuries, but with diminishing force. It is a motif to be found, variously, in sermons and in dramatic speeches attributed to the Virgin and to Christ himself. Rosemary Woolf has shown that 'the theme of a fresh wounding or crucifying of Christ seems to have occurred very early in a spectacular and popular form, that of the *exemplum* of the Bloody Child' (Woolf, 1968, p. 396). She traces the first appearance of the motif to the *Handling Synne* (*c.*1300) of Robert of Brunne, in which the Christ child is the victim of dismembering oaths. In this story the Blessed Virgin Mary shows the sinful swearer her child:

All to-drawn were the guts;
Of hands, of feet, the flesh off drawn;
Mouth, eyes and nose, were all to-knawan [gnawed],
Back and sides were all bloody.

She upbraids the 'rich' [powerful] man who is typical of his class, which 'commonly swears great oaths grisly':

'Thou,' she said, 'has him so shent [damaged],
And with thy oaths all to-rent.'

At this 'the sinner becomes penitent and the Virgin agrees to intercede for him' (Woolf, 1968, p. 396). It is important to realize that these sentiments were not especially English: both Dan Michel and Robert of Brunne were working from French sources. In an English version of one of the most famous compilations of the Middle Ages, the *Gesta Romanorum*, *c.*1440, the literal possibility of wounding words is taken just as seriously; the Virgin upbraids the sinners in these terms:

> 'Why come ye hidder? For to shew the my sone, lo!' she saide, 'here is my sone, lyeng in my lappe, with his hede all to-broke, and his eyen drawen oute of his body and layde on breste, his armes broken a-twoo, his legges and his fete also. . . .' (Woolf, 1968, pp. 396–7)

In the collection of homilies entitled *Festial* by Johannes Mirkus (John Mirk), *c.*1450, Christ upbraids callous and insensitive swearers, using the same motif:

> 'and what particularly grieves me is that you care nothing for my passion which I suffered for you, but I am affronted all day by horrible swearers, who swear by my face, by my eyes, by my arms, by my nails, by my heart, by my blood, and so forth, by my whole body.' (*EETS 96*, p. 113)

Numerous instances of the motif are found in medieval lyrics. Woolf mentions powerful visual analogues in the stained glass of two churches, in Norwich and Broughton, Buckinghamshire. In some of these there are parts of Christ's body actually missing, being grotesquely displayed by some fashionably dressed young men (Woolf, 1968, p. 397). This class gloss is not unique. John Bromyard in his *Summa Prædicantium* observes, under the heading of 'Juramentum', the elements of social aspiration and fashion in swearing:

> These inventors of new oaths, who inanely glory in such things, count themselves more noble for swearing thus. This is to be seen among those who consider themselves of high breeding, or are proud. Just as they invent and delight in everything of the nature of outward apparel, so do they also in the case of vows and oaths . . . . Strange vows and swear-

> words invented by them are already so common that they may be found daily in the mouth of any ribald or rascal you please. (cited in Owst, 1961, p. 414)

These social comments show the extremely diversified reactions swearing produced: sensitive souls interpreted blasphemous invocations seriously and literally as an affront to divine dignity and suffering, while those of a more coarse and callous disposition evidently regarded swearing as no more than a colourful and shocking form of words. These reactions seem in many ways perennial, when one reflects on modern attitudes to sexual swearing. Even in these times the name of the Virgin Mary was being 'minced' into *marry*, a sign that it was no longer used in a powerfully literal fashion. The first recorded instance of the word being used to mean simply, 'Why, to be sure' is *c*.1350O.

For reasons of length, this chapter will consider the topic in relation to only one of the main authors of Middle English by focussing exclusively on Chaucer. Although the *Gawain* poet, Gower and Langland have their various treatments of swearing, only the microcosm of *The Canterbury Tales* explores the whole gamut of human experience and of the lexicon. We are, furthermore, introduced to an extraordinary range of religious charlatans and simoniac opportunists peddling pseudo-sermons and false relics, and uttering blasphemous execrations.

SWEARING IN *THE CANTERBURY TALES*

The puzzling endpiece to the *Canterbury Tales*, the Retractions, show Chaucer the author at the moment of finally unmasking himself to reveal a pious man, very aware of his responsibilities as an author and profoundly earnest in his wish 'that I may be oon of hem at the day of doom that shulle be saved'. Those closing words of his last great work command a serious consideration of ultimate verities which supplants the earlier ironies and the sophisticated literary hide-and-seek of ingeniously created personae. Given this evident belief in the ultimate efficacy of God's word, what can we deduce about the use of swearing in Chaucer's tales?

When one considers the microcosmic variety of the pilgrims, embracing mental and physical antitypes in the Reeve and Miller, the Prioress and Wife of Bath, as well as the ruthless simoniac competitiveness of the Friar, Pardoner and Summoner for the market of indulgences, and the sheer vulgar egotism of so many of the lay artisans and incipient bourgeois, it is to be expected that situations of conflict, and attendant strong language will be one feature of the pilgrimage. Chaucer the ingenious author, who has created the whole multifarious frame narrative, makes Chaucer the naive pilgrim narrator decorously anticipate this problem towards the end of the *Prologue*, introducing it in a rather awkward, slightly embarrassed and long-winded fashion, but gaining courage as he goes along:

> But first I pray yow, of your curteisye,
> That ye n'arette [attribute] it nat my vileynye [ill-breeding]
> Thogh I pleynly speke in this mateere
> To telle yow hir wordes and hir cheere [manner]
> Ne thogh I speke hir wordes properly [in character].
> For this ye knowen al so wel as I
> Whoso shal telle a tale after a man
> He moot reherce [repeat] as ny as evere he kan
> Everich a word, if it be in his charge
> Al speke he never so rudeliche and large [freely],
> Or ellis he moot telle his tale untrewe
>
> Crist spak himself ful brode [plainly] in hooly writ
> And wel ye woot no vileynye is it.
> Eek Plato seith, whoso that kan hym rede
> The wordes moote be cosyn for the dede.
>
> (725–42)

This 'apologia pro labore sua', having earlier models in Jean de Meun and Boccaccio, does not need to be as hesitant as it is.[1] Nor should it distract us from the central point of why some characters swear more violently than others, and what this means. Herbert Starr, in what is probably a conservative estimate, calculated that there are two hundred different oaths in Chaucer (Elliott, 1974, p. 262). Although, as Ralph Elliott has observed in his useful discussion of the topic, 'It is the vulgar characters who swear most and most profanely, with Harry Bailly well out in front, the Wife of Bath some way behind, followed by Pardoner and Miller' (253), one has to distinguish on a more discriminating basis than mere volume. Oaths seem to cascade indiscriminately from the lips of the extraordinary cavalcade of tellers, echoing down the path of pilgrimage. It would appear, however, that Chaucer has created a very sharp differentiation on the basis of character, and that a clear though subtle judgement is being made by the author on his characters on the basis of their oaths and 'brode' language. Furthermore, Chaucer goes beyond the relatively straightforward use of oaths, exploring all kinds of perversions of Holy Writ and blasphemous abuses of religious language, such as curses, mock-blessings, pseudo-sermons and the like. Today, in an age characterized by loss of faith, we are more concerned with obscenity than with blasphemy or profanity. Chaucer's priorities were different. Centuries before Freud, he had perceived that character and personality are revealed, not only in fantasies of wish fulfilment, but in all forms of highly charged language.

The pious modesty of the Knight, to take an extreme example, is reflected in the commendable restraint of his language:

> He nevere yet no vileynye ne sayde
> In al his lyf unto no maner wight
> (70–1)

At the contrary end of the moral scale, the life-lie of bogus evangelism perpetrated by the simoniac Pardoner pours out in a confused mixture of spiritual charlatanism and guilt-stricken, hysterical denunciations of swearing. He seems to be unaware that he is involved in a far more heinous kind of blasphemy. In a topos previously discussed, the drunken revellers of his tale – his own creations – tear Christ's body to pieces, while the author affects moral indignation:

> And many a grisly ooth thanne han they sworn
> And Cristes blessed body they al torente
> (708–9)

In a gentler mode, one of the earliest of many incongruous references to the Prioress in the *General Prologue* is, pointedly, to the mildness of her oaths, the severest of which is, most appropriately, addressed to the patron saint of jewellers:

> Hir grettest ooth was but by Seinte Loy
> (120)

Attitudes towards swearing (or, more properly, false swearing) are strongly counterpointed at the start of the following illuminating exchange between Host, Parson and Shipman in the Epilogue of the *Man of Law's Tale*. The Host invites the Parson to participate in the story-telling game, using provocatively fulsome language; the Parson strongly denounces his blasphemous ribaldry, while the Shipman chimes in, rejecting any possibility of a parsonical sermon, which he castigates as 'glosing'. The Host archly begins:

> 'Sir Parisshe Prest,' quod he, 'for Goddes bones,
> Telle us a tale . . . by Goddes dignitee!'
> The Persone him answerde, 'Bendicitee!
> What eyleth the man so synfully to swere?'
> Our Host answerde, 'O Jankyn, be ye there?
> I smelle a Lollere[2] in the wynd,' quod he.

'Now! goode men,' quod our Hoste, 'herkeneth me,
Abydeth, for Goddes digne passioun,
For we schal han a predicacioun;
This Lollere here wil prechen us somwhat.'
'Nay, by my fader soule, that schal he nat!'
Seyde the Shipman, 'heer schal he nat preche;
He schal no gospel glosen here ne teche.
'We leven alle in the grete God,' quod he.
'He wolde sowen some difficulte,
Or springen cokkel with our clene corn.'
(1166–83)

These three attitudes are not simply a random exchange of character-speeches; they are designed to encapsulate and juxtapose the prevalent views on religious language. The Parson's attitude (which accords with that of Dan Michel and John Bromyard cited earlier) seems, perhaps, unrealistically severe, as are the views on morality and human fallibility which he expresses in his own sermonizing tale. He exemplifies the Wycliffite reformist attitudes which were taking such a hold on the land, and which were in the following centuries to be adopted by the severer sects which tended towards Puritanism and Quakerism. The Host's satirical reduction of the Parson as a 'Lollere' (the first recorded use of the word, criticizing great pretensions to piety and humility) is accordingly sharp, but not undeserved. The Shipman's view shows vestiges of the anti-dogmatic attitudes which were germinating in Chaucer's time and which were to harden in the next century into non-conformist Protestantism. Suspicious of priests, his fundamentalism simply rejects 'glosing' (ingenious or false interpretation) of the gospel. The Host represents the attitude of the balanced, shrewd, commonsensical *homme moyen rationelle*, suspicious of extremes and keen to puncture cant in any form. His own language is, however, fulsome, since he is both passionate and critical.

The originality of Chaucer's swearing is another significant aspect, one which deserves closer scrutiny than it has so far received.[3] In a text of such remoteness, it is clearly hard for us now to recreate accurately, and appreciate properly, the 'newness' of the oaths. To us, secular terms of disparagement like *foul*, *lousy*, *old*, *shrew*, *swine* and *idiot* have lost their 'bite' and wounding sharpness in the intervening centuries. They have undergone the semantic trends known variously as Verbicide, Weakening or Loss of Intensity.[4] Alongside such seemingly spectacular blasphemies as *God's arms!* and *God's bones!* they seem tame. Yet several of these terms would appear, on the basis of the *OED*, to be fire-new, fresh-minted and well able to burn the ears of a contemporary audience. Only those who had their ears very close to the ground would previously have come across such disparaging terms as *lousy* and *idiot*, as well as the fulsome religious ejaculations like *God's arms*, *Christ's passion!*, *Benedicitee!* and the minced forms *pardee* and *cokkes bones!* Even the contemptuous use of *old*, the Wife of Bath's speciality in castigating her elderly spouses in such phrases as *olde barelful of lies, sire olde lecchour*, and the like, seems not to have been very common. Not surprisingly, these instances come from the more aggressive and uncouth speakers, such as the Host, Wife, Summoner and Friar. Yet, as we shall see, even the semantically conservative Man of Law launches the fascinating term *virago* as a new term in the anti-feminist armoury. Furthermore, in his portrait of the one 'good man of religioun', the truly pious and charitable Parson, Chaucer the Pilgrim departs from his primly bourgeois mode to employ four-letter words with uniquely devastating effect. He conveys his detestation of the typically corrupt clergy, referring to them as 'a shiten [defiled] shepherde and a clene sheep' (*Prologue*, 1. 504).

As will emerge in the following brief survey, swearing turns out to be an important index of a character's piety, sensitivity and worth, as reliable as a touchstone as Ruth Nevo has shown in character-attitudes towards material things, and as Arthur Hoffmann has found in a character's quality of love.[5] Furthermore, swearing in various forms, particularly the making and breaking of faith, becomes the theme or turning point of several of the tales, often in revealingly unexpected ways. For instance, both the Wife of Bath's and Franklin's tales focus on the binding quality of oaths, honoured at a considerable cost, examined from a bourgeois pragmatic perspective. The Man of Law's tale is almost wholly concerned with apostasy and treachery, and contains a spectacular punishment for perjury. One aspect of the Knight's tale is the conflict of loyalties between Palamon and Arcite, since they are simultaneously 'brothers ysworn ful depe' and rivals in love. A similar pact between the drunken revellers in the Pardoner's tale is rapidly forgotten and subverted by the finding of gold. The Friar's tale hinges on the point of an oath being binding, provided that it is heartfelt.

When the lot falls to the Knight to tell the first tale (fortuitously or out of respect for 'degree'), he accepts the role with humour and pious modesty:

> . . . Syn I shal bigynnen the game,
> What, welcome be the cut, a Goddes name!
> (853–4)

Interestingly, although the tale is a medieval romance transposed into a classical setting, and although the pagan deities have that major role in manipulating human affairs which is customary in the classical epic, many of the oaths and ejaculations have Christian references. Thus, in a single speech, Palamon berates the 'crueel goddes that governe this worlde' but also uses the phrase 'For Goddes sake', albeit not in the later empty idiom, although the reference is clearly monotheistic (1303–17). Generally, the two rivals speak like modest medieval knights, using asseverations such as '*by my pan, by my fey, for seinte charitee!* and *by God that sit above!* There is only one moment, of extreme passion, when Palamon discovers the deceiving disguise of Arcite and attacks him verbally in a violently personal fashion akin to that of a modern confrontation: 'Arcite, false traytour wikke! . . .' (1580). Coming upon the pair fighting in the grove, Theseus moves from medieval to classical idiom in two lines:

> Namoore, up peyne of lesynge of youre heed!
> By mighty Mars, he shal anon be deed
> That smyteth any strook that I may seen.
> (1707–9)

Subsequently reflecting on the power of love and the ironic futility of the duel, he slips into a more demotic medieval idiom:

> The god of love, a, benedicite!
> How myghty and how greet a lorde is he!
>
> She woot namoore of al the hoote fare,
> By God, than woot a cokkow or an hare!
> (1785–6; 1809–10)

In a conclusion which is also typical of the Knight's generosity, he first bestows a moving benediction on the love of Palamon for Emily, before blessing the fellowship of pilgrims wholeheartedly:

> And God, that al this wyde world hath wroght,
> Sende hym his love that hath it deere aboght
>
> And God save al this faire compaignye! Amen.
> (3099–3108)

As we shall see, the final invocation of a tale is often an important indicator of a teller's religious sensibilities.

The company is united in its opinion that the Knight's tale is 'a noble storie' worthy of memorial, a consensus which is unique in the frame narrative. However, just as the Host is inviting the pseudo-aristocratic

Monk to match the tale, all decorum and polite order cease as the drunken Miller forces himself on the company in a pointedly blasphemous fashion:

> . . . in Pilates voice[6] he gan to crie,
> And swoor, 'By armes, and by blood and bones
> I kan a noble tale for the nones. . . .'
>
> (3124–6)

What follows is not simply 'lewed dronken harlotrye' ('ignorant tipsy smut') as the Reeve primly condemns it, taking a view with which earlier critics generally concurred. It is a brilliant and outrageous parodic performance, mocking both in plot and in stylistic versatility the Knight's noble tale which has sublimated the erotic and aggressive impulses. Some critics have even scented a parody of The Anunciation.[7] Be that as it may, within the compass of our theme, blasphemy is certainly a major feature of the tale, in that a 'divine' prophecy (of a second Flood) is cynically and elaborately fabricated to divert the gullible Carpenter John and ensure his cuckolding. God is further mocked when Nicholas pretends to be possessed, evoking John's touchingly comic attempts at exorcism:

> 'Awak, and thenk on Cristes passioun!
> I crouch [cross] thee from elves and fro wightes [goblins]'.
> Therewith the nyght-spel seyde he anon-rightes
> On foure halves of the hous aboute
> And on the thressfold of the dore withoute
> 'Jhesu Crist and seinte Bendight
> Blesse this hous from every wicked wight
> For nyghtes verye,[8] the white *pater-noster!*
> Where wentestow, seinte Petres soster?'
>
> (3478–86)

Nicholas' eventual resuscitation ('atte laste') prophesying doom, compounds the farce and is very 'near the bone' in its suggestion that the elaborate 'nyght-spel' is a piece of mumbo-jumbo. (The night-spell is discussed further in chapter 2.)

The agonizing silences and enforced separation of the characters in the *Knight's Tale* are replaced in the Miller's bedroom farce by swiftly arranged assignations and a rich diversity of vocal utterance. Less than a hundred lines into the tale, Nicholas has dispensed with the decencies of foreplay and is declaring his secret passion ('deerne love') for Alisoun in a mixture of heavy breathing and religious ejaculation:

And heelde hire harde by the haunchebones,
And seyde, 'Lemman, love me al atones,
Or I wol dyen, also God me save!'
(3279–81)

Even Gerveys the smith, presented as a thumbnail 'character', is given an extraordinary density of religious exclamation packed into what is simply a cheeky 'man of the world' enquiry about Absolon's assumed nocturnal philandering:

'What, Absolon! for Cristes sweete tree [cross],
Why rise ye so rathe [early]? ey *benedicitee!*
What eyleth yow? Som gay[9] gerl, God it woot,
Hath brought yow thus upon the viritoot [gadding about].
By seinte Note [Neot], ye woot wel what I mene.'
(3767–71)

The absurd rival, the precious Absolon, is a character created almost entirely out of religious parody. In many ways summed up by the wonderful vignette of religious kitsch, 'With Poules wyndow corven on his shoos', he is to be found 'on the haliday sensing the wyves of the parrishe faste', which could mean either using the censer or 'groping' them, probably both. His serenade to Alisoun, who is unashamedly *in flagrante dilecto*, is modelled blasphemously on the Song of Songs:

'What do ye, hony-comb, sweete Alisoun,
My faire bryd, my seete cynomome?'
(3698–9)

He eventually manages to express his altogether primmer passion via what is termed in scholarly euphemism, 'the misdirected kiss', or, more classically, *osculum in tergo*, ironically a mode of Satanic worship. When his full discomfiture is apparent to him, his sentiments become truly diabolical:

But Absolon, that seith ful ofte 'Allas!
My soule bitake I unto Sathanas'
(3749–50)

Robin the Miller takes leave of his tale, which has jocularly and cruelly endorsed the law of the jungle, by paying lip service to the convention of a blessing:

Thus swyved [fucked] was this carpenter's wyf,
For al his kepyng and his jalousye;
And Absolon hath kist her nether ye;

And Nicholas is scalded in the towte [arse].
This tale is doon, and God save al the rowte!
(3850–4)

Oswald the Reeve, taking umbrage at what he conceives to be a personal slight, shows vengeful bitterness:

. . . I shal hym quyte [requite] anoon;
Right in his cherles termes wol I speke.
I pray to God his nekke mote to-breke;
(3916–18)

Not for the last time is the Almighty invoked for some personal, trivial vengeance; we are a far cry from the agonized questions about divine justice in the *Knight's Tale*. *The Reeve's Tale*, in common with that of the Miller, indulges in a great deal of 'light' swearing, that is to say, strong oaths are used for minor incidents and problems. When, for example, the students find that their horse is loose, they swear as if this were a major catastrophe:

'Harrow!' and 'Weylaway!'
Oure hors is lorn, Alayn for Goddes banes [bones]
Step on thy feet [get moving]!
(4072–4)

The concentration of oaths is, interestingly, maintained in the passages of assumed Northern dialect:

'Allas,' quod John, 'Aleyn, for Cristes peyne,
Lay doun thy swerd, and I wil myn alswa
I is ful wight [strong], God waat [knows], as is a raa [buck],
By Goddes herte, he sal nat scape us bathe
Why ne had thow pit [put] the capul [nag] in the lathe [barn]?
Ilhayl! [bad luck] by God, Alayn, thou is a fonne [fool]!'
(4084–9)

(The final exclamation seems, interestingly, to be one of the first instances of folly or stupidity being imputed to someone in a swearing form.) The blasphemous low point of the tale is reached, however, when the wife (whose lineage, it has been ironically reiterated, is descended from 'hooly chirches blood') wakes up in the middle of the fracas, imagining that she has been imposed on by an incubus:

'Help! hooly croys of Bromeholm,' she seyde,
'*In manus tuas*! Lord, to thee I calle!
Awak, Symond! the feend is on me falle.'
(4286–8)

It is revealing that the Reeve should conclude his tale, first with a token appeal to God in the image of a distant alien judge, and then reserve the last word for settling his petty score with the Miller:

> And God, that sitteth heighe in magestee,
> Save al this compaignye, grete and smale!
> Thus have I quyt the Millere in my tale.
> (4322–4)

The Cook's Tale is, of course, either truncated, censored or incomplete, no doubt because of its bawdy, decadent matter. In his Prologue there is, however, a memorably sharp vignette, a timeless image of the teller in a paroxysm of mirth combined with religious ejaculation:

> The Cook of Londoun, whil the Reve spak,
> For joye him thoughte he clawed him on the bak.
> 'Ha! ha!' quod he, 'for Cristes passion,
> This millere hadde a sharp conclusion. . . .'
> (4325–8)

Fragment I or Group A of *The Canterbury Tales* shows a quite deliberate diversity of style and register, deriving from classical notions of decorum practised by Virgil, prescribed by Horace, and advocated, for example, by John of Garland in the thirteenth century.[10] The first three tales conform, broadly, to the courtly, bourgeois and rustic styles. As can clearly be seen, styles of swearing are no less differentiated, principally to accord with the characters of the tellers, but also to conform with the characters in their tales. Swearing in *The Knight's Tale* is measured and reserved for serious moments. Appeals to the gods echo desperately through the work. But as we descend from the 'high seriousness' of the courtly romance down to the bedroom farce of the fabliau and the still uglier scenes of low rustic cunning in the Cambridgeshire fens, so the swearing becomes more casual, more mocking and more personal. As Haskins has well put it, 'There is a degree of irreverence for which the modern reader is unprepared.'[11]

PERSONAL VARIATIONS IN OATHS AND INVOCATIONS

The bawdy tales of the Miller and Reeve have a casual immorality encompassing both trivial offences and serious blasphemy. Both are marked by minimal poetic justice, which favours cynical cunning. However, in the sternly moral world of the Man of Law, where treacheries involve the profoundest bonds of individual trust and public faith, judgement is meted out summarily and severely. A spectacular case in point follows the perjury of the evil knight against the innocent Custance:

> A Britoun book, written with Evaungiles,
> Was fet, and on this book he swoor anoon
> She gilty was, and in the meene whiles
> An hand hym smoot upon the nekke-boon,
> That doun he fil atones as a stoon,
> And bothe his eyen broste [burst] out of his face
> In sighte of every body in that place.
>
> A voys was herd in general audience,
> And seyde, 'Thou hast desclaundred [calumniated], giltelees,
> The doghter of hooly chirche in heigh presence;
> Thus hastou doon, and yet holde I my pees!'
>
> (666–76)

The language of the tale has the old-fashioned, dignified formality appropriate to a conservative man of the law. This quality is very apparent in the oaths and exclamations, for instance when the Sultaness vows to prevent her son's apostasy:

> 'But oon avow to grete God I heete [promise],
> The lyf shal rather out of my body sterte
> Or [before] Makometes lawe out of myn herte!'
>
> (334–6)

Heete is a fairly rare archaic survival of A-S *hatan*, to promise or vow, usually confined by this time to formal legal use. Other formal archaisms are *parfay* (110), *God him see*! (156), *He that is lord of Fortune be thy steere!* (448), *thanked be Cristes grace!* (686), *heryed* [praised] *be Goddes grace!* (872), *by God and by seint John!* (1019), *God and alle his halwes* [saints] *brighte* (1060). The teller also indulges in recherché astrological exclamations:

> O Mars, o atazir [influence], as in this cas!
>
> (305)

Yet Custance's prayer when she is set adrift reflects in its resonant symbolism a simple but total faith in the miraculous power of Christ over Satan:

> 'O cleere, o welful auter, hooly croys,
> Reed of the Lambes blood ful of pitee,
> That wessh the world fro the olde iniquitee,

Me fro the feend and fro his clawes kepe,
That day that I shal drenchen [drown] in the depe.'
(451–5)

However, like most of his profession, the Man of Law is no stranger to damning emotive language. The devious sultaness becomes the object of the author's xenophobic and anti-feminist denunciations:

O Sowdanesse [sultaness], roote of iniquitee!
Virago, thou Semyrame the secounde!
O serpent under femynynytee,
Lik to the serpent depe in helle ybounde!
(358–61)

Unwittingly, but not surprisingly, he has launched a new term of misogynist abuse: *virago*. Meaning literally 'manlike', it is the ancient name given by Adam to Eve in the *Vulgate*, and is there intended to be a paternalistic compliment.[12] In the heat of the moment, this previously neutral word has been transformed into a new term of invective. The *Man of Law's Tale* is charged with binary oppositions. Two of the most marked, religious chauvinism and sexual polarization, will be themes to which we shall return in subsequent chapters.

Though the Wife of Bath is not as 'liberated' as she would like to think, she is certainly remarkably free in thought and speech, given the general constraints on women of her status in the Middle Ages. Indeed, the broadness of her language makes her virtually unique as a literary individual in her times. Yet she is quick to claim astrological influence and physiognomical signs as justifications for her make-up:

Gat-toothed[13] I was, and that becam me weel;
I hadde the prente of seinte Venus seel.
As helpe me God! I was a lusty oon . . .
(603–5)

In her casual elevation of Venus, the pagan goddess of love, to the status of a saint, the Wife shows herself to be a Lawrentian long before her time, pointedly praising the mystic power of sex. Chaucer, we observe, does not interrupt her stream of reminiscence in order to question or argue the issue of the proper place of eros in the panoply of deities. Instead, she immediately proceeds, with wonderful broad-mindedness, to invoke the Christian God in her amorous reminiscence: 'As helpe me God! I was a lusty oon'. She then analyses herself (quite accurately) as dominated by Venus and Mars, somewhat like a credulous believer in sun signs. It is only some ten lines later that she returns to her heretical view, commenting: 'Allas! allas! that evere love was synne!' (614).

The Wife's highly subversive views led the American scholar D. W. Robertson Jr. to condemn her as 'hopelessly carnal and literal', even placing her 'firmly among the evil who are in the Church but not of it' (1963, pp. 317, 327). Of her carnality there is no dispute, unless one is to question whether her repeated public self-praise for her copiously experienced *bele chose* does not derive from the same sexual anxiety and insecurity which seems to motivate her own tale. Never the less, perhaps her numerous religious ejaculations and invocations should be looked at a little less dogmatically. It would then appear that Alisoun thanks God fulsomely, but most sincerely, for the mysterious gift of sexuality, and its vigorous dispensation in the institution of marriage:

> Yblessed be God that I have wedded five!
> (44)

> As help me God, I laughe whan I thinke
> How pitously a-night I made hem swynke [labour]!
> (201–2)

> But, Lord Crist! whan that it remembreth me
> Upon my yowthe, and on my jolitee,
> It tikleth me aboute myn herte roote.
> (469–71)

There are, of course, other tones. In the Wife's berating of her various husbands, we start to hear the style of vigorous personal abuse with which we are now familiar, but which was much less evident in medieval times. Among the epithets which cascade from her in her tirades, *old* has a special new vehemence: 'olde dotard shrew!'[14] (291), 'olde barel-ful of lyes!' (302), 'sire olde fool' (357). In an idiom of caustic anger which rings across the centuries, she condemns 'Metellius, the foul cherle, the swyn' (460), using *swyn* as a comparatively new term of abuse. A hectoring and aggressive style is very apparent in her claims to 'maistrie', a term which, ironically, she does not – indeed, cannot – feminize, as well as in her insistence on the communality of property:

> But tel me this: why hydestow, with sorwe,
> The keyes of thy cheste awey fro me?
> It is my good as wel as thyn, pardee!
> What, wenestow [do you hope to] make an ydiot of oure dame
> [i.e. myself]?

Now by that lord that is called Seint Jame,
Thou shalt not bothe, thogh that thou were wood [mad]
Be maister of my body and of my good;

(308–14)

More than once does she resort to tactical provocation to gain the advantage:

What rowne [whisper] ye with oure mayde? *Benedicite!*
Sire olde lecchour, lat thy japes be.

(241–2)

(*Benedicitee!* it appears, is the most widely favoured of Chaucer's ejaculations of annoyance, being used by virtually every teller in the whole gamut of the *Canterbury Tales*.) The Wife can, however, use sacred Christian symbolism in a sharper fashion, which some would consider blasphemous, as when she retaliates for her young husband's dalliances:

I made hym of the same wode a croce [cross]

(484)

Her old, mean, spying husband is roundly cursed:

O leeve [dear] sire shrewe, Jhesu shorte thy lyf!'

(365)

However, perhaps what is finally most illuminating and charming about Alisoun of Bath's religious language are the moments of sincere simplicity, which reveal an unshakable faith in the mystery of the Incarnation:

The hye God, on whom that we beleeve,
In wilful poverte chees [chose] to lyve his lyf.

(1178–9)

Equally obvious is her belief in ultimate salvation, shown in her heartfelt concern for the soul of Jankin, her last husband:

God lete his soule nevere come in helle!

(504)

The wish is repeated in 524 and, most pointedly, when Jankin is exclusively blessed at the conclusion (831) of her 'long preamble', as the Friar calls it:

I prey to God, that sit in magestee,
So blesse his soule for his mercy deere.

(826–7)

In sum, the Wife may indeed be 'hopelessly literal' in her interpretation of Scripture. But perhaps that is her saving grace.

The tales of the Friar and Summoner explore forms of blasphemy and religious charlatanism of an altogether more subtle and opportunistic kind. The Friar's tale is fundamentally concerned with swearing, resting as it does on the traditional belief that an oath was binding if it was heartfelt, but not in cases where a person 'spak oo thing, but he thoghte another' (1570). This observation serves as a valuable gloss on the whole convention of 'light' or loose swearing, since it acknowledges 'slippage' or an accepted latitude in the medieval use of sacred terms. The notion also becomes a narrative stratagem whereby the mysterious diabolical 'yeman' from 'fer in the north contree' outwits and traps the somonour of the tale.

Equally revealing is the sarcastic byplay of the tale's *Prologue*. Being a subtle simulator, adept at playing on people's emotions, the Friar sets out to be deliberately provocative, openly discrediting the Summoner, one of his rivals in the market of 'pay as you sin'. This tactic eventually elicits an angry retort: 'Peter! so been wommen of the styves [brothels]' (1332), in which the exclamation 'Peter!' was comparatively new and rare.

One of the sharpest ironies in the tale lies in the pointed accuracy of the first oath uttered by the devil in disguise; avoiding the minced form *pardee*, he punctiliously uses the correct version, *depardieux* (1395). When piqued, however, he slips into the common form:

> A lowsy jogelour kan deceyve thee
> And pardee, yet kan I moore craft than he.
> (1467–8)

(As was mentioned earlier, this is the first recorded instance of *lousy* in the figurative sense.) The critical moments of swearing in the tale contain the same formula:

> 'The feend,' quod he, 'yow fecche, body and bones.'
> (1544)

Fecche is used where we would now use and expect *take*, which could suggest that the word had a more potent significance in earlier times, or might be the result of alliteration. The diabolical association is found only here and once in the *Canon's Yeoman's Tale*.

The supreme cynicism of the tale emerges at the end, when the Friar plays God in his narrative world, despatching the summoner to hell, and in the same breath turns to the 'real' congregation to give out an unctuously hypocritical blessing:

And with that word this foule feend hym hente [seized];
Body and soule he with the devel wente
Where as that somonours han their heritage.
And God that maked after his ymage
Mankynde, save and gyde us, alle and some
And leve [let] thise somonours goode men bicome!
(1639–44)

The Summoner, his fury caught in a wonderfully graphic image ('lyk as aspen leef he quook for ire'), returns the compliment savagely, after describing his revealingly faecal view of hell: 'God save yow alle, save this cursed Frere!' (1707). He uses against the Friar the same technique of provocation through a devastating exposé of professional misconduct. In the *General Prologue*, Chaucer brilliantly reveals the Friar's religious charlatanism by juxtaposing the languages of confession and flirtation, line by line:

Ful swetely herde he confessioun
And plesaunt was his absolucioun:
He was an esy man to yeve penaunce
Theras he wiste to have a good pitaunce.
(221–4)

There is a clear implication, through the improper linguistic liaisons, that the Friar illicitly mixes business with pleasure. In the tale the character of Friar John is used for similar satirical effect, as Chaucer ingeniously interweaves the ingratiating language of sanctimonious coaxing with that of religious ritual. Nothing becomes him like his entry:

'*Deus hic!*' quod he, 'o Thomas, freend, good day!'
Seyde this frere, curteisly and softe.
'Thomas,' quod he, 'God yelde yow! ful ofte
Have I upon this bench faren ful weel;'
(1770–3)

His greeting of the wife, whom he 'embraceth in his armes narwe [tightly]' and compliments effusively, while gallantly offering to be her 'servant every deel', goes blatantly beyond the limits of ecclesiastical propriety and has obvious tones of propositioning which even hint at an affair. His exploitation of the sermon (illegitimate in itself) pointedly advocates the view contrary to that of the Shipman, cited earlier:

'Glosynge is a glorious thyng, certeyn
For lettre sleeth, so as we clerkes seyn.'
(1793–4)

The travesty of Christ's use of the symbol of the fish to represent the apostolic function gives an old cliché a new materialistic gloss:

> 'I walke, and fisshe Cristen mennes soules,
> To yelden Jhesu Crist his propre rente;'
> (1820–1)

Very much like the 'original' in the *Prologue*, who lisps out of affectation, his confrere's speech is liberally spiced with Biblical tags, Latin and French phrases and plenty of persuasive cant to appeal to his prosperous target market. His charlatanism is nowhere more transparently shown than when, with glib opportunism, he assures the grieving parents of the beatification of their dead child. Even the travel arrangements into the next world have been arranged with quite incredible speed:

> 'His deeth saugh I by revelacioun,'
> Seide this frere, 'at hoom in our dortour [dormitory].
> I dar wel seyn that, er that half an hour
> After his deeth, I saugh hym born to blisse
> In myn avisioun, so God me wisse!'
> (1854–8)

When he eventually receives his desserts in the most concentrated form of hot air, the fart, his whole tone alters abruptly:

> The frere up stirte as dooth a wood [mad] leoun
> 'A! false cherl,' quod he, 'for Goddes bones!'
> (2152–3)

In describing the embarrassing emission to the 'lord of the village', he uses hypocritically loaded terms, especially in his use of *blaspheme*:

> '. . . this olde cherl with lokkes hoore
> Blasphemed hath oure hooly convent eke.'
> (2182–3)

The lord, making light of the whole matter, proposes the preposterous solution of dividing the fart, and concludes with the dismissive comment:

> 'Now ete your mete, and lat the cherl go play;
> Lat hym go honge hymself a devel weye!'
> (2241–2)

The last remark has an interesting linguistic feature, common to modern, rather than medieval swearing, in that idiom is no longer used in a logical or literal fashion. (One thinks here of numerous modern phrases, such as *What the hell! a devil of a mess* etc.) *Devil*, sometimes intensified to *twenty devil*, was a reinforcement in medieval English of 'away'. Recorded from *c.*1300, the idiom often makes little literal sense, though Chaucer has a clearer instance in 'A twenty develewey the wynd hym dryve', from the *Legend of Good Women*, (2177). In this emotive rather than literal use, *devil* was in the following centuries to have a large role to play.

This survey of *The Canterbury Tales* cannot, in view of the scope of this treatment and their overall design, be comprehensive. The intention has been to explore and illustrate various attitudes towards religious language, not to examine each character's performance in detail. However, it has already emerged that the pilgrims are divided into three basic categories: those who take religious language seriously; those who exploit it cynically, and those who use it with a casual looseness. Since, in the nature of things, certain repetitions are bound to occur in the compendium of the tales, it is more economical in the remaining discussion to focus on those areas which are unusual or especially significant.

One aspect, for example, which is revealingly individuated is that of xenophobia. It is notable that the tales of the more conservative characters, such as the Man of Law, Prioress and Franklin, have very strong xenophobic elements either in the plot or the exclamations. The Man of Law, for instance, has the monopoly on the use of *heathen* and *paynim*, given his virulently anti-Muslim tale. On the other hand, it is less predictable that the Prioress, so prim and proper, so very *semely*, should have the monopoly on *Jewes*, which she invariably allies with the adjective *cursed* in her strange tale combining extreme sentimentality and violent xenophobia. She is rivalled in her anti-Semitic outbursts only by the true and false sermonizers, the Parson and the Pardoner.

The Clerk's Tale of the patient Griselde has the pious restraint appropriate to a saint's life. It is only in the final stanzas that the teller indulges in some sarcastic sallies directed at the Wife of Bath, whose earlier provocations, in the forms of anti-clerical comments and whose unorthodox programme of *maistrie*, he has borne in silence. His mock-blessing is, however, as restrained as his ironic allusion to *maistrie*:

> . . . for the Wyves love of Bathe –
> Whos lyf and al hire secte God mayntene
> In heigh maistrie, and elles it were scathe –
> (1170–2)

In this separation of public narrative from private riposte the Clerk demonstrates his severe academic discipline, which places him quite apart from those pilgrims who exploit their tales opportunistically to score points, discredit and even publicly damn rivals and opponents.

The *Merchant's Tale* is as ironic in its treatment of religion as it is about every other aspect of marriage. Surface and reality interact mockingly throughout the narrative. The jaundiced narrator does not leave the reader in much doubt as to whether January's motivation derives from 'hoolynesse or dotage' (1253). The mechanical orisons of the tale's clockwork priest are ironically underscored by a boringly flat beat of the verse as well as the repeated use of *and* in his perfunctory administration of the 'hooly sacrement':

> Forth comth the preest, with stole aboute his nekke,
> And bad hire be lyk Sarra and Rebekke[15]
> In wisdom and in trouthe of mariage;
> And seyde his orisons, as is usage.
> And crouched [crossed] hem, and bad God sholde hem blesse,
> And made al siker ynogh with hoolynesse.
>
> (1703–8)

(The ingeniously cynical insertion of *ynogh*, effectively undermines the *hoolynesse* of the whole ritual, very much in the manner of a modern 'weasel word'.) When January's paradise turns to purgatory (as was forewarned), the ironies intensify. The gods come down (or up) to earth, but behave and speak like churls. In a splendidly humorous play on Biblical and pagan perspectives on religious behaviour, the pagan goddess Proserpine (chosen by Jupiter on the same basis of lust as May was by January) proceeds to give a fishwife's discourse on 'false goddis':

> 'Ey! for verray God, that nys but oon,
> What make ye so muche of Salomon?
> What though he made a temple, Goddes house?
> What though he were riche and glorious?
> So made he eek a temple of false goddis.
>
> He was a lechour and an ydolastre.'
>
> (2291–8)

When the arboreal adulterous climax of the tale is reached, the obsessive drive of the Merchant's soul-baring narrative leads him relentlessly to expose the horror of cuckoldry in the starkest fashion:

> Ladyes, I preye yow that ye be nat wrooth;
> I kan nat glose, I am a rude [unsophisticated] man –
> And sodeynly anon this Damyan

Gan pullen up the smok, and in he throng [thrust].
(2350–2)

When May (who is certainly no lady) attempts to brazen the matter out by recourse to the coy euphemism of 'strugle with a man upon a tree', January's rejection is as summary as is his curse upon them and his asseveration of the truth:

'Strugle!' quod he, 'ye algate in it wente!
God yeve yow bothe on shames deth to dyen!
He swyved thee, I saugh it with myne yen [eyes]
And elles be I hanged by the hals [neck]!'
(2376–9)

May prevails, of course, with the aid of a fair amount of blasphemous protestation ('God woot', 'by hevene king') of the kind that Proserpine herself previously indulged in, with comical excess:

'Now by my moodres sires soule[16] I swere
That I shall yeven hire suffisant answere'
(2265–6)

Significantly, only the oaths of the 'false goddis' come true, enabling the absurdly unrealistic reconciliation to follow. Curiously, the teller, who appears to have exorcized his own loathing and disgust by psychologically re-enacting the betrayal, seems genuinely joyful in his conclusion:

Now, goode men, I pray yow to be glad.
Thus endeth heere my tale of Januarie;
God blesse us, and his mooder Seinte Marie!
(2416–18)

The *Franklin's Tale*, like its teller, is overly concerned with *fredom* and *gentillesse*, ('nobility' or 'magnanimity'), but the narrative is thematically structured round the binding quality of formal oaths, even when these can be abrogated on a technicality, especially when their cost is high. The knight Arveragus, who stands to lose his wife, upholds her bond to Aurelius with admirable idealism, as his suffering makes clear:

'Trouthe is the hyeste thing that man may kepe' –
But with that word he brast anon to wepe.
(1479–80)

Structurally the whole tale arises out of the ambiguity of Dorigen's oath to Aurelius, which requires a physical impossibility, but is framed by serious invocations. These qualities make it both genuine and playful:

'By thilke God that yaf me soule and lyf,
Ne shal I nevere been untrewe wyf'

But after that in pley thus seyde she:
'Aurelie,' quod she, 'by heighe God above,
Yet wolde I graunte to been youre love . . . .'
(983–90)

(Of course, only the audience hear the qualification 'in play'.) In the end, a competitive spirit of *gentillesse* saves the day, and all the obligations are waived. Although the tale ends with the medieval narrative device of a *demande* or ethical question, 'Which was the mooste fre [noble], as thynketh yow?' the socially ambitious Franklin has clearly rubbed in the point that nobility is achieved by actions, not birthright.

The *Physician's Tale* elicits from Harry Bailly a passionate response which gives us an indication of what Chaucer considered outrageous swearing to be:

Oure Hooste gan to swere as he were wood [mad];
'Harrow!' quod he, 'by nayles and by blood!'
(287–8)

His anger assuaged, he starts to load the Physician with ironically bogus compliments and blessings:

'But nathelees, passe over [forget it], is no fors [it's nothing].
I pray to God so save thy gentil cors [body],
And eek thy urynals and thy jurdones [chamber-pots],
Thyn hypocras [aphrodisiacs], and eek thy galyones [remedies],
And every boyste [box] ful of letuarie [remedy];
God bless hem, and oure lady Seinte Marie!
So moot I theen [prosper], thou art a proper man,
And lyk a prelat, by Seint Ronyan![17]
Seyde I nat wel? I kan nat speke in terme [formally];'
(304–11)

The *Pardoner's Tale* is a bizarre exhibition by a lost soul *cum* pseudo-evangelist. The performance is such a concentrated mixture of simoniac opportunism, ambiguous confessioun and hell-fire sermon that it becomes a tour de force of blatant blasphemy:

For though myself be a ful vicious man,
A moral tale yet I yow telle can,
Which I am wont [used] to preche for to wynne [make a profit].
(459–61)

The tale is full of false swearing of various kinds, no doubt to prick the consciences of his captive audience. However, he oscillates unpredictably from voyeuristic replications of grisly swearing to hysterical denunciations of the same sin, creating an extraordinary tension, to use Freudian terms, between the id and the superego. Here is the voice of authority:

> Gret sweryng is a thing abhominable,
> And fals sweryng is yet more reprevable.
>
> But ydel sweryng is a cursednesse.
>
> (631–8)

His profound confusion between triviality and seriousness is perfectly symbolized in the rioters' drunken frenzy, as dicers' oaths and invocations of relics are garbled together:

> 'By Goddes precious herte,' and 'by his nayles,'
> and 'by the blood of Crist that is in Hayles,
> Sevene is my chaunce, and thyn is cynk [five] and treye [three]!'
> 'By Goddes armes, if thou falsly pleye,
> This daggere shal thurghout thyn herte go!'
> This fruyt cometh of the bicched bones two,
> Forsweryng, ire, falsenesse, homycide.
>
> (651–7)

Although the moralistic plot of the tale has a frighteningly stark, geometric simplicity, it is punctuated with absurd, frenzied, centrifugal exclamations on any passing deadly sin. When the rioters have well and truly met Death, the Pardoner launches into his final bout of hysteria:

> O cursed synne of alle cursednesse!
> O traytours homycide, O wikkednesse!
> O glotonye, luxurie [lust], and hasardrie [gambling]!
> Thou blasphemour of Crist with vileynye
> And othes grete, of usage and of pride!
>
> (895–9)

In this welter of exclamations, many are strong, but few are original. The one exception is the strikingly opprobrious phrase for dice, the *bicched bones*, first recorded in this context. Through the strange farrago of ever-increasing passion and incoherence, Chaucer is clearly showing us the final nemesis which awaits the confidence trickster: the total loss of credibility. Rounding off his confession with the 'applause line', 'And lo, sires, thus I preche', he forgets that he has already revealed his technique, and is irresistibly drawn back to the cycle of performance, to play the last two tricks, the moment of 'sincerity', followed up swiftly by the 'hard sell':

> And Jhesu Crist, that is oure soules leche [healer],
> So graunte yow his pardoun to receyve,
> For that is best; I wol yow nat deceyve.
> But, sires, o word forgat I in my tale:
> I have relikes and pardoun in my male. . . .
>
> (916–20)

His nemesis is, ironically, self-chosen. In a shrewd but over-reaching gamble, he first propositions the hard-swearing but hard-headed Host, only to meet with the most devastating public humiliation, as his 'relics' and his virility are openly mocked:

> 'Nay, Nay!' quod he, 'thanne have I Cristes curs!
> Lat be,' quod he, 'it shall nat be, so theech! [may I prosper]
> Thou woldest make me kisse thyn olde breeche [trousers]
> And swere it were a relyk of a seint,
> Though it were with thy fundament [shit] depeint!
> But by the cros which that Seint Eleyne fond,
> I wolde I hadde thy collions [testicles] in myn hond
>
> They shal be shryned in an hogges toord!'
>
> (946–55)

The reference to *collions* (testicles) alludes cruelly to the broad hint in the *General Prologue*: 'I trowe [believe] he were a geldyng [eunuch] or a mare [effeminate]' (691). The Host is the only character to use the word *turd*, in a savagely ironic fashion. Only the intervention of the Knight brings about a charitable conclusion.

Given the Shipman's anti-clerical comments in the Epilogue to the *Man of Law's Tale* (discussed previously), and the observation in the *General Prologue* that he had little time for scruples of conscience ('Of nyce conscience took he no keep', 398), it is entirely appropriate that his contribution should be a cynical tale of adultery in which the co-respondent member of the triangle is a priest. (Indeed, the figure of the priest in *The Canterbury Tales* forms an interesting compendium of vice.) This Daun John is presented as an utterly opportunistic man of the world, indeed an early prototype of Don Juan, who immediately begins a risqué 'wink-wink, nudge-nudge' routine with the wife:

> 'I trowe certes, that oure goode man
> Hath yow laboured sith the nyght began,
> That yow were nede resten hastily.'
> And with that word he lough ful murily,

> And of his owene thought he wax al reed [blushed].
> (107–11)

Hearing of her sexually unsatisfied state and her mooted suicide, Daun John adopts the role of a concerned father-confessor, immediately making a solemn oath of secrecy:

> 'For on my porthors [breviary] here I make an ooth
> That nevere in my lyf, for lief ne looth,
> Ne shal I of no conseil yow biwreye [reveal].'
> (131–3)

The motivation for secrecy is, of course, neatly ambiguous. Does he speak as confessor or seducer? The wife (who turns out to be simply short of money) shows that she is a match for him by completing the pact, even over-topping his protestations:

> 'The same agayn to yow,' quod she, 'I seye.
> By God and by this porthors I yow swere,
> Though men me wolde al into pieces tere,
> Ne shal I nevere, for to goon to helle,
> Biwreye a word of thyng that ye me telle.'
> (134–8)

The slick narrative of betrayal is littered with oaths, several of them appropriate to the French setting, such as 'by Seint Denys of Fraunce'. However, in places Daun John seems actually to revel in the dramatic irony of his blasphemy. Saying to the husband that he needs to borrow the hundred francs to buy some stock (when he intends to 'buy' the wife's favours) he virtually tempts providence in his asseveration: 'God help me so, I wolde it were youres!' (274). The Shipman himself takes leave of his story relating ledger-sheets and bed-sheets with a cheeky blessing that God may send the pilgrimage 'multiple entries':

> Thus endeth now my tale, and God us sende
> Taillynge[18] ynough unto oure lyves ende. Amen.
> (433–4)

The Host accepts the blessing wholeheartedly, even indulging in a rare Latin flourish: 'Wel seyd, by *corpus dominus*!' (435).

The Monk's excruciatingly boring catalogue of tragedies is mercifully cut short by the intervention of the Knight, who speaks without any religious invocation: 'Hoo!' quod the Knyght, 'Goode sire, namoore of this!' (2767). The Host chimes in, but in his characteristically fulsome fashion: 'Ye,' quod oure Hooste, 'by seint Poules belle!' (2780). The subsequent contribution, the Nun's Priest's charming and unpretentious comic tour de force, is as artfully humorous in its use of swearing as it is in its exploitation of learning and rhetoric. Oaths become part of the essential mock-heroic technique, since they are absurdly juxtaposed with mundane trivia: 'For Goddes love,' implores Pertelote, 'taak som laxatyf' (2943). Chauntecleer's attempt to prove that he rules the roost of learning are equally peppered with ungallinacious ejaculations:

> 'By God! I hadde rather than my sherte [I'd give my shirt]
> That he hadde rad this legende, as have I.'
>
> (3120–1)

Even the fox, only really interested in Chauntecleer's succulent flesh, alludes, in a comic blessing, to having sampled the excellent family stock:

> 'My lord your father – God his soule blesse! –
> And eek youre mooder, of hire gentillesse,
> Han in myn hous ybeen to my greet ese [satisfaction];'
>
> (3295–7)

'This sweete preest, this goodly man sir John,' (as Chaucer terms him in a uniquely warm compliment to an ecclesiastic) invokes a splendid array of authorities and deities, but only at the height of the frantic chase does a single *benedicitee!* pass his lips. At his conclusion the Host adopts an attitude pointedly the opposite of his damning remarks to the Pardoner. He compliments the Priest on his manly physique and virile manner, well suited to a secular *trede-foul* or 'stud':

> 'Sir Nonnes Preest,' oure Hooste seide anoon,
> I-blessed be thy breche, and every stoon [testicle]!'
>
> (3446–7)

The last word on swearing comes, of course, from the Parson. Unlike the Pardoner's false sermon, a crudely unpredictable rhetorical firework display which led erratically up 'the croked way', the Parson profoundly changes the whole original narrative plan and reinstates the spirituality of the pilgrimage. He intends

> To knytte up this feeste, and make an ende.
> And Jhesu, for his grace, wit me sende
> To shewe yow the wey, in this viage,
> Of thilke parfit glorious pilgrimage
> That highte Jerusalem celestial.
>
> (47–51)

He includes swearing under Ira in his rigorous *summa* of the Deadly Sins. His treatment is dauntingly comprehensive, encompassing a whole range of false uses of language. These include necromancy, spatulamancy, augury, divination, prophecy, charms, lies and flattery. He reiterates the traditional literal condemnation of swearing examined at the outset of this chapter:

> For Cristes sake, ne swereth nat so synfully in dismembrynge of Crist by soule, herte, bones, and body. For certes it semeth that ye thynke that the cursed Jewes ne dismembred nat ynough the preciouse persone of Crist, but ye dismembre hym moore. (590)

He follows Bromyard in his critical comment relating swearing and class: 'What seye we eek of hem that deliten hem in sweryng, and holden it a gentrie or a manly dede to swere grete othes?' (601). By *gentrie* he would seem to mean 'a mark of good breeding', which corroborates some of the findings of Woolf above, but runs against the implications of *cherles termes*, meaning 'low language'. Turning to swearing and wrath, he introduces a number of set examples and interesting provocations:

> Speke we now of swich cursynge as comth of irous herte. Malisoun [cursing] generally may be seyd every maner power of harm. Swich cursynge bireveth [robs] man fro the regne of God, as seith Seint Paul .... And taak kep [take care] now, that he that repreveth [reproaches] his neighebor, outher he repreveth hym by som harm of peyne that he hath on his body, as 'mesel' [leper], 'croked harlot' [deformed rascal], or by som synne that he dooth. (618–23)

The interesting point which emerges from the second example ('*croked harlot*') is that, contrary to our modern expectations, the Parson means *croked* to be an inflammatory term of insult, since it refers to deformity, not to dishonesty, as it does now. (*Harlot* at this time was applied only to men, in the general opprobrious sense of 'rogue, rascal, villain': the earliest use of the term to mean 'whore' is 1432[O].) However, here he does not seem to regard the word as particularly insulting. Continuing with his theme of chiding, he gives further instances:

> And if he repreve hym uncharitably of synne, as 'thou holour [whore]', 'thou dronkelewe harlot [you drunken bum]', and so forth, thanne aperteneth [belongs] that to the rejoysynge of the devel, that ever hath joye that men doon synne. And certes, chidynge may nat come but out of a vileyns [churlish] herte. (625–6)

The reference to the 'vileyns herte' is pointedly at variance to 'gentrie', discussed a little earlier. *Vileynye* covers a great range of sins, of course, but has particular associations with bad language in the ME phrases 'to speak (or say) vileynye' of someone. The Knight, we recall,

> . . . nevere yet no vileynye ne sayde
> In al his lyf unto no maner wight
> (70–1)

This comment could suggest that the Knight's behaviour was unusual for his class.

The Parson's observations on the relationship between class and swearing are illuminating, because they suggest that the practice was commonest among the aristocracy and the lower orders. As we shall see in the following chapters, this pattern certainly seems to obtain in subsequent centuries. But as with so many aspects of his art, Chaucer has surreptitiously but clearly individuated his characters' swearing on the road to Canterbury.

CONCLUSION

As the Middle Ages drew to a close and the liberating tendencies of the Reformation and the Renaissance started to make themselves felt, so the tenor of swearing changed. As the next chapter will show, the idiom of religious controversy became increasingly violent, with erstwhile terms of authority, like *heresy*, *enormity* and *superstition* becoming the currency of schismatic strife. Another idiom, that of caustic personal abuse, deriving from social referents and emergent through the medieval period, as has been shown in this chapter, started to supplant the religious idiom. Skelton's satire on Cardinal Wolsey, 'Why come ye not to court?', is a virtual catalogue of such terms:

> Lyke Mahounde in a play;
> No man dare him withsay:
> He hath dispyght and scorne
> At them that be well borne;
> He rebukes them and rayles,
> 'Ye horsons, ye vassayles,
> Ye knauves, ye churles sonnys,
> Ye rebads [rascals], not worth two plummis,
> Ye raynbetyn beggars reiagged [tattered],
> Ye recrayed [recreant] ruffyns all ragged!'
> (594–603)

As the tirade continues, other contemporary terms of reproach for people of low class are brought into play; these include the strange trio of *cavel*, *havel* and *javel*, meaning 'low fellow', 'scoundrel' and 'rascal', respectively. All of these terms are essentially secular in origin, with the exception of *Mahounde*, a version of *Mahomet*, which was used throughout the Middle Ages in an abusive fashion to mean variously, 'a devil', 'a false prophet', 'a monster'. In this context he is clearly seen as a dramatic figure, often related to Termagent, 'a violent and overbearing personage' representing a deity supposedly worshipped by Muslims. The various xenophobic connections are discussed in the next chapter.

The first insulting term, *horson*, literally and technically the most wounding insult in English at the time, has a rich and complex history. *Whoreson* is a Middle English swearing term, based on A. F. *fitz a putain*, 'son of a whore' and first recorded in the fourteenth century. It originally had a deadly force, but by the fifteenth century it was clearly losing intensity: Caxton's *Reynard* (1486), has the amusing comment 'I trusted so moche . . . the fals horeson the foxe'. Even more revealing is the inapposite instance cited by Thomas Wilson in his *Rhetoric* (1525): 'The mother merelye [merrily] beyinge disposed, wyll saye to her swete Sonne: Ah you little horeson, wyll you serue me so?'[O] Indeed, from the mid-fifteenth century the word could be used as a 'coarsely abusive epithet', like *scurvy*, *bloody* or *pestilent*, also signalling the loss of literal force. Yet 'son of a whore' could still be taken as the most severe of insults, and was so regarded in Elizabethan and Jacobean times:

> . . . Son of a whore!
> There is not another murdering-piece
> In all the stock of calumny; it kills
> At one report two reputations –
> A mother's and a sons's
> (Middleton, *A Faire Quarell*)

Thus, like Modern English *bugger*, Australian English *bastard* and American Black English *mother-fucker*, the term *could* be used in a jocular or familiar fashion. The modern ambivalence of insult is clearly apparent.

NOTES

1 Cf. *Roman de la Rose*, 1. 15, 159ff. and the 'Conclusione dell' Autore' of the *Decamerone*. Furthermore, Chaucer excuses himself in advance in the *Prologue* to the *Miller's Tale* (3167ff.)

2 *Lollere* is a version of *Lollard*, from Middle Dutch *lollaerd*, 'mumbler' or 'stutterer'. The English application was 'a name of contempt given to certain heretics who followed Wycliffe or held views similar to his'.[O]

3 Other treatments are Herbert W. Starr, 'Oaths in Chaucer's Poems', *West Virginia Bulletin: Philological Studies* IV (1943), pp. 44–63, and R. W. V. Elliott, *Chaucer's English* (London, Deutsch, 1974), pp. 240–84.

4 The terms are used interchangeably in studies of semantics to indicate loss of intensity.

5 Ruth Nevo, 'Chaucer: Motive and Mask in the General Prologue,' *Modern Language Review* LVIII (1963), no. 1, pp. 1–9; Arthur W. Hoffmann, 'Chaucer's *Prologue* to Pilgrimage: The Two Voices,' *ELH* XXI (1954), pp. 1–16.

6 This is the first recorded instance of *Pilate's voice*, signifying a loud, ranting voice, evidently from the style used in the Mystery Plays.

7 See Beryl Rowland, 'Chaucer's Blasphemous Churl', in *Chaucer and Middle English Studies: Essays in Honor of R. H. Robbins*, ed. B. Rowland (London, Allen and Unwin, 1974), pp. 43–55.

8 The meaning of *verye* is disputed; *goblin* and *protect* have been suggested.

9 *Gay* in this context seems clearly to have a sexual innuendo.

10 See John H. Fisher, 'The Three Styles of the Canterbury Tales', *Chaucer Review* 8, pp. 119–27.

11 C. H. Haskins, in Beryl Rowland, 'Chaucer's Blasphemous Churl', cited in footnote no. 7.

12 In his glossing of *Genesis*, ii. 23, Alfric (*c.*1000) kept the name: 'Beo hire nama Uirago, þæt is, fæmne, forðan ðe heo is of hire were genumen' ('Let her name be Virago, that is woman, because she is taken from man.')

13 *Gat toothed* is interpreted variously as 'gap toothed' or 'goat toothed', both being physiognomical signs of lechery.

14 *Shrew* (discussed further in ch. 10) could at this time be used of either sex.

15 There are certain ironies in the priest's choice of exemplary wives.

16 Commenting on oaths sworn upon the souls of parents, B. J. Whiting notes that for two centuries after Chaucer, they were reserved for comic contexts. See his article, 'By my fader soule' *JEGP* XLIV (1945), p. 8.

17 *Ronyan* is unknown as a saint's name, being possibly a mischievous pun on *runnion*, recorded later as 'a coarse woman' or 'the male member'.[O]

18 *Tail* is recorded from the fourteenth century as meaning 'penis or (oftener) the pudendum'.[O] In his somewhat maundering lament for the loss of virility (but not sexual desire), Chaucer's Reeve observes that 'we olde men' have

> . . . an hoor [hoary] heed and a green [vigorous] tayl,
> As hath a leek; for though oure myghte be goon,
> Our wyl desireth folie evere in oon.
>
> (3878–80)

The feminine sense is recorded in a satirical verse (*c.*1515) which runs:

> Many whyte nonnes with whyte vayles,
> That was full wanton of theyr tayles.[O]

4
Schismatic Vituperation: The Reformation

> Catholike being a greeke word signifieth nothing in English but universall or common.
>
> T. Wilson

> The damnable doctrine and pestiferous sect of Reynold Pecock exceedeth in malice and horribility all other heresies and sects of heretics.
>
> R. Pecock

THE Reformation brought about fundamental redefinitions of the notion of religious authority within Christianity, as well as radically changed attitudes among those who had traditionally been termed 'even Christians' (fellow Christians), to use a sadly dated word recorded as far back as the laws of Edward the Confessor. As William Laud, Archbishop of Canterbury, lamented in his last sermon, preached from the scaffold on Tower Hill in 1645: '. . . this poor Church of England . . . is become like an Oak cleft to shivers made with wedges made out of its own body . . . .' (Chandos, 1971, p. 418). In the course of what Geoffrey Hill has called 'the noble, dreadful and at times farcical history of English civil and religious conflict',[1] fellow Christians who had previously been regarded in a fraternal light came in time to be seen as rivals and even enemies. What had previously been a vocabulary of solidarity split into labels of vilification.

As the divisions of the Reformation intensified into sectarian strife, so the increasing vehemence of polemical controversy generated a whole vocabulary of religious abuse. The word-stock was drawn from four major sources: earlier xenophobic terms, some of them used by Wycliffe and his fellow reformers; neutral terms to do with iconography and ritualized worship; terms relating to Rome and the Pope, and those perennial sources of abuse deriving from the categories of crime, demonology and animals. A sense of the hysteria to come is shown by the furious indiscriminacy of that fearless controversialist, John Bale, Bishop of Ossory, in his pamphlet of 1543, *Yet a course at the Romyshe foxe*, wherein he referred to his Catholic opponents as 'fylthie whoremongers, murtherers, thieves, raveners, idolatours, lyars, dogges, swyne .... and very devyls incarnate' (Bennett, 1952, p. 73).

Prior to the Reformation, Christian attitudes towards other religions had been uncomplicatedly chauvinist: their adherents were simply stigmatized as *heathens*, *payens* or *paynims* (pagans).[2] *Infidel*, nicely defined by the *OED* as 'One who does not believe in (what the speaker holds to be) the true religion; an "unbeliever" ', was in its earlier stages applied from a Christian point of view specifically to 'an adherent of a religion opposed to Christianity, especially a Mohammedan' (or *saracen* in its earliest sense). Thus Malory writes (1470–85) of 'Two honderd sarasyns or Infydeles'.[O] *Saracen* is in fact the older word, recorded from Anglo-Saxon times as a general term for 'Arab', before acquiring xenophobic animus in the period of the Crusades. 'Less worth am I then [than] any sarysyne, Whiche is in beleue of sory Mahound [Mahomet]' exclaims a character in *The romance of Partenay* (*c.*1475[O]). Long after the Crusades (so named from their original motivation, which was the recovery of the true Cross), a typically exaggerated travel book called *Wonder Worth Hearing* (1602), describes a man with 'a Sarazins face, his nose too long for his lips, his chekes like the iawes of a horse ....'[O]

The special hatred of the Jews, deriving from their role in the Crucifixion, is conspicuously apparent in medieval times. It is underlined by the frequency of the standard epithet *corsed*, as well as in the consistently hostile semantic history of the word *jew* as noun and verb, sustained even when Jews had been banished from Britain. This term is discussed more fully in chapter 6.

The animus against Muslims has its memorial in various corruptions of the name of Mahomet which have revealing semantic histories. First among these is *Mahounde*, used throughout the Middle Ages in an abusive fashion to mean variously, 'a devil', 'a false god', 'a false prophet', 'a monster'. A character in the Townley Mystery Play (*c.*1460) exclaims: 'Now by Mahowne, oure heven king'. He proves to be a surprisingly resilient figure, appearing in Pope, Scott ('Down with Mahound, Termagaunt, and all their adherents') and other writers up to the mid-nineteenth century. He occasionally makes appearances as a dramatic figure, often related to Termagent, 'a violent and overbearing personage' representing a deity supposedly worshipped by Muslims. 'Lyke Mahounde in a play, No man dare him withsay', writes Skelton of Cardinal Wolsey in his satire, 'Why come ye not to Court?' (quoted at the end of the previous chapter).

Two interesting older terms, *mawmet* and *mawmetrie*, have the same derivation. From as far back as *c.*1205 a *mawmet* signified a false god, or an image of one, an idol, and the word continued to be used in these senses well after Chaucer. The longest surviving sense has been that referring to a doll or puppet: there is a reference in 1892 to a 'Guy Fawkes momet'.[O] In the *Prologue* to his *Æneis* (1513), Gavin Douglas writes: 'Lat Virgyll hald [keep] his maumentis til hym self; I wirschip noder [neither] idoll, stok, nor elf.' However, with the iconoclastic impulses generated by the Reformation, the term was taken over and used by extremist Protestants to stigmatize the images of Christ and the saints. In his *Commentary on Deuteronomy* (1650), John Trapp condemns 'Those mawmets and monuments of idolatry, the Rood of grace, the blood of Hales etc.'[O] The related term *mawmetry* had the linked senses of 'the worship of images, idolatry', as well as that of 'false religion, heathenism'. These words were very current from the fourteenth to the sixteenth centuries, usually in vituperative passages: 'Let the souldiours of Satan and superstitious Mawmetrie, howle, and cry out,' writes Lambarde in 1570, while John Bale fulminates against Holy Church as 'the mother of their olde mammetries'.[O]

The example of *mawmet* has been gone into in some detail, since it shows a semantic shift which came to be repeated many times: xenophobic terms originally relating to heathen practices came to be applied to rival Christian sects. In addition, many previously neutral words were also mobilized in the conflict. As the iconoclastic frenzy seized the land, so terms like *idol*, *image*, *saint* and even *picture* started to take on idolatrous overtones. Tyndale translates *Acts*, xv. 20 as 'Abstayne them selves from filthiness of ymages', whereas the King James Bible prefers *idols*. *Idol* becomes 'applied polemically to images of figures of divine beings and saints' from *c.*1554[O], and is even extended to 'this mischievous idol the mass'. In a typical inventory of destruction dated 1566 we are told that 'One Rood [cross] with Marie and John and the rest of such Idolles was burnt'.

More predictably, accompanying the break with Rome there was a rapid expansion of the word-field describing Rome and the Pope. Terms such as *papist* and *Romish*, laden with hostile overtones of a kind familiar to us in political labels ending in *-ism* and *-ist* sprang into being. Although some, like *Pope-holy*, meaning 'hypocritical', go back to the period of Chaucer and Langland, the mid-sixteenth-century pamphleteers produced a whole swarm of such anti-Catholic terms, as is shown below.

papist	(1521)	*papish*	(1546)
popish	(1528)	*papism*	(1550)
popery	(1534)	*popestant*	(1550)
papistical	(1537)	*popeling*	(1561)
papistic	(1545)		

Adjectival forms (such as *papistic* and so on) are characterized by the *OED* as 'usually hostile and opprobrious', and emerge earlier than the nouns, so that *popish*, for example, is nearly twenty years older than *papism*. This is because adjectives form a useful source of vaguely-defined abuse, as exemplified in *fascist* and *racist* today. The first recorded reference to *papish* makes this point explicit in a marginal gloss: 'They vse the word papish to stop euery mans mouth withal.'[°] A similar reference to *popish* is typical: 'Though popisshe curres hereat do barcke.' *Popery* is apparently coined in a caustic observation by Tyndale in 1534 in which he mocks the capacity 'To beleue the faininges of our moost holy father, al his superstityouse poperye and inuisible blessynges'.[°] The title *Pope*, it should be noted, was used from the fourteenth to the nineteenth century of 'the spiritual head of a Mohammedan or pagan religion'; Purchase's *Pilgrimage* (1613) observes: 'In this Citie dwelleth the chiefe Pope, or High Priest, of that Superstition.'[°]

An assumption of conspiracy often lay behind these coinages. The notion is evident in the title of a pamphlet published in 1534: 'A Litel Treatise agaeynst the Mutterynge of some Papists in Corners'. These feelings were to be greatly intensified by the Gunpowder Plot (1605) and the Popish Plot (1678). Guy Fawkes Day was previously termed Pope Day, since the Pope was burnt in effigy, and is so recorded up to 1903.[°] People are described as *popeing*, i.e. soliciting money, with the formula: 'Please, sir, remember the old Pope!'[°] Though this considerable anti-Catholic armoury is now reduced, both *popery* and *papist* are still occasionally heard and retained in standard dictionaries. Carlyle's enlightened comment (made in 1840), 'The cry of "No Popery" is foolish enough in these days', proved to be rather ahead of its time. Interestingly, the *Pope's nose*, insultingly used of 'the rump of a fowl', dates from post-Reformation times, being first recorded in the 1796 edition of Grose's *Classical Dictionary of the Vulgar Tongue*. (The more domestic variant, the *parson's nose*, emerges about a century later.)

The hostile vocabulary surrounding *Rome* has older roots, going back to the Wycliffite criticisms and reformist initiatives in the fourteenth century. The payment of tribute to Rome in the form of *Peter's pence*, also known as the *Rome penny*, originally attributed to the kings of

Wessex in the seventh century, became a point of increasing contention. This is evidenced in the emergence of such terms as *Rome-runner*, used caustically by Langland and Wycliffe, who comments in 1380: 'þes rome renneris beren þe kyngis gold out of our lond'.[O] *Rome-raiker*, a more critical formation deriving from the flood-tide of Reformation controversy, is first recorded in 1535[O] and put by a contemporary writer in the alliterating company of 'rude Ruffians'. Henry Brinklow added an ironic gloss in 1542: 'Papa means pay pay' (Brinklow, 1874, p. 39). *Romish*, glossed by the *OED* as 'chiefly in hostile or opprobrious use', is first recorded in 1531, in the writings of Tyndale, where he exhorts his readers to 'Examine the Romish bishop by this rule', demoting the Pope to the mere Bishop of Rome in a style which was to become customary for centuries. The modern composite title of *Roman Catholic*, recorded from 1605[O], became necessary because 'simple *Roman*, *Romanist* or *Romish* had become too invidious'.[O]

The Protestant Revolution had the dual effect of neutralizing or disarming the potency of the Catholic sacred names and rituals while at the same time transforming the Catholic Church and its officers into political enemies. Thus while feelings of religious chauvinism and xenophobia (encouraged by the active propaganda of Henry VIII) caused terms relating to Rome and the Pope to become charged with emotion and animus, the name of the Virgin Mary lost its earlier force. The corrupted form *marry*, used in the idiomatic sense of 'to be sure', as in 'Yea, marry, why should we not kepe oure corn in oure barnes?' is recorded as early as *c.*1350[O]. As the *OED* observes, 'By the 16th c., *marry* had probably ceased to be apprehended as anything more than a mere interjection'. One may compare the declining force of *mass* as an oath or asseveration from Chaucer to Kingsley.

As the spiritual power-struggle of the Reformation intensified, so the language of the participants became increasingly virulent in its denunciations. *Devil*, although fundamentally superhuman and monstrous in its original conception, had been applied to human beings from Anglo-Saxon times onwards. A sixteenth-century poet has the bitter line 'Some develles wyll theyr husbandes bete'. But the term was to become part of the verbal stock-in-trade of religious controversialists. The stereotype of the devil-monster is well depicted in John Knox's account of the accusations leading to the martyrdom of John Wishart:

> For right against him stood up one of the fed flock, a monster, John Lauder, laden full of cursings, written on paper, of which he took out a roll both long and full of cursings, threatenings, maledictions, and words of devilish spite and malice, saying to the innocent Master George so

> many cruel and abominable words, and hit him so spitefully with the Pope's thunder, that the ignorant people dreaded lest the earth then would have swallowed him up quick . . . When that this fed sow had read throughout all his lying menacings, his face running down with sweat, and frothing at the mouth like a bear, he spat at Master George's face . . . (*History of the Reformation*, II. 234)[3]

It is interesting that the first use of *devil* as 'merely a term of reprobation', sometimes playfully applied, should occur after the main ructions of the Reformation, in Shakespeare, emanating from that most tolerant of sensualists, Sir Toby Belch, when he compliments Maria on the stratagem to gull the self-styled puritan, Malvolio: 'Thou most excellent devil of wit' (*Twelfth Night*, II. v. 226).

Antichrist shows a similar shift. We now read with amusement the fourteenth-century science fiction fantasy of John of Trevisa: 'The egges of adders . . . ben wonder yelowe, slimy and gleymy: and of thyse egges comyth Cockatrice: and of the venemous juys shall come Antecrist.'[O] But his contemporary Wycliffe attacked papal authority as 'This false heresie and tyrantrie of Antichrist'[O]. Subsequently, both Luther and the Pope were to cast each other in this monstrous role. Indeed, 'the Roman Antichrist' became a set phrase through the sixteenth and seventeenth centuries, and the Pope is still seen in this role by some Presbyterians.

'The Presbyterians called the Independent churches whore, and the Independent Churches called them whore again [in return]', observed William Erbury, before pronouncing his summary conclusion, 'and I say they are all whores together' (Chandos, 1971, xxiv). This comic roundelay of abuse brings home the point that many extreme moral (and especially sexual) terms came to be drawn into the vocabulary of spiritual denunciation. In 1530 Tyndale denounced the Pope as 'The greate baude, the hore of babylon' (the last epithet deriving from the allusion in *Revelation*, xvii). He thereby launched an idiom of abuse which was to remain current for several centuries. Horace Walpole, in a typically gossiping letter of 1743, noted more squeamishly: 'He would have piqued himself on calling the Pope the w---e of Babylon.'

From this seminal metaphor grew the legion of vitriolic terms denouncing spiritual perversion through words with strong sexual overtones, such as *fornication*, *harlotry*, *sodomy* and *carnality*, as well as polymorphously perverse religious practices mutually denounced by rival sects as *profanations*, *enormities* and *abominations*. ' 'Tis a kind of Spiritual Fornication to admit any Creature into a Partnership with him in our Love,'[O] writes John Norris in the late seventeenth century. *Harlot*, a term with a most interesting bi-sexual early history (discussed in chapter 10) becomes embroiled in spiritual controversy. In an unusually even-handed denunciation, George Buchanan condemns 'Godles papistes, harlat protestantis' in 1570.[O] John Knox is not alone in depicting the Church of Rome as 'the Roman harlot' in his *History of the Reformation* (1586/7). It is remarkable that, in the first recorded use of *sodomite*, Wycliffe should apply the term to spiritual, not physical matters: 'þat prelatis ... ben gostly sodomytis worse þan bodily sodomytis of sodom and gomor.'[O] In John Bale's propagandist morality play, *The Thre Laws of Nature, Moses and Christ, corrupted by the Sodomytes, Pharisses and Papystes most wicked* (1538), the direction for the dressing of the parts is instructive: 'Let Idolatory be decked like an old witch, Sodomy like a monk of all sects, Ambition like a bishop ...' etc.

Bale's use of theatrical costume to reinforce religious satire is in many ways an extension of contemporary continental cartoons depicting the religious establishment in various gross guises. One such scurrilous cartoon, published in Germany, depicted Pope Leo as the Beast of Antichrist, his name being conveniently applicable to the leonine creature.

SECTARIAN LABELLING

Today we use the terms *Quaker*, *Presbyterian*, *Methodist* and even *Non-conformist* in a comparatively neutral fashion. However, when these sects were formed, their names were common terms of ironic or vehement abuse. The anonymous author who wrote a history of these Protestant schismatics gave his book the morbid and savage title of *Gangraena*, implying that the sects were cut off from the body of the Church to keep it pure and healthy.

Protestant itself, originally applied (from 1539) to the German princes and free cities who supported the Reformation, was rapidly espoused by the English campaigners against the Papacy, and used in a generally favourable fashion. A title like *The Triumphs of Rome over Despised Protestancie* (1655) stands out as being obviously Catholic. Similarly, *Lutheran* might be used neutrally or vituperatively, depending on the writer's own position: George Cavendish makes an appeal *c.*1562 to 'Depresse [suppress] this newe pernicious sekt of the lutarynauncers', employing a polemical nonce-word modelled, one assumes, on *nigromauncer* meaning a *necromancer*.

Many sect names are first recorded in controversial contexts. Sir Thomas More writes in 1532 in his *Confutation of Tyndale's Answere* of

'Those abominable heresies . . . ye Anabaptistes have added'. Philip Stubbes' contentious *Anatomy of Abuses* (1583) observes that 'Diuers new phangled felows sprong vp of late, as the Brownists'. 'Our Levellers now exclaim against the Parliament,' comments Marchmont Needham archly in 1644.[O]

George Fox, the founder of the Quakers, said that the name was given to himself and his followers by Justice Bennet at Derby in 1650 'because I did tremble at the name of the Lord'. However, a letter written in London in October, 1647 gives a less creditable explanation:

> I heare of a Sect of woemen (they are at Southworke) come from beyond the Sea, called Quakers, and these swell, shiver and shake, and when they come to themselves (for in all this fitt Mahomett's holy-ghost hath bin conversing with them) they begin to preache what hath bin delivered to them by the Spirit.[O]

The name *Quaker* has never been accepted by the Society of Friends itself, and is, in the words of the *OED*, 'now regarded as a term of reproach'. An early study of the sect (1653) is termed trenchantly 'A Brief Relation of the Irreligion of the Northern Quakers'. John Evelyn's entry in his *Memoirs* (1656) describes them as 'a new fanatic sect, of dangerous principles, who show no respect to any man, magistrate, or other'. (He is presumably alluding to their refusal to take any oath.) By the end of the century, another diary (that of De la Pryme) assures us that 'The Quakers do not now quake, and howl and foam with their mouths, as they did formerly.' By the latter part of the century, the opprobrious formations *Quakerism, Quakerish, Quakeristical* and *Quakerly* had sprung up.

The Quakers' use of *thou* and *thee*, which was intended to show humility, became, as George Fox observed in his *Journal* in 1660, 'a sore cut to proud flesh . . . . We were often beaten and abused and sometimes in danger of our lives for using those words to some proud men, who would say, "What, you ill-bred clown, do you *thou* me?" ' (Mencken, 1936, p. 450). *Thou* had been used as an insulting verbal form from *c.*1440; at the trial of Sir Walter Raleigh for treason in 1603, the Attorney General, Sir Edward Coke, harangued Raleigh insultingly: 'All that Lord Cobham did was by thy instigation, thou viper; for I thou thee, thou Traitor!'[O] Ironic comments, such as 'He . . . Quaker-like, thou'd and thee'd Oliver'[O] are common through the seventeenth century.

The alternative term *Shaker* was also current from 1648, explained in this reference from 1694: 'The other sort of Anabaptists are called

Quakers or Shakers, from the Trembling and Quaking, caused in them by Vapours in their Ecstatick Fits.' This variant had certain propagandist advantages for critics of the sect, since *shaker* had an older sense of 'a lascivious person'. Motteux's translation of Rabelais (also published in 1694), comments on 'Those whom Venus is said to Rule, as Wenchers, Leachers, Shakers, etc.' The underlying stereotypical idea is that of demoniality, or indecent intercourse with an incubus or succubus, clearly alluded to in the earlier description ('in all this fitt Mahomett's holy-ghost hath bin conversing with them'). *Conversing* in this context is very much a key term, since it is clearly used in the old sense of 'to have sexual intercourse', of which the first recorded instance (from 1536) relates, fascinatingly, to demoniality, not to human intercourse: 'This Albyne, with her fiftie sisters . . . conversit with devilis in forme of men, and consavit [conceived] childrin.'[O] This stereotypical notion in part explains the application of terms like *harlotry*, *fornication* and *abomination* to 'alternative' religious experience.

'You gave us nothing but the whining piety of a Methodist' is a sharp comment from one of the Junius letters to the Duke of Grafton in 1770.[O] By this time *Methodist* (of uncertain origin) was nearly half a century old, the religious society founded in Oxford by John and Charles Wesley in 1729 having originally attracted the nickname of 'The Holy Club'. The term was applied from the mid-eighteenth century to 'a person of strict religious views', often with the implication of fanaticism: *methodist-mad* has a considerable currency from the 1770s. 'Spare our stage, ye methodistic men!' appeals Byron on behalf of the theatre in 1811. Other disparaging formations are *methodistical*, coined by Fielding in *Tom Jones* (1749), *methodisty* and *methodistico-*, tellingly employed in 'a Methodistico-jacobinal rant' (1805).[O]

We can see in the categorization of sects the same syndrome of hostility, mockery and distorted stereotypes as will be apparent in attitudes towards strangers, discussed in chapter 6.

NOTES

1 Geoffrey Hill 'Common weal, common woe,' *TLS* April 21–7 1989, p. 412.

2 *Pagan* derived from Latin *paganus*, 'villager or rustic', implying that the old idolatry lingered longest in the rural areas. The same notion lies at the root of the older term *heathen*, namely 'a heath dweller'. Both terms were used to stigmatize Jews and Muslims, especially from the fourteenth century, and

then extended to become general terms of abuse for a person of 'heathenish' habits. Shakespeare extended *pagan* to include 'prostitute', and *heathen* was similarly used by Pope in his vicious satire on Narcissa: 'A very heathen in the carnal part', *Moral Essays*: Epistle II, 'Of the Characters of Women', l. 67.

3 Cited in Hillerbrand (1964), p. 367.

5
Creativity and Suppression in the Renaissance

Il jure comme un Gentilhomme: He swears after a thousand pound a yeare; Il jure comme un Abbé, chartier: gentilhomme; prelate. Like a Tinker, say we.

Randle Cotgrave

They wyll say he that swereth depe, swereth like a lorde.

Sir Thomas Elyot

You taught me language; and my profit on't
Is, I know how to curse. The red plague rid you
For learning me your language.

Caliban

Trust none;
For oaths are straws, men's faiths are wafer-cakes.

Pistol

Juliet O! swear not by the moon, the inconstant moon . . .
Romeo What shall I swear by?
Juliet Do not swear at all;

SWEARING in the Renaissance had a rich complexity, combining exuberant creativity and severe restraint. The period saw the last vestiges of flyting, of set-piece tirades, but also of ghoulish punishments for swearing. At a time when a liberated, nominalist view of language was challenging the old taboos, a new wave of repression emanated from the fundamentalist sects like the Puritans and Quakers. Queen Elizabeth seems to have been no stranger to a 'good, mouth-filling oath'; Shakespeare and Ben Jonson amused themselves with 'conflicts of wit'. But in another category of swearing, Guy Fawkes and Father Garnet could knowingly swear false 'in deepest consequence' in that notorious case of high treason, the Gunpowder Plot. It is an ironic circumstance that, during a period considered to be marked by liberation, Chaucer's works would have been unacceptable for any public reading, since they would have infringed the restrictions concerning indecency and profanity on the Elizabethan stage.

The period saw two major developments altering and confining expression. The first was the shift from religious to secular swearing, the continuation of a tendency already developing in the Middle Ages. On the debasement of religious swearing there is this humorous observation by Queen Elizabeth's godson, Sir John Harington, posthumously published in his *Epigrams* (1615):

> In elder times an ancient custom was,
> To sweare in weighty matters by the Masse.
> But when the Masse went down (as old men note)
> They sware then by the crosse of this same grote [value]
> And when the Crosse was likewise held in scorne,
> Then by their faith, the common oath was sworne.
> Last, having sworne away all faith and troth,
> Only God damn them is their common oath.
> Thus custome kept *decorum* by gradation,
> That losing Masse, Crosse, Faith, they find damnation.
> (cited in Montagu, 1973, p. 162)

The second development was the emergence of the first stringently organized forms of secular censorship. These two developments are related: as religious referents were driven underground, so secular terms took their place. The institution by the Crown of the inappropriately named Master of the Revels in 1574 was designed to give the Master the pre-emptive right to censor plays, which the actors had to recite or present to him prior to public performance. The grounds for censorship, usually to do with matters of doctrine and politics, had been the foundation for previous orders against 'players and pipers strolling through the kingdom, disseminating heresy and seditions' in 'naughty plays' (Gildersleeve, 1908, p. 12). There was a special embargo on the staging of scenes which might call the institution of monarchy in question. Thus the deposition scene in Shakespeare's *Richard II* was not permitted to be acted in the latter part of Elizabeth's reign, and was excised from the first and second quartos (1597 and 1598). The staging of the play by the Essex conspirators in 1601 was designed to encourage rebellion. Elizabeth certainly alluded to this piece of agitprop by commenting bitterly: 'I am Richard II, know ye not that?' (Gildersleeve, 1908, p. 99). The staging of two satirical plays, *The Isle of Dogs* (1597) and *Eastward Ho!* (1605), led to authors and actors, including Ben Jonson, being sent to jail.

Linguistic censorship was, however, instituted only after the reign of Elizabeth, in 1606, possibly, Frances Shirley speculates, because the Queen would have been unsympathetic to legislation against Profanity on the Stage: 'Indeed, Elizabeth is said to have sworn "like a man", and certainly would have posed a problem to anyone trying to enforce a new law regulating oaths' (Shirley, 1979, p. 10). (There was, however, a bill 'against usual and common swearing' introduced into the Commons in 1601, but it failed at the first reading in the Lords.) On Elizabeth's abilities as a proponent and exponent of swearing, Nathan Drake observed: 'A shocking practice seems to have been rendered fashionable by the Queen . . . for it is said that she never spared an oath in public speech or in private conversation when she thought it added energy to either' (Shirley, 1979, p. 10). '*God's wounds* was a favourite oath of Queen Elizabeth's', asserts Montagu (1973, p. 139). John Aubrey relates the following naughty anecdote, suggesting a relish for vulgarity:

> This Earle of Oxford [Edward de Vere], making of his low obeisance to Queen Elizabeth, happened to let a Fart, at which he was so abashed and ashamed that he went to Travell, 7 yeares. On his returne the Queen welcomed him home, and sayd, 'My Lord, I had forgott the Fart'. (*Brief Lives*)

Her capacity for sharp and wounding words is attested to in the comment she is alleged to have made Archbishop Parker's wife after having 'greatlie feasted: "And you, *Madam* I may not call you, and *Mistris* I am ashamed to call you, so I know not what to call you, but yet I do thank you."'[1] Elizabeth's penchant for broad language is certainly a likely explanation for the delay until 1606 (in James' reign) of the 'Act to Restraine Abuses of Players':

> If . . . any person or persons doe or shall in any Stage play, Interlude, Shewe, Maygame or Pageant jestingly or prophanely speake or use the holy name of God or of Christ Jesus, or of the Holy Ghoste or of the Trinitie . . . [they] shall forfeite for every such Offence by him or them committed Tenne pounds. (3 Jac. I. c. 21)

This restriction would have completely bankrupted any company which put on, let us say, the religious plays known as the Wakefield Pageants in the Townley Cycle, acted from *c.*1554–76. The Wakefield Master's use of vigorous, even coarse, language in depictions of sacred moments is surprisingly daring. Cain, for example, rudely rejects his brother's good wishes with the crude invitation to *Com kis myne arse!*, or alternatively to *kys the dwillis toute!* (the devil's backside). When the Almighty speaks from above, Cain cheekily enquires, with mock innocence, *Who is that hob* [hobgoblin] *over the wall?* and although he protests *Me list not ban* ('I don't want to curse'), he keeps up a litany of profanity with phrases like *Peasse man, for Godys payn!*, *for Codys sydis* and, ironically, the anachronism *by him that me deere boght!* One of his last anti-social comments is *Bi all men set I nat a fart*. The spectacular ranting part of Herod the Great similarly exploits blasphemous utterance. Oscillating between Christian and pagan referents, Herod swears in the course of a mere twenty lines, *by Gottys dere naylys, What dewill, by Mahowne* [Mahomet] in heuen, the dewill me hang and draw and *by God that syttys in trone* (116–38).

The reaction to the Act of 1606 was twofold. Firstly, there was a marked increase in the use of pagan deities, as will be shown in more detail in the discussion on Shakespeare below. Secondly, 'minced oaths' (as the *OED* refers to them), avoiding direct reference to foul or profane language, grew in profusion. The practice was, of course, well established by this time, as figure 1.1 on Euphemisms demonstrates, with forms like *gog* and *cock* being recorded as far back as the fourteenth century. There was, however, an interesting efflorescence of newly-minced forms (most of them recorded in dramatic contexts) which actually preceded the 1606 Act by several years, as the following table shows:

'sblood	1598	– Shakespeare, *Henry IV, Part I*, I. ii. 82
'slid [eyelid]	1598	– Shakespeare, *Merry Wives*, III. iv. 24
'slight	1598	– Jonson, *Every Man Out of his Humour*, II. ii
'snails	1599	– Hayward, *Henry IV*, I. 19
zounds	1600	– Rowlands, *The Letting of Humours*, V. 72
'sbody	1601	– Jonson, *The Poetaster*, II. i
'sfoot	1602	– Marston, *Antonio's Revenge*, IV. iii

The synchronous quality of these curious mutilations and excisions of the name of God is impressive. In the course of the century this collection was to be augmented by *'sdeath* (1606), *'slife* (1634) and *'slidikins* (1694), a comic diminutive meaning 'God's little eyelids'. The consequent loss of understanding is shown in the re-spelling of *'struth* as *'strewth*. In the case of *zounds*, the form so efficiently obliterated the meaning that within a century the nonsensical alternative pronunciation [zaundz] had grown up. In 1698 the dramatist George Farquhar uses an interesting sociolinguistic distinction as part of a comic exchange in *Love and a Bottle.* Mockmore, an apprentice rake just down from Oxford and anxious to acquire the idiom of a beau, asks:

	... Pray what are the most fashionable Oaths in Town? *Zoons*, I take it, is a very becoming one.
Rigadoon	Zoons is only us'd by the disbanded Officers and Bullies; but Zauns is the Beaux' pronunciation.
Mockmore	Zauns –
Club [servant to Mockmore]	Zauns –
Rigadoon	Yes, Sir, we swear as we Dance: smooth, and with a Cadence. Zauns! 'Tis harmonious, and pleases the Ladies, because 'tis soft. – Zauns madam, – is the only Compliment our great Beaux pass on a Lady.

(II. ii)

A more general prohibition on swearing, the result of Puritan pressures, was incorporated in the year 1623 (21 Jac. I. c. 20):

> For as much as all profane Swearing and Cursing is forbidden by the Word of GOD, be it therefore enacted, by the Authority of the then Parliament, that no Person or Persons should from thenceforth profanely Swear or Curse, upon Penalty of forfeiting one Shilling to the use of the Poor for every Oath or Curse.

Refusal or inability to pay resulted in the offender being set in the stocks (if over twelve years old) or whipped if younger.

The consequent shift in idiom away from religious to secular referents is potently illustrated by comparing the styles of, say, Pandarus and the Wife of Bath in Chaucer with Pistol in *Henry V*. In all cases there is an element of satirical exaggeration. The speech of the Chaucerian characters is littered with religious oaths and asseverations, but the overblown Pistol eschews such referents, preferring such spectacularly provocative terms as *base tike; thou prick-eared cur of Iceland!; egregious dog; O viper vile!; O braggart vile, and damned furious wight!; O hound of Crete.* Only the minced religious form *perdy* finds its way into his vocabulary. He also favours *pish!* a new expression of contempt and disgust seemingly coined by Thomas Nashe in 1592.[O] (*Tush!*, a less provocative expression of impatience and disparagement, goes back to the fifteenth century.) *Cur*, incidentally, is an original Shakespearean contribution to the language of insult, first used in *A Midsummer Night's Dream*, an addition to *hound* (from *c*.1000), *tyke* (from *c*.1400) and *dog* (from *c*.1325). We may assume that Pistol conforms to the contemptible type of 'counterfeit rascal' described by Gower as taking on 'the form of a soldier: They con the phrase of war, which they trick up with new-tuned oaths' (III. vi. 83–5). However, assuredly Pistol's most provocative expressions of contempt are found in this exchange with Fluellen:

Pistol Die and be damned! and figo for thy friendship!
Fluellen It is well.
Pistol The fig of Spain! [*Exit*]
(III. vi. 60–2)

With the references to *figo* and *the fig of Spain*, we pass into more complicated, but quite unambiguous, forms of insulting body language, in this case 'a contemptuous gesture which consisted in thrusting the thumb between two of the closed fingers or into the mouth'.[O] This topic is discussed in the Appendix on Body Language.

Pistol's bravura performances are clearly in the tradition of comic excess. But there were other 'military' parasites who made a living out of verbal aggression. They indulged in 'ruffling' or 'roaring', i.e. extorting money, food, goods or debts by practised cursing and threats. *Ruffler* makes its first appearance in Act. 27 of Henry VIII (1535) in the categorization of 'Idell persons callynge them selues saruing men',[O] aggressive beggars who often pretended to be maimed in the wars. *Roarer* emerges somewhat later, *c*.1586, with a more generalized sense of a 'noisy, riotous fellow'. In *A Fair Quarrell* (1617), by Middleton and Rowley, there are several 'roaring' scenes: 'We'll roar the rusty rascal out of his tobacco' Chough and Trimtram agree in Act IV scene ii. The general sense of *ruffle*, meaning 'to hector, swagger, bear oneself proudly or arrogantly' is described by the *OED* as 'very common *c*.1540 to 1650', but is now entirely archaic.

UNDERGROUND BAWDY

The censorship and institutionalized fines served, as they usually do, to encourage circumvention through enforced ingenuity. The profusion of minced oaths which sprang up as a consequence of the laws against Profanity on the Stage must originally have been 'in-jokes', which guyed the authorities and sailed provocatively close to the wind. Swearing became a self-conscious motif on stage and page. One very stagey instance concerns the scene in *Twelfth Night* (IV. ii) where the Fool

Feste appears disguised in the garb of a clergyman. He is greeted by the libertine Sir Toby with the heavily ironic salutation, 'Jove bless thee, master parson!' Shakespeare is also adept at using a foreign language as a vehicle for obscene puns. An ingeniously bawdy instance is the scene of earnest delicacy in *Henry V* where the French princess is inducted into the rudiments of English:

Katharine *Comment appellez vous le pied et la robe?*
Alice De foot, *madame; et* le coun.
Katharine De foot, *et* le con? *O Seigneur Dieu! ces sont mots de son mauvais, corruptible, gros, et impudique, et non pour les dames d'honneur d'user.*

(III. iv. 55–8)

The innocent English terms which so affront the Queen-to-be are, of course, the ultimate taboos in French, namely *foutre* ('fuck') and *coun, con* ('cunt'). Robert Greene had a few years earlier used *foutre* in the French exclamation 'foutre de se monde!', but Shakespeare was to go further, having Pistol, an outrageously uncensored character, simply take over *foutre* and denounce all and sundry with the variant *foutra*:

A foutra for the world and worldlings base!

(*Henry IV, Part II*, V. ii. 98)

The word was subsequently borrowed as *fouter, footer* and *footling* in a much less vigorous, and, therefore, generally acceptable sense.

A seemingly dry, but actually 'naughty' grammar lesson in *The Merry Wives of Windsor* provides a similar instance:

Sir Hugh Evans . . . What is the focative case, William?
William *O Vocativo, O.*
Sir Hugh Evans Remember, William: focative is *caret* [it is missing].
Mistress Quickly And that's a good root.
Sir Hugh Evans 'Oman, forbear.
Mrs Page Peace!
Sir Hugh Evans What is your genitive case plural, William?
William Genitive case?
Sir Hugh Evans Ay.
William *Genitive, horum, harum, horum.*
Mistress Quickly Vengeance of Jenny's case! fie on her! Never name her, child, if she be a whore.

(IV. i. 53–65)

The comedy of this scene is enriched by Mistress Quickly's eager participation in underlining the sexual innuendoes. Beatrice shows a similar disposition when she observes in *Much Ado About Nothing* that 'With a good leg and a good foot, uncle, and money enough in his purse, such a man would win any woman in the world, if 'a could get her good will' (II. i. 15–18). Here the *double entendres* are *leg* (= 'penis'), *foot* (= *foutre* = 'fuck') and *will* (= 'sexual appetite'). The *Nothing* of the play's title is a coded sexual pun on 'an O thing' (= 'cunt'), already alluded to in William's comment (just quoted) to 'O Vocativo, O'. Hamlet mercilessly pursues this meaning in his public degradation of Ophelia in the play scene:

Hamlet Lady, shall I lie in your lap?
Ophelia No, my lord.
Hamlet I mean, my head upon your lap?
Ophelia Ay my lord.
Hamlet Do you think I meant country matters?
Ophelia I think nothing, my lord.
Hamlet That's a fair thought to lie between maid's legs.
Ophelia What is, my lord?
Hamlet Nothing.[2]

(III. ii. 120–9)

The savageness of Hamlet's word-play shows the attitude of cynical hatred epitomized in his earlier denunciation, 'Frailty, thy name is woman!' As Eric Partridge showed in his pioneering study, *Shakespeare's Bawdy* (1947), the circumvention of Elizabethan restraints on coarse language was achieved by a complex variety of coded evasions and euphemisms.

SHAKESPEARE

From Shakespeare's plays one should, theoretically, be able to build up a patterned series of instances and observations about swearing to use as an index of character, in the manner previously shown in Chaucer's *Canterbury Tales*. However, although Shakespeare shows marked differentiation between characters in terms of oaths and foul language, freedom of swearing was not (as we have seen) a constant condition in his life time. Various forms of government interference designed to stamp out Profanity on the Stage effectively changed regulations and conventions, so that a fair developmental comparison with Chaucer's works cannot be made. The following discussion is extended in the section on the categorization of women in chapter 10.

In the histories the legacy of hatred and betrayal from the Wars of the Roses infuses the early plays of the 'Henriad' with a great chorus of curses which reaches its climax in *Richard III* with the virulent invective of Margaret. Shunning the run-of-the-mill insults such as *dog*, *cur* and *devil*, she employs a spectacular gamut of vituperation, referring to Richard, variously, as a *cacodemon*, as an *elvish-marked, abortive rooting hog*, a *bottled spider*, and, getting into her stride:

> The slave of nature and the son of hell!
> Thou slander of thy mother's heavy womb!
> Thou loathed issue of thy father's loins!
> Thou rag of honour!
>
> (I. iii. 230–3)

All of this fury is compacted into Act I. More sinister are her predictive curses, which, in the mechanical providence of the play, come unerringly true.

Throughout his tragedies Shakespeare explores the dramatic nexus between the most highly charged forms of language (cursing, oaths, prophecy) and deeds or action. It is notable, furthermore, how all the major tragedies hinge on some oath.

In *Hamlet* the duty of vengeance is laid upon the prince in the curious oath-ritual of 'cellarage'. This dramatic emphasis is striking in itself. If the Ghost is a 'good' or 'honest' ghost, why should it be so insistent upon its son taking an oath for what should be a self-evident duty? Hamlet has, in any case, already made his own oath, with an admittedly curious emphasis, to 'wipe away all trivial fond records,' etc., so that

> thy commandment all alone shall live
> Within the book and volume of my brain,
> Unmixt with baser matter: yes, by heaven!
>
> (I. v. 102–4)

Hamlet endeavours to keep his sanity through the maelstrom of his emotions by venting his frustration at his own apparent impotence and inaction, and by expressing his hatred of Claudius in the most virulent oaths. Execration becomes a form of sublimation:

> Bloody bawdy villain!
> Remorseless, treacherous, lecherous, kindless villain!
>
> (II. ii. 616–17)

Yet Hamlet is nothing if not self-critical, of this fault as of others:

> Why, what an ass am I! This is most brave,
> That I, the son of a dear father murder'd,
> Prompted to my revenge by heaven and hell,
> Must, like a whore, unpack my heart with words,

And fall a-cursing like a very drab,
A scullion!

(II. ii. 619–24)

It is a reflection of Hamlet's subsequent self-control that, as he delivers the final death-stroke, there is calculated starkness in his public summary of Claudius' guilt:

. . . thou incestuous, murderous, damnèd Dane

(V. ii. 277)

Assuredly, there is a sense of exultation in that *damnèd* is used, not in a light, but a profoundly prophetic fashion, since Claudius has died in a state of mortal sin. In the course of the play, Hamlet runs through the whole gamut of swearing terms, notably the social and sexual categories. He is especially fixated by *villain*, which the *Concordance* reveals, he uses ten times. His concern with sexual infidelity is reflected in the repeated use of *incestuous* of Claudius and *whore* of his mother. His suspicion of the treachery around him is encapsulated in his cryptic remark: 'I eat the air, promise-crammed' (III. ii. 100).

Ophelia's mad scene (like Lady Macbeth's sleep-walking scene) dramatizes the uncensored mind at work. Ophelia's usual propriety is shown to be a facade by the sexual undercurrents of her speech and its lapses into curiously archaic swearing:

Ophelia By Gis and by Saint Charity,
Alack, and fie for shame!
Young men will do't, if they come to't;
By Cock they are to blame.

(IV. v. 59–62)

Gis is an archaic mutilation of *Jesus*, recorded from *c.*1528°, while *Cock*, a minced form of *God*, is found as far back as Chaucer in the phrase *cokkes bones!*, though there could be a phallic overtone in this context. *Cock* was resuscitated in the nineteenth century by Scott and Longfellow, but *Gis* died out shortly after Shakespeare's lifetime.

The texts of *Hamlet* show some interesting signs of censorship, either by the Master of the Revels, the author or his literary executors, in response to the regulations concerning Profanity on the Stage. Thus, in Hamlet's bitter opening soliloquy, 'O that this too, too solid flesh would melt . . . .' (I. ii. 129), the line, 'O God, a beast that wants discourse of reason', appears in this form in the First and Second Quartos, but in the Folio (1623) is emended to 'Heaven . . .'. Likewise, Hamlet's speech at the end of the tragedy, 'O God, Horatio, what a wounded name . . .' is the reading of the Second Quarto, having been emended to 'O fie . . .' in the First Quarto and 'O good Horatio . . .' in the Folio. *God* is similarly changed to *Heaven*, *'s wounds* is changed to *come*, and *'s bloud* was changed to *why*, or simply omitted. Jespersen noted, very pertinently, that 'such words as *Bible*, *Holy Ghost* and *Trinity* do not occur at all in his writings, while *Jesu*, *Christ* and *Christmas* are found only in some of his earliest plays' (1962, p. 203).

In *King Lear*, verbal horrors are the prelude to barbaric actions. The initial division of the kingdom is the seminal fiat of the play although it is not uttered in formal terms. Indeed, the political insanity of the division is underscored by Lear's peremptoriness. Contrastingly, the violent curses and enraged rejection of his daughters are conveyed in highly formalized statements of passion. The comparison with the 'barbarous Scythian' is an explicit cultural pointer to his regression. So is Shakespeare's dramatic realization of this bizarre situation, in that weird, primitive forces are appealed to in curses framed in highly formal, legalistic language:

> . . . by the sacred radiance of the sun,
> The mysteries of Hecate and the night
> By all the operation of the orbs
> From whom we do exist and cease to be,
> Here I disclaim all my paternal care
> Propinquity and property of blood . . .
> (I. i. 111–16)

The following furious exchange between Kent and Lear dramatizes, in a way which would have had particularly ironic resonances for Elizabethans, Lear's naive faith in pagan deities:

> *Lear* Now, by Apollo, –
> *Kent* Now, by Apollo, king
> Thou swear'st thy gods in vain.
> *Lear* O vassal! miscreant!
> (I. i. 162–3)

Lear's appeals show a fixation with supernatural intervention in the cause of his egocentric notion of 'justice'. He invokes 'all the stor'd vengeances of heaven' (II. iv. 164), a curiously punitive concept. His curses seek, furthermore, horrifically unnatural punishments:

> Into her womb convey sterility!
> Dry up in her the organs of increase . . .
> (I. v. 301–2)

Strike her young bones,
You taking airs, with lameness!

(II. iv. 165–6)

(The cursing language of sterility and destruction is counter-balanced later by Cordelia's healing language of spells and charms.) Edmund, on the other hand, with equal partiality, invokes a panoply of copulatory deities engaged in an orgy of 'divine thrusting-on' to 'stand up for bastards!' (I. ii. 22, 140).

On a different level of invective, generating comedy rather than horror, is Kent's encyclopaedic berating of Oswald as

> a base, proud, shallow, beggarly, three-suited, hundred-pound, filthy, worsted-stocking knave; a lily-livered, action-taking knave; a whoreson, glass-gazing, superserviceable, finical rogue; one-trunk-inheriting slave; one that wouldst be a bawd, in the way of good service, and art nothing but the composition of knave, beggar, coward, pandar, and the son and heir of a mongrel bitch. . . .
>
> (II. ii. 15–24)

(The last epithet seems to be the first version, albeit elaborated, of the subsequent staple American idiom, *son of a bitch*, discussed further in chapter 8).

The play is a great chorus of prayers, curses, blessings and invocations, yet its tragic agony derives from the profound ambiguity of the divinities appealed to and sworn by. Most are overtly pagan (Apollo, Hecate etc.), partly to evoke the primitive era of the action, and partly because the play was written after the period when the edict against Profanity on the Stage had been enforced. There are several instances, however, to the capitalized Christian God.

John F. Danby has justly called *Timon of Athens* 'an unnatural fantasy, a *King Lear* without Cordelia' (1959, p. 195). Timon's alarming curses reveal a comprehensively destructive impulse untempered by sanity, moderation or love. His imprecations, unlike Lear's, are all-encompassing, willing upon Athens a regime of chaos, savagery and disease. They are even more bizarre because they are directed, not at divine or supernatural agencies, but at inanimate objects ('thou wall'), abstractions ('obedience') or social categories (bankrupts and servants):

Let me look back upon thee. O thou wall,
That girdlest in those wolves, dive in the earth,
And fence not Athens! Matrons, turn incontinent!
Obedience fail in children! Slaves and fools,
Pluck the grave wrinkled senate from the bench,

And minister in their steads! *To general filths*
Convert, o' the instant, green virginity!
Do't in your parents' eyes! Bankrupts, hold fast;
Rather than render back, out with your knives,
And cut your trusters' throats! Bound servants, steal! –
Large-handed robbers your grave masters are, –
And pill by law. Maid, to thy master's bed;
Thy mistress is o' the brothel! Son of sixteen,
Pluck the lin'd crutch from thine old limping sire,
With it beat out his brains! Piety, and fear,
Religion to the gods, peace, justice, truth,
Domestic awe, night-rest and neighbourhood,
Instruction, manners, mysteries and trades,
Degrees, observances, customs, laws,
Decline to your confounding contraries,
And let confusion live! Plagues incident to men,
Your potent and infectious fevers heap
On Athens, ripe for stroke! Thou cold sciatica,
Cripple our senators, that their limbs may halt
As lamely as their manners! *Lust and liberty*
Creep in the minds and marrows of our youth,
That 'gainst the stream of virtue they may strive,
And drown themselves in riot! Itches, blains,
Sow all the Athenian bosoms, and their crop
Be general leprosy! Breath infect breath,
That their society, as their friendship, may
Be merely poison! Nothing I'll bear from thee
But nakedness, thou detestable town![3]

(IV. i. 1–33)

The furious indiscriminacy of Timon's appeal for anarchy demonstrates a mind-numbing insanity of a very different order from Lear's 'reason in madness'. However, because the setting of the play is so obviously decadent, rather than simply primitive (as it is in *Lear*), the curses have a frantic, even petulant, impotence. Yet both strike at a notion of order at once precarious and prized.

In *Othello*, the dramatic moment which assures Othello's downfall, signalling his descent into the power of Iago, is his formal vow of punishment through this invocation:

Now, by yond marble heaven,
In the due reverence of a sacred vow, [*kneels*]
I here engage my words

(III. iii. 461–3)

Macbeth, alone of the tragedies, has little focus on swearing or oaths *per se*. It is, however, profoundly concerned with falsity, treachery, what Macbeth finally recognizes as

> . . . the equivocation of the fiend
> That lies like truth
>
> (V. v. 43–4)

which has secured his own 'deep damnation'. A key reference in the central Porter's speech is to the 'equivocator that could swear in both scales against either scale' (II. iii. 10–11). This allusion to the jesuitical prevarication of the conspirators, Father Garnet and Guy Fawkes, who knowingly made false oaths in the investigation into the Gunpowder Plot, had a powerful contemporary resonance.

The play has a stranger emphasis, on prophecy, spells, the weird use of language, and not solely by the Witches. Macbeth and Lady Macbeth seek in their passionate ambition to make the world of man and nature conform to their wishes. Many of their speeches have the force of attempted spells and incantations:

> Stars, hide your fires!
>
> (I. iv. 50)

> Come, you spirits
> That tend on mortal thoughts! . . .
> Come to my woman's breasts,
> And take my milk for gall. . . .
> Come, thick night . . .
>
> (I. v. 41–51)

Weirdly, their words come true, but not always as they had wished.

Shakespeare's Roman plays are highly significant in relation to our theme, since they represent a cultural world in which, apart from *Julius Caesar*, the gods do not have a vital presence. (It seems ironic, in fact, that King Lear can swear far more vehemently by Apollo than can Brutus or Antony or Coriolanus.) In this spiritual aspect the Roman world is quite different from the 'original' classical creations of Homer and Virgil, where the gods constantly manipulate human characters and affairs, and can be appealed to in a meaningful fashion. The consequence is a world of benighted materialism, superficial relationships and ruthless politics largely divorced from loyalty and principle.

Oaths and vows are used with transparent opportunism. One thinks of the political pact between Octavius and Antony, using Octavia as a political pawn in *Antony and Cleopatra*, of the political pact between

Coriolanus and Aufidius in *Coriolanus*, and of the cynical alliance between Antony, Octavius and Lepidus in *Julius Caesar*. Though it may be said that Shakespeare's History plays also have these features of treachery, every character, even the most villainous, has to face the existence of God and the Last Judgement. Thus even the antic villain Richard III has to suffer the knowledge of his crimes in the face of the last things.

Coriolanus, on the other hand, shows the essential imbalance and limitation of the hard, politicized Roman world by largely excluding the numinous and employing almost exclusively the most virulent forms of physical insult. Coriolanus himself shows a limiting fixation with the detestable bodily smells of 'the mutable, rank-scented many' (III. i. 65). The most memorable of many such instances is found in the savage speech of 'reversed banishment' by the hero:

> You common cry of curs! whose breath I hate
> As reek o' the rotten fens, whose loves I prize
> As the dead carcases of unburied men
> That do corrupt my air; I banish you.
>
> (III. iii. 118–21)

The idiom of class hatred and the capacity to see the lower orders only in reified terms seems to have been taken in with his mother's milk. Volumnia, Coriolanus recalls,

> was wont
> To call them woollen vassals, things created
> To buy and sell with groats, to show bare heads
> In congregations.
>
> (III. ii. 8–11)

Apart from his obvious lack of introspection, Coriolanus' tragedy lies in his incapacity to separate registers according to the conventions of polite speech. Menenius alludes to this deficiency in seeking to exculpate Coriolanus' use of soldierly epithets in urbane discourse:

> Consider this: he hath been bred i' the wars
> Since he could draw a sword, and is ill school'd
> In bolted language; meal and bran together
> He throws without distinction.
>
> (III. i. 318–21)

Julius Caesar shows, of all the Roman plays, the greatest degree of swearing by 'the mighty gods', which is the idiom of the patricians; the obverse, of degrading physical insult, is used of the plebs:

> You blocks, you stones, you worse than senseless things![4]
> (*Julius Caesar*, I. i. 39)

Brutus' insistence that the conspirators should *not* be bound by any oath is a rare, albeit naive, instance of his admirable trust. Yet, unlike Macbeth, he remains unaware of the full quality of his treachery, even when Caesar utters the famous despairing and condemning cry: 'Et tu, Brute!' (III. i. 77). In the final act, just before the battle of Philippi, there is an interesting relic, one of the last survivals of the tradition of flyting in an English literary text. Antony, master of many styles, is the most adept at this injurious idiom:

> Villains! you did not so [threat] when your vile daggers
> Hack'd one another in the sides of Cæsar:
> You show'd your teeth like apes, and fawned like hounds,
> And bow'd like bondmen, kissing Cæsar's feet;
> While Damned Casca, like a cur, behind
> Struck Cæsar on the neck.
> (V. i. 39–44)

Casca's response is characteristically contemptuous, mocking Octavius and Antony as:

> A peevish schoolboy, worthless of such honour,
> Join'd wth a masquer and a reveller.
> (V. i. 61–2)

This is fairly polite and subtle when compared with the earlier English and later Scots examples, as we shall see in the next section.

Ben Jonson, with his notoriously aggressive personality, makes swearing and foul language more of an overt feature of his plays. He devotes, for example, a fair amount of *Everyman in His Humour* (1598) to ironic exposés and disapproving commentary on the incidence of swearing in his times. The elder Kno'well observes ironically that infantile education is marked, not by repression of swearing, but by encouragement:

> Their first words
> We form their tongues with, are licentious jests
> Can it call whore? Cry, bastard? Oh then kiss it,
> A witty child! Can 't swear? The father's darling!
> Give it two plums.
> (II. iii. 19–23)

Clement, the major authority-figure in the play, firmly corrects Cob's expletive 'for God's sake' by the sober rejoinder. 'Nay, God's precious'

(III. iii. 103–4). The *miles gloriosus*, Bobadill, is given, predictably, the most exuberant swearing role, with expletives such as *base cullion* [testicle]; *whoreson filthy slave; a dungworm, an excrement! Body O'Caesar* and *by the foot of Pharaoh*. In *Bartholomew Fair* (1614), which has an Epilogue addressed to the King on the subject of profanity and licence, Wasp comes out with such earthy vituperation as *Turd i' your teeth!* and *Shit o' your head!*

While Shakespeare seems to have escaped prosecution under the stringent regulations, Ben Jonson did not. A performance of his play *The Magnetic Lady* (1632) led to a charge of blasphemy. Jonson, by now the victim of stroke, was mystified at the charge, especially since the script had been approved by the Master of the Revels, Sir Henry Herbert (brother of the poet). In the proceedings (from which Jonson was excused) the players at first 'would have excused themselves,' wrote Herbert, 'on me and the poett', but they afterwards confessed that they had found the dialogue insufficiently racy and had larded it with their own interpolations, which apparently included oaths and references to offensive personalities. The Archbishop of Canterbury finally attributed all blame to them (Gildersleeve, 1908, pp. 79, 126).

However, the pressure told, and when Jonson prepared his plays for the press, he toned down many oaths, so that 'by Jesu' became 'Believe me', 'By heaven' is altered to 'By these hilts', 'faith' is replaced by 'marry' or 'indeed', and even the heathen gods are banished, so that 'by the gods' is toned down to 'by my sword' or 'by my life' (cited in Gildersleeve, 1908, pp. 128–9). As a sign of the times, Herbert's certificate of approval was fulsomely given in his Register to a play which has sunk almost without trace or subsequent performance, James Shirley's *The Young Admiral* (1633):

> The comedy called The Yonge Admirall, being free from oaths, prophaneness or obsceanes, hath given mee much delight and satisfaction in the readinge, and may serve for a patterne to other poetts, not only for the bettring of maners and language, but for the improvement of the quality, which hath received some brushings of late. (cited in Gildersleeve, 1908, p. 127)

Royal taste in matters of censorship was not always as strict as that of the Master. Herbert records, with a certain amount of chagrin and pique, the humiliation of being overruled by Charles I in 1634:

> This morning . . . the kinge was pleasd to call mee into his withdrawinge chamber to the windowe, wher he went over all that I had croste in Davenant's playe-booke [*The Wits*] and allowing of *faith* and *slight* to bee

> asseverations only, and no oathes, markt them to stande, and some other few things, but in the greater part allowed of my reformations.

Herbert was not entirely cowed, however, since he proceeds to record his objections:

> The kinge is pleasd to take *faith, death, slight*, for asseverations, and no oaths, to which I doe humbly submit as my masters judgement; but, under favour, conceive them to be oaths, and enter them here, to declare my opinion and submission. (cited in Gurr, 1980, pp. 74–5)

In other areas the royal prerogative was supreme: a satirical passage on royal monetary practices elicited the curt instruction: 'This is too insolent, and to be changed' (cited in Gurr, 1980, p. 75).

As the Puritans gained power, so the war against profanity was conducted on all fronts. 'Not a man swears but pays his twelve pence,' claimed Oliver Cromwell of his Ironsides. A quartermaster found guilty (under military law) of uttering impious expressions was condemned to have 'his tongue bored with a red hot iron, his sword broken over his head, and be ignominiously dismissed the service' (cited in Montagu, 1973, p. 167).

Predictably, throughout this period, treatises against swearing poured from the presses of the land. One Walter Powell, 'Preacher at Standish, neer Gocester,' issued in 1645 a 384-page diatribe, *A SUMMONS FOR SWEARERS, AND A LAW for the lips in reproving them*. Robert Boyle, the scientist, wrote in 1647, at the age of twenty, *A Free DISCOURSE AGAINST Customary Swearing AND A DISSUASIVE FROM CURSING*. It is constructed on a basis of rigorous legalistic logic as 'Pleas' and 'Answers'. Plea VI applies to 'minced oaths':

> Ally'd to this plea, is theirs that will not flatly swear by God, but by certain fictitious terms and abbreviatures, as by Dod, etc. *Ans*. To These I shall only answer with the Apostle, *Be not deceived, God is not mocked*. . . . Well may this childish Evasion cheat our own souls, but never him, who judgeth as well as he discerns Intents . . . since the same credit is both given and expected upon these Mongrel Oaths, that is paid to those they mean . . . 'Tis a pretty flight of these Gentlemen, to cozen the Devil to their own advantage, and to find out By-ways to Damnation, and descend to Hell by a pair of Backstairs. (cited in Montagu, 1973, p. 170).

When the Puritans took up arms, they declared their enemies to be, in addition to the King, 'popery, prelacy, superstition, heresy, schism, and profaneness'. The heaviest of their blows against profanity occurred on 2 September, 1642, when an edict announced that, in 'the Distracted Estate of England, threatened by a Cloud of Blood, by a Civill Warre

. . . publicke Sports do not agree well with publicke Calamities. . . . It is therefore thought fit, and Ordeined by the Lords and Commons in this Parliament Assembled that . . . publicke Stage-playes shall cease.'

THE FINAL EFFLORESCENCE OF FLYTING

While strong language in the South of the British Isles was increasingly marked by politeness, decorum and censorship, the tradition of flyting continued to thrive in the North, presumably because of the tenacity of the Norse influence in those areas. We have traced the tradition back to the skaldic tirades of Erik Skallagrimsson and the medieval debate poems, *The Owl and the Nightingale* (*c.*1250) and Chaucer's *Parlement of Foulys* (*c.*1382). There were, however, various continental antecedents, such as the Provençal *sirvente, tenso* and *partimen*, as well as a tradition of Latin invective from Saint Jerome through some of the fifteenth-century Italian humanists to Erasmus. In his edition of Dunbar, James Kinsley describes flyting (somewhat tamely) as 'a blend of primitive literary criticism and lampoon apparently popular in fifteenth- and sixteenth-century Scotland' (1979, p. 282). In his earlier edition, W. Mackay Mackenzie included as traditional influences 'the *agon* or "altercation", one of the essential elements of the Old Comedy of Greece', as well as parallels in Arabic, Italian and Celtic. Mackenzie defined the genre in more vigorous metaphor as a 'verbal tournament *à outrance*' (1932, p. xxxii), using a figure of speech which seems the more illuminating, since it reminds us that the roots of flyting lie in competition and in the demonstration of skill, not solely in personal execration.

For, in the most famous Scots pieces, such as *The Flyting of Dunbar and Kennedy* (*c.*1503), *The Flyting of Montgomerie and Polwart* (c.1585) and a similar contest between King James V and Sir David Lindsay, we are obviously involved in what can only be called, paradoxically, 'the fine art of savage insult', since the participants are noted authors and their works are neither scrappy nor extemporaneous nor crude. Indeed, Kinsley surmizes that the *Flyting* between Dunbar and Kennedy (which is over 550 lines long) 'may have developed in a series of attacks and counter-attacks circulated in manuscript at court' (1979, p. 284). (Dunbar was a Master of Arts, a Franciscan preaching friar and a priest who was in the King's service for several years and the recipient of a royal pension; Kennedy, who had similar academic qualifications, was greatly admired as a poet, and was of the blood royal.) However, we find in these texts a use of language so sophisticated and so foul that it clearly belongs to a convention of lingusitic versatility quite unfamiliar to us, having been long obsolete. It was presumably designed as a form of entertainment for a sophisticated, not a 'common' audience: 'Montgomerie and Polwart flyted one another in a variety of metres and forms which were designed to demonstrate their versatility to the court audience for whom the whole exercise was presumably staged.'[5]

What makes the Scottish flytings the more striking is that they occur in a country with a vehement tradition against profanity. In 1551, more than half a century before the English Parliament passed such a measure, the Scots Parliament passed an Act

> ... in detestatioun of the grevous and abominabill aithis, sweiring, execrationnis and blasphematioun of the name of God [some egregious examples of which are then listed] and sic uthers ugsume [fearful] aithis ... it is statute and ordanit that quatsumevir persoun or persounis sweiris sic abominabill aithis and detestabill execrationnis as is afoir rehersit sall incur the panis [penalties] efter following als oft as thay failthie respective. That is to say, ane Prelate of Kirk, Erle or Lord, for evereie fault to be committit for the space of thre monethis nixt tocum. That is to say, unto the first day of Maij exclusive xij.d. [twelve pence]. Ane Barrone or benefecit man constitute in dignity ecclesiatik iiij.d. [four pence]. Ane landit man, frehalder, wassal, fewar Burges and smal benefecit men ij.d. [two pence]. Ane craftsman, yeoman, a seward man and all uthers j.d. [one penny]. Item the pure folkis that hes na geir to pay the pane aforeseaid to be put in the stokis or presonit for the space of four houris ...
>
> (cited in Montagu, 1973, pp. 129–30)

This legislation was probably provoked by the works of Dunbar (who died *c.*1520) and by the similar output of Sir David Lindsay (courtier to King James IV and Usher to the infant James V), notably his *Satire of the Three Estates*, which was performed in 1543 at Coupar, which he represented in Parliament. This forthright work contains not only the traditional formulas, such as *be Cokis passion, be the gude Lord* and *be the messe* but *be God's wounds, be God's croce* [cross] and a whole host of curious religious paraphernalia, such as *be God's breid, be God's gown, be Bryde's bell* and other titles, such as *be him that herryit hell, be him that bare the crown of thorn* and, strangely, *be him that our Lord Jesus sauld* [sold, betrayed], i.e. Judas. He attacks prelacy with bitter directness: 'Bischops ... may fuck thair fill and be vnmaryit' (1363).

Dunbar begins the *Flyting* with some hyperbolic threats of how the sea would burn, the moon suffer eclipse and rocks shatter, should he choose to 'flyte'. This provokes from Kennedy the immediate opening insult 'Dirtin [filthy] Dumbar', the first of an astonishing catalogue, which includes

> Fantastik fule. . . .
> Ignorant elf, aip, owll irregular
> Skaldit [scabby] skaitbird and commoun skamelar [sponger],
> Wan fukkit funling [ill-conceived foundling]. . . .
> (35–9)

Dunbar replies in kind, using equally personal insults, such as:

> Cuntbitten crawdon [pox-smitten coward]
> (50)

Crawdon contains a whole resonance of masculine contempt, since the sense of 'coward' derives from a cock which will no longer fight. The singular adjective intensifies the insult by playing on the various meanings of *cock*.[6] In his retort, Kennedy calls Dunbar succinctly, though less subtly:

> A schit but wit [A shit without wit]
> (496)

who would 'like to throw shit by the cartload' (469). (This is one of the earliest recorded personal applications of *shit*.) In the course of the altercation, every conceivable insult is hurled, sexual, religious, natural, social, excretory, (together with many that baffle the imagination or amaze with their directness):

> Thow crop and rute of tratouris tressonable,
> The fathir and moder of morthour and mischeif,
> Dissaitful tyrand with serpentis tung unstable,
> Cuckald cradoun, cowart, and common theif:
> (73–6)

> Sueir swappit swanky, swynekeper ay for swatis
> [lazy great smart-arse, perpetual pig-keeper for small beer]
> Thy commissar Quintyne biddis the cum kis his ers –
> [Your associate Quintin [a Scots poet] bids you come and kiss his arse.]

In all, the work is full of an astonishing variety of register and cultural reference, such as this example of bizarre, surrealistic image:

> Evill fairit and dryit as Denseman on the rattis
> [Evil favoured and desiccated as a Dane on the rack]
> (51)

referring to the 'wheel' on which a criminal was executed and his dead body subsequently exposed.

The work also contains the earliest recorded instances of several current terms, notably *get* (n.) in its old, strong sense of 'bastard':

Fals tratour, feyndis gett.
(244)

An abbreviation of *beget*, *get* is in most of its early history a specially northern and Scottish word, found *c.*1570 in a Scottish poem, 'The Treason of Dunbarton':

Ganylon's gets, relicts of Sinon's seed.
(171)

The word continued to be used in this way in the North, before filtering southwards and losing much of its intensity. Grose (1785) records the term neutrally as 'one of his get; one of his offspring or begetting'. In recent times the pronunciation has shifted to [git].

In the equally scurrilous *Flyting of Montgomerie and Polwart* (*c.*1585), there is the invitation to 'kis þe cunt of ane kow' (817), while the *Answer to Kingis Flyting* (1535-6) contains the frenzied alliteration: 'Ay fukkand [fucking] lyke ane furious Fornicatour' (49).

As can be seen, sexual insults figure in these Northern satires and flytings to a far higher degree than would be expected in the South. In Dunbar's satirical parody of a courtly love debate, 'The Two Married Women and the Widow', the Widow (whose sexual regime is remarkably similar to that of Chaucer's Wife of Bath) shows total contempt for her dominated husband:

I maid that wif carll to werk all womenis werkis
[I made that pansy do all the women's chores]
(351)

I him miskennyt, be Crist, and cukkald him maid
[I deceived him, by Christ, and made him a cuckold]
(380)

I wes laith to be loppin with sic a lob avoir
[I was loath to be screwing with such a clumsy cart-horse]
(387)

Quhen I that grom geldit had of gudis and of natur
[When I had castrated that fellow of his goods and potency]
(392)

Furthermore, C. S. Lewis' insight, termed 'the moralisation of status words' (1960, p. 21), is clearly demonstrated in the Widow's categorization of men. Her husband is contemptuously denigrated in low-class terms as *carl, grome* and *schaik* ('fellow'), *that auld schrew* ('that old bugger'), while she now associates with *knychtis, clerkis [scholars] and cortly persons*. In what, admittedly, seems to be a courtly *cum* erotic fantasy, *the best bourd* is populated by *baronis and knychtis And othir bachilleris blith* who regale her in various ways which give us some insight into late medieval entertainment:

> Sum rownis and sum ralȝeis and sum redis ballatis,
> [Some whisper and some jest and some read ballads]
> Sum raiffis furght rudly with riatus speche;
> [Some rant forth rudely with wanton speech]
>
> Sum stalwardly steppis ben with a stout curage
> [Some step boldly and stout-heartedly into my chamber]
> And a stif standard thing staiffis in mi neiff;
> [And thrust a stiff rampant penis into my fist]
>
> (480–6)

Against this background, it is not surprising to find an Act of 1609 in Scotland (103. Parl. 7. Jam. 6) which ratified the 1551 Act, increased fines and set out stringent policing methods:

> Against Cursing and Swearing, and not delating [reporting], or neglect to Prosecute, the same,
> Abominable Oaths, and detestable Execrations, particularly Swearing in vaine by God's Blood, Body, Passions, and Wounds; saying Devil Stick, Gore, Rost, or Rieve them; and such other Execrations; are Punished as in Act 16. Parl. 5 Q[ueen]. M[ary]. [1551] which is Ratified: The Penalties Augmented: And Censors appointed in the Mercat [market] places of Burrows [boroughs], and other publick Fairs, with power to put the Delinquents in ward till Payment, and Surety for abstaining in time coming: And that by Direction of the Judges Ordinary. And that all House-Holders Delate Transgressors within their Houses, under pains of being punished as offenders themselves. And if the said Majistrates be remiss, they shall be called before the Council, Committed to ward during pleasure, and fined surety for exact diligence thereafter. (cited in Montagu, 1973, pp. 158–9)

When we look at the continuation of flyting in the South, we find that the tradition is considerably atrophied by 1600. It is in the earliest farces, *Ralph Roister Doister* (*c.*1552) and *Gammer Gurton's Needle* (acted 1566) that the most vigorous invective is to be found. In the second of these we find the new idioms of *what the devil, how a murrain [plague], go to, Fie shitten knave and out upon thee, the pox, bawdy bitch, that dirty* *bastard, the whoreson dolt, for God's sake, thou shitten knave* and *that dirty shitten lout*. The violent altercations between Grandma Gurton and Dame Chat show the closest affiliations to flyting:

Gammer Thou wert as good as kiss my tail,
Thou slut, thou cut, thou rakes, thou jakes,
[You whore, you jade, you bawd, you shit-house]
will not shame make thee hide thee?

Chat Thou skald, thou bald, thou rotten, thou glutton,
[You scold, you hairless thing, you rubbish, you pig]
I will no longer chide thee;
But I will teach thee to keep home.

(III. iii)

There are vestiges of flyting, discussed elsewhere in this chapter, in the violent confrontations of Elizabethan tragedy. One thinks here of Hamlet's caustic repartee, of furious exchanges between Lear and Kent and the berating of Oswald by Kent. In all of these there is a savage irony and a bitter humour. And one sees features of flyting in the comic stichomythia of *The Taming of the Shrew* and *Much Ado About Nothing*. But the great scenes of linguistic confrontation are essentially passionate expressions of character conflict in which language is taken in deadly earnest, lives are irrecoverably changed and even destroyed. Flyting, on the other hand, has an essential element of licence, of word-play, since otherwise the insults would lead to duels and other modes of exacting satisfaction.

NOTES

1 Elizabeth was bitterly opposed to the clergy marrying, which in part explains this venomous remark, quoted in J. E. Neale (1958), p. 101, together with the observation by Sir Robert Cecil that she 'was more than a man and (in troth) sometymes less than a woman'.

2 See also E. A. M. Coleman *The Dramatic Use of Bawdy in Shakespeare* (1974) p. 16, who questions this interpretation. Of the many other terms which took on sexual innuendoes at this time, *die* is one of the more remarkable. The sense of 'to experience orgasm' is not immediately apparent in a modern reading of Lear's 'I will die bravely like a smug bridegroom' (IV. vi. 203), but is certainly meant in Samuel Butler's lines 'From Love':

O 'tis a happy and heav'nly death
when a man dy's above and a woman beneath.

3 The italics indicate Bowdler's excisions from his *Family Shakespeare*, discussed more fully in chapter 11.

4 The contemptuous reification of the plebs into mere *things* reflects the patrician view of them as subhuman. Cf. Coriolanus' rejection of them as 'such things as you' (V. ii. 103) and 'You souls of geese That bear the shapes of men' (I. iii. 34–5). 'Hence, rotten thing!' is his dismissal of an ædile (III. i. 178). In the opening scene alone, he refers to the 'mutinous citizens' (to their faces) as *curs*, *foxes*, *hares*, *geese* and *rats*.

5 R. D. S. Jack (ed.), *The History of Scottish Literature* (Aberdeen, Aberdeen UP, 1988), vol. I, p. 51. Jack also makes the point that 'It is not necessarily the case, as is often claimed, that by the time the *Flyting* was written, alliterative verse had become associated only with low styles.'

6 *Craudon*, more commonly *cradden* in Scots and Northern English, has a remarkable similarity to Modern American slang *chicken* in its various senses relating to cowardice. Wright defined it in the *EDD* (1898) as '(1) A coward; (2) A daring feat set by boys such as no "cradden" would undertake; a challenge; (3) (vb.) To betray cowardice.' The wounding alliterating compound, *cuntbitten* is cognate with the aggressive medieval term for 'impotent', namely *cunt-beten*, recorded from c. 1440.

6
Expansionism and Xenophobia

He was the great Hieroglyph of Jesuitism, Puritanism, Quaquerism, and of all the Isms of Schism.

'Heraclio Democritus'

These infernall frogs [Jesuits] are crept into the West and East Indyes.

Lewis Owen

þe Kyng said & did crie, þe pape [Pope] was heretike . . . and lyued in bugerie.

Robert Brunne

He [Tippoo Sultan] was to drive the English Caffers out of India.

Sir T. Munro

'He called me a German and other filthy names.'

Defendant in the Middlesex Police Court, 1915

AS PREVIOUS chapters have shown, xenophobia appears to be an ingrained attitude with a long history. This is understandable when one considers that in the warrior-migration stage of a culture, visitors are likely to be hostile in their intentions, bearing swords rather than gifts. Martial and religious rivalry are the principal forces in the early generation of xenophobic attitudes. In time they become superseded by economic competition and the problems of assimilation in a cosmopolitan society. In both cases, the terms for the 'outsider' or 'stranger' develop hostile overtones of opprobrium and abuse.

The relevant semantic field is set out in the two categories of figure 6.1. The basic conceptual division in the field is between general terms, such as *alien* and *intruder*, and the more specific words of insult, such as *frog, hun* and *gook*. Historically, as is to be expected, the general terms are older, with those of generalized religious hostility (*heathen, paynim* and *infidel*) being the oldest of all. These are discussed in the opening pages

	General Terms	*Specific Terms*
A-S	Heathen	
1500	Infidel Paynim	
1550		Bugger, Turk, Greek Coolie
1600	Savage, Alien, Intruder, Interloper, Barbarian, Foreigner	Blackamoor, Ethiop, Jew, Tartar
1650		Bogtrotter
1700		Vandal, Goth, Macaroni, Dago
1750		Hottentot Yankee Cracker Frog
1800	Native	Kaffir, Nigger, Coon, Frenchy, Wi-wi, Sheeny
1850		Greaser, Gringo, Canuck, Sambo, Jap, Yid, Mick, Limey
1900		Kike, Hun, Chink, Wop, Boche, Fritz, Jerry, Kraut, Pom, Wog, Spic, Eyetie, Ofay, Spaghetti, Wetback, Nip, Gook, Anglo
1950		Slant, Slope, Munt, Honkie, Paki

FIGURE 6.1 The semantic field of xenophobia.

of chapter 4. A second cluster of terms develops *c.*1600, contemporaneously with Renaissance exploration and the economic competition consequent upon this mercantile expansionism. *Interloper* originally signifies (*c.*1590) an unauthorized, trespassing trader, before acquiring the more generalized sense (*c.*1632) of a profiteering opportunist. Likewise, *intruder* carries from *c.*1534 a sense of legal usurpation.[O]

Of the other general terms, *primitive, savage, barbarian* and *native* have, during the modern period during which colonialism and progress have become alike suspect, developed neutral senses where this is possible (as in *native*), or fallen into comparative disuse (as in *savage* and *barbarian*). An historical perspective demonstrates the chauvinist relativity of *barbarian*, since it was used successively of those who were 'non-Hellene', then 'non-Roman', then 'non-Christian', then of 'one of a nation outside Italy'. In the nineteenth century an older civilization, the Chinese, applied the sense (via the character 'I') to the English. Other factors have contributed to the diminished usage, of course. The study of anthropology has encouraged a respectful awareness for the complexity of social and linguistic systems which so-called 'primitive', 'savage', 'barbarian' 'natives' have evolved. Heightened awareness and increased unpopularity of racism have, furthermore, had the effect of self-censorship, driving the more emotive or critical words underground or out of use.

Barbarian supplies a link to a different form of linguistic xenophobia, shown in a desire to mock or belittle a foreign language, making it approximate to infantile babbling. *Barbarian* is a Greek form related to Latin *balbus*, 'stammering', a derisive imitation of the 'primitive' languages encountered. *Hottentot* is, according to Dapper, *Beschryvingh der Afrikansche Gewesten* (1670), 'a word meaning "stutterer" or "stammerer", applied to the people on account of their clicking speech'.[O] To this Dampier (in 1697) added the hilariously implausible, but revealing explanation that 'Hottentot . . . is the name by which they call to one another . . . as if every one of them had this for his name.'[O] There developed subsequently (in the eighteenth century) the predictable deterioration to 'a person of inferior intellect or culture', instanced in Nicholas Amherst's comment in *Terrae filius: or the secret history of the university of Oxford* (1726) that he was 'Surprized to find a place, which he has heard so much renown'd for learning, fill'd with grey-headed novices and reverend hotentots.'[O] This sense the *OEDS* records, but pointedly rejects: 'This derogatory sense, which was based on a failure to understand an alien culture, appears now to be very rare.' The word still survives in this sense in the form *hotnot*, in South African English 'an offensive mode of address or reference to a coloured person' (*DSAE*). The longer and more complex history of *kaffir* is discussed more fully in chapter 8.

The more specific terms grow most abundantly, as the word-field shows, from the nineteenth century, synchronously with the development of nationalism. While most terms are imposed by enemies or rivals, the immediate source of the application of *hun* to the Germans was a speech given by Kaiser Wilhelm II to German troops about to set sail for China on 27 July 1900. It was an extraordinary indulgence in atavistic nationalism:

> No quarter will be given, no prisoners will be taken. Let all who fall into your hands be at your mercy. Just as the Huns a thousand years ago, under the leadership of Etzel (Atilla) gained a reputation in virtue [strength] of which they still live in historical tradition, so may the name of Germany become known in such a manner in China that no Chinaman will ever again even dare to look askance at a German. (*The Times*, 30 July, 1900, p. 3)

Many terms are thrown up, predictably, by the great wars of this century. The promptitude with which hostile terms for the Germans appeared during the First World War is impressive: *boche* is first recorded in 1914, followed by *fritz* in 1915, *kraut* in 1918 and *jerry* in 1919.[S] Xenophobic terms have interesting phonetic similarities, being either short and contemptuous (*pom, yid, frog, wop, wog, boche/bosch*) or conveying a suggestive dislike through an ironic diminutive (*yankee, limey, sheeny, frenchy, wi-wi, whitey, honky, gerry* and *limey*). An expressive, child-like malice is everywhere apparent.

Chapter 4 discussed the terms of opprobrium generated by the Reformation, such as *papist, popery, Rome-runner* and so on. There are, however, many other terms of religious separation which have acquired hostile meanings. *Bugger* is very much a key term in this category. Deriving from French *Bougre*, 'a Bulgarian', it carries the sense of 'a heretic' from the fourteenth century and 'a sodomite' from the sixteenth. The first sense derives from the group's belonging to the Greek Church and subscribing to the Albigensian heresy. Dan Michel (*c.*1340) uses the older form in condemning 'false Christians', who in their unorthodox beliefs are like 'þe bougre, and þe heretike, and þe apostate' (1866, p. 19). However, in Robert Brunne's contemporary *Chronicle* (c.1330) we come across this subversive view: 'Þe Kyng said & did crie, þe pape [pope] was heretike . . . and lyued in bugerie.' The sexual sense appears to be a malicious extension in physical terms of the idea of spiritual perversion. The attribution of 'filthy' sexual practices to freethinkers and religious 'deviants' is, seemingly, an ancient and ingrained propagandist stereotype. Such a religious *cum* sexual ascription is that recorded in 1555: '. . . as rancke bouguers with mankinde, and with beastes, as the Saracenes are.' (There is also a mercantile application, directed against foreign usurers, apparent in the statement of Chamberlayne in 1667: 'The sin of Buggery, brought into England by the Lombards.')[O]

Jesuit provides a parallel example. Denounced by Stubbes in his *Anatomy of Abuses* (1583) as 'the diuels agents', the order's reputation for casuistry and prevarication have, in the words of the *OED* definition, 'rendered the name odious not only in English, but in other languages'.

Even before the Gunpowder Plot and Father Garnet's notorious adherence to the doctrine of equivocation while under oath, William Watson had condemned 'The irremedilesse poyson of the Iesuiticall doctrine'. By 1640 the sense of 'dissembling person or prevaricator' was well established. At this time of vehement religious fanaticism, it also acquires the meaning 'sodomite'; Grose subsequently quotes the comically malicious phrase '*To box the jesuit*', i.e. to masturbate, commenting, 'A crime that is said much practised by the reverend fathers of that society'. The practice of buggery is clearly implied in Rochester's ironic vision of Utopia:

> But Cowards shall forget to rant,
> School-Boyes to Frigg, old whores to paint;
> The Jesuits Fraternity
> Shall leave the use of Buggery . . .
> ('A Ramble in Saint James's Parke', ll. 143–6)

The hostility towards the sect is reflected in the growth of such related opprobrious terms as *jesuit* (vb) (1601), *jesuitish* (1600), *jesuitism* (1609), *jesuitic* (1640) and *jesuitize* (1644).[O]

A great deal of xenophobic malice continued to be concentrated in the noun *jew* from *c.*1600 and the verb from *c.*1850.[O] Both derive from the alleged practices of extortion and cheating of the kind implied in this letter of 1847: 'Some mode of screwing and jewing the world out of more interest than one's money is entitled to.'[O] The *OEDS* adds an early and revealing quotation for *jew-boy* from a Police document of 1796: 'Jew Boys . . . go out every morning loaded with counterfeit copper, which they exchange for bad silver, to be afterwards coloured anew, and again to be put into circulation.' In a commentary on *Deuteronomy* published in 1700, Bishop Patrick observed: 'Better we cannot express the most cut-throat dealing than thus, You use me like a Jew'.[O] Coleridge noted in his *Table Talk* of 16 May 1830: 'Jacob is a regular Jew, and practises all sorts of tricks and wiles.'[O] These fall under the *OED* definition of 'a name of opprobrium or reprobation; *spec.* applied to a grasping or extortionate money-lender or usurer, or a trader who drives hard bargains or deals craftily'. (The controversy which this definition aroused is discussed in the final chapter.) The sense that the Jews were 'different', 'other', 'alien' is shown simply in the great number of compounds, such as *Jew-butcher*, *Jew-physician*, *Jew-pedlar*, and so on. These were followed in the late nineteenth century by *jew-baiting* (1883) and *jew hatred* (1898).[O] The religious animus, deriving from the self-imposed blame for the Crucifixion, is much older and a frequent motif in medieval literature, where the usual qualifying adjective is *cursed*:

> Oure blessed Lordes body they totere –
> Hem thoughte that Jewes rent him not ynough.
> (*The Pardoner's Tale*, 474–5)

There is an anomaly concerning the relation of stereotype and actuality in the later Middle Ages. Although there were virtually no Jews in England from 1290 (when they were expelled by Edward III) to 1655 (when they were readmitted by Oliver Cromwell), vicious stereotypes of rapaciousness, child sacrificers and social saboteurs continued in Chaucer's *Prioress's Tale*, Shylock in Shakespeare's *Merchant of Venice* and Barabas in Marlowe's *The Jew of Malta*. Fagin in Dickens' *Oliver Twist* is a continuation of this tradition, though Riah in *Our Mutual Friend* and Daniel Deronda, the hero of George Eliot's novel, are idealized characters. Ferdinand Lopez, the villain of Trollope's *The Prime Minister* (1876) is the archetypal outsider, 'without a father, a foreigner, a black Portuguese nameless Jew [with] a bright eye, and a hook nose, and a glib tongue' (1983, p. 146).

In addition to the motivation to regard foreigners as objects of contempt and opprobrium, the evidence shows them to be cast in two major threatening roles: the criminal and the diseased. Thus, one of the earlier (and most enduring) low-life senses of *Greek* is 'a cheater at cards', recorded from *c.*1528[O] well into the nineteenth century. Thackeray writes in 1855: 'He was an adventurer, a pauper, a blackleg, a regular Greek.' Less heinously, *a merry Greek* signified a roisterer or drunkard in Elizabethan English, while *Greek fire* came to mean bad whisky or rotgut about a century ago.

Pedlar's French was an old (sixteenth-century) term for cant, and introduces the numerous varieties of *French* insult, which are largely concerned with sordid practices. (Farmer and Henley define *French Vice* as 'A euphemism for all sexual malpractices'.) *French leave* (returned with compliments as *filer à l'anglaise*) dates from *c.*1770, and *French letter* (similarly returned as *capote anglaise* 'English raincoat') is recorded from *c.*1856. The French being, for various reasons, the nationality most associated in the English mind with sex, it is not surprising to find *french prints* recorded from *c.*1850 as a euphemism for pornographic pictures, and *French kiss* (from *c.*1923): John Dos Passos uses the compact verbal form ('she taught him how to frenchkiss . . .') as far back as 1930.[S] Closer to the theme of strong language is the ironic exculpation 'Excuse my French,' recorded from 1895.[S]

THE SYPHILITIC DIASPORA

In the attribution of blame for syphilis, which brought out the most diversified xenophobia, the French easily led the field in England. *French pox* is found as far back as Florio (1598), followed by *French gout, goods, crown, pig* and *crust*, culminating in the grisly dysphemism 'to suffer a blow over the snout with a French faggot-stick', i.e. to lose one's nose by the pox. All these are recorded from the seventeenth century and all appear in Grose (1785). Others which may be added to the list are *Frenchified* ('the mort is frenchified' = 'the wench is infected') and *the Frenchman*. It is hardly surprising that the technical description of the condition in the nineteenth century should have been *morbus gallicus*.

The disease, apparently brought to Europe by Columbus' returning crew, was carried into Italy by the army of Charles VIII and subsequently spread through the length and breadth of Europe by returning camp-followers. One of the standard histories continues, bringing into play the extraordinary etymology of the disease's name:

> In the beginning there was no name for the disease. Each suffering nation blamed it on the outlander. To the French it was the Neapolitan disease because they met it in Naples. [Even Florio calls it *mal di Napoli*, perhaps because he was brought up in England.] The Italians called it the French, or Spanish disease. The English, who caught the infection from France, called it the 'French pox'. The title 'French disease' was current for almost a century. It was used synonymously with the specific name acquired in 1530 when an Italian physician, Fracastor, wrote a long poem in Latin hexameters in which the leading character, a shepherd named Syphilus, was stricken with the disease because of an insult to Apollo. The poem was enormously successful and made the word familiar. (Parran, 1937, p. 36)

The chain of infection which is described makes the nationalistic naming of the disease entirely plausible, although a basic desire to attribute blame elsewhere also plays its part. The imputation of promiscuous sexuality to the Continental nations is also evidenced in the various terms for illicit sexual relations and their locations. *Seraglio* was used of a bawdy house from the late seventeenth to early nineteenth centuries; *bordello* had the same meaning in the same period; while *bagnio* signified a Turkish bath from *c.*1615, before rapidly acquiring the association of 'brothel'. To these may be added *fille de joie* (euphemism for 'prostitute' from *c.*1705), *madame* (for 'female keeper of a brothel' from *c.*1871[S]) and *gigolo* (masculine correlative of *gigole*, 'tall thin woman of the streets or public dance halls', from *c.*1922[S]). *Blowen*, which flourished from the late seventeenth to early nineteenth centuries, was defined by Borrow as 'a sister in debauchery . . . the Beluni of the Spanish Gipsies'[O]. *Liaison*, in origin a term from cookery meaning 'a thickening for sauces', acquires its more intimate human sense in the early nineteenth century, being first recorded, appropriately, in a wicked oxymoron in Byron:

> Some chaste *liaison* of the kind – I mean
> An honest friendship with a married lady.
> (*Don Juan*, III. xxv)

Affair, now Anglicized from *affaire*, acquired its sexual innuendo *c.*1809, though this meaning was unrecorded in the main *OED*.

Many of the terms just discussed now have a somewhat dated quality, since English speakers seem no longer to have to take refuge in foreign euphemisms. ('Escort' agencies continue, however, to blandish their wares with continental or 'exotic' names and services, while their foreign equivalents use the enticing labels *girls, ladies*, and *vamps*.) The amusing native formation *toy-boy*, coined *c.*1984, has largely ousted *gigolo*; the recently publicized sexual diseases, such as herpes and AIDS have not acquired euphemistic variants. (However, the 'malicious attribution factor', previously discussed in relation to syphilis, is apparent in the description of AIDS as 'the gay plague'.) Even *massage parlour*, described by *Colliers* magazine as far back as 1913 as 'an all-too-obvious euphemism', does not resort to foreign terminology, only to misleading terms for the 'treatment'. We may leave the sexual aspect of the field by noting a revealing but ironic Shakespearean quotation alluding to the threatening sexuality of 'the foreigner'. The Porter in *Henry VIII*, responding to *noise and tumult within*, comments '. . . have we some strange Indian with the great tool come to court, the women so beseige us?' (V. iv. 34–5). The overall impression, that foreigners are not to be trusted, since they bring treachery, seductive skills and disease, is unmistakably woven into this part of our semantic legacy.

RACIAL AND ETHNIC INSULTS

It is as well to start by commenting on the terminology used to designate this category. *Race, racial* and *racist* are, of course, the more common terms today, although *ethnic* is, in fact, older. *Race* is of Portuguese extraction, but uncertain ultimate origin, recorded in English only from the late sixteenth century. *Racial* is a nineteenth-century term, and did not originally carry the same prejudicial force of *racialist* and *racist*, which are recorded from 1917 and 1932 respectively.[S] As a consequence of imperialism and nazism, which were based on a pernicious ideology of racial superiority, *racist* has become, like *fascist*, a swear-word in its own right. *Ethnic*, which is currently the more favoured general adjective, being virtually a euphemism, was in origin the more chauvinistically hostile, signifying those nations which were not Christian or Jewish, i.e. Gentile, pagan or heathen. Greek *ethnikos*, meaning 'heathen', was even 'formerly often imagined to be the [etymological] source of English HEATHEN'[O]. The more neutral 'ethnological' sense presently enjoyed by the word emerges only in the mid-nineteenth century.

Racial or ethnic insults cover numerous categories, but have at their base some humorous, ironic or malicious distortion of the target group's identity or 'otherness'. The varieties of this process may be illustrated best from terms applied to American blacks, since this verbal categorization is so numerous and diversified. The principal categories include the following areas of distortion: the name (as in *niggra*, *nigrah* or *nigger* for *negro*); physical characteristics (as in *thicklips*)[1]; traditionally attributed names (as in *rastus* or *Uncle Tom*)[2]; occupational stereotypes (as in *cotton-picker*); animal metaphors (as in *coon*)[3]; distinctive food (as in *buckwheat*); stereotypes of low intelligence (as in *hard-head*) and status diminution (as in *boy*). As we shall see, these categories form the basis for virtually all xenophobic stereotypes.

J. L. Dillard emphasizes the point that the key factor in the development of a term of abuse is not the word itself, but who uses it. He noted that in 'yarning' or telling tales, American mountain men adopted the practice of referring to themselves as 'this beaver', 'this injun', even 'this coon' or 'this nigger'. 'In gauging the significance of these terms,' he continues, 'one must remember that even *nigger* was not offensive to Blacks until whites used it in a derogatory way' (1977, p. 96).

Irving Lewis Allen observes in his study, *The Language of Ethnic Conflict*, that 'Over a thousand usually derogatory terms for more than 50 American groups have been accumulated in scholarly records of slang and of dialectal English'. This accumulation, Allen continues,

> is only seemingly contrary to the common sense that verbal abuse reflects only prejudice. Actually, it shows that both prejudice and verbal abuse heap [sic] in reaction to the history of a group's conflictful contacts with other groups. . . . The words also show something of the dynamism of ethnic diversity and document the strains of assimilation. In what seems a paradox, the stereotypes generated by the plural society underscore its great diversity. (1983, p. 7)

Allen's American Lexicon of Ethnic Epithets reflects these 'strains of assimilation' in that by far the largest categories refer to Afro-Americans, Whites and Jews. While these areas of the lexicon continue to grow, Allen notes that 'no new terms for Yankees have been coined for over a century, which suggests a diminishing image of them as a distinctive ethnic group' (p. 73). On the other hand, in a new theatre of war, he observes (under the terms for Vietnamese): 'All nicknames for Vietnamese originated during the Vietnam War were brought forward from the Korean War and World War II' (p. 69).

Applying Allen's generalizations to the English word-field of ethnic abuse, we find that the nations most consistently involved in martial conflict with Britain (the French and the Germans) and that most consistently seen as an out-group involved in economic competition (the Jews) supply the greater portion of the field. However, the history of the British Isles, having originally been that of a diversity of discrete cultures and languages, has generated a different dynamic field. Notions of ideological and national unity formulated as 'the United Kingdom' and 'Great Britain' evolved comparatively late (officially from 1707), so that problems of assimilation, as well as of in-group and out-group conflict, have not been as significant as in the United States, which has been a 'melting pot' almost since its inception. Less abstractly, it is notable that there are comparatively few terms of abuse between the English, the Scots and the Welsh,[4] but far more are targeted against the obvious out-groups, namely the Jews, the Irish and the 'new Britons', such as the West Indians, West Africans, Indians and Pakistanis, particularly those that have distinctive appearance, food, language, religion and cultural traditions.

Folk etymologies in the form of acronyms figure to a surprising degree. Thus *zip* (for Vietnamese) is supposed to stand for 'zero intelligence potential', while *spick* (for Italian) is supposed to be a coded in-joke for 'No spicka da Engleesh'. The better known American cultural and racist acronyms are WASP (White Anglo-Saxon Protestant) and PIGS (Poles, Italians, Greeks, Slavs). Figure 6.2 shows the considerable abilities of rhyming slang in this regard. On *wog*, often interpreted as 'worthy oriental gentleman', the *OEDS* observes that the origin is 'uncertain; often said to be an acronym, but none of the suggested etymologies is satisfactorily supported by evidence.' It is an interesting aspect of the development of the field that the more recent terms have uncertain or unknown etymologies: examples include *mick, dago, wop, wog, honkie, ofay* and *gook*. Never the less, the lack of a true etymology does not prevent these terms having a powerful impact.

Long version	*Short version*	*Disguised Term*
Army tanks		Yanks
Bubble and squeak	Bubble	Greek
Egg and spoon		Coon
Five to two	Five	Jew
Flour mixer		Shikse
Four by two		Jew
Front wheel skid		Yid
Ham shank		Yank
Harvest moon		Coon
Kangaroo		Jew
Lucozade		Spade
Razor blade	Razo	Spade
Sausage roll		Pole
Septic tank	Septic	Yank
Silvery spoon		Coon
Tea pot/Saucepan lid		Yid
Tiddly-wink		Chink

Notes

1 Dirty Old Jew = Two.
2 *Tisket* = *Bastard* = *Japanese*, via the rhyme:

A Tisket, a Tasket
A little yellow basket.

Basket is a euphemism for *bastard*, and the phrase *little yellow bastard* referred to the Japanese.
3 The marked majority (well over half) of the coded references to foreigners and aliens apply to jews and blacks.
4 Acronyms also feature as disguise mechanisms, e.g. *WASP* (White Anglo-Saxon Protestant) and *PIGS* (Poles, Italians, Greeks, Slavs).

FIGURE 6.2 Codes for foreigners and aliens in rhyming slang.

The capacity of specific xenophobic terms to become generalized depends largely on the recognizability of their origins. Thus, *Jap* or *Hun*, being recognizable, are now likely to remain specific terms, whereas *Gook* or *Wog*, having no true or obvious 'etymological anchor', show, predictably, the greatest mobility. The fact that some of the fairly 'specific' terms are capable of generalized xenophobic meaning suggests that the hostility or aggression is not specific, except in times of war. For instance, in reading the following remarks on *frog* in Fanny Burney's *Evelina* (1778), we immediately recognize today's meaning: 'Hark you,

Mrs Frog, . . . you may lie in the mud till some of your monsieurs come to help you out of it.' But a century and a half earlier (in 1626) we find a quite different sense: 'These infernall frogs [Jesuits] are crept into the West and East Indyes.'[O] In 1652 it is applied to the Dutch; in 1785 Grose records *froglander* for Dutchman.

Dago, though generally supposed to be a corruption of *Diego*, is first recorded in a very different application in a New England context of 1723: 'The negro Dago hanged for fiering Mr Powell's house.'[S] In the American provenance it has since been applied to Spaniards, Mexicans and Italians. *Wog*, though very inadequately recorded, is possibly (but not certainly) from *golliwog*, and thus has a specific sense of 'African' or 'oriental' (used insultingly by colonial whites), while at the same time being used contemptuously of foreigners in general in the insular observation, 'The wogs begin at Dover'.

Sambo is derived from *zambo*, a Latin American term for a person of mixed Negro and Indian parentage. Commenting on the gradations of colour and their parallel status, Captain Marryat observed in 1833: 'A quadroon looks down upon a mulatto, while a mulatto looks down upon a sambo, that is, half mulatto and half negro.'[O] It is also recorded from *c.*1860 (with a capital letter) as a nickname for a negro, and has, during the course of this century, become a derogatory term in English for a black person. The paternalistic colonial set-phrase 'little black sambo' has, assuredly, reinforced the meaning. However, in Japan the term is quite neutral, probably because the term arrived there before the end of the nineteenth century from the Philippines, then a Spanish possession. The feminine form, *zamba*, is also applied to the popular ethnic dance, anglicized to *samba*.

Coolie, thought originally to be derived from Tamil *kuli*, meaning 'a hireling', is recorded in this sense since 1638, in a reference in Hakluyt's *Voyages*.[O] As tends to happen with role-words of low status, it acquired an opprobrious sense. In 1826 one W. Elliott noted: 'Coolie means a porter, but is often used reproachfully to other servants of superior rank.'[O]

Gook ('origin unknown, mainly American'[S]) is the perfect example, so to speak, of a word which has been used flexibly as 'a term of contempt for a foreigner, specifically, a coloured inhabitant of (south-) east Asia or elsewhere'[S]. It has in a short time performed all the xenophobic roles, expressing hostility towards the interloper, the business rival and the martial enemy. Thus, in 1935 it was applied to the Filipinos; in 1947 to the Koreans; in 1959 to the Japanese (also found in *gook* car), and most recently, to the Viet Cong: 'This is a gook grave'[S] (from the *Brisbane Sunday Mail Magazine*, 1969).

In conclusion, we may sum up by observing that the field shows a number of interesting developments. Most significantly, the categories change from those of strong moral stereotyping (with religious connotations) in earlier times to comparatively superficial characteristics of diet and appearance in modern times. Thus stereotypes of savagery, cruelty and treachery surround *Vandal, Goth, Hun, Tartar* and *Turk*, that of primitiveness surrounds *Hottenot* and *bog-trotter*, dishonesty is associated with *Greek* and *Jew* and immorality with *French*. However, food and diet generate *macaroni, spaghetti, frog, limey* and *kraut*, while distinctive appearance is emphasized in *slope, slant* and *squarehead*. Many modern terms are without any stereotypic associations. We may also notice that the field shows marked general growth in modern times and (as is unusual in the case of slang and colloquialisms) several terms have survived for over a century. Furthermore, as English has grown from being exclusively the language of the colonial imperialist to a world vernacular, so the Anglocentric or Eurocentric view-point has given way to other perspectives. Notable among these has been the growth of critical words for whites such as *gringo, ofay, honkie* and *cracker*.

NOTES

1 *Thicklips* seems first to have been used in 1604 (as a 'contemptuous appellation for a negro') in *Othello*, I. i. 66.

2 *Uncle Tom* was originally in Harriet Beecher Stowe's novel (1852) a patient, suffering negro slave. The contemptuous sense of a sycophantic or subservient 'sell-out' seems to be first recorded *c.*1943.[S]

3 Captain Frederick Marryat seems to have been the first person to record the use of *coon* in application to a person. He observes in his *Diary in America* (1839): 'In the western states, where the racoon is plentiful, they use the abbreviation coon even in speaking of people.'[O]

4 *Welsh*, meaning 'to cheat', derives from the slang of the turf and has no derogatory connection with the Welsh.

7
The Reign of Decorum: Augustan and Victorian Attitudes

What then can we think of those who make use of so tremendous a Name [that of God] in the ordinary expressions of their Anger, Mirth, and most Impertinent Passions?

Addison

Damns have had their day.

Sheridan

Johnson	I am afraid that I may be one of those who shall be damned (looking dismally).
Dr Adams	What do you mean by damned?
Johnson	(passionately and loudly) Sent to Hell, Sir, and punished everlastingly.

Boswell

'Why, because you have the capital or the command of it, why screw us?'

Dr F. J. Furnivall

'"Hosscar" Wilde is a fatuous fool, a tenth-rate cad, an unclean beast.'

Henry James on Oscar Wilde

WHEN we read the following lines from 'A Ramble in Saint James's Parke':

Much wine had past with grave discourse
Of who Fucks who and who does worse

But tho Saint James has the Honor on't
Tis Consecrate to Prick and Cunt.

Whence Rowes of Mandrakes tall did rise
Whose lewd Topps Fuckt the very Skies
(ll. 1–20)

we are immediately aware that neither the sentiments nor the language could be publicly uttered during the lifetime of Shakespeare nor between 1700 and 1900. Both the cynical assumptions of human behaviour and the coarseness of the expression – not to mention the surreal sexual imagery – limit the location of the utterance to a period when notions of gentility and decorum could be fearlessly affronted. The lines are by 'the most brilliant wit and the most accomplished rake' of Charles II's court, Rochester. His poems were published, in pirated and inadequate texts, 'meerly for lucre's sake' when he died in 1680 (Walker, 1984, p. xii). But by 1703 the comment could be made that

> One man reads *Milton*, forty *Rochester*.[1]

Rochester epitomizes the licentiousness of the Restoration, which was in its way as extreme as the restriction of the Puritanism to which it was a reaction. Although there is not a great deal of sexual swearing *per se* in his work, Rochester clearly enjoys juxtaposing sacred and profane language in a deliberately shocking fashion:

> I' th'Isle of Britain long since famous growne
> For breeding the best cunts in Christendome
> ('A Satire on Charles II', ll. 1–2)

Rochester's is a world seen from crotch level, a world stripped of pretence to leave the sole dominating force that of frantic sexual energy. Though he accepts his own involvement, he describes the participants in the terms of contemptuous animal insult:

> So a proud Bitch does lead about
> Of humble Currs the Amorous Rout
> Who most obsequiously do hunt
> The savory scent of salt swoln Cunt.
> ('A Ramble in Saint James's Parke', ll. 83–6)

The actors in this sexual roundelay are caustically described, as 'Some stiff prickt Clown or well hung Parson', 'Three Confounded Asses' and a 'damn'd abandon'd Jade'. However, when He wishes to exclaim with emphasis, Rochester resorts to the tame and conventional:

> Gods! That a thing admired by mee
> Shou'd fall to so much Infamy.
> (*Ibid.*, 89–90)

Although Rochester is deservedly given prominence in the Restoration reaction to Puritan censorship, he was not alone in this respect. It is one of the major ironies of English cultural history that during the period when Puritanism was so signally in the ascendant, there should have appeared (in 1653) the first two volumes of the English translation of that bizarre encyclopaedia of humorous obscenity, François Rabelais' *Gargantua and Pantagruel.* The original had appeared a century previously, so that Urquhart (initially) and Motteux (subsequently) felt obliged to translate the coarse language of the original into the idiom of their own times. Even this elasticity in the selection of terms did not greatly alleviate the burdensome search for suitable synonyms, as these encyclopaedic extracts show:

> The bun-sellers or cake-makers . . . did injure them most outrageously, calling them prattling gabblers, lickorous gluttons, freckled bittors, mangy rascals, shite-a-bed scoundrels, drunken roysters, sly knaves, drowsy loiterers, slapsauce fellows, slabberdegullion druggels, lubberly louts, cozening foxes, ruffian rogues, paltry customers, sycophant varlets, draw-latch hoydens, flouting milksops, jeering companions, staring clowns, forlorn snakes, ninny lobcocks, scurvy sneaksbies, fondling fops, base loons, saucy coxcombs, idle lusks, scoffing braggarts, noddy meacocks, blockish grutnols, doddipol-joltheads, jobbernol goosecaps, foolish loggerheads, flutch calf-lollies, grouthead gnat-snappers, lob dotterels, gaping changelings, codshead loobies, woodcock slangams, ninny-hammer flycatchers, noddypeak simpletons, turdy gut, shitten shepherds, and other suchlike defamtory epithets. (Book I, chapter xxv)

An even greater tour de force of unfamiliar terms pours forth when Gargantua's governesses take 'you know what' and dandle it:

> One of them would call it her little dille, her staff of love, her quillety, her faucetin, her dandilolly. Another, her peen, her jolly kyle, her bableret, her membretoon, her quickset imp: another again, her branch of coral, her female adamant, her placket-racket, her Cyprian sceptre, her jewel for ladies. And some of the other women would give it these names, – my bunguetee, my stopple too, my bush-rusher, my gallant wimble, my pretty borer, my coney-burrow-ferret,[2] my littel piercer, my augretine, my dangling hangers, down right to it, stiff and stout, in and to, my pusher, dresser, pouting stick, my honey pipe, my pretty pillicock[3], linky pinky, futilletie, my lusty andouille, and crimson chitterling, my little couille bredouille, my pretty rogue and so forth. (Book I, Chapter xi)

In reading that splendid contemporary compendium of gossip and personalia, John Aubrey's *Brief Lives* (1669–96), we are also struck by the freedom of language as he gives out nothing but 'the naked and plaine trueth, which is here exposed so bare that the very pudenda are not covered, and affords many passages that would raise a Blush in a young Virgin's cheeke' (1972, p. 161). Accordingly, Aubrey relays the view that 'Mr Selden had got more by his Prick than his practise. He was no eminent practiser at the Barre' (1972, p. 434). Sir Walter Raleigh, we are told, was 'damnable proud' and when severely embarrassed by his son at a great table, gave him 'a damned blow over the face' (1972, pp. 417, 419). Yet he sees Sir Philip Sidney as 'a reviver of Poetry in those darke times, which was then at a very low ebbe: there is not 3 lines but there is *by God* or *by God's wounds*' (1972, p. 440). Aubrey's winning way of writing about sexual congress in a humane and direct fashion is the essence of this marvellous anecdote about 'this Hero' (Raleigh):

> He loved a wench well; and one time getting up one of the Mayds of Honour up against a tree in a Wood ('twas his first Lady) who seemed at first boarding to be something fearfull of her Honour, and modest, she cryed, sweet Sir Walter, what doe you me ask; Will you undoe me? Nay, sweet Sir Walter! Sweet Sir Walter! Sir Walter! At last, as the danger and the pleasure at the same time grew higher, she cried in the extasey, Swisser Swatter Swisser Swatter. (1972, p. 418)

The next generation of poets, the Augustans, like the lexicographers of their age, rigorously maintained a strict separation of registers, upholding the principle of decorum even in the most virulent satires. For instance, in his savage denunciation of the Lord Hervey, castigated as Sporus, Pope studiously avoids common terms of abuse:

> Let Sporus tremble – A [rbuthnot]: What? that thing of silk,
> Sporus, that mere white curd of ass's milk?
> Satire or sense, alas! can Sporus feel,
> Who breaks a butterfly upon a wheel?
> P [ope]: Yet let me flap this bug with gilded wings,
> This painted child of dirt, that stinks and stings;
> (*Epistle to Dr Arbuthnot*, 1. 305–10)

A direct gloss on swearing is supplied by the splendidly idiotic Sir Plume (cast in *The Rape of the Lock* as the role of defender of Belinda's honour). Pope creates this caricature of a knight to represent the decline of aristocratic chivalry from a vital force for honour and justice to an impotent blusterer mouthing empty oaths:

> (Sir Plume of amber snuff-box justly vain,
> And the nice conduct of a clouded cane)
> With earnest eyes, and round unthinking face,
> He first the snuff-box open'd, then the case,
> And thus broke out – 'My Lord, why, what the devil?
> 'Z—ds! damn the lock! 'fore Gad, you must be civil!

'Plague on't 'tis past a jest – nay, prithee, pox!
'Give her the hair' – he spoke, and rapped his box.
(Canto IV, ll. 123–30)

In his 'Epistle to Burlington on the Use of Riches', he satirizes the decline of the Church into time-serving politesse. In Timon's chapel

To Rest, the Cushion and soft Dean invite,
Who never mentions Hell to ears polite.
(149–50)

In his *Purity of Diction in English Verse*, Donald Davie made a valuable distinction between two poetic practices concerning diction. There are the linguistically receptive poets (Davie cites Hopkins and Shakespeare) in whose work 'one has no sense of English words thrusting to be let into the poem and being held out of it by the poet'. Alternatively, there are the selective and literally exclusive poets, in whose work 'a selection has been made and is continually being made, [in] that words are thrusting at the poem and being fended off from it' (1952, p. 5). The Augustan literary ethos preferred brute fact to be presented, not in a genuinely catholic selection of diction, but as an artificial 'poetic diction' or, in prose, in polysyllabic, opaque abstraction. Hence Pope's *finny prey* for 'fish', his *feathered race* for 'birds' and Johnson's pedantic, almost facetious formations like *exdigitate* for 'to pull one's finger out', his omission of a basic word like *shit* (as well as most of Sir Plume's ejaculations), and his definition of a network as 'anything reticulated or decussated, at equal distances, with interstices between the intersections'.

Swift was pre-eminently the violator of Augustan decorum, spectacularly and rudely resuscitating the silenced four-letter terms, most famously in the climax to 'The Lady's Dressing Room' (1730):

O, Celia, Celia, Celia shits![4]

In his so-called *Polite Conversation* (1738) he uses the astounding bathos: 'Why, Miss, You shine this Morning like a sh-- Barn-Door,' according to Partridge 'a proverbial saying of the 17th-mid-19th century' (1963, p. 85). In this work, he generally omitted oaths, arguing in the introduction that 'a just Collection of Oaths, repeated as often as the Fashion requires, must have enlarged this Volume, at least to double the Bulk' (1963, p. 30). Among the 1074 'Flowers of Wit, Fancy, Wisdom, Humour, and Politeness, scattered in this volume' are the following: 'She rises with her ---- [arse] upwards' (p. 167); 'keep your filthy hands to yourself' (p. 158); '. . . you hit yourself a devilish Box of the Ear' (p. 64); 'Od so, so I have cut my Thumb with this cursed Knife' (p. 66), and 'Out upon you for a filthy Creater' (p. 83). Even in a more private and less satirical vein he could write to Stella on 28 May 1711, that it was 'bloody hot walking to-day', using *bloody* as the coarse intensive of the times. And, in a notable rejoinder on first meeting Arbuthnot (who asked if he had sand to blot a letter) he replied quizzically, 'No, but I have the gravel, and if you will give me your letter I'll piss upon it.' Johnson's magisterial (or rather, magistrate-like) response was to judge that Swift had an 'unnatural love of dirt'.[5]

Johnson's own attitudes were more complex, perhaps because he was more of a public figure. When Garrick asked him what was the greatest pleasure in life, Johnson 'answered fucking and second was drinking. And therefore he wondered why there not more drunkards, for all could drink though all could not fuck.'[6] In spite of this splendid *mot*, perhaps because a strong puritan streak ran through him, Johnson was not a noted exponent of either art. Furthermore, his *Dictionary* was a model of decorum.

The two sides of the age are well juxtaposed in Boswell's 'official' biography of Dr Johnson and his intimate, and altogether less creditable, *Journal*, which came to light in a cache of papers in a loft in an outbuilding of Malahide Castle near Dublin in 1939. Yet even in this private record Boswell never descends to the demotic, and only occasionally to the risqué. Just prior to sexual congress with 'Louisa' (Mrs Lewis, an actress) he jokes: '"How curious would it be if I should be so frightened that we should rise as we lay down."' The love-making itself is Olympian, largely athletic in its metaphors (and largely self-centred): 'Proud of my god-like vigour, I soon resumed the noble game. I was in full glow of health. Sobriety had preserved me from effeminacy and weakness, and my bounding blood beat quick and high alarms. A more voluptuous night I never enjoyed. Five times I was fairly lost in supreme rapture' (1950, pp. 138–9).

Even when Boswell discovers, to his fury and chagrin, that he has encountered 'Signor Gonorrhea', his outburst is almost comically tame: 'Am I, who have had safe and elegant intrigues with fine women, become the dupe of a strumpet? . . . O dear, O dear! what a cursed thing this is! What a miserable creature am I!' (1950, p. 156). Subsequently, his mood changes: 'Enraged at the perfidy of Louisa, I resolved to go and upbraid her most severely.' In the ensuing frigid interview, recorded like a play, he eventually breaks out:

BOSWELL 'But by G-D, Madam, I have been with none but you, and here I am very bad'.

However, his own thoughts are more savage:

BOSWELL (to himself): What the devil does the confounded jilt mean ...? (1950, p. 160)

John Cleland's notorious excursions into pornography were similarly couched, not in the language of the street, but in sensual metaphors of a high poetic quality and mechanical figures of speech rendered in equally elevated register, sometimes oddly juxtaposed: 'The platform of his snow-white bosom, that was laid out in a manly proportion, presented, on the vermilion summit of each pap, the idea of a rose about to blow' (1986, p. 57). He writes of *exudations* from *impassionable parts*, of *volcanic eruptions*, of *ungovernable passions* generated by the conjunction of the *engine, machine, battering ram* or *stiff gristle of 'amour'* with its *conduit pipe* and *tender globular reservoirs* and the *orifice, pleasure-thirsty channel* or *Venus mound* (a direct translation of the classical *mons Veneris*).[7] Masturbation is termed variously *the solitary vice, inferior gratification, pollution* or *digitation*. As figure 7.1 shows, this was the period when latinization became *de rigueur* in referring to 'rude' subjects and objects. He even uses the word *pego* (thought to be a borrowing from the Greek word for 'a fountain') for 'penis'. But he also uses the basic verb denoting orgasm in this times, namely *go*.[8] Very occasionally does Cleland descend to incongruously direct or familiar words such as *rod* and *clit*. The sexuality of the underworld is as steadfastly excluded as its argot: 'Avoiding the company of jades and w---, I was thus constant in my fidelity,' writes his Oxford Scholar in his *Memoirs* (1969, p. 99). Peter Quennell observes in his Introduction to a modern edition of *Fanny Hill* that the book '... treats of pleasure as the aim and end of existence, and of sexual satisfaction as the epitome of pleasure, but does so in a style that, despite its inflammatory subject, never stoops to a gross or unbecoming word. Fanny Hill would have shuddered at *Lady Chatterley*' (Beer, in Enright, 1986, p. 110). Yet in its time the book was considered extremely licentious, and Cleland, who received only twenty guineas for it, was summoned before the Privy Council. A bookseller, Drybutter, who is said to have altered the language for the worse, was made to stand in the pillory.

OATHS AS OBJECTS OF COMMENTARY

Throughout the period, there are commentaries to be found on the varieties of swearing. They vary from provocative denunciations to urbane analyses. The most controversial of the first kind was Jeremy

Anglo-Saxon	*Middle English*	*Renaissance*	*Augustan*	*Victorian*	*Modern*
shit(n) turd	**ordure**	**excrement**	crap*	**defecation**	
	piss(v)	**urinate**	**micturate**[1]		pee
sleep with	swive	fuck*	**copulate** screw	make love	bonk
	pollution	frig[2]	onanism **digitation** **self-abuse masturbation**		wank
arse	bum* buttocks	**fundamental anus**	bottom **posterior**(s)		
	cunt thing[3]	**coney pudendum**	twat* **vagina**	quim*	
weapon[4]	cock yard tool	prick **penis**	**(privy)member**		

Notes

Bold type indicates Romance origin.
* Origin uncertain.
1 'The sense is incorrect as well as the form' (*OED*).
2 *Frig* overlapped with *fuck* in the seventeenth and eighteenth centuries.
3 *Thing* has served for both male and female genitalia since Middle English.
4 OE *wæpened* ('weaponed' or 'armed') has the basic sense of 'male' in many compounds including gender in children and plants.

FIGURE 7.1 The semantic field of 'rude' words.

Collier's tirade, *A Short View of the Profaneness and Immorality of the English Stage*, published in 1698. As figure 7.2 partly shows, Collier's articulate puritanism surveyed, with little sense of irony or humour, the decadence of current productions in which (in contrast to the severe morality of the classical theatre) there was wholesale profanity, the clergy was abused, libertines were rewarded and immorality flourished. It immediately attracted ripostes from Dryden, Congreve, Vanbrugh and others, to which Collier peremptorily responded, so that within three months the broadside was in its third edition. Most commentators were less fulminatory. Steele, in one of several essays discoursing upon idiomatic preferences, makes the distinction betwen the *Low* phlegmatic type (who prefers tame minced forms such as *fackins* and *Odsbodikins*) and the *High* choleric coxcomb, who never omits to be 'magnificently passionate' at trivial nuisances:

> We were stopped by a train of coaches at Temple-bar. 'What the devil!' says my companion,' cannot you drive on, coachman? D---n you all for a set of sons of whores; you will stop here to be paid by the hour! There

A

SHORT VIEW

OF THE

Profaneness and Immorality

OF THE

ENGLISH STAGE, *&c.*

With the Several

DEFENCES of the Same.

In ANSWER to

Mr. CONGREVE, Dr. DRAKE, *&c.*

BY

JEREMY COLLIER, *A. M.*

LONDON,

Printed for SAMUEL BIRT at the *Bible* and *Ball* in *Ave-Mary-Lane*, and THOMAS TRYE near *Grays-Inn-Gate* in *Holborn*.

MDCCXXXVIII.

FIGURE 7.2 Fulmination from the Pulpit: Jeremy Collier's controversial *Short View of the Profaneness and Immorality of the English Stage* (3rd edition, expanded, 1738).

Profaneneſs of the Stage. 39

ſweep the *Box:* And the *Stage* muſt either reform, or not thrive upon Profaneneſs.

3dly. Swearing in the *Playhouſe* is an ungentlemanly, as well as an unchriſtian Practice. The *Ladies* make a conſiderable part of the *Audience.* Now Swearing before Women is reckon'd a Breach of good Behaviour; and therefore a civil Atheiſt will forbear it. The Cuſtom ſeems to go upon this Preſumption; that the Impreſſions of Religion are ſtrongeſt in Women, and more generally ſpread. And that it muſt be very diſagreeable to them, to hear the Majeſty of God treated with ſo little Reſpect. Beſides, Oaths are a boiſterous and tempeſtuous ſort of Converſation; generally the Effects of Paſſion, and ſpoken with Noiſe, and Heat. Swearing looks like the beginning of a Quarrel, to which Women have an Averſion; as being neither arm'd by Nature, nor diſciplin'd by Cuſtom for ſuch rough Diſputes. A Woman will ſtart at a Soldier's Oath, almoſt as much as at the Report of his Piſtol: And therefore a well Bred Man will no more Swear than Fight in the Company of Ladies.

II. A *Second* Branch of the Profaneneſs of the *Stage* is their Abuſe of Religion, and *Holy Scripture.* And here ſometimes they don't ſtop ſhort of Blaſphemy. To cite all that might be collected of this kind would be tedious. I ſhall give the *Reader* enough to juſtify the Charge, and I hope to abhor the Practice.

To begin with the *Mock-Aſtrologer.* In the Firſt *Act*, the *Scene* is a *Chapel.* And that the Uſe of ſuch Conſecrated Places may be the better underſtood, the Time is taken up in Courtſhip, Raillery, and Ridiculing Devotion. *Jacinta* takes her Turn among the reſt. She interrupts *Theodoſia*, and cries out: *Why Siſter, Siſter----will you pray? What Injury have I ever done you that you ſhould pray in my Company? Wildblood* ſwears by *Mahomet*, rallies ſmuttily upon the other World, and gives the Prefe-

D 4 rence

> is not such a set of dogs as the coachmen, unhanged! But these rascally cit --- Ounds. . . .' (*The Tatler*, no. 137, 23 February, 1710)

This lengthy satirical tirade occasions the judgement that 'In a word, a few rumbling words and consonants clapped together without any sense, will make an accomplished swearer'. Addison showed more of the moral earnestness of the Augustans by recounting (in what sounds like a fictitious anecdote) the enterprising example of a host who had an amanuensis take down verbatim the conversation of a group of friends who 'were addicted to the foolish habitual Custom of Swearing':

> After the second Bottle, when Men open their Minds without Reserve, my honest Friend began to take Notice of the many sonorous but unnecessary Words that had passed in his House since their sitting down at Table, and how much good Conversation they had lost by giving way to such superfluous Phrases. What a Tax, says he, would they have raised for the Poor, had we put the Laws in Execution upon one another? (*The Spectator*, no. 371, 6 May 1712)

This laudable scheme for the charitable exploitation of profanity was taken up by Swift and turned into one of his brilliantly satirical 'projects'. In 1720, the year of the South Sea Bubble, he published the prospectus for *The Swearer's Bank*, the title page of which appears as figure 7.3. With his characteristically cool irony, Swift indefatigably draws up a perfectly viable financial scheme. The bank's income will be derived from the one shilling fine exactable by Act of Parliament for profane swearing. After the defrayment of expenses, the profits will be devoted to the erection and maintenance of charity schools. The principal sources of income will be the gentlemen, the farmers, and pre-eminently, the army, which might possibly bankrupt itself. This draws the ironic speculation that 'it would be a matter of great joy to Papists, and disaffected persons, to see our militia swear themselves out of their guns and swords . . .' (1945, p. 45).

Although the drama of the time is comparatively restrained in its language, Sheridan has some amusing sallies on the subject of swearing in *The Rivals* (1775). When Bob Acres comes out with the strange minced oath, 'odds triggers and flints!', Absolute observes that he has got 'an odd kind of new method of swearing'. Bob explains, with ironic gravity in the style of Aristotle and Horace:

> *Acres* Ha! ha! you've taken notice of it – 'tis genteel, isn't it? – I didn't invent it myself though; but a commander in our militia,

THE

Swearer's-BANK:

OR,

Parliamentary Security

FOR

Eſtabliſhing a new BANK

IN

IRELAND.

WHEREIN

The Medicinal Uſe of OATHS is conſidered.

(WITH

The *Beſt in Chriſtendom.* A TALE.)

Written by Dean SWIFT.

Si Populus vult decipi decipiatur.

To which is prefixed,

An ESSAY upon *Engliſh* BUBBLES.

By THOMAS HOPE, *Eſq*;

DUBLIN:

Printed by THOMAS HUME, next Door to the *Walſh's-Head* in *Smock-Alley.* 1720. Reprinted at *London* by J. ROBERTS in *Warwick-Lane.*

FIGURE 7.3 Jonathan Swift's ironic project, *The Swearer's Bank* (1720).

a great scholar I assure you, says that there is no meaning in the common oaths and that nothing but their antiquity makes them respectable – because, he says, the ancients would never stick to an oath or two, but would say, 'by Jove!' or 'by Bacchus!' or 'by Mars!' or 'by Venus!' or 'by Pallas!' according to the sentiment' so that to swear with propriety, says my little major, the oath should be an echo to the sense; and this we call the *oath referential* or *sentimental swearing* – ha! ha! 'tis genteel, isn't it?

Absolute Very genteel and new indeed! – and I daresay will supplant all other figure of imprecation.

Acres Ay, ay, the best terms will grow absolute – Damns have had their day.

(II. i)

The prophecy is premature. Ironically pursuing the maxim that 'the oath should be an echo to the sense', Sterne contrives a brilliantly ironic divertissement when Dr Slop cuts his thumb and overreacts in *Tristram Shandy* (1760–7):

Small curses, Dr Slop, upon great occasions, quoth my father (condoling with him first upon the accident) are but so much waste of our strength and soul's health to no manner of purpose. . . . For this reason, continued my father, with the utmost Cervantic gravity, I have the greatest veneration in the world for that gentleman, who, in distrust of his own discretion on this point, sat down and composed (that is at his leisure) fit forms of swearing suitable to all cases, from the lowest to the highest provocation which could possibly happen to him – which forms . . . he kept ever by him on the chimney-piece, within his reach, ready for use. (*Tristram Shandy*, Book III, chapter x)

This counsel does not prevent Dr Slop from insisting 'The devil take the fellow,' namely Obadiah, who tied the intricate knots of the doctor's instrument bag, and in his view was the cause of all the trouble. He solemnly reads out in full 'a form of excommunication of the Church of Rome', over two pages long. Sterne's capacity to reduce everything to absurdity is also shown in the oath which begins Book IV, chapter xxvii:

Zounds! ——————————————————————

————————————————————————————

————Z----ds! cried Phutatorious, partly to himself – and as yet high enough to be heard –

In his *History of Modern Colloquial English*, Professor H. C. Wyld explored with greater diligence and seriousness than most of his academic contemporaries the vagaries of 'sub-standard' speech and writing. Under the heading of 'the Decay of the Older Profanity', he observed that 'From the beginning of the nineteenth century it would seem that nearly all the old oaths died out in good society, as having come to be considered, from unfamiliarity, either too profane or else too devoid of content to serve any purpose' (1936, p. 391). Clearly, this is true of most of the old religious oaths, such as *zounds! gadzooks! odsbodikins!* and the like, of which '*struth!*, subsequently corrupted to *strewth*!, is a sole survivor. However, stalwarts like *bloody, damn* and *hell* continued, though not, as Wyld has it 'in good society'. Hugh Rawson, in discussing the modern onset of euphemism, dates the process somewhat earlier than Wyld:

> The beginning of the period of pre-Victorian prudery is hard to date – as are most developments in language. . . . one can only say that fastidiousness in language became increasingly common from about 1750, and that this trend accelerated around the turn of the century . . . (1981, p. 6)

VICTORIAN ATTITUDES

The schizophrenic quality of Victorian culture is equally apparent in the separation of linguistic registers. The divisions of 'The Two Nations', as Disraeli called them, have clear linguistic correlatives. More than at any other stage of English culture, the elite neither recognized nor accommodated the underworld. For instance, the humane and diligent researches into the lower reaches of the underworld by Henry Mayhew and William Acton were presented in a form cleansed of impolite language: in the demotic domain, Mayhew 'made no specific mention of rhyming slang, with which he must have been familiar' (Franklyn, 1975, p. 5). His explorations into the twilight world of prostitution employ such terms as *convives, prima donnas, ladies of intrigue, chères amies* and even *female operatives*. Several of his interviews are edited with blanks, notably that of the 'soldiers' woman' who said brusquely, 'Get along with your questions. If you give me any of your cheek, I'll—— soon serve you the same' (1983, p. 75). However, Mayhew properly exposes a bookseller's jargon: 'He puts at the end of his catalogue two pages that he calls *Facetiæ* – indecent books indeed.'

Mayhew and Acton were typical. In many Victorian authors the opaque latinisms and ingenious metaphors virtually obscured the subject:

> The Tree of Life, then, is a succulent plant, consisting of one only straight stem, on the top of which is a *pistillim* or *apex*, sometimes of a glandiform appearance, and not unlike a May-cherry, though, at other seasons more resembling the Avellana or filbeard tree. Its fruits, contrary to most others, grow near the root; they are usually two in number; in size somewhat exceeding that of an ordinary nutmeg, and are both contained in one Siliqua, or purse, which, together with the whole root of the plant, is commonly beset with innumerable fibrilla, or capillary, tendrils. (from *The Exquisite*, 1842)

Not every reader would perceive this to be a description of the penis.

Dickens, whose life epitomized the Victorian schism, being first bourgeois *paterfamilias* and then sexual adventurer, bounder and cad, showed a similarly ambivalent attitude towards the lower registers of the language. The creative artist familiarized his readers with such rhyming slang forms as *Barnaby Rudge* ('judge'), *Artful Dodger* for 'lodger' and much of the argot of lower classes and criminal slang, such as *beak* (magistrate), *brat* (child), *crack* (break open, burgle), *do* (swindle), *fence* (receiver of stolen goods), *gonoph* (thief), *lifer* (one sentenced to transportation for life), *nab* (arrest), *peach* (to turn informer), *prig* (a thief), *put-up job* (burglary arranged beforehand by conspiracy with the servants), *quod* (prison), *shop* (send to prison), *split upon* (to inform against), *stone jug* (prison) and *trap* (a policeman). But in the persona of *Vox Populi*, Dickens denounced 'the sewerage and verbiage of slang' in *Household Words*, no. 183, 24 September 1853.[9]

Swearing does not figure largely, with *jiggered* (damned) being Dickens' favourite and *drat* (curse) being the speciality of Mrs Gamp. Indeed, the following exchange from *Nicholas Nickleby* is fairly risqué for 1838:

> 'What's the dem'd total?' was the first question [Mr Mantalini] asked.
> 'Fifteen hundred and twenty-seven pound, four and ninepence ha'penny,' replied Mr Scaley, without moving a limb.
> 'The halfpenny be dem'd,' said Mr Mantalini, impatiently. (chapter 21)

But, by and large, euphemisms predominate. In *Pickwick Papers* Sam Weller resorts to this comic circumlocution to avoid the word *damned*: 'he says if he can't see you afore tomorrow night's over, he vishes he may be somethin'-unpleasanted if he don't drownd hisself' (Chapter 39). Elsewhere we find *National participled* and '. . . [he] demanded in a surly tone what the – something beginning with a capital H – he wanted.' In *Sketches by Boz*, *inexpressibles*, *indescribables* and *inexplicables* do comic service in upholding the Victorian taboo against mentioning the word *trousers*. The same mechanism is at work in this passage from *Oliver Twist* as Giles the butler recounts a nocturnal disturbance:

> 'I tossed off the [bed] clothes,' said Giles . . . looking very hard at the cook and the housemaid, 'got softly out of bed; drew on a pair of —'
>
> 'Ladies present, Mr Giles,' murmured the tinker.
>
> '— of *shoes* sir,' said Giles, turning on him and laying great emphasis on the word. (chapter 28)

Trollope, on the other hand, overtly shares with the reader the amusing spectacle of self-righteous anger struggling with decorum, and being ultimately stifled by it. Nowhere is this conflict more comically shown than in Archdeacon Grantly of *The Warden* (1855):

> 'Why not!' almost screamed the archdeacon, giving so rough a pull at his nightcap as almost to bring it over his nose; 'why not!' – that pestilent, interfering upstart, John Bold – the most vulgar young person I ever met! Do you know that he is meddling with your father's affairs in a most uncalled for – most ——' And being at a loss for an epithet sufficiently injurious, he finished his expressions of horror by muttering, 'Good Heavens!' in a manner that had been found very efficacious in clerical meetings of the diocese. (chapter 2)

But in *The Prime Minister* (1876), the villain Ferdinand Lopez (lacking the restraint of Dr Grantly of Barchester) utters the word *damned* in front of his young wife Emily, with shattering effects, which Trollope discourses on for over a page: 'It was to her a terrible outrage. . . . The word had been uttered with all its foulest violence, with virulence and vulgarity. It seemed to the victim to be the sign of a terrible crisis in her early married life. . . . She was frightened as well as horrified and astounded' (chapter xliv).

In contrast to the traditional view of decorous Victorian order, George Gissing gives us an unflatteringly sharp picture of 'the vulgarity of the people' on a typical Bank Holiday: 'Their notion of a holiday [he writes in a letter of 1882] is to rush in crowds to some sweltering place, such as the Crystal Palace, and there sit and drink and quarrel themselves into stupidity. . . . Places like Hampstead Heath and the various parks and commons are packed with screeching drunkards, one general mass of dust and heat and rage and exhaustion.' An article published in *Household Words* in 1857 describes the region of Piccadilly: 'At night it is absolutely hideous, with its sparring snobs, and flashing satins, and sporting gents, and painted cheeks, and brandy-sparkling eyes, and bad tobacco, and hoarse horse-laughs, and loud indecency. . . .' (Mayhew, 1983, p. 21). Acton is equally critical about 'unvirtuous women': 'Stupid from beer, or fractious from gin, they swear and chatter brainless stuff all day. . . .' (Mayhew, 1983, p. 24).

The other side of Victorian attitudes towards swearing and coarse speech is nicely illustrated in Browning's hilariously catachrestic howler concerning the word *twat*. Apparently coming across this unfamiliar term in a caustic context in the *Vanity of Vanities* (1660):

> They talk't of his having a Cardinalls Hat,
> They'd send him as soon an Old Nuns Twat

Browning erroneously used it in *Pippa Passes* (1848) 'under the impression that it denoted some part of a nun's attire'[9]:

> Then owls and bats
> Cowls and twats
> Monks and nuns, in cloister's moods,
> Adjourn to the oak-stump pantry.
> (IV. ii. 96)

Research into the works of another pillar of Victorian society, Henry James, has shown how he uses terms like *intercourse, ejaculation* and other words which were starting to move from sexual overtone to denotation. Some would say that this is an unconscious 'Freudian slip' by James, the stern celibate.[10] Yet other writers had a Johnsonian directness, at least in private. Pearsall recounts the anecdote of a composer visiting Tennyson, who read some of his verses to him. 'That's an awfully jolly stanza,' enthused the composer during a pause. 'Don't say "awfully",' admonished Tennyson. 'What shall I say, then?' asked the composer. 'Say "bloody",' replied Tennyson (1969, p. 409).

As has been shown by Steven Marcus in *The Other Victorians* and Ronald Pearsall in *The Worm in the Bud: The World of Victorian Sexuality*, behind the staid Victorian façade, some riotous sexuality persisted. The documentation comes from such *sub rosa* biographies as the revealingly titled *My Secret Life* (*c.*1888–94), which was anonymous, and *My life and Loves*, by Frank Harris, written around the turn of the century, but not published until 1923–7. In opening up the taboo subject of his sexual initiation at school, Harris' vocabulary shows the division of registers, apparent in the incongruous mixture of slang and technical terms such as *'nigger', seed, semen, anus, prick, cock, unruly member, frig, self-abuse, orgasm, randy, sex, vagina, cunt, pussy* and *clitoris* (also termed the *tickler*). Polite observances still apply to swearing: Harris will write of someone having 'a d—— bad temper' (1966, p. 541). He seems to be one of the first writers to use the term *sex-life*

(1966, p. 53). The second volume, published in France, provoked a prosecution on the grounds of its being an 'outrage aux bonnes moeurs', 'an outrage against good morals'. One of the offending passages describes no more than a society dinner party being disrupted by one of the participants repeatedly inflicting on the company 'a loud unmistakable noise and then an overpowering odor' (1966, p. 395).

Within the genre of Victorian pornography, the division of registers is generally apparent, quintessentially revealed in this description: 'I could see the lips of her plump pouting cunny, deliciously feathered, with soft light down, her lovely legs, drawers, stockings, pretty boots, making a *tout ensemble*, which as I write and describe them cause Mr Priapus to swell in my breeches.' The title itself contains the same linguistic mélange: *Sub-Umbra, or Sport Amongst the She-Noodles* (1879); others were more to the point: *Lady Pokingham: Or They All Do It* (1880). Classically-derived or foreign euphemism contributed *academician* for 'whore', *ballum rancum* or *ballum ranorum* for 'a dance of naked whores' and *pose plastique* for 'strip tease'. Elsewhere writers gave way to direct dysphemism, as in this piece of absurd lyricism:

> 'My adored one, how lovely you are! What admirable hips! What an adorable – ARSE!'
> 'Oh! Alfred! What is that naughty word?'
> 'Don't be frightened, darling; lovers can say anything. Those words, out of place in colder moments, add fresh relish to the sweet mystery of love. You will soon say them too, and understand their charm.' (from *Voluptuous Confessions of a French Lady of Fashion* (1860))

Occasionally, wild, prurient fantasy took over, as in this letter from Swinburne to Rossetti, dated 1 March 1870:

> This is a dildo the Queen used
> Once in a pinch in an office,
> Quite unaware that it had *been* used
> First by a housemaid erratic.
> Soon, though obese and lymphatic,
> Symptoms she felt all that month as it went on
> What sort of parties had used it and spent on.

The spiciness of this wicked vision is enhanced by *office* being a euphemism for 'lavatory' and *spend* including the sense of 'ejaculate'.

Ronald Pearsall's study reminds us that extreme Victorian reticence and restraint produced all manner of perversions. These qualities also produced a curious legal accident: 'When the Criminal Law Amendment Act of only to men – no one could think of a way to explain to Queen Victoria what homosexual acts between women were' (1969, p. 474).

DIVIDING THE WORD-FIELD

Slang dictionaries (albeit of a rudimentary nature) antedated even the first 'respectable' glossary or *Table Alphabeticall of Hard Vsuall English Words* published by Robert Cawdrey in 1604. They were not dictionaries in a true sense, but were rather guides to the clandestine and criminal 'cant' or argot of the underworld, the territory of *coney-catchers* (cheats and swindlers, especially at cards) who practised *cosenage* or *coosnage* (trickery). (*Cant* is here used in the sense defined by *OED* 4 (a) as 'The secret language or jargon used by gipsies, thieves, professional beggars, etc.') Many of the titles make use of this 'alternative' cant, trading on a certain illicit excitement, and yet claim to be doing a public service by explaining to the honest citizenry the linguistic ways of the criminal classes, described with a great range of contemptuous language. The works are also significant as sociolinguistic phenomena, since they show the antiquity of interest in differing linguistic milieux, an interest which appears to be perennial.

Works of this kind appeared in 1552, 1561, 1566 and 1591; in the following year some half-dozen were printed. Most of them exhibited the market-catching features mentioned earlier, with enticing titles which typically incorporate the 'blurb'. One of the first of these underground glossaries, by Thomas Harman (1567), advertises itself as *A Caveat or Warening, For Commen Cursetors vulgarely called Vagabones, set forth by Thomas Harman Esquiere, for the utilitie and proffyt of his natural Cuntrey, Augmented and inlarged by the fyrst author here of.*

Cursetors are subsequently defined by Harman (since this is the first recorded use of the word) as 'runners or rangers', rather vagabonds or tramps. A detailed account of the various species follows: 'A prigger of prancers be horse stealers' (p. 103); 'these Abraham men be those who feign themselves to have been mad' (p. 108); 'These freshwater mariners, their ships were drowned in the plain of Salisbury' (p. 109). 'These that do counterfeit the crank be young knaves and young harlots that deeply dissemble the falling sickness' (p. 111); 'These doxies be broken and spoiled of their maidenhead by the upright men' [fradulent servingmen and labourers] (p. 135). A criminal 'black list' of 'the most notorious and wickedest walkers' is included, followed by a glossary of 'the lewd, lousy language of these loitering lusks and lazy lorels' (p. 146). Of the 120 words listed, most have proved to be ephemeral. Survivors include *booze*, *prat* in the sense of 'buttock' and *niggle*, 'to have to do with a woman carnally'. Robert Greene, 'Maister of Arts', a notable contributor to the genre, touted his work of 1591 with calculating criminal salacity as *A Notable Discovery of Coosnage, Now daily practised by sundry lewd persons, called Connie-catchers, and Crosse-biters* [whores]. Less severely moralistic in his tone, he distinguished 'the eight laws of villainy' (varieties of cheating), with their ironic appellations, formed by metaphor, inversion or high register euphemism:

> The [highway] thief is called a *high-lawyer*;
> The bawd, if it be a woman, a *pander*;
> the bawd, if man, an *apple-squire*;
> the whore, a *commodity*;
> the whore-house, a *trugging-place*
> (1972, p. 176)

Over a century later the titles are suggestive of both the *beau monde* and the underworld: the secrets of the boudoir are offered by *Mundum Muliebris; or the ladies dressing room unlocked. . . . Together with the fop-dictionary*, by John and Mary Evelyn (1690). The older tradition, exposing the threatening jungles of the underworld and the highway are to be found in *The Memoirs of the Right Villainous John Hall, the Late Famous and Notorious Robber, Penn'd from his Mouth some time before his Death* (1708) and 'Captain' Alexander Smith's *Compleat History of the Lives and Robberies of the Most Notorious Highwaymen, Footpads, Shoplifts, & Cheats of Both Sexes*, particularly the fifth edition (1719), which contains a thieves' *Canting Dictionary, Grammar and Key*. Elisha Coles added a pragmatic reason for including canting terms in his *English Dictionary* of 1676: 'Tis no disparagement to understand the Canting Terms: 'It may chance to save your Throat from being cut, or (at least) your pocket from being Pick'd.'

During the Augustan period, however, the principal energies of lexicographers were devoted to trying to define or 'fix' the literary language, with underworld slang being regarded, in Johnson's terms, as 'a fugitive cant, unworthy of preservation'. Johnson included several of the 'four letter' words, but avoided the most taboo, unlike his contemporary, Nathan Bailey, who included all.[11] That he was, never the less, aware of his audience's interest in such language is shown in this splendid anecdote:

> He called on them [Mrs Digby and her sister, Mrs Brooke] one day, soon after the publication of his immortal dictionary. The ladies paid him due compliments on the occasion. Among other topics of praise, they very much commended the omission of all naughty words. 'What! my dears! then you have been looking for them?' said the moralist. The

ladies, confused at being caught, dropped the subject of the dictionary. (Beste, *Memorials*, p. 11–12)[12]

Johnson's exclusion of the grosser demotic language is shown up by a comparison with Grose's *Classical Dictionary of the Vulgar Tongue* (1785), a major slang dictionary continuing the older tradition. Grose has several entries under *flash*, such as *flash lingo*, 'The canting or slang language', *to patter flash*, 'to speak the slang language', and *flash ken*, 'a house that harbours thieves'. Though he omits *damn*, Grose includes *blast*, 'to curse' and notes that *bloody* is a 'favourite word used by the thieves in swearing'. *Sh-t sack* is defined as 'a dastardly fellow', and *sh-t-ing through the teeth* is a colourful metaphor for 'vomiting' which sounds like an anticipation of Barry McKenzie. Both *piss* and *fart* have a variety of entries, including *fart-catcher* for valet or footman, *fartleberries* for 'excrement hanging about the anus' and *pissburned* for 'discoloured'. The distinguishing quality of Grose's work is its robust man-of-the-world wit, as can be seen from the following:

BEARD SPLITTER A man much given to wenching.
BURNING SHAME A lighted candle stuck into the parts of a woman, certainly not intended by nature for a candlestick.
BUTTERED BUN One lying with a woman that has just lain with another man, is said to have a buttered bun.
DRAIN Gin: so called from the diuretic qualities imputed to that liquor.
DUCK F-CK-R The man who has the care of the poultry on board a ship of war.

A larger sample is to be found in figure 7.4.

Substantial dictionaries of the lower register started to reappear regularly in the nineteenth century. In a practice common in those times, Grose's work was recycled as the *Lexicon Balatronicum* (1811): the title page, forming figure 7.5, shows that it was tailored for a smarter market. Likewise, *The Flash Dictionary* (1821) was recycled, with a few additions and illustrations by George Cruikshank, as *Sinks of London Laid Open* (1848), to be followed by *The Vulgar Tongue* (1857) and Hotten's *The Slang Dictionary* (1869). However, the definitive work of the century was *A Dictionary of Slang and its Analogues*, by Farmer and Henley, issued in seven volumes from 1890 to 1904.

This massive work (running to nearly three thousand pages) gives an extraordinary insight into the burgeoning demotic argot of Victorian times. Although it is historical in framework and includes continental synonyms, it also covers contemporary usages normally found only in

BIDDY, or CHICK-A-BIDDY. A chicken, and figuratively a young wench.

BIDET, commonly pronounced BIDDY. A kind of tub, contrived for ladies to wash themselves, for which purpose they bestride it like a French poney, or post-horse, called in French bidets.

BIENLY. Excellently. She wheedled so bienly; she coaxed or flattered so cleverly. *French.*

BILL AT SIGHT. To pay a bill at sight; to be ready at all times for the venereal act.

BILBOA. A sword. Bilboa in Spain was once famous for well-tempered blades: these are quoted by Falstaff, where he describes the manner in which he lay in the buck-basket. Bilboes, the stock; prison. *Cant.*

TO BILK. To cheat. Let us bilk the rattling cove; let us cheat the hackney coachman of his fare. *Cant.* Bilking a coachman, a box-keeper, and a poor whore, were formerly, among men of the town, thought gallant actions.

BILL OF SALE. A widow's weeds. See HOUSE TO LET.

BILLINGSGATE LANGUAGE. Foul language, or abuse. Billingsgate is the market where the fishwomen assemble to purchase fish; and where, in their dealings and disputes, they are somewhat apt to leave decency and good manners a little on the left hand.

BING. To go. *Cant.* Bing avast; get you gone. Binged avast in a darkmans; stole away in the night. Bing we to Rumeville: shall we go to London?

BINGO. Brandy or other spirituous liquor. *Cant.*

BINGO BOY. A dram drinker. *Cant.*

BINGO MORT. A female dram drinker. *Cant.*

BINNACLE WORD. A fine or affected word, which sailors jeeringly offer to chalk up on the binnacle.

BIRD AND BABY. The sign of the eagle and child.

BIRD-WITTED. Inconsiderate, thoughtless, easily imposed on.

BIRDS OF A FEATHER. Rogues of the same gang.

BIRTH-DAY SUIT. He was in his birth-day suit, that is, stark naked.

BISHOP. A mixture of wine and water, into which is put a roasted orange. Also one of the largest of Mrs. Philips's purses, used to contain the others.

BISHOPED, or TO BISHOP. A term used among horse-dealers, for burning the mark into a horse's tooth, after he has lost it by age; by bishoping, a horse is made to appear younger than he is. It is a common saying of milk that is burnt too, that the bishop has set his foot in it. Formerly, when a bishop passed through a village, all the inhabitants

ran

FIGURE 7.4 A glossary of underworld slang: a page from the 1811 edition of Captain Francis Grose's highly popular work, *A Classical Dictionary of the Vulgar Tongue* (1785).

Lexicon Balatronicum.

A

DICTIONARY

OF

Buckish Slang, University Wit,

AND

PICKPOCKET ELOQUENCE.

Compiled originally by Captain Grose.

AND NOW CONSIDERABLY ALTERED AND ENLARGED,

WITH

THE MODERN CHANGES AND IMPROVEMENTS,

BY A

MEMBER OF THE WHIP CLUB.

ASSISTED BY

Hell-Fire Dick, and James Gordon, Esqrs. of Cambridge; and William Soames, Esq. of the Hon. Society of Newman's Hotel.

LONDON:

PRINTED FOR C. CHAPPEL,

Pall-Mall;

SOLD BY J. JOHNSTON, CHEAPSIDE; GODDARD, PALL-MALL, AND ALL OTHER BOOKSELLERS.

1811.

FIGURE 7.5 More of the same: Francis Grose's *A Classical Dictionary of the Vulgar Tongue* (1785) remarketed as the *Lexicon Balatronicum* ('Jester's Dictionary').

the 'underground' literature of the time. For example, few people would deduce from their reading of the period that *fucking* could then be defined as 'A qualification of extreme contumely' and 'a more violent form of BLOODY', which corresponds to the modern practice. More surprisingly, both words are described as 'common', an observation which is difficult to corroborate from written records. It is also remarkable to find the vigorous variety of compounds, such as *fuckable, fuck-finger, fuck-fist, fuck-hole, fuckish* and *fuckster*, an array which certainly matches the modern equivalents. Farmer and Henley's work makes it clear that, so far as 'home' English is concerned (as opposed to the colonial varieties), the great modern expansion of swearing occurred much earlier than one would suppose, namely in late Victorian times. But, like so many 'underground' features of the culture, it was suppressed by decorum.

Meanwhile, over at the Scriptorium at Oxford, Murray and his team were edging their way round 'the treadmill of the alphabet', as Johnson called it. In his splendid Introduction, Murray had observed: 'The circle of the English language has a well-defined centre but no discernible circumference. Yet practical utility has some bounds, and a Dictionary has definite limits: the lexicographer must, like the naturalist, 'draw the line somewhere' (p. xvii). Farmer, who had become involved in a law suit with his publishers 'for breach of contract occasioned by their refusal to publish obscene words,' observed in correspondence with Murray, 'I am, in a small way, fighting your own battle in advance' (Murray, 1977, p. 195). In her biography of the great lexicographer, Elisabeth K. Murray concluded that 'contemporary opinion forced him to omit' the offending terms: 'James really had no choice but to leave them out of his Dictionary' (Murray, 1977, p. 195). Clearly taboos were far more stringent a century ago than now. Yet the *OED* is by no means consistent. *Fuck* was excluded, but *wind-fucker* and *fuck-wind* appear, as regional names for the windhover or kestrel. *Cunt* was similarly excluded, but the echoic slang euphemism *coney* (pronounced and often spelt *cunny*, discussed in footnote 2, was included). So was *twat* and the remarkable nonce-word, *lick-twat* (found in a translation of Martial in 1656). The curious histories of *bugger* and *bloody* were elucidated, but *condom* was excluded: a voluntary reader, James Dixon, felt that the word was 'too utterly obscene' for inclusion (Murray, 1977, p. 195). (One of the few linguistic consequences of the spread of AIDS in the late 1980s has been the open use of the word in prophylactic advertising.) Murray, like Johnson before him, was a strong-minded rationalist, and it is a measure of the force of decorum that he ultimately omitted these 'two ancient terms', as Robert Burchfield termed them in his Preface to volume I of the *OEDS* (1972).

NOTES

1 Marvell regarded Rochester as 'the best English satyrist' and thought that he 'had the right vein'. See Walker (1984) p. xi.

2 *Coney*, *cony*, meaning a rabbit, was spelt *cunny* and regularly rhymed with *money* up to the eighteenth century. However, the word obviously developed an association with *cunt*, as is shown in this saucy verse from 1720: 'All my Delight is a Cunny in the Night'.[S] *Cony-burrow* had clearly developed this association as far back as 1652: 'Can he not . . . read Cupids Conyberie, the Park of Pleasure . . .?[O] The *OED* observed, on the change of pronunciation: 'It is possible, however, that the desire to avoid certain vulgar associations with the word in the *cunny* form [which the *OED* did not print] may have contributed to the preference for a different pronunciation in reading the Scriptures. (*Rabbit* originally applied only to the young animal).

3 *Pillicock* is the ancestor of the modern slang term *pillock*: in an early fourteenth-century text a character complains 'Mi pilkoc pisseth on mi schone [shoes]'.

4 Swift technically avoids the obscenity by a dash, but the matching rhyme (*fits*) makes his meaning unmistakable. He repeated this line (118 in the quoted poem) as the climactic conclusion to 'Cassinus and Peter: A tragicall Elegy'. Elsewhere in his poetry he uses *p--s*, *leak*, *stink*, *quean* and *whore*, but resorts to *z-ds*.

5 In his generally unsympathetic *Life of Swift*: Boswell observed on more than one occasion that Johnson was biased against Swift.

6 Quoted (circumspectly) in Christopher Hibbert's excellent study, *The Personal Life of Samuel Johnson*, p. 68. Boswell noted the remarks, but did not print them in his *Life*.

7 *Fanny Hill* is, one assumes, a humorously low-register version of *Mons Veneris*.

8 For several centuries the verbs *come* and *go* have competed for the sense of 'to experience orgasm'. *Come* is recorded as far back as 1650 (in one of *Bishop Percy's Loose Songs*): 'Then off he came, & blusht for shame, soe soon that he had endit.'[S] Equally, when Charmian says (somewhat spitefully) in *Antony and Cleopatra* (I. ii. 61): 'O, let him marry a woman that cannot go', she seems to have a similar meaning. *Go* seems to have faded out (together with *spend* and *swive*) around the turn of the last century, though Lawrence wrote of Connie Chatterley '. . . the consummation was upon her, and she was gone' (1960, p. 181).

9 See G. L. Brook's excellent study, *The Language of Dickens*, in the Language Library (Deutsch, 1970).

10 Tony Tanner, in *The Reign of Wonder* (1965, p. 273), writes of James '. . . concealing, perhaps unconsciously, a hint of forbidden and frightening sexual orifices'. His section on *What Maisie Knew* ('The Reign of Wonderment') is also very pertinent.

11 Bailey, it is true, uses various euphemisms by way of explanation. In his *Dictionarium Britannicum* (1730), *fuck* is designated as 'a term used of a goat'; also (somewhat chauvinistically) *subagitare fœminam; cunt* is rendered as *pudendum muliebre*, which has become traditional.

12 Cited in the *Oxford Book of Literary Anecdotes*.

8

Quakers to Convicts: Swearing in the New Worlds

> In the more southerly colonies [of the United States] there must have been an even more lavish use of cuss-words.
>
> H. L. Mencken

> The operative words are 'pig', 'bullshit', 'motherfucker'. It is the language of left militant students . . . the 'alma-mater fuckers'.
>
> E. Goodheart

> Profane swearing prevails throughout the interior of New South Wales to an extent hardly credible but by those who have actually witnessed it.
>
> H. W. Haygarth

THE English-speaking settler populations which established themselves in the various corners of 'the New World' varied greatly in terms of their linguistic mores, from the staid and dignified Puritan sects of the Pilgrim Fathers to the verbally coarse convicts transported to Botany Bay. These founders and pioneers set the tone, whether restrained, flamboyant or mixed, for the subsequent verbal style of their speech communities. The extent to which they were politically independent of the 'mother country' also clearly affected their linguistic freedom and the degree of their observance of the generally constricting correctness of British models.

In America, the sparse 'plain speech' of the Puritans, and the even more attenuated speech style of the Quakers of Pennsylvania with their insistence on truth and sincerity, can be seen as a reaction against Restoration dandyism, foppishness and decadence, which led Swift to complain that the Court had 'become the worst school in England'.[1] The model of 'plain speech' also retains, curiously, the sober dignity and reticence so admired as an ideal in Anglo-Saxon times. Particularly significant is the Quaker emphasis on Christ's words in Matthew v. 34:

'Do not swear at all' and their consequent refusal to utter or take any oath, even those required by legal procedure. However, one of the earliest English travellers in America, Ned Ward, observed in 1699 that the New England Puritans were 'notwithstanding their sanctity, . . . very prophane in their common dialect' (Mencken, 1936, p. 313). At the other end of the world, about half a century after the establishment of the penal colonies in Australia, H. W. Haygarth commented (in 1848) in now-familiar terms on Antipodean verbal fashions: 'Profane swearing prevails throughout the interior of New South Wales to an extent hardly conceivable but by those who have actually witnessed it' (*Bush Life in Australia*, cited in Hornadge, 1980, p. 134).

OATHS IN THE USA

It is an interesting speculation to reflect on how America might have developed linguistically in the nineteenth century had convicts continued to be transported there, instead of being 'marinated' (after the American War of Independence) to Australia. The contrast between the Pilgrim Fathers and the 'Convict' Fathers is designed to emphasize extremes, and is, of course slightly unfair, since it leaps across two centuries of intervening time. For by the mid-nineteenth century, particularly as a result of the opening up of the West, American speech had started to acquire its own colourful slang and devil-may-care raciness. Within the linguistic spectrum of America, one wonders how Henry James, the elegant Bostonian mandarin 'with the beautiful manners' would have communicated with his outlaw namesake from the Wild West, Jesse, born four years later.

Mencken catches very well the pioneering spirit of exploration which infused the expansion of America:

> Thousands of youngsters filled with a vast impatience of all precedent and authority, revilers of all that had come down from an elder day, incorrigible libertarians . . . swarmed across the mountains and down the great rivers, wrestling with the naked wilderness and setting up a casual, impromptu sort of civilization where the Indian still menaced. Schools were few and rudimentary; there was not the remotest approach to civilized society. (Mencken, 1936, p. 133)

In these conditions, 'a wild and lawless development of the language went on, and many of the uncouth words and phrases that it brought to birth gradually forced themselves into more or less good usage' (Mencken, 1936, p. 138). Similar conditions would apply in many other newly colonized areas, especially Australia. 'In the United States, probably because of the decay in the legal concept of blasphemy, there has been little organized opposition to profanity' (Mencken, 1936, p. 313). Consequently, the mainstream of American swearing is more concerned with obscenity than with profanity.

In 1744, Alexander Hamilton, a Scottish traveller in New Jersey, recorded in his diary: 'I was waked this morning before sunrise with a strange bawling and hollowing without doors. It was the landlord ordering his Negroes, with an imperious and exalted voice. In his orders the known term or epithet *son-of-a-bitch* was often repeated' (Mencken, 1936, p. 313). Clearly the visitor regarded the term as remarkable, although the epithet was first recorded in England in 1707, and is found in variants such as *biche-sone* as far back as *c.*1330.[S] In a more elaborate form, the epithet is found in *King Lear* (II. ii. 22), where Kent calls Oswald 'the son and heir of a mongrel bitch'. Although plain *bitch* had previously been 'common in literature'[O] and first recorded from *c.*?1400 in a spirited exchange in the *Chester Play*, 'Whom calleste thou queine [whore], skabde biche?' it had subsequently fallen out of polite use. Indeed, Grose (1785) described it unequivocally as 'The most offensive appellation that can be given to an English woman, even more provoking than that of whore'.

'The early Americans showed that spacious disregard for linguistic nicety which has characterized their descendants ever since,' wrote Mencken (1936, p. 117). The general attitude of liberation derived in part from the increasingly aggressive sense of independence from the motherland, particularly after the war of 1812. Mencken saw Andrew Jackson as epitomizing the 'archetype of the new American who appeared after 1814 – ignorant, pushful, impatient of restraint, an iconoclast, a Philistine, and Anglophobe in every fiber' (1936, p. 132). Frances Trollope's *Domestic Manners of the Americans* (1832) tended to find these qualities in the population at large. In 'her two volumes of tart fault-finding and rather superior approval' (as Michael Sadleir calls them in his Introduction) she enumerates the gaucheries of the military company on a Mississippi steam-boat:

> The total want of all the usual courtesies of the table, the voracious rapidity with which the viands were seized and devoured; the strange uncouth phrases and pronunciation; the loathsome spitting, from the contamination of which it was absolutely impossible to protect our dresses; the frightful manner of feeding with their knives . . . The little conversation that went forward while we remained in the room was entirely political, and the respective claims of Adams and Jackson to the presidency were argued with more oaths and more vehemence than it had ever been

> my lot to hear. Once a colonel appeared on the verge of assaulting a major, when a huge seven-foot Kentuckian gentleman horse-dealer asked of the heavens to confound them both, and bade them sit still and be d---d. (1927, p. 15)

Although she does not comment upon it, she is clearly surprised at the fulsome response of a prospective domestic in Cincinnati: '"O Gimini!" exclaimed the damsel, with a loud laugh, "you be a downright Englisher, sure enough. I should like to see a young lady engage by the year in America!"' (1927, p. 44). Mrs Trollope also commented on the style of a Presbyterian service in Ohio; 'the prayer was extravagantly vehement, and offensively familiar in expression . . . the sermon had considerable eloquence, but of a frightful kind' (1927, p. 64).

There was, furthermore, a considerable change in the speech-community as immigrants of all kinds poured into America in the nineteenth century, all contributing their loan-words and moulding the language to their own idiom. Henry James epitomized the Eastern purist when he commented, not with entire approval, on the silent revolution taking place in the American language:

> All the while we sleep the vast contingent of aliens whom we make welcome, and whose main contention, as I say, is that, from the moment of their arrival, they have just as much property in our speech as we have, and just as good a right to do what they choose with it . . . are sitting up (*they* don't sleep!) to work their own will on their new inheritance and prove to us that they are without any finer feeling or more conservative instinct of consideration for it . . . (cited in Boorstin, 1969, p. 363)

The idiom of western expansion was 'tall talk' which, in Daniel Boorstin's words, 'blurred the edges of fact and fiction' in its emphasis on the remarkable and extravagant (1969, p. 364). Mencken puts it more strongly, observing that 'It ran to grotesque metaphors and far-fetched exaggerations' (1936, p. 136) which became current in self-consciously humorous writers. Mark Twain's *Life on the Mississippi*, *c.*1852, contains this example:

> Whoo-oop! I'm the old original iron-jawed, brass-mounted, copper-bellied corpse-maker from the wilds of Arkansaw! Look at me! I'm the man they call Sudden Death and General Desolation! Sired by a hurricane, dam'd by an earthquake, half-brother to the cholera, nearly related to the smallpox on my mother's side! Look at me! I take nineteen alligators and a bar'l of whiskey for breakfast when I'm in robust health, and a bushel of rattlesnakes and a dead body when I'm ailing. I split the everlasting rocks with my glance and I squench the thunder when I speak!

> . . . Blood's my natural drink, and the wails of the dying is music to my ear! (cited in Mencken, 1936, p. 137)

Exuberant imagery and violently juxtaposed registers are well captured in Davy Crockett's 'Celebrated War Speech', popular between 1835 and 1856:

> While the stars of Uncle Sam, and the stripes of his country wave triumphantly in the breeze, whar, whar, whar is the craven, low-lived, chicken bred, toad-hoppin', red-mounted, bristle-headed mother's son of ye who will not raise the beacon light of triumph . . . (cited in Boorstin, 1969, p. 368)

It would appear that as the pioneers moved West, so their 'tall talk' started to take on a more violent and more blasphemous airs. Commenting on the Montana mining towns of the mid-century, Thomas J. Dimsdale observed: 'One marked feature of social intercourse, and (after indulgence in strong drink) the most fruitful source of quarrel and bloodshed, is the all-pervading custom of using strong language. Men will say more than they mean' (Boorstin, 1969, p. 372). In such exclusively male domains, bravado became a natural idiom. 'Black Bart' was the *nom de crime* in California of Charles E. Bolton, a dandified highwayman (*fl.*1877–83) who specialized in leaving light insulting verses to infuriate those he had robbed:

> I've labored long and hard for bread
> For honor and for riches
> But on my corns too long you've tred
> You fine haired sons of bitches.
> (Cited in Elman, 1975, p. 217)

'Black Jack' Ketchum, a noted desperado, is reputed to have accepted the hangman's noose in Santa Fe in 1901 with the nonchalant remark: 'I'll be in hell before you start breakfast, boys. Let her go!' (Cited in Elman, 1975, p. 226).

In his observations on 'Expletives', Mencken tends to endorse the view of Robert Graves, that there has been a noticeable decline of swearing and foul language. Commenting that 'All expletives tend to be similarly dephlogisticated by over-use', Mencken found that a similar stage of verbal exhaustion seemed to exist in American, observing archly:

> Our maid-of-all work in that department [profanity] is *son-of-a-bitch*, which seems as pale and ineffectual to a Slav or a Latin as *fudge* does to us . . . when uttered with a wink or dig in the ribs, it is actually a term of endearment, and has been applied with every evidence of respect by

one United States senator to another. . . . Worse, it is frequently toned down to *s.o.b.*, or transmogrified into the childish *son-of-a-gun*.[2] (Mencken, 1936, p. 317)

Graves then makes the apposite comparison with *whoreson*, which by Elizabethan times had lost most of its force, though *son of a whore* was still a deadly insult.

'*Hell* fills so large a part of the American vocabulary, that it will probably be worn out in a few years more,' wrote L. W. Merryweather in 1931, with more irony than naieveté (*American Speech*, August 1931). It was most memorably used in public by Adlai Stevenson, then Ambassador to the United Nations, at the time of the Cuban missile crisis in 1961, when he said that he was prepared to wait 'till hell freezes over' for the Russian Ambassador's response to a leading question.

Mencken notes that *bugger* is 'not generally considered obscene in the United States' (Mencken, 1936, p. 314). Today the word is generally uncommon there, *bugger off!*, for example, being 'minced' into *bug off!* More revealingly, he has virtually nothing to say of *fuck*, which is coyly coded as 'one of three obscene auxiliaries' and 'a word of sexual significance' (Mencken, 1936, p. 314). (Since the fourth edition of *The American Language* was published in 1936, this omission is not surprising, even from so trenchant and frank an observer.) As chapter 9, 'The Modern Explosion', will illustrate, perhaps the most remarkable development in the modern period has been the shattering of the taboos concerning sexual swearing.

Commenting on the wholesale borrowing of *goddam* from English into American, Mencken claims that the process of 'integration' or 'infixing' was an American invention:

> The American custom of inserting *goddam* into other words, to give them forensic force, is generally believed by the learned to have been launched by the late Joseph Pulitzer, of the New York *World*, a great master of profanity in three languages . . . 'the trouble with you, Coates [Editor of the *World*] is that you are too inde*goddam*pendent!' (Mencken, 1936, p. 315)

'This ingenious device,' continues Mencken chauvinistically, 'has been borrowed by the Australians, who are great admirers of the American language, but they use *bloody* instead of *goddam*, no doubt as a concession to Empire solidarity.' Mencken is assuredly on safer ground when he claims that 'The insertion of infixes into *Jesus Christ* also seems to be an American invention. The common form is *Jesus H. Christ* [but] *Holy*

Jumping Jesus is also heard' (Mencken, 1936, p. 316). The use of these enclitic forms clearly shows the semantic downgrading of the term in question.

As subsequent chapters show, sexuality, so suppressed in earlier times, has come to the fore in American varieties of swearing in forms such as *mother-fucker*, *cocksucker*, *dickhead* and *brown-nose*. This feature is not so apparent in the other varieties of swearing we are to consider.

AUSTRALIAN OATHS: FROM BOTANY BAY TO EARLS COURT

The stern morality and extreme restraint of the American Puritans and Quakers stood at the furthest remove from the 'marinated' criminality and underworld verbal mores of the founders of the Australian penal colonies. According to Sidney J. Baker, 'Between 1788 and 1868 nearly 160,000 convicts were shipped to Australia from Britain' (McLeod, 1963, p. 103). It has been estimated that within two generations of the arrival of the First Fleet in Botany Bay, 'a staggering 87 per cent of the Australian population were either convicts, ex-convicts or of convict descent' (McCrum *et al.*, 1986, p. 288). Indeed, in 1837 James Mudie coined an ironic new social classification, *felonry*, to describe the social make-up of the colony:

> The author has ventured to coin the word FELONRY, as the appellative of an order or class of persons in New South Wales – an order which happily exists in no other country in the world. A legitimate member of the tribe of appellatives . . . as peasantry, tenantry, yeomanry, gentry. (cited in Hornadge, 1980, p. 78)

The distinctive dialect of the convicts was a criminal argot called *flash*, a term for underworld slang which had been current in England from around 1750. A Captain of the Marines, Watkin Tench, in his *Complete Account of the Settlement at Port Jackson*, commented on this linguistic feature as early as 1793:

> A leading distinction, which marked the convicts on their outset in the colony, was the use of what is called 'flash', or 'kiddy' language. In some of our early courts of justice, an interpreter was frequently necessary to translate the deposition of the witness, and the defence of the prisoner. This language has many dialects. The sly dexterity of the pickpocket; the brutal ferocity of the footpad; and the deadly purpose of the midnight ruffian, is each strictly appropriate in the terms which characterize it. (cited in Hornadge, 1980, p. 78)

A thrice-transported convict, James Hardy Vaugh, compiled in 1812 a glossary of the argot during his 'solitary hours of cessation from hard labour' and published it in his *Memoirs* in 1819 under the title of *A New and Comprehensive Vocabulary of the Flash Language.* In view of the nature of the speech community, it is not quite clear whom he could have had in mind as a target market. Vaugh defined *kiddy* (mentioned above and commonly defined as a 'professional thief') as 'a thief of the lower order, who . . . dresses in the extreme of vulgar gentility'. The term was probably related to *kid* meaning 'to deceive', which is included in the vocabulary, together with *grub* ('food'), *lark* ('fun' or 'sport'), and *to queer*, ('to spoil'). One of the most distinctive flash words to have passed into the mainstream of Australian English is *swag* for 'stolen wearing apparel, linen or piece-goods'. (The term was transported from the mother country, where it had meant 'stolen goods in general' since *c.*1785.) It was from this criminal provenance that the deadliest Australian insult, *bludger*, emerged. Originally meaning a street bully or prostitute's pimp, it has become extended through army usage to mean a parasite, idler, skiver or freeloader.

As in America, there seems to have been little separation of registers on the basis of social class in Australia. Within half a century of Captain Arthur Phillip's founding of the first colony in 1788, Edward Gibbon Wakefield observed in his *Letter from Sydney*:

> Bearing in mind that our lowest class (the convicts) brought with it a peculiar language, and is constantly supplied with fresh corruption, you will understand why pure English is not, and is unlikely to become, the language of the colony. . . . Terms of slang and flash are used, as a matter of course, from the gaols to the Viceroy's palace, not excepting the Bar and the Bench. No doubt they will be reckoned quite parliamentary, as soon as we have a parliament. (cited in Hornadge, 1980, p. 76)

The Great Australian Adjective

One of the first writers to comment on the astonishing currency of the word *bloody* in the settlement was Alexander Marjoribanks, in his *Travels in New South Wales* (1847). By noting the fact that a bullock driver used the word twenty-seven times in a quarter of an hour, Marjoribanks was probably not the first outsider to be sufficiently impressed to record the performance of an Australian native speaker giving tongue. Obviously astonished, he went further, extrapolating the incidence to show that over fifty years the driver would have used 'this disgusting word no less than 18,200,000 times' (pp. 57–8).

Marjoribanks' criticism of the word, which seems rather precious to us now that it has been superseded by various apparently stronger copulatory and excretory terms, is very much in tune with the sensitivities of the time. Other contemporary commentators referred to it as 'the crimsonest of adjectives' and 'this odious word' (Hornadge, 1980, pp. 141–2). The *OED* entry (originally in a fascicle published in March, 1887) makes the following class comments on the usage: 'In general colloquial use from the Restoration to *c.*1750; now constantly in the mouths of the lowest classes, but by respectable people considered "a horrid word", on a par with obscene or profane language, and usually printed in the newspapers (in police reports, etc.) "b---y".' Emphasizing the distinctive English abhorrence for the word, Mencken observed in his classic (but slightly chauvinist) study, *The American Language*: 'Perhaps the most curious disparity between the vocabulary of the two tongues is presented by *bloody*. The word is entirely without improper significance in America, but in England it is regarded as indecent, with overtones of the blasphemous.' His comments on the dual attitudes towards the word are shrewdly observed and widely applicable: 'The more it is denounced by the delicate, the more it is cherished by the vulgar' (Mencken, 1936, pp. 311–12).

Things were different in the outback, and by the end of the century the term was starting to acquire the sobriquet of 'the great Australian adjective'. (On 18 August, 1894, the *Sydney Bulletin* referred to *bloody* as 'the Australian adjective'.) No doubt the currency of the word reflected the convict origins of the settlers, for Grose observes in his *Classical Dictionary of the Vulgar Tongue* that *bloody* was 'a favourite word used by thieves in swearing'.

The word gained institutional status (if it needed it) in C. J. Dennis' marching song, called 'The Australaise', originally written in 1908. The third version, published in 1915, was dedicated to the Australian Expeditionary Force and widely distributed among them. More commonly known by its first line, 'Fellers of Australia', it was sung to 'Onward Christian Soldiers' and ran:

Fellers of Australier
    Blokes an' coves an' coots
Shift yer --- carcases,
    Move yer --- boots.
Gird yer --- loins up
    Get yer --- gun
Set the --- enermy
    An' watch the blighters run

Chorus
Get a --- move on,
Have some --- sense
Learn the --- art of
Self de---fence

The uncharacteristic reticence of taking refuge in the omitted, 'unprintable' but obvious code-form is revealing. Equally interesting is the Australian speciality of integrating the adjective into an adjoining word: 'self de[bloody]fence. Subsequent verses have the forms 'Australi---ar', 'enthusi---asm', 'Pos---terity', 'Spiffler---cate' and 'Kingdom---come'. The process, which shows that the word has lost all semantic force and is being used as an enclitic for the purposes of syncopation, has proved very fruitful. In spite of Mencken's remarks (cited above) the feature seems to be more characteristically and enthusiastically Australian than American.

Although there continued to be resistance to, and even outrage at, the common use of the word in the early part of the century, all commentators conceded its wide use. One judge wittily observed that 'If vulgar and uneducated people were debarred from using the word their conversation would be seriously impaired' (Hornadge, 1980, pp. 144–5). In a significant judgement given in the Sydney Divorce Court on 22 June 1942, Mr Justice Halse Rogers held that 'the word *bloody* is so common in modern parlance that it is not regarded as swearing' (Hornadge, 1980, p. 144). Wakefield's prophecy about the word becoming parliamentary has been amply fulfilled. In 1970 a Member of the House of Representatives announced: 'I never use the word "bloody" because it is unparliamentary. It is a word I never bloody well use' (Hornadge, 1980, p. 145). A colleague, the Minister of Transport, made no such claims to reticence, commenting (in 1973) on the forthcoming budget:

> There is going to be some bloody mammoth changes – some mammoth changes which the Budget will disclose. Bloody mammoth changes, that is the only way you can describe them. I think that Frank Crean has done a bloody good job to stand up to the pace. Bloody oath, he has done a marvellous job in standing up to the bloody pace. (cited in Hornadge, 1980, p. 145)

Parliamentary exchanges are often laced with highly insulting language, as is shown in this example, which occurred in the House of Representatives in 1975:

Dr R. T. Gun (Labour) 'Why don't you shut up, you great poofter?'

Mr J. W. Bourchier (Liberal) 'Come round here, you little wop, and I'll fix you up.'

(cited in Hornadge, 1980, p. 166)

Terms of Colour

The Aborigines, originally termed *natives* or *blacks*, were soon stigmatized as *niggers*, a term which gained currency in the course of the last century but became obsolescent in the course of this, having been replaced by *abo* and *boong* (an aborigine word). The currency of *abo* was accelerated by the term's copious use in the Sydney *Bulletin*, which uttered such views as this: 'No nigger, no Chinamen, no lascar, no kanaka, no purveyor of cheap coloured labour, is an Australian' (1887) (cited in Hornadge, 1980, p. 163). *Coon* has been borrowed from America, and though 'not extensively used by white Australians', is 'sometimes used by Aborigines to describe other Aborigines of whom they disapprove' (Hornadge, 1980, p. 163). The opprobrious names for the Chinese are *chows, chinks, paddies, opium smokers, slit-eyes, quangs, slants* and plain *yellow bastards*. In his book *Our Australian Cousins* (1879), J. Inglis noted that the Chinese were, for some reason, especially incensed by the use of *paddy*. The other immigrant nations have been generally labelled by their current terms of opprobrium, *dago, wop, eytie, jap, hun* and *frog*.

Barry McKenzie

Although 'Bazza' McKenzie has a large (and sophisticated) audience, Barry Humphries describes him as 'a pastiche figure. His vocabulary is borrowed from a diversity of national types, and words like "cobber" and "bonzer" still intrude as a sop to Pommy readers, though such words are seldom, if ever, used in present day Australia' (1988, p. 134). Superficially, the picaresque adventures of Barry 'the Chunderer' McKenzie (*fl.*1963–) might seem to be an ironic instance of the return of the native son of Oz mouthing uncouth convict-speak and shocking the indigenous population no less than his forebears did their bourgeois British governors. The lexis of this satirical institution has, however, revealing limited foci evoked in charmingly picturesque metaphors which have gained a considerable currency. The vast majority of the terms concern urination (*drain the dragon, point Percy at the porcelain* and *syphon the python*), defecation (*strangle a darkie*) and vomiting (*technicolour yawn* or *liquid laugh down the great white telephone*). Sexual activity is similarly alluded to by means of humorously graphic (and uncomplicatedly chauvinist) figures of speech, copulation being rendered variously as *sink the sausage* and *spear the bearded clam*, alternatively by means of coy euphemisms (*to feature, exercise the ferret* or *dip the wick*). *Flog the lizard* or *jerking the gherkin* are the preferred terms for masturbation. The use of Cockney rhyming slang is fairly common: thus *mulligatawny* is pedantically glossed as 'in a state of heightened sexual erethism', while *to take a Captain Cook* is 'to look' and thirst is melodramatically rendered as being *as dry as a kookaburra's khyber*. In short, 'Bazza' may be risqué, but is always reassuringly 'decent' and 'proper', eschewing gross or 'four-letter' words. In the more spirited exchanges it is invariably the upper-class 'Poms' who come out with 'Good God!' 'Christ!' and 'shit!', while Bazza generally limits himself to 'Jeez!', 'Cripes', 'flaming', 'bloody oath' and the ambivalent 'bastard'.

McKenzie shows, furthermore, a typical prissiness in taboo genital areas, as is seen in the saying 'dry as a nun's nasty' for 'to be quite thirsty'. Indeed the lack of 'liberation' of the Australian male is well illustrated in the standard joke involving a loud, brash character from the outback who regales his drinking companions with variations of the following commentary, always with the same punch-line: 'My colonial oath,[3] we had a bloody terrific time! Won some money on the races. Me and Dawn (that's my sheila) partied all evening. After a fucking great steak and a lot of snorts we went upstairs for a naughty.' In one of his rare passionate outbursts, McKenzie exclaims: 'Jeez you look bonzer tonight. I reckon I could go a little celebration naughty before we adjourn inside.' As the link-piece after this episode observes, 'Intimacy is an ugly word' (1988, p. 19).

Yet, curiously, both *naughty* and *nasty* are ancient euphemisms, which McKenzie and his fellowmen of Oz are merely perpetuating long after their disappearance in the homeland. *Naught* and *naughty* used to have a strong sense of 'wickedness' or 'evil', but the phrase *to do naught* is clearly used with sexual innuendo as far back as Shakespeare's *Richard III*, where Gloucester makes a 'man of the world' comment on the King's affair with Mistress Shore:

> Naught to do with Mistress Shore! I tell thee fellow,
> He that doth naught with her, excepting one [her husband],
> Were best to do it secretly, alone.
>
> (I. i. 98–100)

In *Measure for Measure*, Mistress Overdone's brothel is variously described by Elbow as *a hot-house, a very ill house* and *a naughty house*. The term *naughtypack* was used of women (and men) of bad or dissolute character from the mid-sixteenth century, while the phrase *to go naughty* for 'to indulge in illicit sexual intercourse' is found in a note in the *EETS* text of Lyndsay's *Satire of the Three Estates* (1869) where the original text (1602), 'some of our dochtours, I dreid, salbe miscaried' is glossed as 'some of them [our daughters] go naughty' (p. 498). Farmer and Henley also record the phrase *to do the naughty*: ('Shop and working girls in large towns sometimes say that they work for their living, but do the naughty for their clothes'). Both variants, as well as *have a naughty*, have become the specialty of Australian and New Zealand English, where they are applied even to marital intercourse, long after *naughty* has become trivialized in relation to its old strong sense. *Nasty* is less easily traced, but under *C**t*, Grose (1785) observes, presumably with a pun, that the word is 'a nasty word for a nasty thing'.

Despite the Barry McKenzie column acquiring an institutional status, what Barry Humphries called 'a puritanical backlash' led to it being embargoed with consequent legal proceedings in Australia in 1970. A film, 'The Adventures of Barry McKenzie', was banned in New Zealand in 1973 on the grounds that it was verbally indecent' (1988, p. 138).

Less well known outside the shores of Australia is the character of type known as *Ocker*, deriving from a stereotypical character portrayed in a television comedy series from the early 1970s. The type is defined in the *Australian Pocket Oxford Dictionary* as a 'Boorish person; person who is aggressively Australian in speech and behaviour, often for humorous effect'. Both Barry McKenzie and Ocker fall into the category of satirical or cartoon national self-image also seen in Andy Capp and Van der Merwe.

The tradition of Australian swearing shows little sign of atrophying. In a case of drunken driving heard at the Magistrate's Court of Bundaberg, Queensland, the words *clown, clot, ratbag, nit* and *dickhead* formed part of the proceedings, issuing from the lips, not of the defendant, but of the Stipendiary Magistrate, Mr R. Tully. When the Appeal Court commented that his language was inappropriate for his judicial capacity, Mr Tully's rebuttal was at once blunt (and slightly naive in its examples): 'If you're talking to a politician you use reserved language and correct English. If you're talking to a mob of hoons [louts] you have to get down to their level before they can understand' (cited in Hornadge, 1980, p. 155). Be that as it may, the Australian speech community has developed its distinctive array of insults and swear-words.

BOERS, KAFFIRS AND ROOINEKS

Although there had been some English settlement at the Cape of Good Hope as a consequence of the annexation of the Cape from 1795–1803, the main body of immigrants were the group known as the 1820 Settlers, who were encouraged by the British government to take up land in the Eastern Cape. The four thousand settlers who landed at Algoa Bay from 10 April of that year were mainly respectable men of education and some means, farmers, tradesmen and artisans from various parts of the British Isles. There was a considerable Methodist element among them: by 1844 five of the ten churches built in the area were Methodist. These various factors perhaps explain why South African English speakers, unlike Australians, for example, have never been noted for the flamboyance or distinctiveness of their swearing.

There has, in fact, developed a marked inclination for *ESSAs* (an acronym for 'English-speaking South Africans' as Professor Guy Butler has termed them) to prefer Afrikaans terms to English equivalents in areas of strong, foul or picturesque language. This may be because the Afrikaans equivalents are used more freely in that language, or as an evasion of what is taboo in English. This would seem to be a unique characteristic among English speech communities of the Empire. The principal borrowings include the following: *kak* ('shit': 'He talked a lot of absolute kak'); *doos* (literally 'box' or 'chest' → 'cunt', as with French *boîte*: 'Smith is a real doos'); *moer* (also 'cunt', usually in the straight personal expletive, *Jou moer!* described by Athol Fugard as 'the ultimate obscenity: contraction of *Jou ma se moer*, your mother's womb') (*DSAE*). The word can also be used as an intensifier in various idioms, such as 'He gave me a moer of a clap' (as in English *a hell of a* ——, *a helluva* ——; ('He gave me a hell of a smack'). Another term for the same thing (but not used as a personal insult) is *poes* [puss]: a Dutch Professor issues the warning (in 1884) that 'the new arrival from Holland takes a risk if he addresses a Cape cat' (*DSAE*). Others are *gat* ('hole', especially 'arsehole'), hence *gatkruiper* 'arse-creeper', 'brown-nose': 'Smithers is an ingratiating little *gatkruiper*.' *Poep*, meaning 'fart' (as in 'What a poep!') figures in a number of interesting hybrid combinations, such as *poephol* (equivalent of the insulting use of 'arsehole'), and *poep-scared*, equivalent of 'shit-scared'.

Also borrowed from Afrikaans is *voetsak!*, roughly equivalent of 'get lost!', now assimilated as a verb: 'I simply told him to voetsak'. Less physical, but equally wounding is *bobbejaan*, literally, 'baboon' but signifying 'idiot': 'the bobbejaan caught the wrong train'. Interesting because of its diversification is *bliksem*, the Afrikaans word for lightning. It can be used as a straight expletive of annoyance or frustration: '*bliksem!*' or as an emotive adjective: 'now the bliksem car won't start!' or as a term of personal abuse roughly equivalent of 'bastard': 'that bliksem is up to no good.' Religious expletives are also much in evidence. These include *jissus!*, *yessus!* and even *yislaik!*, all corruptions of *Jesus!*, *Here!* for *Lord!* and *God!* in its more guttural Afrikaans pronunciation.

All of these terms could be commonly heard on the lips of *ESSAs* (both artisan and professional) in the course of a day's informal discussions concerning, say, local or office politics. (Few of these speakers would, however, use the English equivalents.) By contrast, there is a comparative paucity of English swear-words borrowed into Afrikaans. The principal instance is *blerry*, a corruption of *bloody*, but none of the 'big six' have crossed the linguistic barrier. The movement has been entirely in the opposite direction. This dependence on Afrikaans perhaps explains why there is no 'great South African swearword' which has passed into the mainstream of world English. Perhaps the only claimant for this dubious title would be *kaffir* (discussed below), which is probably the best known of the opprobrious terms which have emanated from the sub-continent.

The traditional animosity which has existed between the British and the Boers has its semantic correlatives in many insulting terms. From the British side there are *hairyback, rockspider, crunchie* and plain *Dutchman* (which, never the less, carries a great deal of contempt). All of these are comparatively recent coinages recorded back only as far as around 1973, though *Dutchy* was in use by 1837.[5] In addition, several terms have been borrowed from Afrikaans; these include *gawie, takhaar* ('unkempt' or 'dishevelled' in appearance, literally, 'with branches of hair') and *japie* or *jaap*, derived from the name Jakob. (According to *DSAE*, the term has apparently travelled as far as Australia.) All denote or imply a boorish or rustic stereotype, a hairy heeled, mealie (maize) crunching backwoodsman or troglodyte. Among Afrikaaners the greatest insult (in this category) would be to call someone 'a real jaap', while among blacks the term of greatest contempt is still, interestingly, *boer*. It is used among urban blacks as a term of abuse even for someone of mixed blood. The term has also become politicized in that it is used of those in the institutions of power: it is prison slang for the police or prison warders, and SWAPO used it for the South African forces in their war of liberation; radical elements in South Africa often criticize (and intimidate) 'non-whites' who 'work with the Boere'. Afrikaans has not been as creative in its terms for the British: *rooinek* ('red neck'), coined in the Boer War, graphically represented the sunburnt British troops, but did not imply a lack of culture, as the American *redneck* does. Though still current, the term has lost a great deal of its animosity and has not really been replaced.

The insult most notoriously associated with South Africa is *kaffir*. The initial spread and subsequent obsolescence of the word is a reflection of colonial categorization and subsequent censorship mechanisms. The land which the 1820 Settlers were granted bordered on an area which had been called Caffir-land or Cafraria at least as far back as 1599. In its earlier spelling, *cafre*, the term was a borrowing from Arabic *kafir*, meaning 'infidel', 'unbeliever', 'heathen' (from the Muslim point of view). A letter written in 1799 notes that Tipoo Sultan 'wished to drive the English Caffirs out of India,' an expression which seems highly ironic in view of later developments. In V. S. Naipaul's novel, *Suffrage of Elvira* (1958), the usage is maintained in this exchange: '. . . he lifted up his arm and pinched the skin . . . "this is pure blood. Every Hindu blood . . . is pure Aryan blood." Baksh snorted. "All-you is a just a pack of Kaffir"' (*DSAE*).

Kaffir subsequently became associated with the Xhosa-speaking peoples living in the North-East of the Cape Colony, and developed the generalized sense used in the names of places (*Kaffirstad*, *Kaffirskraal*), flora (*kaffirboom*), fauna (*kaffir finch*) and food (*kaffir corn*, *kaffir beer*). In the early 1890s the term was applied in the London Stock Exchange to South African mining shares. The sector was originally termed, not very complimentarily, 'the Kaffir Circus', but this application is now virtually unheard.

The derogatory personal use of the word (like that of 'nigger') was commented upon as far back as 1847, when William Shaw observed that '"Kaffir" is not a term used by the natives themselves . . . The Border Kaffirs know that the white nations apply the term to them, and many of them regard it as a term of contempt' (*DSAE*). This offending usage has, of course, continued, becoming one of the most notorious of insults. Although the most publicized cases involve blacks being insulted by whites, *kaffir* is also used by blacks of other blacks, and by Muslims of non-Muslims, as has already been noted. The usage has only recently been curtailed by legal restraints and by awareness amongst sensitive people that the word should be taboo.

There have been various responses to this awareness. The word was banned in Namibia within months of that territory gaining independence. Legally the usage is now actionable, constituting *crimen injuria*, and has been the cause of several court cases in the Republic. The place names (controlled by a government committee) are no longer allowed to proliferate. However, as tends to happen when taboo terms are driven underground, they emerge in disguised forms. In this case the term has surfaced as an abbreviation, namely *k*, used in *k-taxi*, *k-beer* and, most insulting, *k-factor*, meaning an allowance made for stupidity or incompetence, e.g. 'This machine has a high k-factor'.

The racial divisions of apartheid have, not surprisingly, brought semantic correlatives. Afrikaans has, however, persisted in the use of the insulting racist terms *kaffir* and *coolie*, and generated many others for 'non-white' peoples, such as *klonkie* and *kleurling* for 'coloured'. The contemptuous compound *kaffirboetie* ('black man's chum', the local equivalent of *nigger-lover*) is an insult directed at a white person 'thought to be a negrophile, or to one who works for or attaches importance to the welfare of black people' (*DSAE*). *Coon*, seemingly borrowed from the insulting American usage, can be applied to black people, often in the paternalistic compounds, *coon-boy* or *coon-girl*. The term is also used, apparently without disrespect, of the *Coon Carnival*, held at New Year in Cape Town by choirs and bands of coloured people, 'so named from the black and white racoon-style make-up similar to that of negro Christie minstrels' (*DSAE*). All of these terms can be heard on the lips of *ESSAs*, but not (generally speaking) with the frequency that they would be encountered in Afrikaans.

Summing up, one notices the interesting difference in the degree of taboo in dealing with sexual and political matters. The *ESSAs* have borrowed quite heavily into Afrikaans in the currency of sexual insults, while the *ASSAs* (Afrikaans Speaking South Africans) have borrowed and maintained the currency of racial insults.

THE EMPIRE STRIKES BACK

As might be expected, the colonies and outposts generated their own terms for their original homeland. In the course of the 1830s the letters P.O.M.E. (standing for 'Prisoner of Mother England') were carved on the walls of the Port Arthur jail in New South Wales. According to one theory, they were later formed into the acronym *pom*, which has become the basic Australian term for the British. (It is hard to see, however, why what was originally a term for a convict should have become that for the colonial power.) The rival interpretation resembles that for Afrikaans *rooinek* ('red neck'), deriving the application of *pom* to the British because their rosy cheeks supposedly resembled the pomegranate. Writing of the period before the First World War, Xavier Herbert recalls: 'When we kids saw people on the street dressed like that [in heavy clumsy British type of clothing] we would yell at them 'Jimmygrants, pommygranates, Pommies!'[5] Whatever its origin, *pom* has become an ambivalent label, varying in tone from affectionate to critical, depending on the qualifying adjective or following noun. When Mrs Mary Whitehouse visited Australia in 1978, the Attorney General of South Australia referred to her as 'a notorious pom', which was denounced by the *Australian* in an editorial as 'A Stinkardly Insult'. *Pommie bastard* would have elicited a similar response. The American term *limey* dates from at least 1910, originating *c.*1880 in *lime juicer*, from the limes issued to British sailors to prevent scurvy. Curiously, the term had been previously used (at least from 1859) by the English to signify an Australian.

PIDGINS

An expected consequence of Empire has been the growth of pidgins throughout the world. In her recent study, *Modern Englishes: Pidgins and Creoles* (1984), Loreto Todd distinguishes no less than thirty-one varieties of English pidgins and creoles, principally located in West Africa, the West Indies and the Pacific. Pidgins are rudimentary communication systems developed between groups who do not share a common language, a makeshift simplified nucleus of a language in which most of the vocabulary is, expectedly, drawn from the language of the dominant group.

Less predictable is the interesting fact that in a number of these varieties, what would be regarded as swear-words in 'Standard English' (broadly conceived) are used as inoffensive general terms. The most prevalent of such terms in Papua New Guinea Tok Pisin [Talk Pidgin] is *baga*, from *bugger*, meaning simply and generally 'a man' in its noun form and 'destroy' as a verb. It has generated *lesbaga* ('lazy bugger') and the highly generalized verb *bagarap*, from 'bugger up', defined in its intransitive uses as 'break, become impaired, have an accident happen to, become exhausted or injured, disintegrate'; the transitive variant *bagarapim* encompasses the senses 'to destroy, break etc., rape, render useless'. Thus this advice in the *Road Safety Guide to New Guinea*: 'If you have an accident, get the other driver's number' is translated as *Sapos yu kisim bagarap, kisim namba bilong narapela draiva*. In the *Nupela Testamen*, God's destruction of Sodom and Gomorrah is rendered by the same term. Other surprisingly central words are *bulsitim* (from 'bullshit'), meaning 'to deceive or cheat' and the general use of *sit* ('shit') to mean 'residue', as in *sit bilong faia* for 'ashes' and *sit bilong lam* (lamp) for 'soot'. *As* (from *arse*) is similarly very generalized, including the senses 'buttocks, bottom, stump, underlying cause, place of origin, underside, rear', while *baksait* means 'back' or 'rear' and not 'buttocks'.

Although the precise circumstances of the origins of Tok Pisin are uncertain, it is known that from the late nineteenth century Papuans worked as indentured labourers in Queensland and thus acquired Queensland Plantation Pidgin English. The central location of these derogatory terms in the lexis indicates, as Loreto Todd puts it, that 'the local people were disparaged by their overseers' (1984, p. 253). They also remind us of the truism that all linguistic use is a matter of convention. For the native speakers, these 'strong' terms have been defused, just as for Standard English speakers *gorblimey!* and *he gets on my wick* are not shocking since the original meanings of the phrase ('God blind me!') and ('He gets on my prick!') are now quite opaque. Pidgins shock and amuse outsiders because the separation of registers formalized in most varieties of English is consistently violated: slang and taboo terms jostle and rub shoulders with polite words without any sense of incongruity. Thus, in Cameroon Pidgin, the basic bodily vocabulary consists of *anus*, which is technical, *bɛlɛ ('belly')* and *bobi* ('bubby', 'breast'), which are informal, *pis* and *shit*, which are vulgar. Terms of insult are, however, drawn from the archetypal motifs of incest and bastardy: *chuk yu mami!* ('fuck your mother!') is the strongest insult in Cameroon Pidgin, followed by *Yu mami i pima!* ('your mother was promiscuous!'). It would seem that terms like *shit* and *piss*, since they are 'defused', are not used in the standard idioms of insult, such as *'You shit!'* and *'Piss off!'*

A convenient point of conclusion is suggested by the experience of Captain Basil Hall when he visited the Sandwich Islands in the 1820s. An islander greeted him with an odd series of salutations: 'Very glad see you! Damn your eyes! Me like English very much. Devilish hot, sir! Goddam!' The man was simply repeating the essential points of communication left by Captain Cook's expedition in 1778.[4]

NOTES

1 From Swift's 'Proposal for Correcting, Improving and Ascertaining the English Tongue' (1712).

2 *Son of a gun* is a euphemism originally applied to a bastard born on board ship.

3 *My colonial oath!* has become one of the most distinctive Australian ejaculations. In the form *My kerlonial oath!* it is found in 'the Bastard from the Bush', a poem written by Henry Lawson near the turn of the century. (He

subsequently toned down the obscenities in the work (which had been circulated privately) and published it as 'The Captain of the Push'.) The use of *oath* in place of some more egregious term is also a feature of Australian swearing.

4 B. Hall, *Fragments of Voyages and Travels* (Edinburgh, 1831) p. 89.

9
The Modern Explosion and its Accompanying Restraints

'Not bloody likely.'

Eliza Doolittle

'Mr T.,' he [Noel Coward] said crisply, 'you are a cunt. Come and have dinner with me.'

Kenneth Tynan

I do not claim to be a literary critic, but I know dirt when I smell it and here it is in heaps – festering putrid heaps which smell to high heaven.

W. Charles Pilley

'Is it [*Lady Chatterley's Lover*] a book that you would wish your wife or even servant to read?'

Mervyn Griffiths-Jones

'I could kill them. When I'm with a woman who's really Lesbian, I fairly howl in my soul, wanting to kill her.'

Oliver Mellors

About half a century ago, Robert Graves published his speculative monograph, *Lars Porsena, or The Future of Swearing* (1927), subsequently *The Future of Swearing and Improper Language* (1936). He took the controversial view that both forms of discourse were atrophying:

> Of recent years in England there has been a noticeable decline of swearing and foul language, and this, except at centres of industrial depression, shows every sign of continuing indefinitely until a new shock to our national nervous system – envisageable as war, pestilence, revolution, fire from Heaven, or whatever you please – may (or may not) revive the habit of swearing, simultaneously with that of praying. (1936, p. 1)

With somewhat feline irony, Graves first predicts a continuing dearth of swearing, then withdraws the prediction, suggests plausible and specific causes in a variety of social upheavals, only to 'pass the buck' to the reader with the phrase 'or whatever you please', finally positing a pertinent linkage between swearing and praying, implying that the first is the debased currency of the second. It is a passage rich with suggestive observations.

The dénouement of Graves' study is equally ironic: 'As for *The Future of Swearing*, who is going to write about it? Not I. To begin with, I cannot believe that it has a future, at least, not one worth setting beside its past' (1936, p. 65). He proceeds to suggest a title (his own), proposes to 'leave someone else to do the dirty work', but offers a synopsis of themes and causative factors which vary from the cogently plausible to the plainly ridiculous. They include:

> The imaginative decline of popular swearing under industrial standardization and since the popular Education Acts of fifty years ago; the part played in this decline by the rise in the price of liquor and the shortening of drinking hours; following the failure of the Saints and the Prophets, and the breakdown of orthodox Heaven and Hell as supreme swearing stocks, the questionable compensation offered by newer semi-religious concepts as the League of Nations, Pacifism and Social Credit, by such superstitious objects as hammers, sickles, swastikas and shirts of different single colours, and by Freudian symbolism; the effect on swearing of the spread of spiritistic belief, of golf, of new popular diseases such as botulism and sleepy-sickness, of new forms of scientific warfare . . . ; of gallantly foul-mouthed feministic encroachment on what has been hitherto regarded as a wholly male province. (1936, pp. 65-6)

Although time has hardly borne out Graves' basic speculation, the following chapters will deal with some (but not all) of the factors which he posited. There is, one surmises, a biographical factor at work in Graves' pronouncements on the decline of foul language. We can well imagine that for a literary man who had been immersed in the linguistic miasma of war, everything subsequent would have seemed a bit tame. He records in his superb memoir of the war, *Goodbye to All That* (published in 1929) a number of such episodes:

> The greatest number of simultaneous charges that I ever heard brought against a soldier occurred in the case of Boy Jones, at Liverpool in 1917. They accused him, first, of using obscene language to the bandmaster. (The bandmaster, who was squeamish, reported it as: 'Sir, he called me a double effing c---.') (1929, p. 70)

As we can see, there was some squeamishness even in 1960. Graves was writing, however, in a period when censorship and self-censorship were both widespread. In *Lars Porsena* he often alludes to 'the Censor' and admits that 'I have let a learned counsel go through these pages with a blue pencil and strike through paragraph after paragraph of perfectly clean writing' (1936, p. 69). In terms of our theme, we could regard this period as an interregnum between two landmarks, the first being Eliza Doolittle's scandalous ejaculation, 'Not bloody likely' in Shaw's *Pygmalion*, the sensation of the 1914 theatre season. The second was the protracted trial which led to the unbanning of D. H. Lawrence's *Lady Chatterley's Lover* in 1960.

Readers of the *Daily Sketch* of 11 April 1914 were greeted with the following remarkable news:

> TONIGHT'S 'PYGMALION' IN WHICH MRS PATRICK CAMPBELL IS EXPECTED TO CAUSE THE BIGGEST THEATRICAL SENSATION FOR MANY YEARS ...
> *One word in Shaw's new play will cause sensation.*
> Mr Shaw introduces a certain forbidden word.
> WILL MRS PATRICK CAMPBELL SPEAK IT?
> Has the censor stepped in or will the word spread?
> If he does not forbid it, then anything might happen!
> It is a word which, although held by many to be merely a meaningless vulgarism, is certainly not used in decent society.
> It is a word which the *Daily Sketch* cannot possibly print, and tonight it is to be uttered on the stage. (cited in Huggett, 1969, pp. 127–8)

What was subsequently alluded to by the press as 'SHAW'S BOLD, BAD WORD', 'the Unprintable Swearword', 'THE "LANGWIDGE" OF THE FLOWER GIRL', 'the Word', and numerous other evasions provoked 'a few seconds of stunned disbelieving silence' and then hysterical laughter for at least a minute and a quarter (Huggett, 1969, pp. 136–7). The performance occasioned such headlines as 'THREATS BY DECENCY LEAGUE', 'THEATRE TO BE BOYCOTTED', 'I SEE NO OBJECTION SAYS PRIME MINISTER' and 'SIR HERBERT [Tree] CENSURED BY THEATRE ASSOCIATION' (Huggett, 1969, p. 141). Although the Bishop of Woolwich took the view that 'The Word should be banned,' *bloody* became the catchword of the season (Huggett, 1969, p. 142). Shaw, who had rightly intuited that the Censor would not interfere (having twice passed *bloody* before) commented a week later in a statement for the *Daily News*:

> I have nothing particular to say about Eliza Doolittle's language. ... I do not know anything more ridiculous than the refusal of some newspapers (at several pages' length) to print the word 'bloody', which is in

> common use as an expletive by four-fifths of the English nation, including many highly-educated persons.

Shaw proceeded to note that 'It is, however, a class word' and to congratulate himself on the incongruous juxtaposition of style and content, for the text and stage directions of the crucial delivery in Act III run:

> *LIZA* [with perfectly elegant diction]: Walk! Not bloody likely. [Sensation]. I am going in a taxi.

In the New York performance, however, the word 'failed to cause any stir' (Mencken, 1936, p. 311). Huggett comments that 'the Americans . . . were not in the least shocked by The Word, regarding it as a charming and delightful piece of English slang' (1969, p. 171).

Self-censorship by an author is not usually apparent to the reader, but in the following passage from *The Moon and Sixpence* (1930), Somerset Maugham wryly admits to indulging in it. He has been describing an altercation between his Gauginesque hero, Charles Strickland, and a local bully, Tough Bill:

> Charlie stuck it for a bit, then he stepped forward and just said, 'Get out, you bloody swine'.

Later, the author comes out of hiding and admits:

> Strickland, according to Captain Nichols, did not use exactly the words I have given, but since this book is meant for family reading, I thought it better – at the expense of truth – to put into his mouth language familiar to the domestic circle. (chapter 47)

Looking back over the intervening half century with the benefit of hindsight, we can see that Graves' 'noticeable decline' did not continue long, that 'the habit of swearing' and the use of 'foul language' now thrive with positively indecent health. Both forms are increasingly encountered in public discourse, where they are given considerable publicity. Noted participants of recent years include ex-President Nixon (for his expletives in the Watergate tapes in 1972–3), Princess Anne (for her invitation to the Press to 'Naff off!' in 1982), the English cricket captain, Mike Gatting (for calling a Pakistani umpire a 'bastard' in 1987), Prince Charles (for complaining that English 'is taught so bloody badly' in 1989) and the tennis player, John McEnroe, whose long and shameful record of public obscenity culminated in his being ejected from the Australian Open Championship in 1990 for telling the umpire, amongst other things, to 'fuck off!'

A fair number of these instances could be justified as being expletives uttered in the heat of the moment. But there are plenty of deliberate cases to be found in less predictable locales. As we have seen, few English poets after Rochester dared to use the 'four-letter' words or the crude argot of the street. Of the Modernists, Pound alone ventured into this area, for instance, in this cryptic passage from the 'Pisan Cantos':

> 'wd.' said the guard '*take* every one of them g.d.m.f. generals
> c.s. all of 'em fascists'
>
> (Canto LXXIV)

Although one would have expected writers of anger and robustness like John Osborne, John Braine, Alan Sillitoe, Sylvia Plath and Ted Hughes to have been more daring in their use of what Wordsworth called 'the language of ordinary men', it was, somewhat ironically, Philip Larkin, the shy, withdrawn academic librarian, who modulated his persona to accommodate such startling demotic idioms as:

> They fuck you up, your mum and dad.
> They may not mean to, but they do.
>
> ('This Be The Verse', 1971)

and

> When I see a couple of kids
> And guess he's fucking her and she's
> Taking pills or wearing a diaphragm
> I know this is paradise
>
> ('High Windows', 1967)

We may modify Larkin's ironic observation on 'the sexual revolution' to apply as much to words as to deeds:

> Sexual intercourse began
> In nineteen sixty-three
> (Which was rather late for me) –
> Between the end of the *Chatterley* ban
> And the Beatles' first LP.
>
> ('Annus Mirabilis', 1967)

In his use of the defiant idiom, 'stuff your pension!' in *The Less Deceived* (1955), Larkin is credited with a first recorded instance by the *OEDS*.

Even public academic discourse, normally conducted in a decorously high register, has shown some signs of a lowering of tone. In a letter to the *London Review of Books* (21 November, 1985, p. 4) Professor Terence Hawkes curtly dismissed Professor Graham Hough with the words 'piss off'. In fact, Hawkes' notoriously churlish performance combined cowardice with insult, since his whole letter was, technically, directed to the Editor, who was thereby obliged, amongst other indignities, to 'tell him [Hough] to piss off.' Interestingly, this outrage led to no controversy whatever (over the offending phrase) in England, but did provoke an ironic comment on the lavatorial idiom from a professor in Germany and an ingenious, but slightly specious justification from Brazil: '. . . Hawkes was doing nothing more than altering the level of discourse – varying the code, as it were – in order to undermine the ritual of civilised insults typically exchanged by learned Guardians in their more disputatious moods' (*LRB*, 17 April 1986, p. 4).

Swearing in public is now encountered in press columns (especially those of the British tabloids) far more commonly than half a century ago. A notable outburst was that of the *Daily Mirror* when it castigated Mr Kruschev's hammering the rostrum of the United Nations with the demotic reprimand, 'MR K! DON'T BE SO BLOODY RUDE!' The same paper asked the question 'IS EVERYBODY GOING BLOODY MAD?' in 1974, at the depth of one of Britain's financial crises. 'MURDERING BASTARDS!' was the headline which denounced the assassination of Lord Mountbatten in 1980, while in 1978 the *Evening Standard* reported a message from the Labour Party Conference in the summary terms: 'JIM [CALLAGHAN] TOLD: GET STUFFED.' The Appendices in this book on the language of graffiti and comics, show the same decline. In all, the modern efflorescence has reached the point that many figures in authority, some elected, some accepted and others self-appointed, feel that curbs are necessary. How has this change come about?

It is notable that most of Graves' posited social catalysts are traditional. Indeed, in using the archaisms *pestilence* and *fire from Heaven*, he is almost self-consciously alluding to the traditional kinds of social factors in his explanation, not that these are to be despised. As chapter 6 has shown, war traditionally generates large vocabularies of opprobrium, such as *Hun, Bosch, Yankee, Limey, Gook* etc. Similarly, syphilis and the plague generated *pox, pestilence* etc., set out in figure 9.1; the English Revolution produced *Puritan* and *Cavalier*, and the Russian produced *bolshie* etc. 'Fire from Heaven' has, mercifully, not yet materialized. But when we survey the past half-century, it is notable that – apart from the catalyst of war – few of these factors have had much play. Disease and revolution have left few semantic memorials: people do not use *flu!* or *counter-revolutionary!* as imprecations, in the way that their ancestors used *pox!* or *radical!* The nightmare of nuclear war and the spread of AIDS have alike left the idioms of swearing unaffected.[1] Instead, new

literal sense	*word*	*imprecatory sense*
1303	pestilence	1386
1350	pocky	1598
1398	pestilential	1531
1542	pestiferous	1458
1548	plague	1566
1550	pox	1588
1568	pest	1570
1604	plaguey	1574

Notes

1 The main infestations of the Plague occurred in the fourteenth century (especially 1348–9, 1360 and 1379) and in 1664–6. These devastations yielded such uses as *the death* and *the great death*. The *Black Death* appears to have been 'introduced into English history by a Mrs. Penrose in 1823'.[O] Syphilis is believed to have been introduced into Europe in 1493.

2 The most interesting feature of the table is the general concentration of imprecatory usages between 1531 and 1588, even though some of the literal applications are two and a half centuries older. Two terms, curiously, generate an imprecatory sense *prior* to their literal sense. They are *pestiferous*, in which the imprecatory sense precedes the literal by almost a century, and *plaguey*, which shows a similar anticipation by some thirty years. Both these features suggest that the plague became such a fashionable topic in swearing that the emotive use became dominant.

FIGURE 9.1 The semantic correlatives of the plague and the pox.

factors to do with broadcasting and film, new terms deriving from political and racial confrontations, have come into play. As the previous catalogue of notable participants indicates, swearing and foul language have become news. One assumes that earlier generations of public figures and reporters alike would have been less inclined to indulge in and publicize breaches of traditional verbal etiquette. Furthermore, the upsurge of swearing has occurred, not simultaneously with praying, but as a virtual consequence of the decline of religion as a vital force in most people's lives.

THE RELAXATION OF CENSORSHIP

As previous chapters have shown, restraints on swearing have a long history, going back to the Saxon kings. Subversion and profanity on the stage were subsequently policed by the Master of the Revels, institutionalized in the reign of Henry VII. The Licensing Act of 1737 (by which virtually absolute powers were invested in the office of the

Lord Chamberlain via 'the Examiner of the Stage') derived directly from attacks by Fielding on Walpole at the Little Theatre in the Haymarket earlier that year. Powerful initiatives to limit censorship were made in 1832 and 1843, resulting in the directive that the Lord Chamberlain was forbidden to withold his licence unless on the grounds of 'the preservation of good manners, decorum or of the public peace'. Petitions by dramatic authors of note, made in 1865 and 1907, resulted in greater flexibility, but the responsibilities of the Lord Chamberlain for theatrical censorship were abolished only in the Theatres Act of 1968.

In the past century censorship has been exercized to prevent the publication of a considerable number of works, including Charles Baudelaire's *Fleurs du Mal* (1857), James Joyce's *Ulysses* (1922), Henry Miller's *Tropic of Cancer* (1934) and *Tropic of Capricorn* (1939) as well as D. H. Lawrence's *The Rainbow* (1915) and his *Lady Chatterley's Lover* (1928), to name the more obvious *causes célèbres*. (The exhibition of Lawrence's scandalous nude paintings was closed and the paintings confiscated by the police in 1929.) Censorship has increasingly been less concerned with ideological or political issues and has focussed on the question of 'obscenity' (technically 'obscene libel' or 'matter tending to deprave or corrupt'), usually taken to mean the explicit depiction of sex and use of 'dirty' or taboo words. This notion of 'obscenity' was so broad in definition that, as Shaw wrote in a letter in 1928, 'There is not a work of literature in existence which Counsel would defend as being outside that all-embracing definition' (Moore, 1955, p. 47). It derived from a key judgement by Lord Chief Justice Cockburn in 1868:

> . . . the test of obscenity is this, whether the tendency of the matter charged as obscenity is to deprave and corrupt those whose minds are open to such immoral influences and into whose hands a publication of this sort may fall. (cited in Moore, 1955, p. 46)

'I feel that one has to fight for the phallic reality, as against the non-phallic cerebration unrealities,' wrote Lawrence in a letter to Witter Bynner (13 March 1928). 'So I wrote my novel, which I want to call *John Thomas and Lady Jane*', he continued, somewhat naively. 'But that I have to submerge into a subtitle, and call it *Lady Chatterley's Lover*.' Subsequently, in *A Propos of Lady Chatterley's Lover* (1930), he wrote: 'If I use the taboo words, there is a reason. We shall never free the phallic reality from the "uplift" taint till we give it its own phallic language, and use the obscene words' (Moore, 1955, p. 267). When he was half way through the novel he described it to Kotelianski as 'the most improper novel ever written' (*Collected Letters*, 1028) but always denied that it was pornography. The early publishing history and critical responses are revealingly contradictory. The book was published privately in Florence in July 1928, and by April of the following year five pirated editions had appeared all over the Continent and in America. Under the headline 'Famous Author's Shameful Book', an unsigned review in *John Bull* (20 October 1928) denounced the work as wicked, decadent, corrupt and tainted by its foreign origin:

> ... the most evil outpouring that has ever besmirched the literature of our country.
>
> The sewers of French pornography would be dragged in vain to find a parallel in beastliness. The creations of muddy-minded perverts, peddled in the back-street bookstalls of Paris, are prudish by comparison. (cited in Draper, 1970, p. 278)

The onslaught continued, mocking 'the fetid masterpiece of this sex-sodden genius', 'the abysm of filth', 'the foulest book in English literature', culminating in the call that 'The circulation in this country of *Lady Chatterley's Lover* must be stopped' (cited in Draper, 1970, p. 280). The book was suppressed for immorality, and though Lawrence attempted an expurgated version, he found it impossible: 'I might as well try to clip my own nose into shape with scissors. The book bleeds' (cited in Draper, 1970, p. 21).

In 1959 the Obscenity Act was revised in various important respects. It required that the book in question had to be regarded 'as a whole' and that the courts had to listen to the evidence of experts who could be called to justify the work as being 'for the public good on the grounds that it is in the interests of science, literature, art or learning' (cited in Rolph, 1961, p. 4). However, the old core was retained, since the book was 'deemed to be obscene if its effect ... [is] such as to tend to deprave and corrupt persons who are likely ... to read it' (cited in Rolph, 1961, p. 10).

These became the main issues in the pivotal trial of the unexpurgated edition of *Lady Chatterley's Lover* (*Regina v. Penguin Books Ltd.*) in 1960. The fairly length and expensive proceedings in this important test-case, designed to bring matters to a head, were mainly concerned with the artistic suitability of terms denoting the genitalia and copulation. Whereas in the case against the paintings in 1929, expert defence witnesses such as Augustus John, Sir William Orpen, Arnold Bennett, Glyn Philpot and others had not been allowed to testify, many influential literary figures were able to give their views in the *Chatterley* trial. They included E. M. Forster, Richard Hoggart, Helen Gardner, Raymond Williams, Graham Hough, Kenneth Muir and the Bishop of Woolwich. In all some thirty-five defence witnesses were called. The outcome of the trial hinged more on the weight of these critical and literary expert witnesses than on points of strict law.

Aldous Huxley reflected in *The Genius and the Goddess* on the problematic relationship between 'four-letter words' and 'four-letter acts': 'In silence, an act is an act is an act. Verbalized and discussed, it becomes an ethical problem, a *casus belli*. . . . (1955, p. 103). Much comment was expended both in the early criticism and in the trial on the notorious 'four-letter' words, especially when used by the gamekeeper Mellors in dialect:

> 'Th'art good cunt, though, aren't ter? Best bit o' cunt left on earth. When ter likes! When tha'rt willin'!'
>
> 'What is cunt?' she said.
>
> 'An' doesn't ter know? Cunt! It's thee down theer; an' what I get when I'm i'side thee, and what tha gets when I'm i'side thee; it's a' as it is, all on't.'
>
> 'All on't,' she teased. 'Cunt! It's like fuck then.'
>
> 'Nay nay! Fuck's only what you do. Animals fuck. But cunt's a lot more than that. It's thee, dost see: an' tha'rt a lot besides an animal, aren't ter? – even ter fuck? Cunt! Eh, that's the beauty o' thee, lass!' (1960, p. 185)

F. R. Leavis, though a champion of Lawrence, wrote (after the trial) of 'turning on the dialect', of its being used as 'a way of putting over the "four-letter words" – of trying to make the idea of their being redeemed for non-obscene and undefiant , or "normal", use look less desperate', trenchantly concluding, 'I find these performances on Mellors's part insufferable' (Coombes, 1973, pp. 416–17). During the trial Graham Hough also criticized this part of the text, saying 'I don't think that this passage comes off at all', whereas Helen Gardner took the wider view that 'by the end Lawrence has gone very far . . . to redeem this word from low and vulgar associations'. Richard Hoggart brought out the paradox that 'They are used, or seem to me to be used, very freely indeed, far more freely than many of us know', concluding that in the course of the book 'they were being progressively purified as they were used' (Rolph, 1961, pp. 49, 60, 98, 99). (He was the only participant to use the word *fuck* personally.) Perhaps the most poignant view (invoked more than once in the trial) was the profound and sympathetic judgement of Yeats when he wrote in a letter (in 1933) that 'the coarse language of the one, accepted by both, becomes a forlorn poetry uniting their solitudes, something ancient, humble and terrible' (Draper, 1970, p. 298).

Yet even Lawrence, who wrote (in *Collected Letters*, 967) of his 'positive belief that the phallus is a great sacred image' and of the necessity to use 'the obscene words', seems to have been reticent at the most crucial union, in chapter xvi. Here he writes symbolically of 'Burning out the shames, the deepest, oldest shames, in the most secret places,' of 'the sensual flame [that] pressed through her bowels and breast' to 'the core of the physical jungle, the last and deepest recess of organic shame. The phallos alone could explore it.' Furthermore, 'She had to be a passive, consenting thing, like a slave, a physical slave' (1960, pp. 258–9). John Sparrow, in a noted article in *Encounter* 101 (February, 1962), subsequently caused something of a furore, questioning the acuteness of some of the 'expert' witnesses and accusing Lawrence of 'This failure of integrity, this fundamental dishonesty' (p. 41) by arguing cogently from the passage that 'The practice approved by Lawrence is that known in English law as buggery . . . [of which] the "full offence" involves *penetratio per anum*' (p. 36). Andrew Schonfield had previously argued that such an interpretation seemed 'a reasonable guess' (*Encounter*, 96, September, 1961, pp. 63–4). Frank Kermode later concurred, implying that there had been a conspiracy of reticence on the point: 'The fact that it describes anal intercourse was long ignored; nobody mentioned it at the 1960 trial . . . As in *Women in Love*, the climactic sexual act is an act of buggery, conceived as a burning out of shame' (1973, p. 130). The upshot of the trial, however, was that Penguin Books was acquitted, but without costs. Five years later, *The Rainbow* was prescribed for school study.

Some would say that this judgement was a 'watershed' which made possible an atmosphere of moral licentiousness now known by the journalistic cliché of 'the permissive society'. Be that as it may, within a few years there was a radical change in the freedom of language and sexuality depicted in publications and public entertainment. Some of the newly emergent organs were unambiguously pornographic, advertising their wares under such titles as *Screw, Ban, Orgy, Pleasure, Suck, Cunts and Grunts, The Whipping Post* and *Kinky Komiks*. Kenneth Tynan's dionysiac celebration 'Oh! Calcutta!' featured mass stage nudity and simulated stage sex for the first recorded time.[2] The show became the longest-running musical on Broadway, and was seen by some 85 million people in productions all over the world between 1969 and 1989. Tynan insisted that there would be 'no crap about art or redeeming literary merit: this show will be expressly designed to titillate, in the most elegant and outré way'; it was to be a 'cool, witty and sophisticated tease'; however, for legal reasons, 'indecent exposure is out, and so are 4-letter words' (Tynan, 1987, pp. 278–9). Tynan also provoked a scandal through the first broadcast utterance of *fuck* on the BBC (in 1965). Asked in an interview if he would allow a play in which there was sexual intercourse on the stage to be put on at the National Theatre, he replied 'Oh I think so, certainly,' adding mischievously, 'I doubt if there are very many rational people in this world to whom the word "fuck" is particularly diabolical or revolting or totally forbidden.' Some of the ensuing barrage of headlines ran: 'That Word on TV'; 'Insult to Womanhood'; 'Is this Moral?'; 'the War on BBCnity' and 'Sack 4-letter Tynan' (Tynan, 1987, pp. 236–7). Others regarded it as an utterance of considerable éclat: 'As becomes a great pioneer,' wrote Ashley Montagu, 'his stock has considerably risen in the world' (1973, p. 312). Indeed, for a short while his name became synonymous with the word, so that people would say, jocularly, 'Shut the Tynan door!', just as a previous generation had said 'Not Pygmalion likely!', alluding to Eliza Doolittle's famous sanguinary outburst.

We may assume that in earlier periods, Celtic, Germanic, Roman and Greek, both these 'innovations' of sexual licence would have been regarded as unremarkable. Indeed, W. H. Parker, in his anthology *Priapea: Poems for a Phallic God* (1988), has shown that virtually every major Roman author composed one or two poems celebrating the phallic deity. While considering other cultural perspectives, we should recall the highly public totemic figure of the naked Cerne Abbas giant, complete with rampant penis, cut into the turf of a Dorset hillside in prehistoric times. Regrettably, we do not know how the society which created (and presumably worshipped) him spoke of him.

So far as general parlance in the 1960s is concerned, the so-called 'four-letter words' were not audible on the lips of the populace with obviously greater currency than previously, even though they were certainly articulated with greater frequency on film and television. Traditional attitudes still prevailed in many quarters, and sanctions continued to be exacted for violations of propriety.

By the end of the 1960s there were clear signs of hostility to the freedom of the post-*Chatterley* years. The *New York Times* of 1 April 1969 carried an editorial commenting on 'the *reductio ad obscenum* of the theatrical art.' 'Obscenity now struts openly in the market place,' wrote Edward J. Mishan in an article, 'Making the World Safe for Pornography'.[3] The expansion of the market was reflected in the growth of such related terms as *porn, porno, pornobiography, pornocrat, pornogram, porno-film, porno-magazine, pornomania, pornophile* and *porny* in the course of the 1960s. The focal point was the trial (in the summer of 1971) of the magazine *Oz* on a charge of obscenity. The organ was openly 'alternative' in advocating sex and drugs as forms of liberation, as well as satirical (and fairly subversive) in carrying on extensive campaigns discrediting the police, the judiciary and the establishment in general. 'The statement of our values is "dope, rock'n'roll and fucking in the streets". We know what we mean by this even if straights don't,' wrote Warren Hague in *Oz 42*, p. 54. In an article entitled 'Here Come De Judge' in *Oz 38* by one 'Ned Ludd', the writer focussed on the supposed inherent injustice of 'the system': 'Such however is the skill of legal brains that 90% of the actions of the ruling bastards to steal the wealth from the workers is law . . .' (p. 22). There is, furthermore, systematic complicity between 'his lordship mafia in ermine' and the 'piggies': 'Pigs are sexually repressed, politically ignorant, psychologically stunted persons who do a very good job being atomations [sic] of state repression' (p. 23).

The prosecution focussed on *Oz 28*, the 'Schoolkids Issue'. In an interesting article covering all aspects of the case, Keith Botsford summarized the contents, among which were:

> *pp. 8–9*, continued guerrilla action [against schools] with cartoons whose balloons include 'cunt' and 'bollocks'. *pp. 10–11*, school atrocities including notorious portrait of schoolmaster and schoolboy post fellatio (?) . . . *pp. 14–15*, exams, sex freedom and Rupert Bear in congress with Gypsy Granny.[4]

Few were entirely surprised when a verdict of guilty was returned, but the severity of the sentences, in which Judge Michael Argyle, QC, meted out a fifteen-month prison term for the Editor, Richard Neville (with twelve and nine months respectively for his associates) provoked outrage from a variety of quarters, including several authors and commentators not sympathetic with *Oz* itself. Although Mrs Mary Whitehouse took the view that 'It is a very good thing that the line has been drawn,' Kenneth Tynan saw the judgement in terms of a different metaphor: 'The battle has been joined between Judge Argyle's England and a free England.' (These were quoted on the front page of *Oz 42*.) Although the sentences were revoked by the Court of Appeal, many took the view that the trial was in essence more political than linguistic, in view of the essential confusion over the legal definition of 'obscenity' and the lack of prosecution of the rampant pornography all around.

Botsford, however, concludes that 'The real martyrs' were not the editors, but 'the words we use, which in the Ozzian mouth become meaningless' (1971, p. 72).

The *Oz* trial was significant in that it encapsulated the conflict of forces and social attitudes involved in extremes of free expression. The swashbuckling libertarianism of the early 1960s received something of a rebuff as traditional attitudes of propriety reasserted themselves. Lawrence Durrell's Preface to an American edition of *Lady Chatterley's Lover* in 1968 even employed the reverse code forms 'kcuf', 'tnuc', 'kcirp' and 'sllab' for the taboo words. In the same period an ode published in the Cambridge literary magazine *Granta* beginning 'God, God, the silly sod' led to the Editor, Mark Boxer, being sent down for a spell and the magazine suppressed. In 1975 Peregrine Worsthorne uttered a four-letter word on television and was temporarily suspended from duties on *The Daily Telegraph*. In a very interesting article, 'Four-letter words and the *OED*' (*TLS*, 13 October, 1972, p. 1233) Robert Burchfield traces the changing attitudes prior to the inclusion of these terms in the *Supplement*. It includes a polite exchange of letters in 1969 between *Oz* and OUP on the 'curious omission' of the word *fuck* from the *Shorter Oxford Dictionary*. In 'Linguistic Milestones' he recounts the following anecdote:

> But when the time came for the verification in the Bodleian Library of some of the richer uses of the words *cunt* and *fuck* I was told by the library research assistant at the time that she had had 'quite enough of the kind of filth found in Partridge and other dictionaries of slang'. It seemed tactful not to insist, and I therefore had the doubtful privilege of looking out the material myself. (1989, p. 16)

THE REBIRTH OF AMERICAN SWEARING

In the United States the change in the conventions of swearing has been swift and dramatic. In the course of a mere two decades, from 1950 to 1970, a radical shift in attitudes occurred, marked by spectacular and often scandalous instances of public profanity. Although there were fewer institutionalized restraints in the past (since the American Constitution underwrites freedom of speech), what can only be called a Puritan survival seems to have left its mark in attitudes towards swearing. Earlier chapters have alluded to the general censorship of *cock*, which seems to have been largely unconscious. Few of the 'big six' are easily traceable before the Second World War, while *bugger*, *bloody* and *bastard* have never found much of a foothold across the Atlantic. Mencken saw the taboos of Victorian England as having become even more severe in America, where Noah Webster went to the extreme of bowdlerizing the Bible. This amounted to replacing traditional euphemisms by more recent. Thus *stones* (testicles) became *peculiar members* and *in the belly* became *in embryo*, while *to give suck* became *to nourish* and *whore* became *lewd woman* or *prostitute*. Mencken notes that 'He got rid of *womb* by various circumlocutions, and expunged many verses altogether . . .' (1936, p. 303).

In a lengthy discussion under the arch heading of 'Forbidden Words', Mencken included *cock, bull, leg, bitch, ram, boar, stallion, buck, sow, ass, castrate, womb, nipple, pregnant, whore, virgin* and *seduce*. The removal of such specific words necessitated the substitution of bizarrely vague euphemisms, such as *inexpressibles* for *pantaloons*, *blood-poison* or *blood-disease* for *syphilis*, *public comfort station* for *lavatory* and *cone* for *nipple*. On the semantic antics used to avoid *stomach*, he wittily observed that the word '. . . then under ban in England, was transformed, by some unfathomable magic, into a euphemism for the whole region from the nipples to the pelvic arch' (1936, p. 302). As a consequence of these attitudes, he pointed out, '. . . we have nothing properly describable as a vocabulary of indecency. Our maid-of-all-work in that department is *son-of-a-bitch* . . .' (1936, p. 317).

The influence of Hollywood has become a dominant factor, initially for restraint, but subsequently for licence. In 1934 a self-regulatory code of ethics known as the Production Code was drawn up by Will H. Hays and put into strict effect by Joseph I. Breen. Excluded themes were revenge in modern times, illegal drug traffic, miscegenation and sex perversion. 'Excessive and lustful kissing, lustful embracing, suggestive postures and gestures are not to be shown,' the Code continued. 'Pointed profanity (this includes the word God, Lord, Jesus, Christ – unless used reverently – Hell, S.O.B., damn, Gawd), or other profane or vulgar expressions, however used, is forbidden' (Katz, 1979, p. 934). Breen's strict execution of the Code resulted in his name being given to the rule whereby 'if a man and a woman were on a bed together, at least two feet had to be on the floor at all times. (It was a standing joke that this rule only encouraged perversion.)' (Latham, 1972, p. 152). He rejected the script of *Raffles* because it was 'a violation of the Production Code' in that it showed 'a criminal, who is permitted to outsmart the police, and go off "scot free".' In sanitizing the script, he further recommended that the producer should 'eliminate the expression . . . "Good Lord"' (Latham, 1972, pp. 234–5). However, Rhett Butler's famous parting line in *Gone With the Wind* (1939), 'Frankly, dear, I don't give a damn,' was a notable breach of the Code which was eventually sanctioned.

Within the cultural institution a régime of rigorous self-censorship originally obtained. There was a rigid code of 'family decency' imposed by the film moguls such as Louis B. Mayer. As he pronounced patronizingly to Hedy Lamarr:

> We have an obligation to the audience – millions of families. We make clean pictures . . . of course . . . if you like to make love . . . fornicate . . . screw your leading man in the dressing room, that's your business. But in front of the camera, gentility. You hear, gentility. (cited in Latham, 1972, p. 154)

Mayer concluded this conversation with a revealing comment on Miss Lamarr's talents: '. . . you have a bigger chest than I thought! You'd be surprised how tits figure in a girl's career.' Mayer's oscillations of register, revealed in his gauche mixture of prissiness and coarseness in *make love, fornicate, screw, chest* and *tits*, show his essential hypocrisy.

The erosion of the Production Code was initiated by competition with television, which had started to be broadast in the United States in 1939 and which had expanded to twelve channels by 1952. Since television was essentially a family medium, it was constrained by even more rigorous prohibitions against nudity, profanity and immorality than film. As cinema audiences started to decline in the face of the competition of television, so film-makers saw their opportunity to make films which were 'alternative', 'adult' entertainment. Furthermore, advertisers could pressurize television networks to keep their programmes 'clean', withdrawing their revenues if there was no co-operation, but had no such influence over film-makers. Consequently, all the television networks now have in-house censors (termed the Standards and Practices Office) whose function it is to eliminate or ration 'offensive' material, whereas the film studios are no longer bound by any such 'Production Code'. The divergence between the two media has accordingly increased.

As Partridge observed, 'War is the greatest excitant of vocabulary'. J. L. Dillard certainly regards the Second World War as a significant factor in the acceptance of slang and expletives.[5]

> The big watershed insofar as explicit terminology was concerned was probably World War II; many of America's readers were shocked at the realistic reporting of serviceman's talk in Norman Mailer's *The Naked*

> *and the Dead* (1948) and in James Jones's *From Here to Eternity* (1951). (Dillard, 1985, p. 213)

The liberation from censorship has been surprisingly slow, given the American belief in individual liberty, the glorification of the maverick and the constitutional endorsement of freedom of speech. When, for example, the Third edition of *Webster* came out in 1961, the year after the *Chatterley* trial in England, it sought to justify *ain't* and *floozy* on the grounds that they were standard in American speech, but excluded *fuck* and *cunt*, reportedly because the publishers feared adverse repercussions and boycotts. On these developments, see Gary Jennings (1965, p. 116).

However, in the course of the 1960s, the floodgates opened. The various libertarian movements journalistically termed the Hippies and the Flower Children consciously rejected and even violated the traditional values of family decency of middle America by advocating a lifestyle of dyonisiac sexuality, drug-taking and a general freedom from bourgeois restraint. The war in Vietnam acted as a major catalyst in social division, provoking violent protests in which the liberation of the sexual vocabulary proved to be a corollary, and many confrontations between the upholders of order and the shakers of the foundations were marked by verbal slogans such as 'Fuck the Pigs!' The politicization of foul language was one of the tactics used by radical students at Berkeley, resulting in the so-called Filthy Speech Movement, the successor of the Free Speech Movement: students voiced and published obscenities as a form of protest. Commenting on the new vocabulary of protest in an article entitled 'the Rhetoric of Violence', E. Goodheart wittily observed: 'The operative words are "pig", "bullshit", "motherfucker". It is the language of left militant students. . . . The "alma-mater fuckers". . .'[6] *Pig*, which has a surprisingly long semantic history as a slang term for a policeman, being recorded in this sense from *c.*1785, came to be used for virtually any unsympathetic authoritarian figure and then virtually any (male) figure in authority. It was then appropriated by the feminist movement to pillory the obdurately sexist stereotype, the *male chauvinist pig*, recorded from *c.*1970.[7]

Needless to say, these developments had certain consequences in court proceedings wherein jurists were required to make awkward judgements, such as the following:

> For while the particular four-letter word being litigated here ['Fuck the draft'] is perhaps more distasteful than most others of the genre, it is nevertheless often true that one man's vulgarity is another man's lyric. (*Cohen v. California*, 403 US. 15, 25, 1971)

This slogan initially led to the conviction of the man who was displaying it on the back of his jacket in the Los Angeles courthouse, but an appeal court voted 5 to 4 to overturn the verdict.

The Black Consciousness movement also mobilized a language of animus, mainly in slogans. The 'alternative' newspaper, *The Black Panther* of 14 November 1970 carried the galvanizing front-page headline: 'DEATH TO THE FASCIST PIGS/SHOOT TO KILL.' The metaphor was developed quite bizarrely:

> ... the so-called White House building should be seized and all of the pigs who presently occupy it should be taken out on the lawn, and we should set up pits – bar-b-que pits. And we should take long stakes and drive them through their bodies and put them on those stakes, put some charcoal down, put a match to it and have a massive, pig bar-b-que session. ...[8]

An equally virulent combination of the antithetical types of sloganeering insult and 'poetic' form was 'TCB' by Sonia Sanchez, which consisted of three-line 'verses' demonstrating the following 'incremental repetition' (as it is fashionably called):

wite/motha/fucka
wite/motha/fucka
wite/motha/fucka
whitey

The burden is repeated six times, the only significant variation being a sequence of insulting terms (following *whitey*) taken from the argot of the street, namely *ofay, devil, pig, cracker* and *honky*. The ending is a rather hollow call for collaboration: 'now. that it's all sed / let's get to work.' (*Mother-fucker* appears to have developed initially in negro communities, proliferated in the Vietnam War and then spread across America socially and geographically with the returning troops.)

This idiom may owe something to modern American forms of verbal duelling which show affinities to flyting. Known variously as 'playing the dozens', 'sounding' and 'signifying', the genre, which is largely confined to usage among black male youths, has been researched for the past half century. In his substantial article, 'Rules for Ritual Insults', William Labov observes that 'the activity is remarkably similar throughout the various black communities' (1972, p. 307). Instances typically involve sexual insults directed at the victim or hearer's mother, using a concentrate of vigorous metaphor and savagely chauvinistic humour, often set in couplets:

> I hate to talk about your mother, she's a good old soul
> She got a ten-ton pussy and a rubber asshole
> (Labov, 1972, p. 307)

Others rely solely on the black humour of a pun: Your mother's like a police station – dicks going in and out all the time. (Labov, 1972, p. 320)

'Many sounds *are* obscene in the full sense of the word,' Labov continues. 'The speaker uses as many 'bad' words and images as possible – that is, subject to taboo and moral reprimand in adult middle-class society' (1972, p. 324). Though many of these features might apply to the flytings of Dunbar and Kennedy, there is no sophisticated range of register and little use of blasphemy.

In 1975 there began a significant case deriving from a Citizen's Complaint against the Pacifica Foundation Radio Station WBAI, New York, concerning the broadcast in the early afternoon of a comedy routine called 'Filthy Words'. It was a monologue by 'George Carlin, Occupation: Foole', consisting of a generally humorous but designedly shocking discourse on the words *shit, piss, fuck, cunt, cocksucker, mother-fucker, fart, turd, twat* and (less obviously) *tits*. Much of the humour arose from the terms being applied to incongruous circumstances: 'Who are you? I am FUCK. (laughter) FUCK OF THE MOUNTAIN. Tune in again next week to FUCK OF THE MOUNTAIN. (laughter)'. (One does not know whether the 'laughter' was in the script or the transcript.) The case was of particular interest since freedom of speech is protected by the First Amendment to the US Constitution, and previous judgements had diverged, some courts holding that obscene speech was not constitutionally protected, others, such as that involved in the case of the jacket bearing the legend 'Fuck the Draft' (*Cohen v. California*, cited above), ruling that the utterance was protected speech. The upshot was that the complaint was upheld by the Supreme Court.

From the early 1970s the popular music world has been augmented by the genre of 'rap', a predominantly black form of social and political commentary which is rhythmically accentuated and uses markedly strong language. Fascinatingly, the present meaning is taken as an extension of *rap* in the sense of 'to strike smartly'. As far back as the sixteenth century the word took on the sense of 'to utter sharp words or an oath' ('I am wont sometime to rap out an oath,' confessed Wyatt in 1541[O]). By the eighteenth century a related sense of 'to swear' was in vogue: 'I scorn to rap against a lady,' says a character in Fielding's *Amelia* in 1752.[O] It developed related northern dialect senses including 'to speak angrily and quickly; to use bad language' (*EDD*). Contemporary rap artists who can be included in this category are 'ice T', 'easy E' and 'LL cool J'. A sample from 'easy E' runs:

> I said 'Fuck it, I know what should be done.
> Just pull your panties down and I'll fuck the biggest one.
> And then I'll get the other pussy and put it in the freezer,
> So I can always have my own hostesser.'[9]

Though not common, such material can be heard on many radio stations. Today many American films rated as 'family entertainment' contain a degree of swearing which shows a total rejection of the old studio constraints. The Production Code, in response to pressures for social change, Supreme Court decisions concerning obscenity, and civil liberties groups, was revised in the course of the 1960s. The remarkable verbal frankness of Edward Albee's *Who's Afraid of Virginia Woolf?* (1966) led to substantial relaxations in the Code and subsequently to the present 'rating' system. The spate of Vietnam war films such as *Apocalypse Now!* (1979), *Platoon* (1987) and *Full Metal Jacket* (1988) was marked by a verbal bombardment quite as devastating as the fire-power of weaponry. Swearing and soldiership have an ancient association, borne out in Shakespeare's line from 'the seven ages of man' speech in *As You Like It* describing the young blood as 'Full of strange oaths and bearded like the pard' (II. vii. 150). But many other modern films, such as Milos Forman's version of the musical 'Hair' (1979) and the sado-masochistic extravaganza, *Blue Velvet* (1986) have been characterized by gratuitously strong language. National varieties of swearing are often exploited opportunistically for comic purposes. A signal example occurred in the film *A Fish Called Wanda* (1989), in this highly caricatured exchange between Otto, an American, and Archie, a very English solicitor:

> *Otto* You pompous, stuck-up, snot-nosed, English, giant twerp, scum-bag, fuck-face, dick-head, arsehole!
> *Archie* How very interesting. You are a real vulgarian, aren't you?

So far as American drama is concerned, the pattern of 'verbal liberation' has been more gradual. The aforesaid major milestone, Edward Albee's *Who's Afraid of Virginia Woolf?* (1966), had less of a following on the stage than on the screen. However, a powerful, but less subtle torrent of 'verbal copulation' occurred in David Mamet's play *Glengarry Glen Ross* (1983). Set in a real estate office, it contained many exchanges such as the following, in which a newcomer is introduced to the office argot:

Williamson . . . my job is to marshall the leads.
Levene Marshall the leads . . . marshall the leads? What the fuck, what bus did *you* get off, we're here to fucking *sell. Fuck* marshalling the leads. What the fuck talk is that? Where did you learn that? In school . . .?

(Scene i. 11. 95–100)

By the end of the play, Williamson is as fluent in the copulatory idiom as the other characters. 'There is, however, very little profanity and little explicitly sexual talk on network television, and virtually none in movies rated "G" or "PG",' observes J. L. Dillard, who continues,

> Nevertheless, the four-letter words, known to virtually everyone over the age of eight but not generally used in "mixed company" . . . are not blatantly imposed upon the public ear. Nevertheless, there has been a striking increase in the public use of relatively explicit terms for bodily functions, apart from the taboo words. (1985, p. 213)

It is perhaps ironic that the most spectacular incident of swearing of recent times should have involved, not a radical nor a consciousness raiser nor a feminist, but an American President.

NOTES

1 Apart from the unsympathetic styling of AIDS as 'the gay plague', virtually no derogatory names (along the lines of *poxed* and *pestilential*) seem to have emerged. The euphemistic abbreviation *PWAs* (for People With AIDS), invented at a convention at Denver, Colorado, in 1983, has been equally ignored.

2 The name of the show was a pun on the saying of a French surrealist painter: 'Oh quel cul que t'as!' ('Oh what an arse you have!'). For an interesting contemporary reaction, see John Weightman's article, 'Flashing the Old Job' in *Encounter*, October 1970, pp. 38–40.

3 In *Encounter*, March 1972, p. 11. The number contains four interesting and topical articles on 'Sex and Culture'.

4 'The Innocence of *Oz*', *Encounter*, November 1971, p. 68. See also Tony Palmer, *The Trials of Oz* (London: Blond and Briggs, 1971).

5 A considerable explorer of underworld argots, David W. Maurer, traced developments between the wars in his article, 'Language and the Sex Revolution: World War I through World War II' in *American Speech* 51 (1976), pp. 5–24.

6 E. Goodheart, 'The Rhetoric of Violence', *The Nation*, 6 April 1970, p. 399.

7 The rapid extension of *pig* in the 1960s to apply to virtually any male in authority or exhibiting undesirable political attitudes can be paralleled by *fascist* in earlier times and *racist* in later.

8 M. J. L. (Melvin J. Lasky), 'In the margin: A Reading of *The Black Panther*', *Encounter*, January 1971, pp. 92–4.

9 In June, 1990 an American rap group, '2 Live Crew', were arrested by a Florida sheriff on charges of obscenity. Their album, 'As Nasty As They Wanna Be,' carried the warning 'Explicit Language Contained' and included numbers with titles such as 'Bad Ass Bitch' and 'Get The Fuck Out of My House (Bitch)'.

10
Sexuality in Swearing

He is a schrewed byche
In feyth, I trow he be a wych.

*EE Misc, c.*1500

Language is the most intense and stubborn fortress of sexist assumptions, [which] crudely enshrines the ancient bias against women.

Susan Sontag

A phallocentric cockocracy.

Gary Taylor

Women are now talking seriously dirty.

Rosalind Coward

THE issue of sexism or sexual categories in swearing invites two perspectives, namely an analysis of modern idioms and a study of the historical evolution of the word-field relating to the categorization of woman. As was mentioned in the Introduction, the starting point for such a discussion lies in the considerable amount of 'consciousness-raising' in feminist circles in recent years concerning sexism in swearing. This was part of a broader debate centred on the view of language as a male-derived system of chauvinist bias, which is, therefore, equally open to semantic engineering by chauvinists. The point is articulated neatly, but somewhat glibly, by Simone de Beauvoir: '[Language] is inherited from a masculine society, and it contains many male prejudices. . . . Women simply have to steal the instrument; they don't have to break it, or try *a priori*, to make it something totally different. Steal it and use it for their own good.'[1] As Gary Taylor's mischievous parody in the epigraphs shows, it is a view which can be, perhaps deservedly, travestied for its simplistic notion of language as no more than a mechanical cultural artefact. On swearing the general feminist view is that, since language is generated in a 'patriarchal' or 'phallocratic' dispensation, there has developed, especially in male swearing, a prevalence of the terms of feminine anatomy, such as *cunt* and *tit*.[2] This aspect forms the theme of the latter part of this discussion.

What has been less closely examined is whether, in general terms, these derogatory words, as well as *bitch* and *cow*, have greater currency or potency than the equivalent male terms *prick* and *balls*, *pig* and *swine*. The discussion should, properly, include both the way that gender terms (such as *bitch* and *pig*) are used, as well as neutral terms, such as *moron* and *bastard*. Accordingly, figure 10.1, 'Gender in Swearing', explores the distribution of categories in the main terms of vehement personal abuse.

This field reveals the interesting distributional dynamic that the great majority of terms, from whatever provenance, are applied exclusively to the male sex. (It is true, of course, that until comparatively recently, most of the words in question were used almost entirely by men.) This currency is particularly paradoxical in the genital area, where gender of origin and application do not relate at all. It turns out that it is only in the animal category that origin and application follow each other logically. These imbalances in the origin and application of terms create what can be termed 'lexical gaps', which can be as revealing as lexical concentrations. In the general category, obviously *bugger* and *sod*[*omite*] are determined by sexual role, but, on the other hand, *bastard* and *fucker* need not be exclusively male. The other curious point is that no term in the field can be used of either sex, with the possible exception of *pig*, and then only in the context of eating. It is also generally true that all the terms in the genital category have developed quite a strong sense of 'a worthless person' or 'fool'. In this respect, it is worth noting that *prat* had an old slang sense of 'arse' or 'buttocks', though it subsequently developed the same anatomical ambiguity as exists in the modern usage of *fanny*.[3]

Thus far the discussion has dealt only with the distribution or application of terms. The aspect of 'potency', or the 'wounding capacity' of these insults, is, of course, also pertinent, but is too problematic and filled with variables for any generalizations to be made. Some would place *cunt* at the acme of insult and affront, others *bastard*, but most would concede that context, tone, social codes and degree of deliberation would be the crucial factors. The form of words 'You old bastard!' could convey hatred, envy, even affection.

The issues are complex, since there are conflicting criteria. One has to balance intensity of insult against range. For instance, *cunt*, *tit* and *bitch*, all feminine-derived, are obviously more potent than the singular

	Gender of terms			Application of terms		
	male	*female*	*indeterminate*	*used of male*	*used of female*	*used of either sex*
genital						
	prick			X		
		cunt		X		
		twat		X		
	pillock			X		
anatomical						
		tit		X		
			arsehole	X		
excretory						
			shit	X		
			turd	X		
			fart	X		
imbecilic						
			idiot	X		
			imbecile	X		
			moron	X		
			cretin	X		
			prat	X		
animal						
		cow			X	
		bitch			X	
		sow			X	
			swine	X		
	pig			X		
general						
			bastard		X	
			fucker		X	
	bugger				X	
	sod				X	

FIGURE 10.1 Gender in swearing.

male-derived *prick*, but on the other hand *all* the indeterminate terms, such as *bastard*, *shit* and *idiot*, which should logically be 'bisexual' in application, are invariably applied only to males. Consequently, the differing 'levels of injury' sustained or inflicted by these words would vary greatly from speaker to speaker and hearer to hearer.

The semantic history of the field shows, as does that for women in general, one significant trend: several of the more severe words, like *bitch* and *harlot*, were first used of males (or of either sex) and only later applied exclusively to women. This point, discussed more fully below, raises the question of whether these shifts suggest a 'patriarchal' conspiracy against women, or are simply fortuitous.

There is also the point that sexual and genital terms can be used in a symbolic fashion. Thus *balls* and *spunk* (sperm) can be used to suggest virility, as in 'He's got balls'. Indeed, probably the greatest compliment a chauvinist can pay to a woman is to say 'She's got balls.' Margaret Atwood makes fun of this idiom (not as successfully as she would like) by observing: 'Work by a male writer is often spoken of admiringly as having "balls"; ever hear anyone speak admiringly of a work by a woman as having "tits"?'(1982, p. 198).

SWEARING IN WOMEN

It is obviously difficult to generalize on the extent of women's swearing in the past, and the related restriction on men from swearing in their presence. Although John Fletcher wrote critically (in 1619) of 'Rack[ing] a maid's tender ear with dam's and Devils',[O] the Wife of Bath, Gammer Gurton and many characters in Elizabethan drama constitute a line of redoubtable feminine swearers. Indeed, figure 10.2, 'Bywords of Swearing', shows the sexes to be fairly evenly matched. Yet Defoe took the view in *An Essay on Projects* (1697) that 'The Grace of Swearing has not obtain'd to be a Mode yet among the Women; *God damn ye*, does not sit well upon a Female Tongue; it seems to be a Masculine Vice, which the Women are not arrived to yet . . .' (in Montagu, 1973, p. 185). Lady Brute in Vanbrugh's *The Provok'd Wife*, produced in the same year, observes: 'Men have more Courage than we, so they commit more Bold, Impudent Sins. They Quarrel, Fight, Swear, Drink, Blaspheme, and the like. Whereas we, being Cowards, only Backbite, tell Lyes, Cheat at Cards, and so forth' (V. ii). Swift, however, suggested in his delightfully ironic *Polite Conversation* (1738) that the assumed offence of swearing in front of a lady might be exaggerated or even hypocritical:

> I have been assured by some judicious Friends, that themselves have known certain Ladies to take Offence (whether seriously or no) at too great a Profusion of Cursing and Swearing; even when that Kind of Ornament was not improperly introduced: Which, I confess, did startle me not a little; having never observed the like, in the Compass of my own Female Acquaintance, at least for twenty years past. (1963, p. 30)

Traditionally, women's access to the language of power and assertion

Bear-garden

1678	'He speaks Bear-garden.' John Ray, *English Proverbs.*
1697	'This is brave Bear-garden language.' Jeremy Collier, *A short view of the immorality and profaneness of the English stage.*

Billingsgate

1652	'With down-right Billingsgate Rhetoric.' Nicholas Culpepper, *The English Physitian.*
1676	'With sharp Invectives.' William Wycherley, *The Plain Dealer.*
1750	'Low, Billingsgate invectives.' John Wesley, *Works.*
1683	'Neither have we any Billings-gates, all that sort of People are our hewers of VVood and drawers of water.' Tryon, *The Way to Health.*
1721	'*Billingsgate*: A scolding, impudent Slut.' Bailey, *Dictionary.*

Fishwife

1662	'They abuse one another like Fish-wives.' J. Davies, trans. *Olearius's Voyage.*

Lord

1531	'They wyll say that he that swereth depe, swereth like a lorde.' Elyot, *The Governour.*

Tinker

1608	'He swore like a dozen of drunken Tinkers.' J. Dekker, *The Honest Whore.*
1611	*Il jure comme un Abbé* etc. 'He swears like a tinker, say we.' Cotgrave. (*OED* note: 'The low repute in which [tinkers], especially the itinerant sort, were held in former times is shown by the expressions *to swear like a tinker, a tinker's curse* or *damn, as drunk* or *as quarrelsome as a tinker*, etc.')

Trooper

1810	'The fellow swore . . . like a trooper.' *Sporting Magazine.*

FIGURE 10.2 Bywords of swearing.

has been severely limited. Although, as this study has shown, there have been signal swearers among women, they appear to have been the exception, not the rule. In her influential study, *Language and Woman's Place* (1975), Robin Lakoff made the point, often repeated, that 'If a little girl "talks rough" like a boy, she will be ostracized, scolded, or made fun of' (p. 5). Tracing the development of this feminine acculturation, she offered this example:

> (a) Oh dear, you've put the peanut butter in the refrigerator again.
> (b) Shit, you've put the peanut butter in the refrigerator again.
>
> It is safe to predict that people would classify the first sentence as part of 'women's language', the second as 'men's language'. (1975, p. 10)

Although much of Lakoff's thesis (not to mention her examples) have a dated air in terms of the current debate, much of what she says probably still applies to the mass of society. One consequence of the feminist movement, notably in modern America, has certainly been the growth of a more 'liberated' attitude towards swearing. On this point, J. L. Dillard observes:

> Another change, toward use of 'objectionable' language by women, has taken place as a by-product of the same [feminist] movement. Erica Jung's [sic] *Fear of Flying* [1973] was a striking example of writing by a woman in a genre which had been almost the exclusive property of men and in which they had exercised considerable restraint before World War II. (1985, p. 215)

These developments are not accepted uncritically or blandly, as is shown in the following review (by Val Henessey of Andrea Newman's *Triangles*):

> 'She screamed with the joy of it, and he stopped just before it began to hurt and smiled up at her, doing it again and again until she was sobbing with exhaustion and each time she thought she couldn't come again but somehow she did. . . .' God Almighty! Stone the crows! It amazes me that mature, middle-aged Andrea *Bouquet-of-barbed-wire* Newman has the audacity to continue churning out crass pap of this sort. (*The Listener*, 1 March 1990, p. 30)

'Women are now talking seriously dirty,' wrote Rosalind Coward in a review article in *New Statesman & Society* (9 June 1989, p. 42). Though she did not validate the generalization, she reviewed and discussed women's fiction which frankly depicts 'alternative' forms of female sexual behaviour, such as lesbian pornography, fantasies of humiliation, rape, masochism and sadism, themes which clearly do not conform to the feminist 'phallocratic' interpretation of sexual dynamics.

Perhaps these forms of behaviour might be considered too 'abnormal' to be relevant to the issue under debate. In modern times there is, however, plenty of evidence that women are swearing to a greater extent than previously. This is unquestionably the case in contemporary American films. Dillard is not entirely convinced, however, that usage always indicates familiarity or habit:

> An occasional female speaker at a scholarly conference very pointedly, aggressively, and rather self-consciously uses one of the 'four letter' words in order to demonstrate her freedom to do so. In such a case, however, the calling attention to the usage is tantamount to an admission that it is not really commonplace for women to use such words in public. (Dillard, 1985, p. 216)

This raises the question of whether women use the 'traditional' vocabulary or generate their own distinctive vocabulary and idioms. By and large, it would appear that there is no obviously new feminine vocabulary of abuse.

THE ANGEL/WHORE DICHOTOMY: BINARY OPPOSITION IN THE CATEGORIZATION OF WOMEN

When one turns to the historical aspect of sexism in swearing, one is immediately struck by the significant fact that the semantic field categorizing women reveals an extreme dichotomy of praise and abuse in the feminine archetypes. It seems valuable, therefore, to broaden the argument to include this variety of terms, and not simply to focus on swear-words. The terms are legion, and those set out in figure 10.3, 10.4, 10.5 and 10.6 do not exhaust the possibilities. In the schematic representation, the line code is as follows: a solid bar indicates the historical extent of the present dominant meaning; a 'slashed' bar indicates the period when the term in question was not exclusively feminine in application, as in the cases of *wench* and *harlot*. (This highly significant category will be the object of subsequent analysis.) A dotted bar indicates a neutral or favourable sense in the word over the period demarcated. The symbol 'OE' signifies that the word derives from Old English. The word-field for 'man' has not been set out, since it would be too vast, cumbersome and complicated. Most of the germane points of the argument can be made in terms of generalizations set against, and illuminated by, the field for 'woman'.

In comparing the word-fields for 'man' and for 'woman', two imbalances are immediately apparent, in terms of both lexical gaps and –

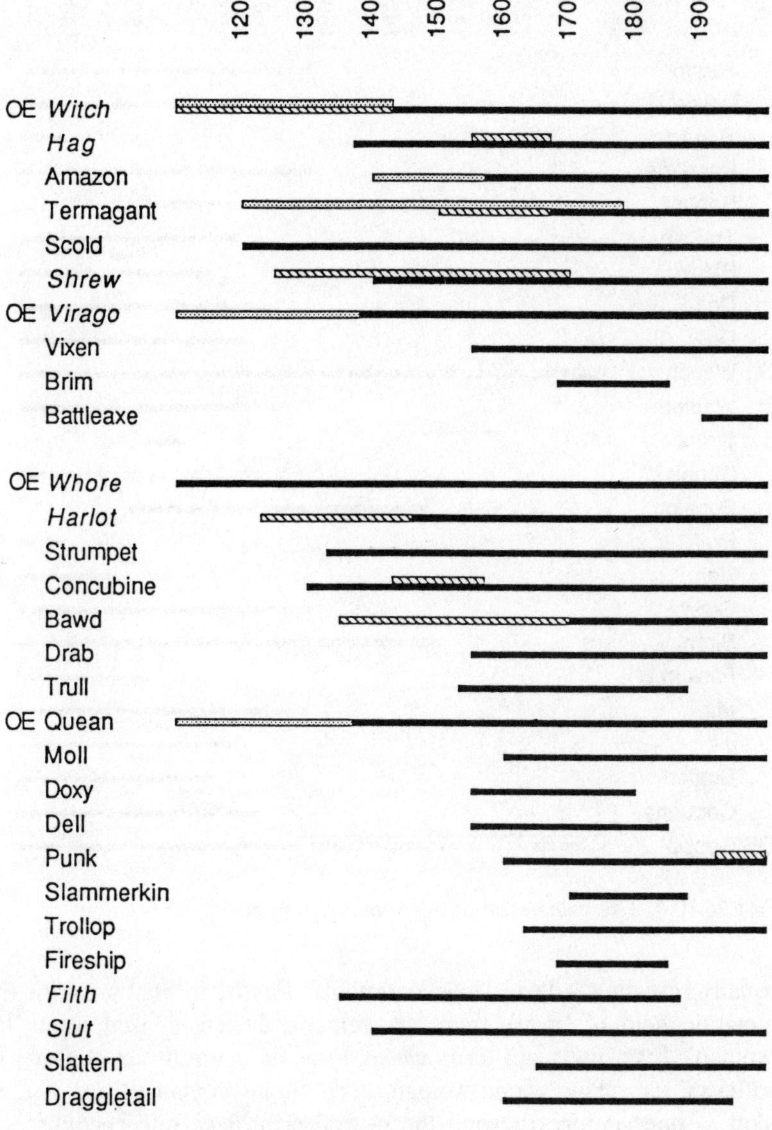

FIGURE 10.3 The categorization of women.

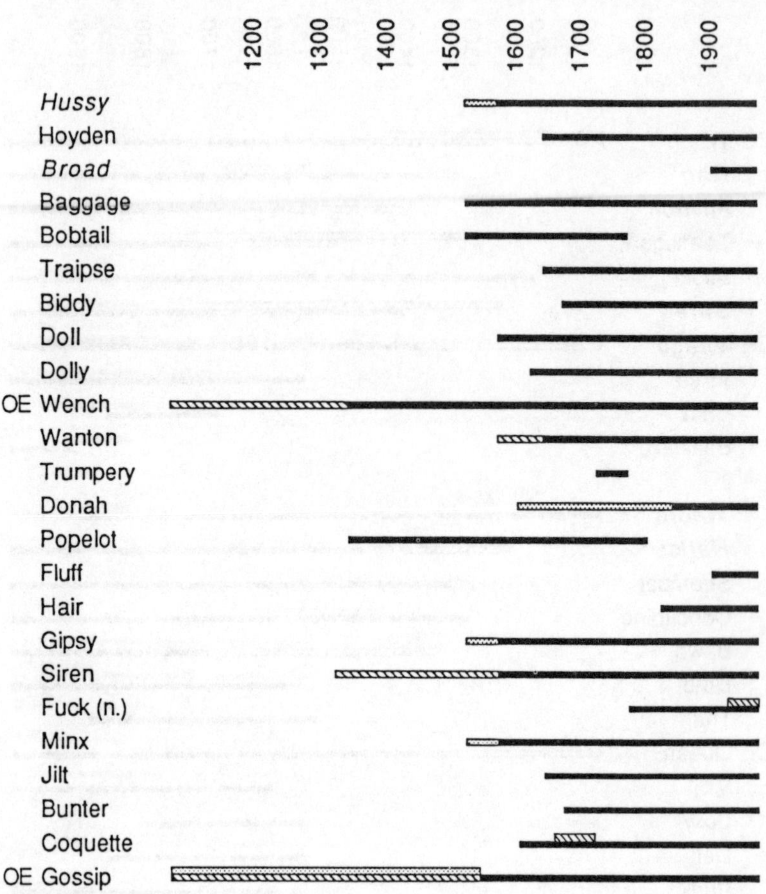

FIGURE 10.4 The categorization of women (continued).

equally revealing – lexical concentrations. Firstly, in contrast with the semantic field of 'man', there are remarkably few neutral terms for 'woman'. Even the plain term *woman* loses its neutrality in contexts of criticism, e.g. 'This stupid woman. . . .', 'Some woman driver. . . .' As soon as one ventures beyond the central term *man*, one encounters a host of informal terms, such as *bloke*, *chap*, *fellow*, *cove* and *guy*. These derive from a great diversity of sources, several of them from dubious quarters of society: *cove* comes from sixteenth-century underworld slang and *guy* from the publicized treason of Guy Fawkes. However, whatever their origins, they have now moved to roughly the same level of usage and, more significantly, have acquired generally favourable overtones.

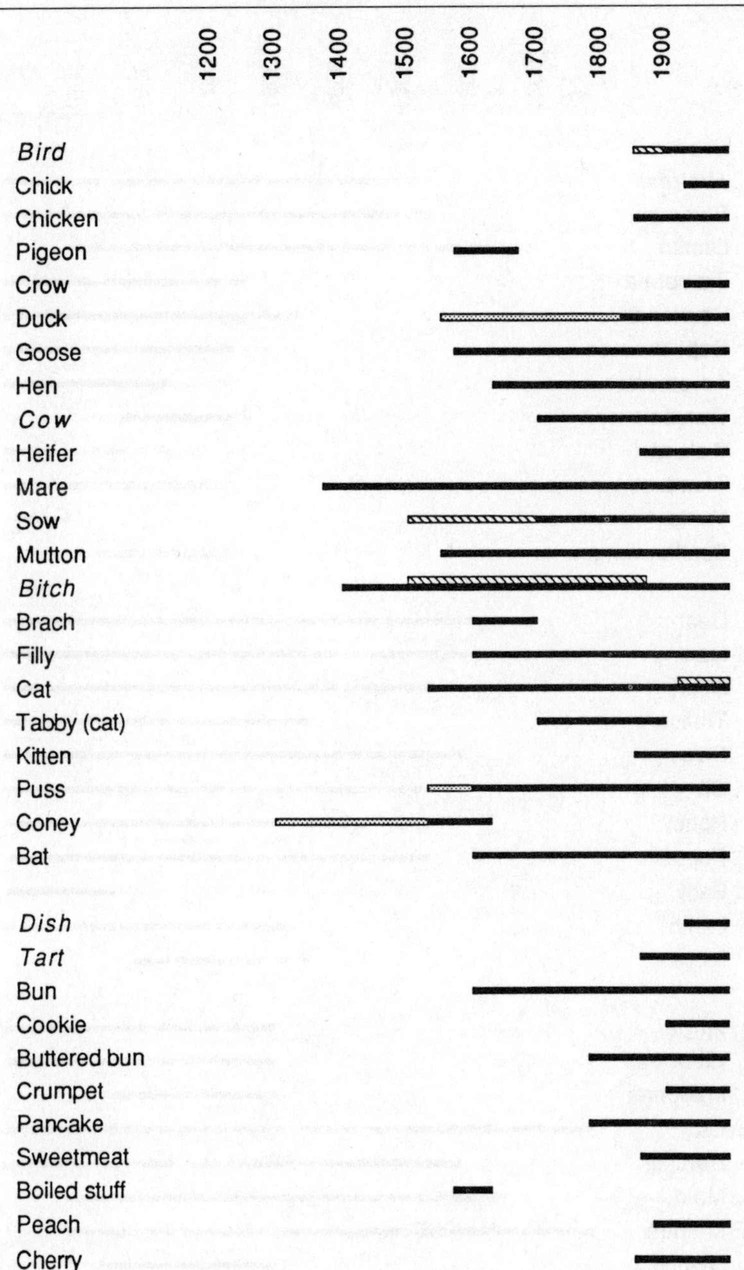

FIGURE 10.5 The categorization of women (continued).

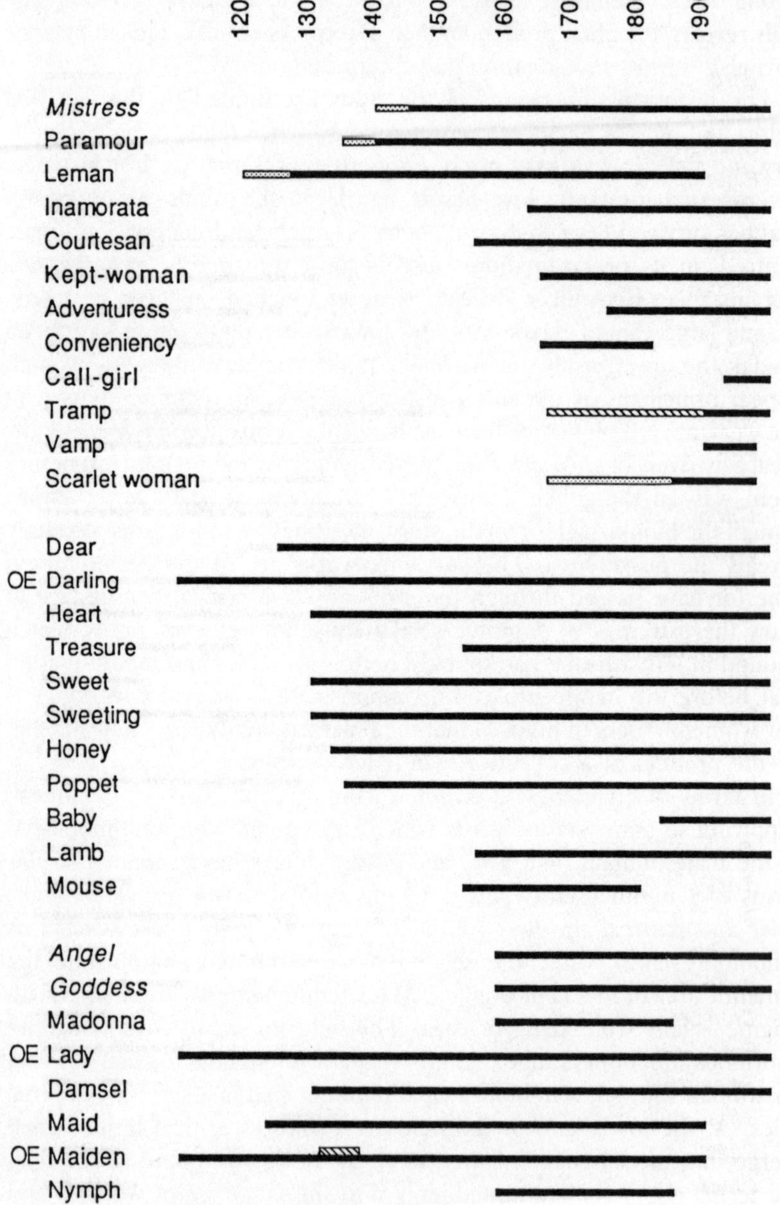

FIGURE 10.6 The categorization of women (continued).

Contrariwise, virtually every term for woman, formal or informal, has a strong moral or emotive overtone. Furthermore, as figure 10.7 dramatically reveals, the great preponderance of terms is critical. This imbalance obviously invites investigation and interpretation.

The historical dimensions of the study are limited by the fact that before the time of Chaucer the semantic evidence tends to be fragmentary and the survivals may not be properly representative. For instance, heterosexual, romantic love hardly figures in the Anglo-Saxon poetry that has survived.[4] Anglo-Saxon poetry is largely 'androcentric', or 'male centred' in its preoccupations, just as most romance is 'gynocentric'. For instance, Beowulf's love-life is never touched on, even remotely. By and large, Anglo-Saxon attitudes towards women seem to have been feudal: the lower orders are virtually unmentioned, while noble women appear principally as queenly consort (*healsgebedda*), commonly used in the weaving of diplomatic alliances, hence the terms *freoðuwebbe*, literally 'peace-weaver' or *friðusibb folca*, 'peace-pledge of the people'.[5] Whether there was anything like a misogynist tradition we shall never know, though the monkish gloss on the story of Orpheus and Eurydice certainly reveals the possibility.[6] The surviving works are of too high a moral tone (or have passed through too strict an ecclesiastical censorship) to show the extremes of damning sexual abuse and etherial praise which abound in, say, Elizabethan times. There is also the important limitation that before the eighteenth century there were – as far as we know – few women writers of note, so that the polarization of terms may, indeed, be the product of a collective male consciousness.

In terms of etymology, it is noteworthy that the Norman Conquest, supplying so many status-words which subsequently became moralized in the male domain (like *noble* and *gentle*) should have supplied so few terms of feminine status and refinement. Of the two principal terms, *dame* and *mistress*, the first has passed out of common use (except as schoolboy slang), while the second has deteriorated sharply into the semantic area of the 'kept woman'. Many feminine terms are of uncertain origin, usually from slang or cant. The field for 'man' covers such an enormous functional range that it is virtually impossible to analyse. That for woman shows her to be principally stereotyped in a series of extreme roles. At the lower end of the field are countless critical terms which merge into the language of the gutter; at the opposite end of the field the terms rise steeply and suddenly into the language of worship and the superhuman. More specifically, one can see the outer limits of human identity being plumbed in clusters of terms focussing on, respectively: the diabolical woman in the *witch/hag* group, which overlaps with the unnatural, aggressive or 'manlike' woman, the *virago/shrew* group; the woman seen as the superhuman, spiritual creature of salvation, the *angel/goddess* group; the woman seen as an endearing pet in the *mouse/lamb* group; the woman castigated in the animal terms of the *bitch/cow* group; the woman seen as the available object of delight, the *dish/tart* group; the woman seen as an object of physical revulsion, the *filth/slut* group, and by far the largest category, the *whore/harlot* group, which tails off into the *hussy/broad* group. The question which these extremities and imbalances poses is whether their causes are psycholinguistic or sociolinguistic.

Resonating behind the dominant stereotypes of the angel/whore dichotomy there can be detected certain potent and deeply embedded role models, especially those generated by the religious figures of Eve and Mary, referred to by Sheila Delany as 'the opposed examplars of the feminine character'.[7] The one half of the antithesis is epitomized in the disobedient, earth-bound, seductive origin of sin, suffering, guilt and shame; the other is the submissive, etherial, immaculate vehicle of the redemption. Eve, limited to carnal knowledge and sublunary good and evil, is tied to the Myth of the Fall; Mary is the instrument of a Grace which is potentially limitless. The one is the pure mother-figure in whom conception is the source of blessing; the other is the stained mistress-figure in whom conception is a sorrow, a curse. Interestingly, the role of Eve is symbolically continued at the scene of the Crucifixion by the fallen Mary, Magdalene the *maudlin* prostitute.[8]

The profundity of these stereotypes can be demonstrated via the fecundity of their use in seminal works of literature in Middle English and the Renaissance. It seems more than a coincidence that Chaucer's first two tales should introduce these two stereotypes, in the form of Emily, the idealized, distant, angel-goddess singing etherially in her *hortus conclusus*, followed immediately by the vibrantly physical and eager adulteress in Alisoun. The only full-length portraits of women in the *Prologue* are of the precious, sentimental, attitudinizing Prioress immured from the world, and the aggressive, self-made, much-married widow, who 'koude muchel of wandrynge by the weye', a potent combination of Venus and Mars. Within Shakespeare's 'world of women' the two antitypes are also clearly apparent. The virginal innocent (invariably wronged by deluded man) is exemplified by Hero, Ophelia, Desdemona, Isabella and Hermione, while the ruthless virago is strongly represented by Tamora, Lady Macbeth, Volumnia, Goneril and Regan.

SHAKESPEARE

It might be illuminating to consider first Shakespeare's most versatile creation, Cleopatra. Here he sets the two languages, that of mythic paean and the insult of the street, in parallel, the one counterpointing the other. The queen who wears the regalia of the goddess Isis (and Antony's 'sword Philippic'), who is praised as surpassing both Nature and fancy, is also degraded as a *strumpet*, a *whore*, *a right gypsy at fast and loose*.[9] Often the two aspects are brought into a juxtaposition which is oxymoronic, as in 'Royal wench!' and 'My serpent of old Nile' (II. ii. 235 and I. v.25). Cleopatra is also unique in her appropriation of the male idiom of extreme praise and abuse: her contemptuous dismissal of Caesar as *ass unpolicied* anticipates Charmian's posthumous compliment: *lass unparallelled* (V. ii. 309 and 318). *Antony and Cleopatra* is Shakespeare's most developed treatment of categorization because the whole gamut of both male *and* female terms is richly used.

Shakespeare particularly focussed on the dramatized perceptions of the hero. He perceived that the stronger the character's projection, the more violent the dualistic antimony and the oscillation from idealism to cynicism, from love to hate. The highest spiritual aspirations thus turn to extreme physical disgust; 'lilies that fester smell far worse than weeds':

> The bonds of heaven are slipp'd, dissolv'd and loos'd;
> And with another knot, five-finger tied,
> The fractions of her faith, orts of her love,
> The fragments, scraps, the bits, and greasy relics
> Of her o'er-eaten faith are bound to Diomed.
>
> (*Troilus and Cressida*, V. ii. 153–7)

More than any other of the tragedies, *Othello* epitomizes this split vision, with 'yond high marble heaven', the harmonious, idealistic world-view of the hero, set against the 'cistern for toads to knot and gender in',[10] the product of the diseased and infecting cynicism of Iago. These world-views are, furthermore, intimately related to the view of women in the play. The 'divine' Desdemona of Act II, suspending the laws of nature, is the product of Cassio's gallant imagination and winning charm. In the course of Act III she is converted into a *strumpet*, a *whore* and even a *devil*[11] through the corrosively cynical innuendo of Iago, and consistent play on such key words as *honest*, *devil* and *hell*. It is Iago, the cunning chameleon of language, who plays with the idea of projection in this *jeu d'esprit*, part of his own role as the bluff ancient entertaining the ladies:

> You are pictures out of doors,
> Bells in your parlours, wild cats in your kitchens,
> Saints in your injuries, devils being offended,
> Players in your housewifery, and housewives in your beds.[12]
> (II. i. 109–12)

Dichotomized images of woman proliferate in *Hamlet*. Sickened by his mother's behaviour, Hamlet savagely denounces all womankind:

> Frailty, thy name is woman!
> (I. ii. 146)

Yet Ophelia, dead, becomes promoted in her brother's imagination, to the role of 'ministering angel' (V. i. 263). Probably the most striking scene relevant to this theme occurs when Ophelia is converted, in a mere thirty lines, from an ostensibly praying *nymph*[13] to someone fit for a *nunnery*: the ambiguities of this word, referring simultaneously to the convent and the brothel, impressively epitomize the angel/whore dichotomy. An equally savage, but more deserved, piece of word-play is deployed when Pandarus refers to Helen twelve times in sixty lines as *queen*. An Elizabethan audience would certainly pick up the pun on the homophonic moral opposite *quean*, 'prostitute'.[14] This dualism reaches its most Zoroastrian form in Lear's seminal misogynist tirade:

> Down from the waist they are Centaurs
> Though women all above;
> But to the girdle do the gods inherit,
> Beneath is all the fiend's.
> There's hell, there's darkness, there is the sulphurous pit
> (IV. vi. 127–31)

THE FEMINIZATION OF AMBISEXUAL TERMS

The exclusive feminization of terms which were originally male or ambisexual in application is a highly significant development in the semantic field. *Scold* has its origins in *skald*, the Old Norse word for a poet, with probable associations of a lampooner, which possibly derive from the practice of flyting. However, in English the feminine application has always been dominant: 'in early use a person (especially a woman) of ribald speech; later a woman (rarely a man) addicted to abusive language. The phrase a *common scold* has always been applied to a woman, certainly since 1476, when the Court Rolls announced that "Eadem Katerina est communis scolde."'[O] Blackstone commented in 1769: 'Our law-latin confines it to the feminine gender.' *Shrew*, a curiously exclusive Anglo-Saxon word within the Germanic family, is extended metaphorically from its rodent referent, possibly enriched by 'superstitions as to the malignant influence of the animal'. The word had been used in the senses of 'a wicked, evil-disposed or malignant man, a rascal or villain, specifically the Devil', from *c.*1250. The feminine application starts to emerge during the lifetime of Chaucer, memorably when his Merchant ruefully describes his wife as a perfect example of the species: 'She is a shrewe at al' (*Prologue* 1222), which would translate into modern parlance as 'She is an absolute bitch'.

Analysing this group of words, one can see in them a semantic link which might be termed the feminization of the monstrous: woman is categorized as something alien, the recipient or agent of supernatural powers. Thus *hag*, is 'an evil spirit, dæmon, or infernal being in female form', virtually unrecorded before Elizabethan times, when we find 'Hegges, or nyght furyes, or wytches like unto old women . . . whyche do sucke the bloude of children in the nyght-*striges*'.[O] *Dragon*, so formidable in its mythical potency, was applied to Satan from the fourteenth century, was humanized generally before taking on its feminine specialization from the eighteenth century, being applied to 'a fierce violent person, especially a duenna', first recorded in Johnson's Dictionary (1755). *Termagent* is well established, over four centuries before being applied to a quarrelsome woman, as 'the name of an imaginary deity held in medieval Christendom to be worshipped by Mohammedans: in the mystery plays represented as a violent and overbearing personage'. A certain xenophobic malice would also seem to lie behind the similar borrowing of *tartar*, 'an old cant name for a strolling vagabond, thief or beggar', then 'a rough, violent, irritable or intractable person', especially applied to women from *c.*1663, as in one of Dryden's plays: 'I never knew your grandmother was a Scotchwoman: is she not a Tartar too?' Male *witches* are recorded earlier (from *c.*890) than the female variety. *Harpy* seems to epitomize certain misogynist views of woman: 'a fabulous monster, rapacious and filthy, having a woman's face and a bird's wings and claws'. Though the term has associations with the legal fraternity, and Johnson referred to 'the harpies of taxation', in society discourse of the eighteenth and nineteenth century, most people used the word as did Thackeray in 1859: 'Was it my mother-in-law, the grasping, odious, abandoned, brazen harpy?' *Siren*, dating from *c.*1340, is originally 'an imaginary species of serpent', derived from glossarial explanations of Latin *sirenes* in the Vulgate text of Isaiah, xii. 22. By Chaucer's time it had evolved into a variety of fabulous, seductive monsters, part woman and part bird (but sometimes confused with the mermaid), and had developed the associations which make the modern sense inevitable.

Within the human sphere proper, the process of feminization is apparent in several other terms. *Wench*, in the sense of 'mistress', goes back to Langland, but has a confused earlier relationship with OE *wencel*, 'a child of either sex'. The connection with what is minor or diminutive is significant here. The sense of *doll* and *dolly* as a child's plaything is first recorded over a century after the primary meanings, which are given as follows: 'A pet form of the name Dorothy. Hence given generically to a female pet, a mistress. Also the smallest or pet dog in a litter (dial.).' *Biddy* is given the following, somewhat embarrassed, etymology in the *OED*: 'conjectured to be an instinctive sound used in calling chickens'. Also deriving from a farmyard ambience is *coquette*, in origin *coquet*, a young cock, notable for what the *OED* calls its 'strutting gait and amorous characteristics'. In *The Beggar's Opera* (1728), Gay refers to 'The coquets of both sexes'. Even *sow* does not have an exclusively female application: 'applied to a person (male or female) as a term of abuse'. As late as 1803 a Scottish song carries the mocking line: 'Ye're a sow, auld man.' *Minx*, of obscure origin, is used of a pet dog from *c.*1540, a pert girl or hussy from *c.*1592 and a whore from *c.*1598°. One of the few terms to move from a female provenance to the male is, strangely, *hunk*, which was originally a Scottish dialect word meaning 'a sluttish indolent woman', as in 'a lazy hunk' or 'a nasty hunk', recorded from *c.*1825. It is notable that in its newer male sense it has acquired favourable overtones as an attractive, rugged well-built male, though possibly somewhat unintelligent.

We come now to the area where moral deterioration is linked to sexual specialization. The previously accepted derivation of *harlot* from Arlette, mother of William the Conqueror, is now dismissed as a 'random conjecture of the sixteenth century'. From *c.*1225 the word carries the senses of 'vagabond, beggar, rogue, rascal', one of the most memorably scathing uses being the application to Chaucer's sexually ambivalent Summoner: 'He was a gentil harlot and a kynde' (*General Prologue* 647). There is a fascinating comment in Ranulph Higden (1432–50): 'The harlottes at Rome were called *nonariæ*', which explains the origin of the debased sense of *nunnery*, as used by Hamlet. *Bawd*, of uncertain origin and first found in *Piers Plowman*, is a procurer/ess, though it is masculine in the majority of early passages. By *c.*1700 it has become exclusively feminized. *Harridan* has previous French associations of 'an old jade', but in English these are sharpened into 'a haggard old woman; a vixen; and in Johnson 'a decayed strumpet'. *Gipsy* arose in the early sixteenth century from the appearance of the Romanies (a wandering race of Hindu origin) and the supposition (on the basis of their complexion) that they came from Egypt. A male sense of 'cunning rogue' is briefly established in the early seventeenth century, whereafter feminization and sexual deterioration set in. A similar pattern can be seen in the semantic development of *tramp* from 'a male vagrant' to 'a sexually promiscuous woman'.

The semantics of deterioration or pejoration in feminine terms is clearly considerable. Apart from those already mentioned, the words affected include *mistress, hussy, donah, puss, coney*, and *lemman*. All of these previously had a neutral or even a favourable significance before declining into their various senses of 'kept woman', 'whore', 'loose woman' or plain 'genitalia'.[15] The field has been traversed many times since Bréal made this psycholinguistic observation in 1897:

> The so-called pejorative tendency has yet another cause. It is in the nature of human malice to take pleasure in looking for a vice or a fault behind a quality. . . . We remember what a noble signification *amant* and *maîtresse* still possessed in Corneille. But they are dethroned, as was *Buhle* in German. Here we see the inevitable results of false delicacy; honourable names are dishonoured by being given to things which are dishonourable.[16]

The most obvious objection to Bréal's first suggested cause is that 'the nature of human malice' would, presumably, prevent words like *amant* and *maîtresse* from acquiring 'noble significations' in the first place. The attribution to 'false delicacy' has greater plausibility, and is supported by Stephen Ullmann:

> Thus the notorious deterioration which has affected various words for 'girl' or 'woman', such as English *hussy*, *quean*, French *fille*, *garce*, or German *Dirne*, was no doubt due to genuine or pseudo-euphemism rather than to any anti-feminine bias. (1964, pp. 90–1)

In the first place, the difference between 'genuine' euphemism and 'pseudo-euphemism' is very important, since it is the difference between tactful vagueness and malicious innuendo. In view of the prevalence of deterioration in feminine terms, the causes are likely to be general. Attention has to be paid to the manner in which derogatory words or deteriorated meanings fit into the whole semantic field.

HISTORICAL DEVELOPMENT OF THE SEMANTIC FIELD

An examination of the historical development of the semantic field shows that, contrary to what is often stated or supposed, deterioration is *not* the main trend, properly speaking, since many terms critical of women actually originate with unfavourable denotations or connotations and retain those senses throughout their history. The proportion is four to one *against* deterioration, in fact. Many are frank terms of abuse in which no euphemistic impulse (or 'false delicacy') has ever been registered. The great number, variety and general hostility of these words can, in short, only be interpreted as showing a decidedly 'anti-feminine bias'. They can be used, and are, to mobilize the hypocritical complex of envy, suspicion and disapproval which extra marital sexual relations traditionally arouse.

If we consider the broad subdivisions of the semantic field in the historical perspective schematized in figure 10.7, we find that the oldest groups are the *whore/harlot/strumpet* and the *witch/hag/virago* complexes. As has been demonstrated, several of these terms are also the least stable and consistent in gender in the earlier stages, possibly because the aggressive or martial element involves male implications. The *harlot/hussy* group is much larger and, generally speaking, more recent, undergoing marked expansion from the Renaissance period. The *mare/bitch/cow* group, also well established by 1600, would seem to be a contemptuous reinforcement of the feudal attitude whereby woman was regarded as man's chattle.[17] The food group (*dish/tart/sugar*) is, comparatively speaking, the most recent and the most affectionate, provided that the gustatory associations do not stick in one's throat. The connotations of sweetness are the obverse of the dirt and ugliness heavily underwritten in *filth, slut, slattern* and so on. The smaller group of *paramour/mistress/courtesan*, in which the notion of a permanent extramarital arrangement is assumed, is not always easily separable from the casual carnality of the *harlot/hussy* group. Several of the terms (*inamorata, paramour* and *courtesan*) are of foreign origin, suggesting an element of xenophobia at work.

The most prominent feature of the field is the imbalance in favour of terms of abuse, especially the glaring hiatus in the creation of favourable terms between 1600 and 1850. Partial sociolinguistic explanations might be found in the Puritan Revolution, Restoration cynicism[18] and Augustan austerity. But it is strange that no Elizabethan poet seems to have made any substantial contribution to the favourable side of the field. Shakespeare's contribution is not as opulent as one might expect; he is the first to apply *angel* to an earthly woman via the ecstatic Romeo in the great love scene:

> O, speak again, bright angel!
> (II. i. 26)

Date	*Favourable*	*Unfavourable*
	Lady	
900	Darling	
950		
1000	Maiden	Witch
1050		
1100		Whore
1150		
1200		Scold
	Maid	
1250	Dear	
1300	Damsel, Sweet, Sweeting	Quean, Lemman, Concubine, Strumpet
1350	Heart, Honey	
1400	Poppet	Hag, Shrew, Virago, Popelot, Wench, Mare, Bitch
		Paramour
1450		Harlot, Slut, Filth, Mistress
1500		
1550	Treasure, Lamb	Gossip, Drab, Dell, Doxy, Trull, Mutton
	Nymph, Mouse, Coney	Cat, Courtesan
1600	Angel, Goddess, Madonna	Moll, Punk, Bobtail, Doll, Wanton, Baggage, Goose, Bat, Vixen, Brach, Pigeon, Draggletail, Bun, Siren
		Amazon, Minx, Boiled stuff
1650		Termagent, Dolly, Hussy, Trollop, Gipsy, Filly, Hen, Slattern, Inamorata, Puss, Coquette
1700		Brim, Fireship, Bawd, Bunter, Hoyden, Biddy, Traipse, Cow, Tabbycat, Kept-woman, Conveniency, Sow, Jilt
1750		Trumpery, Slammerkin
1800		Buttered bun, Pancake, Fuck (n.)
1850	Baby, Kitten	Blowen, Duck, Heifer, Sweetmeat, Hair, Scarlet woman
1900		Donah, Bird, Chicken, Tart, Cherry, Battleaxe
		Vamp, Tramp, Femme fatale
1950	Sugar, Sweetie pie	Broad, Crow, Chick, Dish, Cookie, Cunt, Call-girl
		Crumpet, Escort

FIGURE 10.7 The historical evolution of the categorization of women.

Yet there are complications. The solid materialism of *angel's* Renaissance monetary connotations is surely no accident, as intentional a deflationary effect as Juliet's endearing practicality and literalism in the face of wild hyperbole:

> O swear not by the moon, the inconstant moon . . .
> *Romeo* What shall I swear by?
> *Juliet* Do not swear at all;
>
> (II. ii. 109–12)

Shakespeare's own sonnets record his own struggle with sincerity and hyperbole. He exploits the high Pertrachan style satirically rather than positively: 'My mistress' eyes are nothing like the sun' (Sonnet 130). In matters of the heart it is better to be 'rude in [one's] speech', to 'love and be silent' and maintain a 'gracious silence'.[19]

One important factor which might, perhaps, come into play and explain this great swing to feminine abuse is the spread of venereal disease. As the discussion of the topic in chapter 6 has indicated, the disease is a powerful factor in 'name-calling'. D. H. Lawrence asserted in his remarkable essay, 'Introduction to His Paintings' (1929), that syphilis caused a fundamental rupture in the emotional life of Renaissance England:

> What appeared to take full grip on the northern consciousness at the end of the sixteenth century was a terror, almost a horror of sexual life . . . this extra morbidity came, I believe, from the great shock of syphilis and the realization of the consequences of the disease . . . by the end of the sixteenth [century], its ravages were obvious, and the shock of them had just penetrated the thoughtful and imaginative consciousness.[20]

Though the disease would certainly provide a motivation for misogyny, the taboo against direct mention of a condition so intimately acquired would, in the normal run of circumstances, excite the creation of risqué euphemisms. In general, however, the semantic evidence does not seem to merge with strong definition at the right time. The effect on *pox*, already an established term, is catalytic: it produces the syphilitic specialisms, *French pox*, *Great pox* and *Spanish pox* timeously, the earliest emerging *c.*1503. However, most terms are first recorded well after the outbreaks of the sixteenth century, though this may be because they had previously been 'underground' terms. *Goose*, for example, meaning a 'venereally diseased whore' (especially in *Winchester goose*) is first recorded in 1591 in *Henry VI Part I* (I. iii. 53). *Fireship*, a more explicit term for the same thing, is recorded only from 1670 (in Wycherley), while a similar interpretation could be put on *brim*, (from *c.*1730) and *brimstone* (from *c.*1751)[O]. The semantic problem is that *burning*, *heat* etc., have already acquired such strong amatory associations that the added discomforts of venereal disease cannot be conveyed through established metaphor without a laboured explicitness which is wearisome. In general the evidence of the word-field does not suggest that venereal disease was a major factor in the categorization of women. It did, however, generate many other exclamations, such as *pox!*, set out in figure 9.1, as well as xenophobic categorizations, discussed in chapter 6.

Drawing these various threads together, it would seem that in recent times there has been a diminution of the extreme terminology, and of the intense dualism which characterizes the earlier stages of the field. Potential reasons are numerous and complex. Among them could be cited the decline in religious and superstitious belief, causing religious metaphors, such as *witch* and *goddess*, to atrophy. In addition, the increasing awareness of psychological processes, particularly projection, mania and wish-fulfilment, would, logically, curtail the use of the more extreme and judgemental terms. Furthermore, an increasingly permissive attitude towards sex has diminished the feelings of guilt and mysticism traditionally associated with the act. Finally, feminist writings and awareness groups have, in recent years, made some progress in the eradication of those prejudices which are verbally impacted. Germaine Greer's influential study, *The Female Eunuch* (1970), incisive and sharply ironic, deserves a special mention in this respect.[21]

Never the less, the tenacity and resilience of stereotypes is reflected in a variety of hostile terms and phrases. *Battleaxe*, dating from *c.*1896, was originally US slang but is now a general colloquialism. *Hooker*, from a similar provenance, and recorded from around the time of the Civil War, has also generalized, as have *vamp*, an abbreviation of *vampire*, recorded from 1911, and *tramp* (from 1922). Modern dictionaries of slang abound in terms which diminish woman to a disembodied sexually available object, terms such as *piece of ass*, *pussy*, *lay* and the stereotype of the edible object, *honey-pot*, *hair pie* and *jelly-roll*. *Scarlet woman/lady*, an older censorious term which originally mobilized feelings of religious xenophobia as 'an abusive epithet for the Church of Rome'[22], started to take on the more literal sense of 'whore' around the turn of the last century, while *femme fatale* was borrowed into English *c.*1912. The antitype, the *angel of the hearth* is especially associated with Dickens, particularly.[23]

There seem to have been virtually no instances of amelioration, and very few shifts whereby hostile feminine terms have been extended to apply to men. *Punk*, a prostitute from Elizabethan times, has in the past decade or so become ambisexual and in some quarters means a catamite. Another instance concerns *bitch*, recorded from *c.*1400. Here the observation of Grose (1785) certainly carries weight: 'The most offensive appellation that can be given to an English woman, even more provoking than that of whore.' Yet in earlier times the word could be acceptable in literary contexts. Thus in Hobbes' *Odyssey* (1675) we find: 'Ulysses looking sourly answered, "You Bitch".' There are rare instances (recorded from as far back as *c.*1500) of the word being used of a man, as in the highly coloured speech of Squire Western in *Tom Jones*: 'I can tell you, landlord is a vast comical bitch.'[24] After centuries of feminine specialization, the word has started to be applied to things ('Life's a bitch') and occasionally to men: 'Truman [Capote] was a bitch'.[25]

It is clear, never the less, that the preponderance of unfavourable terms continues unabated, and that this imbalance, deriving mainly from sexist assumptions, seems to be constant and unaffected by, or unresponsive to, social developments. The apparent permanence of this imbalance suggests that it is a mass psycholinguistic phenomenon.

HOMOSEXUALITY

Most of this chapter has been concerned with the heterosexual roles of women and their semantic correlatives, since these aspects have become major areas of debate. The topic of 'Sexuality in Swearing' would not be complete, however, if it did not consider an aspect which has been more openly discussed in recent times than previously, namely homosexuality. At the time when the *OED* was compiled, there was no neutral term for the condition, which was generally regarded with hostility and abhorrence. Consequently, there had grown up, as can be seen in figure 10.8, a number of underground slang terms. The coy appellation of 'the love that dare not speak its name' (from Lord Alfred Douglas' poem, given prominence in the trial of Oscar Wilde in 1895) no longer applies. It has not only 'come out of the closet', to use the American idiom; it now makes its claims as an 'alternative' way of life, free of guilt, shame and prejudice.

The term *homosexual* seems to have been coined by a Hungarian physician named Benkert in 1869, though it was given currency by Krafft-Ebing in his classic study of sexual disorders, *Psychopathia Sexualis* (1886), translated into English by C. G. Chaddock in 1892. It is, perhaps, a measure of the misinterpretation of the term as deriving from Latin *homo*, 'a man', as opposed to Greek *homos* 'the same' (as in

Male

1300	sodomite
1548	bardash
1552	buggerer
1555	bugger
1591	ganymede
1592	ingle (also ningle)
1593	catamite
1603	pathic
1613	pæderast
1694	he-whore
1708	huffler
1745	molly
1818	sod
1824	miss nancy
1850	poof
1895	fairy
1890s	gay
1891	cocksucker
1904	nancy
1910	poofter
1914	faggot
1923	fag
1924	queen
1929	homo
1929	pansy
1932	queer

Female

1601	tribade
1890	lesbian
1902	sapphist
1942	dyke
1954	butch
1956	lezzie

Common term

*c.*1970	gay

Notes

1 The field has grown enormously in recent years, as reference to Green (1988) will show. This is, therefore, only a representative collection of the more generally known terms.

2 *Cocksucker* is defined by Farmer and Henley (1891) as '*A feliatrix*'.

FIGURE 10.8 Terms for homosexuals.

homogeneous) which has brought about the situation whereby it has been widely assumed that the term referred exclusively to males and that homosexuality is entirely confined to males. Indeed, as the word-field set out in figure 10.8 makes clear, the curious fact is that for centuries there were words only for male homosexuals, most of them highly critical. (The exceptions were very recherché.) Not only is the male field far larger, virtually every word in the field is far more virulent and contemptuous than any in the female equivalent. Furthermore, the clear imbalance in the relative size of the fields represents a striking reversal of the imbalance previously seen in the terms categorizing women.

Krafft-Ebing devotes a whole section (pp. 255–79) to 'Homo-Sexual Individuals, or Urnings'. This curious latter term, which is the headword for the section, had been coined in German in 1864, and related to *Uranism* or *Uranian*, deriving from the reference in Plato's *Symposium*: 'This is noble, or heavenly love, which is associated with the heavenly muse, Urania' (1951, p. 56). The word acquired a brief and limited currency in English around the turn of the century, when there was enormous interest in the subject. It represents one side of the split in the word-field, already alluded to: the terms derive either from classical references or from underground slang. Among those preferring 'the decent obscurity of a learned language' are *pæderast* ('boy lover'), *ganymede* ('a Trojan youth, whom Zeus made his cup-bearer'), *catamite* (which is, extraordinarily, 'a corrupt form of *ganymede*') and *pathic*. The majority are from the lower category, although (like *fairy* and *pansy*), they may have quite charming or innocent origins, being examples of what Ullmann calls 'pseudo-euphemism' (1964, pp. 90–1). Of course, respectable origins (etymologically speaking) do not ensure the same status for the subsequent history of the term. In an early use of *ganymede* (in 1649), Drummond of Hawthornden uttered the prayer, 'I crave Thou wilt be pleased, great God, to save my sov'reign from a Ganymede.'[O]

Sodomite is the oldest term, deriving from the vicious rapacity of the men of Sodom in Genesis, xviii–xix who 'pressed sore upon Lot' and called upon him to bring out the men of the house 'that we may know them'. The term retained its potency as a term of opprobrium, appearing in polemical passages in the company of various criminal categories, as is seen in this barrage from 1705: 'An Adulterer, Simonist, Sodomite, Murtherer, Arian.'[O] However, from the early nineteenth century, the abbreviation *sod* became current. In some contexts the sense of *sodomite* was clear: 'Beware of Sods!' appeared on bills in respectable houses in Charing Cross, according to a record of *c.*1855.[S] But when a court session (of 1818) records: 'As he passed me by he said that the other was a b---y s--d', the meaning is uncertain. *Sod* had acquired centuries before, through association with *sot*, the contemptuous sense of 'drunkard', which probably diversified the meaning to its generalized present sense of 'fellow' or 'chap'. *Bugger*, discussed in greater detail in chapter 6, has followed very much the same pattern. It also qualifies for ambiguity, since legally *buggery* can refer both to intercourse with a person or an animal. The same problem of specificity surrounds *cocksucker*. As the notes to figure 10.8 indicate, the term was defined by Farmer and Henley as 'a *feliatrix*', although the popular conception of the time and subsequently would regard the term as describing a homosexual practice. When E. E. Cummings wrote (in a letter of 1923) of 'the cocksucking leisure classes', his meaning is not certain, but could certainly include the weakened modern sense of contemptuous disapproval. The term could never be used of a woman now.

It would appear from the word-field that homosexual activity was openly acknowledged around 1600. Ben Jonson's works, in particular, carry several observations. The first (in *Sejanus*, 1603) is simply: 'He was the noted Pathick of the time,' while the *Poetaster* (1601) contains the exclamation: 'What, shall I have my sonne a stager now? an enghle [ingle] for players?' Samuel Purchas's *Pilgrimage* (1613) contains an account, no doubt tinged with xenophobia: 'He telleth of their Pæderastie, that they buy Boyes at an hundred or two hundred duckats and mew them vp for their filthie lust'.[O] Holland's *Pliny* (1601) mentions a place 'called Cinedopolis, by reasons of certain Catamites and shamefull baggages left there by Alexander the Great'. (John Florio had defined *cinedo* in his *Worlde of Wordes* (1598) as '*a bardash, a buggring boy, a wanton boy, an ingle*.') A character in Thomas Heywood's *Captives* denounces 'That ould catamiting cankerworm'.[O] A writer of 1795 elaborates: 'The persons who suffered this abuse were called pathics, and affected the dress and behaviour of women.'[O] Both *nancy* and *molly* were previously attended by the ironic title *miss* before acquiring independence. *Molly* is a good candidate for sexual ambiguity, set out in figure 11.2, since in the course of less than a century it meant a prostitute, a sodomite and an effeminate person.

The modern terms have phonetic similarities to those previously discussed under the heading of xenophobia, being short and laden with hostility. *Homo* represents an example of a term which was originally neutral having become abbreviated and critical. Some also show great flexibility. In the course of this century, *sod*, for example, has generated *sod it!*, *sodding*, *sod all*, *sod off*, *not give a sod* and *sod's law*, virtually the same range previously noted in *fuck* in figure 1.5.

When we turn to terms for female homosexuals, the reticence over explicit reference to lesbian activity (mentioned in the section on 'Victorian Attitudes' in chapter 7) probably explains the remarkable 'gap of time' between the emergence of the male and female categories. Although *buggeress* and *sodomitess* are recorded during the early hiatus, they are really nonce-words, the first being found only in a glossary of 1450, the second used marginally in the King James Bible. The translators obviously had a problem with a lexical gap, in a context which is fairly explicit: 'There shall be no whore [marg. *sodomitesse*] of the daughters of Israel, nor a sodomite of the sons of Israel' (Deuteronomy, xxiii. 17). Ben Jonson is again a prominent early contributor: in the Prelude to *The Forest* (1601), he writes of 'Light Venus . . . with thy tribade trine, invent new sports'. (*Tribade* comes from a Greek root meaning 'to rub'.)

As with the male field, the early terms are also classical, both *lesbian* and *sapphist* revolving round the figure of the famous Greek poet Sappho, who lived on Lesbos *c.*600 BC and who was 'accused of this vice', as the *OED* puts it. (Virtually every detail of Sappho's life seems, however, to be in dispute.) Although Krafft-Ebing observed that 'The homo-sexual woman offers the same manifestations, *mutatis mutandis*' (1892, p. 256), the term *homosexual* was seldom applied to women, and even now this use is something of a rarity. Clearly, the growth of opprobrious abbreviation *homo* (applied only to men) has reinforced this situation. By and large, terms for lesbians are, however, less critical than those for male homosexuals, since the practice is more tolerated, and, as Anthony Storr observed, 'there are very few cases recorded of women soliciting homosexually or seducing minors' (1964, p. 70).

It hardly needs to be stressed that, historically speaking, both varieties of homosexuality have provoked hostility and been condemned in such vocabulary as *abominations*, *perversions*, *aberrations*, *deviations* or worse. The Cleveland Street Scandal of 1889 (involving a homosexual brothel frequented by many respectable London gentlemen) was denounced by the *Birmingham Daily Post* as 'this hideous and foetid gangrene' (Pearsall, 1969, p. 469). The case was interesting for a semantic reason, in that during the proceedings a male prostitute by the name of John Saul, one of the key witnesses, described his associates as 'gay'. He was evidently using the word in both the time-honoured heterosexual fashion of 'the gay ladies on the beat' meaning 'sexually active' (found as *gay girl* as far back as Chaucer), as well as referring to his male friends. As Howard (1977) and Rawson (1981) point out, this seems to be the first recorded usage of the term to refer to homosexuals.

The subsequent appropriation of *gay* by homosexuals of both sexes (notably by the Gay Liberation Movement in the late 1960s) has been the object of much comment in the past two decades, most of it hostile. This was largely because this piece of semantic engineering was so successful that it drove the older senses out of use. Philip Howard noted archly: '. . . it is a paradox that it has been expropriated by one of the sadder groups in society' (1977, p. 34). Paul Johnson denounced the process in much stronger language:

> Finally, must we also be stuck with 'gay' for male homosexuals? I can see why these people wanted to designate themselves by some non-pejorative term. But it was a monstrous piece of verbal larceny to appropriate one of the most delightful and useful words in the language, which even in its ancient criminal-slang sense (quite unknown to most people anyway) had a wider meaning and applied to harlotry of both sexes. The homosexual lobby on both sides of the Atlantic has successfully sold the term to what might be called the sub-editorial establishment. (*Spectator*, 5 July 1986, p. 22)

Never the less, the upshot has been that *gay* has become the accepted term, both as noun and adjective. The older critical terms have become taboo, as attitudes have changed in the direction of tolerance. One cannot imagine the following sentiments being uttered in the same terms during the past decade: 'Everything is controlled by the sods. The country is riddled with homosexuals who are teaching the world how to behave – a spectacle of revolting hypocrisy.'[26] It remains to be seen whether *gay* will retain its neutrality as a term, or whether, like its predecessors, it will acquire such negative overtones that it will need to be replaced.

NOTES

1 Alice Jardine, 'Interview with Simone de Beauvoir', *Signs* 5:2, 1979, pp. 229–30.

2 Germaine Greer's excellent chapter on 'Abuse' in *The Female Eunuch* (1970) was one of the first of many studies, including Muriel Schultz, 'The Semantic Derogation of Women,' in *Language and Sex: Differences and Dominance*, ed. B. Thorne and N. Henley (Rowley, Mass., Newbury House, 1975), pp. 64–73.

3 As figure 11.2 reveals, both *prat* and *fanny* show considerable semantic instability over time. In the case of *fanny*, ambiguity persists since the term means 'backside' in America, but 'cunt' in British English, although in some contexts (e.g. 'to fall on your fanny') only backside would be possible.

4 There could be exceptions in the fragmentary and cryptic poems *Wulf and*

Eadwacer, *The Wife's Lament* and *The Husband's Message*. However, the poems have been subjected to a great diversity of interpretations.

5 H. Van der Merwe Scholtz, in his study, *The Kenning in Anglo-Saxon and Old Norse Poetry* (Doctoral Thesis, Utrecht, 1927), gives only two examples of kennings for 'queen', but over two pages for 'king'.

6 In King Alfred's translation of Boethius, Eurydice is made to stand allegorically for the hellish sins which a man must constantly renounce; Orpheus' backward glance symbolizes sinful backsliding.

7 Sheila Delany, 'Womanliness in *The Man of Law's Tale*', *Chaucer Review*, vol. 9, no. 1, Summer 1974, p. 68.

8 *Maudlin* is, of course, a phonetic variant of *magdalen*(*e*), and the word's association with weeping grew out of the traditional role in which Mary Magdalen is cast in artistic depictions of the Crucifixion. Connotations of penitential tearfulness emerge strongly in both noun and adjective in the first decade of the seventeenth century.

9 *Antony and Cleopatra*, I. i. 13, III. vi. 67, IV. xii. 13 and IV. xii. 28.

10 *Othello*, III. iii. 460 and IV. ii. 61.

11 *Othello*, II. i. 73, IV. ii. 82 and III. iv. 43. *Strumpet* is used nine times in *Othello* and *whore* a dozen, in both cases far exceeding the use in any other Shakespearean play.

12 In the last line Iago is giving *housewife* a cynical push downhill towards *hussy*, the role of infidelity which he has attributed (psychologically) to his wife, and the one he is about to foist on the heroine.

13 *Nymph* is, of course, an ambiguous term by this time. Though the old 'divine' sense is current even today, Richard III uses the word in its antithetical, debased sense in the phrase 'a wanton ambling nymph' (I. i. 17). There is also a very bawdy reference in *The Tempest* IV. i. 137–8: 'And these fresh nymphs encounter every one/In country footing.' The euphemism for 'whore', especially in the phrase *a nymph of the pave*, was current by *c.*1859.

14 Edmund Leach mentions the *queen/quean* pairing in his classic article 'Anthropological Aspects of Language: Animal Categories and Verbal Abuse'. In *New Directions in the Study of Language*, ed. Eric H. Lenneberg. Cambridge, Mass.: MIT Press, 1964, pp. 25–6.

15 *Coney* (from Latin *cunniculus*, a rabbit) and its venereal associations, are discussed in detail in chapter 7, footnote 2.

16 Bréal (1900) p. 101. Other psycholinguistic explanations of deterioration are offered by Schlauch, Burgess and Barber.

17 This notion is elaborately satirized in *The Taming of the Shrew*, III. ii. 233–6.

18 'Allardyce Nicholl reports that the society comedies of the restoration period in England tended to vilify any and all words applied to women, even the most sacred and dignified [such as *sister* and *mother*].' From M. Schlauch, *The Gift of Tongues*. London, Allen and Unwin, 1960, p. 119.

19 The quotations are from *Othello*, I. iii. 81, *King Lear*, I. i. 64 and *Coriolanus*, II. i. 194.

20 *Selected Essays* (1950), pp. 307–9. Lawrence also emphasizes (p. 310) the significance of the disease in swearing: 'How the word "pox" was in every mind and in every mouth'.

21 See especially Dale Spender, *Man Made Language* (London, Routledge, 1980). Numerous studies subsequently appeared in the same vein (but without Greer's flair), such as *Words and Women* and *The Handbook of Non-Sexist Writing*, both by Casey Miller and Kate Swift.

22 The association, from Revelation xvii. 1–6, is exploited from *c.*1648.[O] Hawthorne's title *The Scarlet Letter* (1850) shows that the adulterous associations of *scarlet* were established well before the nineteenth-century uses.

23 On dualism in Dickens see Edmund Wilson's seminal essay 'Dickens: The Two Scrooges,' in *The Wound and the Bow*. London, Secker and Warburg, n.d., pp. 1–104.

24 *Tom Jones* (1749), Book XVII, chapter iii.

25 *The Spectator*, 28 May 1988, p. 40.

26 Sir Thomas Beecham, quoted in Charles Reed, *Beecham. An Independent Biography*. (Cited in Frank S. Pepper (ed.), *Twentieth Century Quotations*. London, Sphere Books, 1987, p. 185.)

11
Conclusion

> For, now-a-days, Men change their Oaths,
> As often as they change their Cloaths.
>
> Swift

> Oaths are the Children of Fashion.
>
> Swift

> It seems to be the case that the serious oaths survive longest, or at any rate die hardest, while each age produces its own ephemeral formulas of mere light expletive and asseveration.
>
> H. C. Wyld (1930)

> *Effie* What's the Problem?
> *Blind* These fucking new BBC restrictions on dialogue . . .
>
> *The Listener*

> Beware of the community in which blasphemy does not exist; underneath, atheism runs rampant.
>
> Antonio Machado

> How difficult it is, in these days when you can discuss orgasms over the soup and flagellation with the ice cream, how extraordinarily difficult it is to remember the strength of the old taboos, the depth of the silence by which they were surrounded!
>
> Aldous Huxley

THE word-field of swearing is, as Swift and many others have observed, in constant flux, as older terms of weight and force are trivialized, to be replaced by modish newcomers. The frequently posited similarity between linguistic currency and fashion is clearest in the language of swearing. Consequently, an historical study such as this has to deal with an astonishingly large field in which virtually no single term has managed to retain its place in the panoply of insult. The few exceptions to this generalization lie in those timelessly calumniating terms of immorality, such as *coward, thief, whore*, and so on.

Looking back over the many centuries which this study has covered, it would appear that the major shift in mode which can be detected is that various forms of personal abuse, or swearing *at*, have assumed the dominant mode, while asseveration and the invocation of higher powers, or swearing *by* and *to*, have correspondingly diminished. In fact, apart from casual use in 'light swearing', the mode of swearing *by* is reserved, for the most part, for formal legal proceedings such as taking an oath or issuing an affidavit.

More specifically, it would appear that in Western society the major shifts in the focus of swearing have been from religious matters (more especially the breaching of the commandment against taking the Lord's name in vain) to sexual and bodily functions, and from opprobrious religious categorization, such as *heathen* and *pagan* to national and racial insults, such as *coolie* and *kike*.[1] Both of these trends reflect the increasing secularization of Western society.

Furthermore, there has been a decline in the varieties of socially framed terms of opprobrium, such as *traitor*, *renegade* and *coward* (in which the primary notion is that of 'in-group loyalty'). The point is made quite forcibly when we consider this exchange:

> ... what I speak
> My body shall make good upon this earth,
> Or my divine soul answer it in heaven.
> Thou art a traitor and a miscreant. ...
>
> I do defy him and I spit at him;
> Call him a slanderous coward and a villain:

These challenges are uttered by Bolingbroke and Mowbray in the opening scene of Shakespeare's *Richard II* (lines 36–9 and 60–1, respectively). We are very aware that the moral categories here invoked are no longer current; neither is the very physical emphasis in the exchange. Bolingbroke's quaintly forcible accusation

> With a foul traitor's name stuff I thy throat
> (44)

is countered by Mowbray's asseveration

> Then, Bolingbroke, as low as to thy heart,
> Through the false passage of thy throat, thou liest.
> (124–5)

Likewise, terms originally based on notions of social superiority or class differences, such as *churl, knave, cad, blackguard, guttersnipe* and *varlet* have undergone what C. S. Lewis analysed as 'the moralisation of status words' (1960, p. 21). First, the class sense was, over the centuries, replaced by a moral sense, which has in turn weakened to the point that the words are virtually obsolete. A curious example is supplied by *snotty-nosed*: the earlier meaning (in the late sixteenth century, deriving from the literal sense) was 'dirty, mean, paltry, contemptible'; it has since 'changed class', so to speak, to mean 'pert, saucy, proud, impudent, conceited', first (in the nineteenth century) in dialect use, but now generally. Hence the related term *snotty*. An interesting shift is also apparent, in the course of the past century or so, in that terms like *villain*, *rotter*, *bounder* and *cad*, which used to have a strong moral basis, have been displaced by more physically and sexually based terms, such as *bastard*, *bugger*, *shit* and *fucker*.

The work ethic has also played a continuing part, intensifying the opprobrium attaching to those accused of shirking work, stigmatised as *vagabonds*, *beggars*, *tramps*, *bums*, *skivers*. As was seen in chapter 5, this shift was very apparent in Elizabethan times when the whole social problem of 'upright' men and 'sturdy beggars' assumed considerable proportions.

These various changes reflect increasing attitudes of fairly cynical nominalism, regarding words as having no intrinsic, let alone absolute, value, far removed from the idealized medieval notions of linguistic 'realism' (philosophically speaking) and individual *troth* or personal commitment. It is a notable innovation that a judge will on occasion ask a witness taking the stand a question which would have been superfluous in earlier times, namely, 'Do you regard this oath as binding upon your conscience?'

SEXUAL AND RACIAL TABOOS

One index of the change of sensitivity concerning sexual and racial categories is the dictionary. It seems significant that the original *OED* (1884–1928) should have included all the religious and racial swear words, but have omitted several of the most genital, signally *fuck* and *cunt*. This fact passed virtually without comment, being alluded to only in a review of the first *Supplement* (1933) by A. S. C. Ross:

> Other omissions consist chiefly of modern slang . . . [and] (to use the more usual term, obscene) words. As regards, the latter there appears to have been a definite policy of omission; it certainly seems regrettable that

> the perpetuation of a Victorian prudishness (inacceptable in philology beyond all other subjects) should have been allowed to lead to the omission of some of the commonest words in the English language (e.g. *cunt* 'female sex organs'; *the curse* 'menstrual period'; *to fuck* 'to have intercourse with'; *roger* = *fuck*). (*Neuphilologische Mitteilungen* XXXV, 1934, Nr 3/4, p. 9)

Although the subsequent *Supplement* (1972–86) made good this omission, other forms of censorship came into play: the Oxford University Press was harrassed and pressurized over a number of political and racial definitions. The most determined campaign was that to suppress the opprobrious senses of *jew*, even though these had been current for centuries and continue to be used. This resulted in an action in the High Court of Chancery in 1972 (*Shloimovitz v. The Clarendon Press*). The case was rejected with costs on 5 July 1973, and the opprobrious senses stand. The consequence was that the following sociolinguistic explanation was added to the definition:

> In medieval England, Jews, though engaged in many pursuits, were particularly familiar as money-lenders, their activities being publicly regulated for them by the Crown, whose protégés they were. In private, Christians also practised money-lending, though forbidden to do so by Canon Law. Thus the name of Jew came to be associated in the popular mind with usury and any extortionate practices that might be supposed to accompany it, and gained an opprobrious sense.

Such has been the increased sensitivity on this point that one cannot imagine the following passages appearing in any popular modern fiction:

> The capitalists would rake in the shekels, and make fortunes by buying up wreckage. Capital, he said, had no conscience and no fatherland. Besides, the Jew was behind it, and the Jew hated Russia worse than hell. . . . 'The Jew is everywhere, but you have to go far down the backstairs to find him . . . if you're on the biggest kind of job and are bound to get to the real boss, ten to one you are brought up against a little white-faced Jew in a bath-chair with an eye like a rattlesnake.'

This is part of Scudder's crass conspiracy theory as explicated to Richard Hannay in the opening chapter of John Buchan's highly popular political thriller, *The Thirty-Nine Steps* (1915).[2]

It is remarkable to reflect that at the time of the Reformation the most virulent religious insults (*antichrist*, *devil*, *superstition* and *profanation*) could be freely employed, whereas in modern times comparatively less wounding ethnic terms (from a literal point of view) have become far more highly charged and offensive. Thus today *nigger* and *kaffir*, which were originally descriptive terms simply relating to colour (blackness) and to faith (*kafir* originally meaning an infidel), are considered so provocative that they may not be used without serious legal consequences, since they form grounds for *crimen injuria*. On the other hand, one can now refer to a person as a *devil* or a *witch* without such consequences.

Sensitivity to the issue of colour has also become a major political and social issue, especially in the United States, and was very apparent in the furore consequent upon the American Secretary of Agriculture, Earl Butz, making these remarks in 1976:

> I'll tell you why you [the Republican Party] can't attract coloreds. Because coloreds only want three things. You know what they want? I'll tell you what coloreds want; it's three things: First, a tight pussy; second, loose shoes; and third, a warm place to shit. (cited in Strentz, 1989, p. 95)[3]

Although the comment had been made privately, and though Butz had technically avoided any opprobrious label (even using the dated euphemism *coloreds*), his stereotype was in itself so outrageously insulting that he was subsequently forced to resign. Many newspapers preferred to use euphemisms like *vulgarism* and *obscenity* (in brackets) in place of Butz's original terms.

The shift in taboos from sexual to racial terms is also well reflected in the following comment in an American magazine article on race relations in the police, 'Black and White in Blue', published in 1970:

> The kind of racism that has separated him from his fellow white officers is so commonplace that it's scarcely noticeable. 'You drive down the street and the other guy says, "Look at those fucking n------s!" But they don't do that too much around me anymore.' (*San Francisco Magazine*, June, 1970, p. 16.)

The modern hypersensitivity to racist (or even racial) terms is highlighted by a comparison with earlier practice. In 1952 Kenneth Tynan satirically referred to Orson Welles' performance of Othello as 'Citizen Coon', a witticism (parodying 'Citizen Kane') which one cannot imagine being repeated in the 1980s. In 1973, in his prescriptive glossary *Don't Say It*, Professor Alan S. C. Ross made this pertinent comment about the differing degrees of offensive racist terms:

> CHINK, meaning 'Chinaman'. This rather old-fashioned word is, like *wog*, essentially taboo on racial grounds, though, for some reason, to disparage the Chinese is not considered as heinous as to disparage black people.

The perpetuation of racist categorizations has, however, also been exploited as a politicizing device: thus the NAACP (The National Association for the Advancement of Colored People) has intentionally retained the stigmatizing label 'colored' as a tactic to remind people that racial inequalities and prejudice persist. A more militant usage is to be found in the savagely ironic names of some modern American black rap groups, e.g. 'Nigger With Attitudes'.

At least one dictionary has responded to these opprobrious terms by the unrealistic, old-fashioned evasion of expungement. Dr David B. Guralnik, Editor-in-Chief of *Webster's New World Dictionary*, Second College Edition, published in 1970, justified the exclusion of such words as *dago*, *kike*, *wop* and *wog* in the following editorial statement:

> It was decided in the selection process that this dictionary could easily dispense with those true obscenities, the terms of racial or ethnic opprobrium, that are, in any case, encountered with diminishing frequency these days. (Foreword, p. viii)

Most dictionaries would not agree with the policy, the justification, or the final observation. Dr Robert Burchfield, Editor-in-Chief of the *OEDS*, in setting out some guidelines concerning 'Controversial Vocabulary in the *Oxford English Dictionary*' (in 1973) was emphatic on the point: 'Most particularly I want to stress the importance of rejecting Guralnikism, the racial equivalent of Bowdlerism, as a solution as far as historical and "unabridged" dictionaries are concerned' (Burchfield, 1989, p. 100). His essay, 'The Turn of the Screw: Ethnic Vocabulary and Dictionaries' (1989, pp. 109–15) also discusses the problem. Dr Guralnik's semantic extension of *obscenity* (discussed below) to include racial insult is also singularly noteworthy.

To a large extent, the dictionary reflects attitudes towards language which derive from the invention of printing. Most people would agree with Victor Hugo's observation that 'printing is the mother of all revolutions.' They would, however, interpret 'revolution' from a libertarian point of view, since assuredly, printing has had a major effect in mobilizing mass support for popular causes. However, when William Caxton made such substitutions as *buttocks* for *arse* in his *Morte d'Arthur*, he was making a revolutionary and far-reaching editorial decision on the notion of language which was 'fit to print'. From that time, the separation of registers was *de rigueur*, so that, as C. S. Lewis put it trenchantly, 'As soon as you deal with [sex] explicitly, you have to choose between the language of the nursery, the gutter and the anatomy class'

(Tynan, 1975, p. 154). In the majority of instances, only the last variety is acceptable in print.

But less than a century before Malory, Chaucer's *Canterbury Tales* had contained, without censorship, the whole available thesaurus, from *spatulamancy, calcinacioun, maat* (a rare Arabic word meaning 'dead') to *fart, shit, queynte* and *swyve*. Shakespeare's work was denied the same freedom, as was that of virtually all major writers down to Lawrence and Joyce. Chapter 7 has traced the development of this tradition of decorum and its notable breachers.

In Modern English there is, consequently, an enormous imbalance between 'acceptable' and 'underground' vocabulary. Using the traditional hierarchical thinking in these matters to set out the terms schematically, starting at the high-register ceiling and working down to the language of the street, or, as some would have it, the gutter, one might come up with the following separation:

reproduction
generation
copulation
coition
intercourse
congress
intimacy
carnal knowledge
coupling
pairing
mating

at roughly which point the line is drawn, below which are found:

shagging
banging
bonking
fucking

This picture, which seems sound enough, is actually misleading, in that it suggests that the majority of terms are 'acceptable' and the minority are 'unacceptable'. In fact, when the whole word-field is taken into account, the imbalance is reversed, in that the majority of terms, like the proverbial iceberg, are out of sight, even if they are not always out of earshot. Farmer and Henley cite in their *Dictionary of Slang* (1890–1904), under the relevant heading, curiously termed GREENS, an astoundingly vigorous thesaurus of copulation, from the opaque *act of darkness* to the mercilessly explicit *beast with two backs, bum dancing, bottom wetting* and *a squirt and a squeeze*. In all, the category contains some 500 items. Even Jonathon Green's recent and splendidly comprehensive collection, *The Slang Thesaurus* (1988) lists only approximately 200 items.

The basic point, however, is that the 'line of acceptability' has shifted. For instance, one would be very surprised to read in a modern medical text-book that 'In women the bladder is short, and is made fast to the cunt,' since classical terminology is now universal in the medical field. However, in medieval times, when registers could be mixed more freely, that description occurs, in Lanfranc's *Cirurgery* (*c.*1400). An anonymous contemporary manuscript in Gloucester Cathedral informs us that '[the urine] passith out by the ȝerde', using an ancient term for the penis, the *yard*, for the first time.[O] John of Trevisa writes in similar vein a contemporary passage, 'Emoroides ben fuyue veynes whyche stretche out atte the eeres' ('Haemorrhoids are five veins which stretch out at the arse').[O]

We have seen that, from an historical perspective, the Crown has been the traditional censor in matters of language. However, in the past two centuries, there has been a significant new actor, who might be termed 'the self-appointed supervisor of bourgeois morals'. This role can be extended back to William Prynne and Jeremy Collier, who launched savage attacks on the decadence of the English stage in the seventeenth century. Prynne's *Histriomastix* (1633) (which might be loosely rendered as 'actor-bashing') and Collier's *Short View of the Immorality and Profaneness of the English Stage* (1698) provoked much controversy. But neither of them acquired the institutional force of their successor, the personage of the mythical Mrs Grundy, an imaginary character in Thomas Morton's play, *Speed the Plough* (1798). Though (significantly) she never appeared, she was still able, *in absentia*, to pressurize the other characters, who asked the anxious, persistent question, 'What will Mrs Grundy say?' Her formidable influence is reflected by the growth of *Grundyism* (1836), *Grundyites* (1845) and *Grundyist* (1883).[O]

However, within a generation, her cause had been championed collectively by the Bowdler family, notably by Dr Thomas Bowdler (1754–1825), who took the uncompromising view that 'Words which give an impression of obscenity should not be spoken, written or printed.'[4] Bowdler put his views into practice by producing in 1818 an edition of Shakespeare from which, as is announced on the title page (figure 11.1) 'those words and expressions are omitted which cannot with propriety be read aloud in a family'.

> Many words and expressions occur which are of so indecent a nature as to render it highly desirable that they should be erased. . . . neither the vicious taste of the age, nor the most brilliant effusions of wit, can afford an excuse for profaneness or obscenity; and if these could be obliterated, the transcendent genius of the poet would undoubtedly shine with more unclouded lustre. (1827, p. xvi)

In this vein of total assurance, Bowdler turns more specifically to the expungement of profanity: 'The most sacred Word in our language is omitted in several instances, in which it appeared as a mere expletive; and it is changed into the word Heaven in a still greater number' (1827, p. xvii).

Yet Bowdler, like most censors, was inconsistent. In *Othello* he retains (curiously) *impudent strumpet! cunning whore of Venice* and *demi-devil* (but predictably removes *an old black ram is tupping your white ewe*). Yet, contrary to what is sometimes maintained, Lady Macbeth's agonized line 'Out, damned spot!' is not altered to 'Out, crimson spot!' In *Hamlet*, *whore* is deleted but *drab* retained, 'bloody, bawdy villain' is emended to the somewhat déclassé 'bloody, *murderous* villain'. Generally speaking, Bowdler retains the violence but excises the sex. Unsurprisingly, *Timon of Athens* comes in for the greatest swathes of excision. In Timon's great curse, quoted in chapter 5, the deletions are indicated by italics. Looking for fresh fields to mow, Bowdler then proceeded to *bowdlerize* (to use his eponymic verb, which appeared in 1836) a far less fruitful text, namely Gibbon's *Decline and Fall of the Roman Empire*. His semantic legacy is also found in *bowdlerism* (1869), *bowdlerized* (1879) and *bowdlerization* (1882).[O]

The most recent (and most influential) figure in this sanitizing establishment is Mrs Mary Whitehouse, who was provoked by the strong language and low morality of such television comedies as 'Till Death Us Do Part' (1966–8), to start a campaign to 'Clean Up Television'. She published a book, *Cleaning-Up TV* (Blandford Press, 1966) and subsequently became something of a 'watchdog' agency, agitating against pornographic material, bad language and blasphemy to the point of putting pressure on producers and even bringing the occasional lawsuit.[5]

It would be misleading to regard these initiatives as lacking public support or as being a thing of the past. Although the figure of the Lord Chamberlain is unlikely to be resuscitated, a similar role is fulfilled by official enquiries such as the Mogg Commission.[6] Evidence also accumulates from other official sources. In February, 1990, the report of the Lord Justice Taylor into the state of English soccer (consequent upon the crushing to death of 94 football fans at Hillsborough on

THE

FAMILY SHAKSPEARE,

In Eight Volumes;

IN WHICH

NOTHING IS ADDED TO THE ORIGINAL TEXT;

BUT THOSE WORDS AND EXPRESSIONS ARE OMITTED WHICH CANNOT WITH PROPRIETY BE READ ALOUD IN A FAMILY.

——— exemit labem purumque reliquit
Æthereum sensum, atque aurai simplicis ignem.
VIRGIL.

BY

THOMAS BOWDLER, Esq. F.R.S. & S.A.

THE FIFTH EDITION.

VOL. I.

CONTAINING

TEMPEST;
TWO GENTLEMEN OF VERONA;
MERRY WIVES OF WINDSOR;
TWELFTH-NIGHT: OR, WHAT YOU WILL;
MEASURE FOR MEASURE;
MUCH ADO ABOUT NOTHING.

LONDON:

PRINTED FOR
LONGMAN, REES, ORME, BROWN, AND GREEN.
PATERNOSTER-ROW.

1827.

FIGURE 11.1 Victorian excision: Thomas Bowdler's sanitized *The Family Shakespeare* (originally published in 1818).

15 April 1989) recommended, amongst other measures, the banning or suppression of 'obscene and racist chanting' by football spectators. As has been seen in this study, prohibitions are often as revealing as breaches.

Traditionally, pressure groups and institutional censors have sought to suppress swearing on religious grounds; in modern times their policies and activities have become far more complex, since they have become more politically aware. In areas of the culture concerning explicit sex, the older forms of repression have given way to permissiveness. In areas of sexual insult, traditional heterosexual terms like *fucker*, *bugger*, etc., have achieved a certain acceptance, but homosexual insults, such as *queer*, *homo*, *poof*, etc. have been increasingly suppressed: in May 1990, the Press Council of the United Kingdom went so far as to classify *poof*, *poofter* and *woofter* as 'impermissible'.[7] (No such ban applies to insulting terms for lesbians.) In racial areas, double standards have come to surround references to blacks. Insulting terms for blacks have acquired a special taboo (as A. S. C. Ross observes) but pro-Black lobbyists (like the NAACP) and black 'rap' groups have deliberately maintained them as a form of protest. Things are more complicated than they were when this horrifying report emanated from Ruleville, Mississippi in 1965:

> [The two highway patrolmen] stood me against the wall. 'You a nigger or a nigra?' one asked. 'A Negro,' I said. The other hit me across the mouth. Then he asked, 'You a nigger or a nigra?' 'A Negro,' I said again. The first punched me hard on the ear, and I fell down. They took me by the shirt and the arm, and they pulled up. I could feel two teeth were loose. The first patrolman asked me again, 'You a nigger or a nigra?' I looked at their faces, and I knew what they wanted me to do.
>
> 'A nigger,' I said. Then they smiled, because it was what they wanted to hear.[8]

CHANGES IN TERMINOLOGY

The change in the focus of swearing is also reflected in the terminology used to describe swear-words. The older terms, like *blasphemy*, *profanity* and *obscenity* originally had a strong religious denotation. Thus *blaspheme* meant from Middle English times 'to utter impious or profane words' and was usually followed by *against*, as in John Wycliffe's stricture that 'freres by gabbings [twaddle] blasfeme upon Christ'.[O] From Elizabethan times, the word (and its other forms) could be used to mean simply 'abuse'. Likewise, *profane* carried over into its Middle English sense its Latin etymology of 'to desecrate or violate a temple', before its meaning was extended to more secular objects. Even John Donne, Dean of St Paul's, could use *profanation* (coined in *The Book of Common Prayer* of 1552) in the context of love, *c.*1610:

> T'were prophanation of our joyes
> To tell the layetie our love.[9]

In the United Kingdom the blasphemy law has been invoked only at irregular intervals in modern times. Previously, since Christianity was legally conceived as being part of the law itself, blasphemy was construed as subversion. There were, consequently, more prosecutions and stricter punishments. Up to 1677 the offence was punishable by burning at the stake, though the last instance of a burning took place in 1612. The death sentence remained in Scottish law until 1825, by which time the pillory or a fine was in force in England. Shelley's joint publication of a pamphlet, *The Necessity of Atheism*, in 1811 led to his being sent down from Oxford, but not to a prosecution. There are cases brought by the Crown dating from 1882 (for the publishing of comic cartoons ridiculing Christianity) and 1921. In 1977 Mrs Mary Whitehouse brought a private prosecution against the editor of *Gay News* for publishing a poem by Professor James Kirkup suggesting that Jesus was a promiscuous homosexual. Mr John Mortimer, who conducted the defence, subsequently observed: 'At the trial it was ruled that we could call no evidence on the poet's sincerity or the poem's literary merit (so blasphemers are far more harshly treated than pornographers)' (*Spectator*, 21 April 1990, p. 7). The editor was fined £500 and given a prison sentence of eighteen months, suspended for nine months. In 1989 an attempt to invoke the law against Salman Rushdie's controversial novel, *The Satanic Verses*, failed on the grounds that the law covers only Christianity, its personages and articles of belief. This led to two contrary approaches, one to extend the law to cover other religions, the other to abolish it entirely. In April, 1989 a bill for abolition introduced into the House of Commons fell without debate.

Obscene, given as 'of doubtful etymology' by the *OED*, is explained thus by Robert Graves in his essay, 'Poetry and Obscenity':

> The word 'obscene', from the Latin *obscenus*, which means 'inauspicious' or 'ill-omened', consists of the words *ob* meaning 'against' and *scæne* (from the Greek *scene*) meaning 'a theatrical performance'. It won [sic] its secondary meaning of 'depraved' or 'indecent' when plays, originally performed in honour of deities and heroes under the protection of Dionysus, god of the Mysteries, came to include scenes of indecent buffoonery offensive to the gods themselves. . . . When public sexual

> handling of one another by Roman actors – the 'actresses' being boys – became fashionable, this was at first considered anti-religious and therefore unlucky by the old-fashioned public. (1972, p. 63)

In tracing the English meanings, it is often difficult to know, without full knowledge of the context, which senses are conveyed by *obscene* and *obscenity*, since they cover 'abominable', 'disgusting', 'filthy', 'indecent' and 'lewd'. It would seem that both terms started to acquire a sexual specialization in the course of the seventeenth century, for by 1725 Pope could use *obscene parts* to signify 'private parts' in his translation of the *Odyssey*: 'Her [Scylla's] parts obscene the raging billows hide.'[O] This sexual association has also been emphasized by the legal category of 'obscene libel', discussed in relation to the *Chatterley* trial in chapter 9.

It is a fascinating point that the semantic history of *obscene* and *obscenity* represents in miniature the thesis which this study has traced in the wider developments in swearing, in that the words have progressed through four basic stages in meaning: first religious, then sexual, finally political and racial. The political *cum* racial sense was alluded to earlier in this chapter in the discussion of 'Guralnikism', notably in the reference to racist swear-words as being 'those true obscenities'.

The same development can be seen in *indecent* and *indecency*. 'Public indecency' now has an explicitly sexual overtone. It could never now be used of, say, exhibiting one's wounds or setting fire to oneself. Other terms which have developed in a similar direction are *foul*, *filth* and *filthy*, as well as *dirty* and *smutty*. The most recent addition is *four-letter word*, dating from 1934.[S] (One can hardly imagine this euphemism being used of *pish* and *tush*.)

Summing up these developments, we may note that the terminology has become increasingly imprecise as the terms have lost their original religious sense and continued to be used in application to sexual, social, sexist and racist idioms. Thus the statement, 'The man was furious, blaspheming and uttering obscenities', gives us now no sense of the content of the utterance. Philip Howard makes this apposite comment: 'Starvation and mass unemployment are detestable. To describe them as "obscene" erodes the meaning of "obscene", without making one's detestation any more emphatic' (1985, p. 13).

In leaving the topic, we may note that a highly significant shift in terminology has been that from specific labels to general categories. Thus, in earlier times of religious ruction, vilifying labels, such as *papist*, *methodist* and *puritan* became the stock-in-trade of schismatic abuse. However, once the period of frenzy had passed, it was the general notion of 'extremist' which generated the term of abuse, in the form of *fanatic* and *enthusiast* (in its seventeenth-century sense). Thereafter, chauvinist labels like *frog*, *yankee*, *limey* and *dago* produced *nationalistic* and subsequently *fascist*. Similarly, *nigger*, *kaffir*, *ofay*, *wop* and *yid* are currently being concentrated in plain *racist*. Chauvinist labels *bitch*, *tart*, *dish*, *doll* and *bird* have in their turn generated *sexist*. (The term is, of course, still usually applied only to men, even though there is a matching range of female chauvinist epithets such as *hunk*, *cheesecake*, *stud* and *jock*.) In all cases, the specific label becomes highly motivated through friction and controversy, and then, as the period of confrontation passes and reasonable people start to stigmatize the extremists, the generalized term acquires emotive disapproval. The problem is, of course, that the newly motivated terms like *fascist*, *racist* and *sexist* become so generalized as to be labels themselves.

These lexical and semantic changes obviously reflect social developments. As we have seen, swearing in religious terms increased from medieval to Victorian times in direct proportion to the decline of the Church as a major force in Western society, while the corresponding increase in the currency of sexual swearing seems to reflect liberation from inhibitions traditionally suppressing the sexual drive and direct reference to it. The growth of nationalism is reflected in terms which Eric Partridge has called 'Offensive Nationality', while racist sentiments have found ready expression in many opprobrious terms. Very often the growth of these vocabularies of abuse is the consequence of mercantile expansion, military conflict or problems of social competition or assimilation. As is shown in the discussion in chapter 6, terms concerned with strangers or outsiders depict them as rivals, invaders, pagans and perverts.

It would appear from an analysis of these mainsprings of swearing that people swear by what is most potent to them. Hence the decline in religious swearing in Protestant societies reflects the decline of the influence of the Church. By contrast, in Catholic societies the grisliest imaginable religious invocations are still current. The decline of the invocation *Mary!* in English, first to *marry!*, and then to oblivion, is in sharp contrast to the such grotesque Catholic variations as Italian *Porca Madonna!* ('that sow of the Virgin Mary!') and *Madonna puttana!* ('that whore of the Virgin Mary!').

Sexual swearing is initially concerned with roles, rather than genital parts: hence the oldest terms of abuse are *quean* and *whore*, both going back to late Old English. As the discussion on 'The Categorization of Women' in chapter 10 has shown, there has been a constant supply of these terms over the past thousand years. The metaphorical use of sexual parts is a more recent and more complicated development.

The 'modern explosion' (as it is termed in chapter 9) has undoubtedly been the most significant development of recent times. Although swearing is certainly not yet acceptable in public, and still occasions fines, law suits and censure, one is very aware of a great change of attitude having taken place between our own times and the period in which the following words were written.

> There is a certain adjective, most offensive to polite ears, which plays the chief rôle in the vocabulary of large sections of the community. It seems to argue a certain poverty of linguistic resource when we find that this word is used by the same speakers to mean absolutely nothing – being placed before every noun, and often adverbially before all adjectives – and also to mean a great deal – everything indeed that is unpleasant in the highest degree. (Wyld, 1936, p. 387)

Wyld's painstaking but knowing evasions now seem quaint. (He pays a price for his delicacy, however: while his audience would have known that the taboo word alluded to was *bloody*, many modern readers might read the passage and, being uncertain, conclude that Wyld was alluding to *fucking*.) His notions of taboo have increasingly been replaced by attitudes of insensitivity, indifference or sophisticated *laissez-faire* of the kind superbly satirized by David Lodge in the following piece of academic enlightenment:

> 'But doesn't it bother you at all?' Robyn said. 'That the things we care so passionately about – for instance, whether Derrida's critique of metaphysics lets idealism in by the back door, or whether Lacan's psychoanalytic theory is phallogocentric, or whether Foucault's theory of the episteme is reconcilable with dialectical materialism – things like that, which we argue about and read about and write about endlessly – doesn't it worry you that ninety-nine point nine per cent of the population don't give a monkey's?'
>
> 'A what?' said Charles.
>
> 'A monkey's. It means you don't care a bit.'
>
> 'It means that you don't give a monkey's fuck.'
>
> 'Does it?' said Robyn, with a snigger. 'I though it meant a monkey's nut. I should have known: "fuck" is much more poetic in Jakobson's terms – the repetition of the "k" as well as the first vowel in "monkey" . . .' (Lodge, 1989, p. 217)

In his contemporary work of fiction, *Oscar and Lucinda*, Peter Carey recreates attitudes towards obscene swearing which are manifestly

Victorian. His narrator describes a confrontation between his parents in the middle of a power cut:

> I cannot explain how frightening this was. My father did not speak like this. He liked life to be quiet. . . . But for some reason this announcement seemed to outrage him. He clasped his head. He put the candle on top of the Kelvinator where it promptly went out again.
>
> 'Oh, Christ,' he said. 'Jesus, Joseph and fucking Mary.'
>
> In the lightning I saw my sister's mouth drop open.
>
> My mother stood up. She never made gentle or gradual movements. She stood so quickly her chair fell backwards. It crashed to the floor. The phone rang – two short bleats, then stopped.
>
> 'Kneel,' my mother said. She meant for God to forgive my father his blasphemy. We understood her meaning, but we were outside our normal territory. Only 'divorce' could have frightened me more, only 'sex' been more embarrassing.
>
> 'Kneel,' she shrieked. (Carey, 1988, p. 5)

DIFFERENCES WITHIN THE SPEECH-COMMUNITY

Although there have obviously been major changes since Wyld's delicately conspiratorial passage was written, the developments have not been entirely in the direction of the 'liberation' which Lodge so amusingly depicts. It is all a question of the conventions within the 'speech-community', which may be divided on many lines, including those of race, class or gender. Swearing among women has been discussed in chapter 10; the conventions of 'sounding', or ritual insults among American blacks have been discussed in chapter 9. So far as class distinctions are concerned, much has been made of the differing linguistic mores categorized (nearly half a century ago by A. S. C. Ross) as 'U' and 'non-U' usage. However, that study, which was undoubtedly accurate in many respects, omitted any discussion of swearing. The situation is more complicated than the simplistic 'U'/'Non-U' dichotomy suggests, in that within the English class system, both the upper and the working classes, preferring directness to euphemism in most things, maintain traditions of fairly heavy swearing, so that most of the 'four-letter' words thrive in these socially separated circles. On the other hand, the bourgeoisie maintains strict taboos against any such utterance. These attitudes are not new. As chapter 3 recorded, several medieval writers comment on swearing being a feature of upper-class speech. We recall that Chaucer, in the guise of the bourgeois pilgrim narrator, was embarrassed by the 'cherles terms' of the Miller, while Harry

Hotspur, that embodiment of aristocratic *sprezzatura*, enjoined his wife to

> Swear me, Kate, like a lady as thou art,
> A good mouth-filling oath; and leave 'in sooth,'
> And such protests of pepper-gingerbread,
> To velvet-guards and Sunday citizens.[10]
> (*Henry IV, Part I*, III. i. 257–60)

Defoe, castigating (in 1712) the profanity of beaux talking 'senseless stuff' in a coffee house, continues: 'But take them in in any other discourse 'tis the same; at play 'tis G---d damn the cards; a-hunting, G---d damn the hounds; they call the dogs sons of whores, and men sons of bitches (1951, p. 260). It is surely no coincidence that the two most notorious breaches of decorum in modern literature should have involved a Cockney flower-girl and a rustic game-keeper. A more recent gloss on being studiously un-bourgeois is wittily made by Jilly Cooper in *Class*: 'I once heard my son regaling his friends: "Mummy says that *pardon* is a much worse word than *fuck*"' (1981, p. 39).

One consequence of the dispersal of English as a world language has been the creation of such a great variety of linguistic attitudes and idioms that the notion of 'an English-speaking community' now seems questionable. Swearing, being the most emotive form of the language, is that most easily misinterpreted; there is always the possibility of a form of words (such as *bastard*, *bugger* and *mother-fucker*) being taken literally when it may be intended in a mild, familiar or even jocular fashion. Not only that. The sheer volume of terms is now so enormous (as a consequence of wholesale borrowing and regional growth) that few people can now travel the world and be sure of understanding the diversity of insults. A simple test case may be devised from the following list: *addlepate, airhead, BF, berk, birdbrain, bozo, brenda, cement-head, clodpoll, clunk, coot, dickhead, dildo, dingbat, dipshit, dork, drongo, dumb-bell, dumbo, dummy, fruitcake, gink, git, goof, ig man, klutz, kook, lunchbox, lunkhead, mutt, nit, noodle, nutter, prat, prawnhead, puddinghead, rookie, schlemiel, schmeggege, schmuck, screwball, section eight, shitkicker, silly-billy, spaz, squarebrain, stupe, thickie, thicko, toolhead, twit, zipalid*. No reader would be uncertain, by the end of the list, that it related to those stigmatized for being 'stupid or unintellectual'; but, equally, no reader would be familiar with *all* of these terms in this sense. The list comprises, incidentally, only about one third of the category listed in Jonathon Green's *The Slang Thesaurus* (1988).

The profusion of terms listed above shows a certain creativity in this area of abuse. However, much modern swearing qualifies as verbicide and little more, so that its omission is often more effective than its inclusion. The point is well made in *Songs and Slang of the British Soldier, 1914–18*, by John Brophy and Eric Partridge:

> From being an intensive to express strong emotion it became a merely conventional excrescence. By adding *-ing* and *-ingwell* an adjective and an adverb were formed and thrown into every sentence. It became so common that an effective way for the soldier to express emotion was to omit this word. Thus, if a sergeant said, 'Get your ---ing rifles!' it was understood as a matter of routine. But if he said, 'Get your rifles!' there was an immediate implication of urgency and danger. (1930, p. 15ff. Cited in Mencken, 1936, p. 315)

The semantic tendencies known as 'Loss of Intensity' and 'Verbicide' would seem to be a major feature in the development of swear-words. (Here there is an interesting contrasting pattern to the process of Euphemism: euphemisms multiply because they become too explicit and have to be replaced at regular intervals, whereas swear-words need periodic reinforcements since they become weakened through repetition.) Although *fuck, shit* and *cunt* have not lost all their original potency, many of the terms in the word-field are now enfeebled: these include *bloody, bastard, damn, hell, blast*, indeed nearly all the religious terms, and a surprising number of erstwhile sexual terms, such as *frig, frigging* which meant both 'copulation' and 'masturbation' from the seventeenth century. Similarly, *footle* and its Scots relation, *footer*, 'to muck about, waste time', derive from French *foutre*. These instances alert us to the curious imprecision of many anatomical terms. We have already noted the ambiguity of orifice referred to in *fanny* and noted that *prat* and *roger* (vb) had in earlier times a similar genital confusion. Here the cause doubtless lies in the deliberate vagueness and unfamiliarity of the terms, which would lead to confusion. The relevant terms are set out in figure 11.2 on 'Instability of Sexual Terms'.

What of the language of genuine vehemence and urgency? Can it be argued that the profusion of 'light' swearing has had the ultimate effect of undermining this idiom? When one looks back to Chaucer, for example, to the moment of comic panic in the *Nun's Priest's Tale*, when Chauntecleer is being abducted, one is struck by the richness of the language of exclamation in medieval times:

> [They] cryden 'Out! harrow! and weylalway!'
> (3380)

Bugger

1 A heretic 1340
2 A sodomite 1555
3 A practiser of bestiality 1555
4 A chap, fellow, customer 1719

Fanny (not in *OED* or Grose)

1 (UK): 'The female *pudendum*' (Farmer and Henley)
The sense is surely implied in John Cleland's *Fanny Hill* (1749), a punning reference to Latin *Mons Veneris*
2 (US): 'The buttocks, rump = ASS from 1920s' (Chapman) 'from 1860s' (Flexner)

Frig

1 To masturbate 1598 (Florio)
2 To copulate 1707

Merkin

1 'the female *pudendum*' 1535
2 'Counterfeit hair for the privities of women' 1736 Bailey (from *c.*1620)
3 A pubic wig, generally 18th c.
4 An artificial vagina 1886 (Burton)

Prat

1 Buttocks 1573 (Harman)
2 The female *pudendum* 19th c. (Partridge)
3 A fool, idiot 1960s

Punk

1 A whore 1575
2 A catamite 1904
3 A worthless fellow 1917

Roger

1 Penis 1653
2 (vb) Copulate 1709
3 (vb) Rape (US) 1930s

Tail

1 Backside 1303
2 'The female *pudendum*' 1362
3 Penis 1386

Notes

One surmizes that these terms have acquired ambiguity through being used euphemistically or through being slang or underworld terms not readily understood by those unfamiliar with them. *See also the note on *jere* in FIGURE 1.2 (p. 17).

FIGURE 11.2 Instability of sexual terms.

A modern translator is hard put to it to convey this emotion adequately because of the paucity of terms. *Harrow* (originally *haro!*), was a call for help in emergency legally defined under Norman law. *Wei la wei!* is the most poignant of Anglo-Saxon laments, which later became trivialized into *wellaway*. It seems significant that T. S. Eliot found it necessary to invoke the older form in *The Waste Land* (1922), ll. 277–92. Both words have passed away, leaving us with such feeble alternatives as *help!* and the archaic *alas!*

What of the language of sexual passion? In spite of Lawrence's valiant attempts at reclaiming or 'redeeming' the four-letter words, most people would agree with Frank Kermode that

> They can hardly be said to have acquired a tender, let alone a numinous quality; acceptable in common use, whether as expletives or as part of a genuinely sexual language . . . they remain part of sex-in-the-head, or as instruments of the wrong kind of letting-go. . . . Hence Mellors's use of them, though it may impress liberal bishops, strikes most people as a bit comic, doctrinaire almost – at best the language of a lost paradise. (1973, pp. 123–4)

Although the view that there has been considerable liberation in modern times has much truth in it, the interpretation of a steady advance to enlightenment is simplistic. Such a view would hold that the constraints of medieval times were overthrown in the Renaissance, that there was a steady liberalization through the Enlightenment, a Puritanical regression in Victorian times, and a final throwing off of the shackles in the post-war era. Curiously, nearly all of these generalizations are inaccurate. Chaucer and many medieval writers had more freedom than their Renaissance successors; the Enlightenment saw a steady clamping down on strong or risqué language, while the Victorian era showed a remarkable efflorescence of strong and foul language, in some ways surpassing that of modern times. However, it took place out of earshot of 'polite society'. The trials of *Oz* and *Gay News* show that modern tolerance has its limits. Most people are more 'comfortable' with *bonk* rather than *fuck*, and even battle-hardened combat troops talk of being *wasted* rather than being *killed*.

It may, of course, be argued that ever since slang dictionaries started to appear in England, in the late sixteenth century, they demonstrated that the underground language of coarse abuse was growing with such luxuriance that it could not be controlled, and that this proliferation has simply continued. Curiosity in this linguistic area seems to be perennial. Modern interest in 'bad language' is evidenced in the remarkable upsurge in the publication of 'alternative' dictionaries (and such organs as *Maledicta: the International Journal of Verbal Aggression*) in recent times.[11] These would seem to have an anomalous function, in that those readers unfamiliar with the 'underground' obscenities will presumably not use them, while those who know the words have no need of the dictionaries. One thing is clear. The profusion of foul language and swearing in modern times represents the ultimate triumph of informal language over formal, a development which can be paralleled in many areas of social change.

Attitudes towards swearing are not constant. Like those towards sexuality, they seem to oscillate in cycles between acceptance and repression. However, the energy generating swearing is constant. The comparison with sexuality is apposite in that, during periods of sexual repression, prostitution and perversion flourish. In the same fashion, during the periods of Puritan, Augustan and Victorian repression, the underworld lexicon flourished to a quite remarkable degree. Within the American provenance, a long period of restraint has led to the counterbalancing modern explosion.

When one looks at the contemporary scene, it would appear that the axiom of Vico is clearly fulfilled. Historically, swearing has indeed moved down from the domains of gods and heroes, and is now largely indiscriminate, with sacred, profane, sexual, political and racist modes coexisting in a farraginous conglomeration. Hence such absurdities as 'Jesus fucking Christ!' and this verified oddment from Australia: 'You rotten, bloody, poofter, commo, mongrel bastard' (Hornadge, 1980, p. 136).

Much of this study has, of necessity, concerned itself with taboos, since swearing in its ambivalent fashion both violates and respects taboos through shocking directness or euphemistic evasion. Aldous Huxley's epigraph to this chapter emphasizes a major shift in the sexual area. Today, when nothing seems sacred, what taboos can still be invoked? Twenty years ago John Weightman considered the question à propos the mass stage nudity of Kenneth Tynan's *succès de scandale*, 'Oh! Calcutta!':

> What one wonders now is where the taboo will reassert itself in Western civilization, if it has really been removed from sex. Will one be perfectly in order in showing one's nakedness and yet obscene, for instance, if one develops a rational argument? (*Encounter*, October 1970, p. 38)

The question remains unanswered. Which suggests that *anomie*, the normlessness which Durkheim diagnosed as being the distinctive malaise of modern western society, is as apparent in the extremes of linguistic behaviour as any other.

NOTES

1 See A. S. C. Ross (1973) pp. 6–7.
2 Most of such 'theories' of 'Zionist plots' derive from a document called *The Protocols of the Elders of Zion*, ostensibly a record of secret agreements by 'world Jewry' aimed at global domination. The document was first published in book form in Russia in 1905, used during the pogrom after the 1917 Revolution, but shown by a judicial enquiry in 1934 to be a forgery by the Okrana (Russian Secret Police).
3 I am obliged to Professor Strentz for supplying me with the original version, which I have used in the text in place of euphemistic forms.
4 Philip Howard points out (1984, pp. 107–8) that Bowdler's mother, Elizabeth Stuart Bowdler, published an edition of the *Song of Solomon* in which she emended, amongst other terms, *bed* to *bridal chariot*. He also states that much of the censorship in *The Family Shakespeare* was, in fact, carried out by Bowdler's sister, Henrietta Maria, known as Harriet.
5 Mrs Whitehouse brought the action for blasphemy (mentioned below) against *Gay News*.
6 Part of the brief of the Mogg Commission (inaugurated in 1988) concerned broadcast language.
7 The ban on *woofter* seemed especially absurd, since the word was virtually unknown. See Paul Johnson, 'Storm in a Powder-Puff' (*Spectator*, 26 May 1990), p. 25.
8 *Encounter*, November 1965, p. 95.
9 'A Valediction: Forbidding Mourning,' ll. 7–8. Donne is notable for his daring use of religious terms like *martyr*, *hermitage* and *canonized* in amorous contexts.
10 In Elizabethan times, *gingerbread* had the figurative meaning of 'showy but insubstantial'; a *velvet-guard* would wear such soft trimmings, while by a *Sunday citizen* Hotspur would seem to be referring to one in 'Sunday best', assuming a temporary urbanity.
11 *Maledicta* started publication in 1965, and has published annual collections since 1977. As the Bibliography to this study shows, similar works have appeared since 1987 by Chapman, Green, McDonald, Morton and Paros.

Appendix A
Body Language

> Some cried, some swore, and the tropes and figures of Billingsgate were used without reserve in all their native zest and flavour; nor were those flowers of rhetoric unattended with significant gesticulation. Some snapped their fingers, some forked them out, some clapped their hands, and some their backsides.
>
> Tobias Smollett, *Humphry Clinker* (1771), pp. 53–4

SMOLLETT'S wonderfully graphic description of the rude exchanges which occurred at a party in Bath has a timeless zest. It also reminds us of the obvious point that swearing is not simply a matter of words, but of tone and 'significant gesticulation'. Offensive body language or 'gesticulatory swearing', as Montagu calls it (1973, p. 344), has become the focus of considerable discussion in modern times, often carrying the misleading implication that such behaviour is a recent phenomenon. This interest has presumably arisen as tourists have increasingly become aware of curious foreign codes and modes of insulting behaviour. The Queen has, on her recent visits to New Zealand, often been subjected to the *whakapohane*, a Maori insult or gesture of protest which takes the form of exhibiting one's naked buttocks. An expert in local customs describes it as 'the ultimate culturally sanctioned Maori way of displaying opprobrium' (Mort, 1986, p. 212). The practice, which is ancient and widespread in Oceania, was recorded by Captain Cook in 1774. He required no 'local expert' to get the point: 'One fellow shewed us his back side in such a manner that it was not necessary to have an interpreter.'

The same practice has become quite well known on college campuses in the US as *mooning*, with the important differences that it is more of a prank or taunt, variously intended to impress, protest against or affront, and is often confined to women. *Moon* has a surprisingly extended history in the sense of 'buttocks'; there is a tantalizing quotation from 1756 which runs: 'But his Moon shall never be covered by me or Buck 'till they put down the Ready [cash] – and no Brummagums [counterfeit coins].'[O]

Whether or not such forms of behaviour are more common in certain cultures or at particular stages of a culture is a moot point. One would assume that the further back one went in a culture, the more gesture would accompany (and possibly even replace) language. About half a century ago, R. G. Collingwood made these observations about cultural differences in communication:

> A dispute between Italian peasants is conducted hardly more in words than in a highly elaborated language of manual gesture. Here again, there is no physiological basis for the difference. Italians do not possess more sensitive fingers than northern Europeans. But they have a long tradition of controlled finger-gesture, going back to the ancient game of *micare digitis*. (1938, p. 242)

Yet Smollett shows us that 'gesticulatory swearing' was well developed in the eighteenth century, a period normally thought to be highly formal. Snapping of fingers would not qualify now as a mode of insult, but we are still familiar with forking them out. Indeed, the tradition is encapsulated in the phrase 'to fork the fingers', recorded, remarkably, as far back as 1640, in a collection called *Witts Recreations*: 'His wife . . . behind him forks her fingers'.[O]

Body language shows considerable instability over time, as well as the capacity to transfer to different cultures. Even the clapping of the hands, now the traditional sign of applause, was in earlier times also a gesture of derision: Miles Coverdale translated Job, xxvii. 23 as 'Than [then] clappe men their hondes at him, yee and ieaste [jest] of him.' The King James version is rather more contemporary in its symbolism: 'Men shall clap their hands at him, and shall hiss him out of his place.' The wagging of the head was also a gesture of contempt in earler times: 'They that passed by revyled hym waggynge ther heeddes' is Tyndale's version (1526) of the mocking of Christ on the Cross. All three modes are found in the King James version of Lamentations, ii. 15: 'All that pass by clap their hands at thee; they hiss and wag their head at the daughter of Jerusalem. . . .' To *hiss* someone, incidentally, is recorded as far back as Wycliffe's translation of the Bible in 1388. In the theatre this action by an audience is known, of course, as 'getting (or being given) the bird', previously 'the big bird' (i.e. the goose), recorded as far back as 1825.[S] The verb *goose* dates from the same period, but has probably been driven out of use by the abbreviated form of rhyming slang *goose* (= *goose and duck* = *fuck*), more recently 'grope'.

Another familiar gesture of contempt is to stick out one's tongue. This is related to sticking one's tongue in one's cheek, or speaking 'tongue in cheek', recorded from *c.*1748[S], to which a derisive significance was previously attributed. The action also yielded the contemporary verb *to tongue*. (Today, of course, the idiom is metaphorical and simply denotes irony.) As with most of such behaviour, it is hard to trace its origins, but the practice probably lies behind such old corrective idioms as 'Mew thy tongue, or wee'll cut it out' (in Lyly, 1594) and to have 'a tongue too long for one's teeth' (in Barham, 1859).[O]

There seems to be virtually no record of offensive body language in the Old English records and literature which have survived, other than the aggressive shaking of a spear while uttering a battle-speech (alluded to in chapter 2). In Middle English there appears to be a similar paucity, even though we know other forms of body language (such as playing 'footsy-footsy' alluded to by Chaucer's Wife of Bath).

Some of the clearest indicators of insulting gestures emanate from the rituals of duelling. The famous exchanges of veiled provocation between the Montagu and Capulet servants in *Romeo and Juliet* provide a notable early example:

Sampson	I will bite my thumb at them; which is a disgrace to them, if they do bear it.
Abram	Do you bite your thumb at us, sir?
Sampson	I do bite my thumb, sir.
Abram	Do you bite your thumb at us, sir?
Sampson[Aside to Gregory]:	Is the law of our side if I say ay?
Gregory [Aside to Sampson]:	No.
Sampson	No, sir, I do not bite my thumb at you sir; but I bite my thumb, sir.

(*Romeo and Juliet*, I. i. 47–57)

Randle Cotgrave defined the action in his English/French Dictionary (1611) in the entry for *nique* as 'to threaten or defie by putting the thumbe naile into the mouth and with a jerke (of the upper teeth) make it to knack [make a cracking sound]'. This is quoted by the *OED*, which appends the allusion 'to give the "fico," to insult'.

FICO

Dr Johnson defines this both linguistically and physically as 'An act of contempt done with the fingers expressing "a fig for you"'. (He cites the phrase 'to give the *fico* to an adversary' from Carew.) The

OED defined the action more specifically as 'A contemptuous gesture which consisted in thrusting the thumb between two of the closed fingers or into the mouth,' comparing the whole complex with French *faire le figue*, Italian *fica* and Spanish *dar la higa* ('give the fig'). Curiously there is no reference in Grose, but Farmer and Henley carry a long, colourful derivation of the etymology from an anecdote concerning the Emperor Barbarossa and his Empress, and the 'extraction of a fig from the fundament of a mule', with allusions in Ben Jonson and other writers. One of Pistol's numerous bellicose ejaculations in *Henry V* is 'Die and be damned! and figo for your friendship', which he subsequently identifies as 'The fig of Spain!' (III. vi. 62). In another piece of typical bluster he vows, with obvious emphatic gesture:

> I speak the truth:
> When Pistol lies, do this; and fig me, like
> The bragging Spaniard
> (*Henry IV, Part II*, V. iii. 120–2)

However, the word has a confused relationship with *fig*, which in Elizabethan slang *fig* was a minced version of *fuck*. We may be sure that Charmian has this meaning in mind when says to the Soothsayer 'I love long life better than figs' (*Antony and Cleopatra*, I. i. 34).

CORNUTO

The thriving semantic history of the term and its extended family in the fifteenth and sixteenth centuries is discussed in chapter 1. During this period the word *horn* carried acute associations of cuckoldry, but neither *cornuto* nor the accompanying gesture ever conveyed anything like the same gravity of insult that surrounds them in Italy.

CONCLUSION

Body language obviously continues to supply significant forms of aggressive and insulting behaviour. While some gestures, like mooning, flashing and streaking, have no semantic extensions, others show a continuing cross-fertilization between gesture and language. Continuing the tradition of *figo* and *cornuto*, an insulting phrase such as 'Up yours!' is simply a verbalization of what the *OEDS* coyly terms 'an impolite gesture, a shortened form of "Up your arse"', itself an abbreviated imperative of 'Shove [it] up your arse!' For the uninitiated, Norman Moss's *British/American Dictionary* (1984) illustrated the difference between the British (forked fingers) and American (single finger) styles.

Appendix B
Graffiti

IT IS, perhaps, significant that the word originally existed in its singular form, *graffito* and was used mainly in contexts of antiquarianism and art history to describe a method of decoration by incising, as well as writing or drawing on a wall, of which perhaps the best known are the scribblings found in Pompeii and Rome. A caricature of Christ on the cross was found on the walls of the Domus Gelotiana on the Palatine Hill in 1856. One of the earliest records of the modern use of the term is found in 1877, when a traveller up the Nile mentions monuments which have been 'visited by crowds of early travellers who have, as usual, left their neatly-scribbled graffiti on the walls'.[O]

Graffiti, especially in its political dimension, is a new sociological phenomenon of protest, a symbolic demonstration in language which commonly exploits forms of linguistic aggression and extreme freedom in swearing. Being simultaneously public and anonymous, it forms an outlet for individual anger, humour, protest, subversiveness and wit, expressed with a gloating outrageousness.

In some ways the spray-paint can is now used with the same purpose that the pamphlet was exploited in earlier times. Previously, the bulk of the population was static, but could be reached by means of moveable type. Nowadays, with the bulk of the population commuting, it is possible to place one's message in some locale where it will perforce be seen by the commuting public. Clearly the message is highly abbreviated and reliant on slogans or succinct statement. But, being anonymous, it often employs taboo language or unconventional sentiments. Since graffiti always carries the tinge of the illicit, it can only be used for subversive views: graffiti endorsing a bank or some establishment institution would be counter-productive. The initial message is, however, itself vulnerable to subversion, since subsequent 'authors' often contribute witty put-downs of the original statement. One such instance (from a university in Germany) ran: 'FUCK THE AMERICAN WARMONGERS', to which had been added the riposte: 'I PREFER REDHEADS MYSELF.' It is a genre (if that is the right word) in which all taboos are broken.

Appendix C
The Language of Comics

SINCE the language of comics is one to which most western children are exposed, it is worth considering briefly how it has changed (or remained static) over the past few decades. Clearly, *comic* is something of a misnomer, in view of the diversity of the genre, including 'war comics', 'cowboy comics', 'adventure comics', those dealing with politics, space exploration, social questions and so on. It is useful to bring into play the perspective supplied by George Orwell's classic attack on the genre in his essay, 'Boys' Weeklies' in 1939.

Up to the past decade or so, the language remained generally sanitized. In the established English organs the occasional *heck* or *flaming* appears as a concession to changing mores, but by and large they depict a world where, in Orwell's words, 'Everything is safe, solid and unquestionable' (1958, p. 131). This insulation is even more true of America, where most comics are certified 'Approved by the Comics Code Authority'. Thus situations of conflict and discomfiture are marked, not by realistic responses from the victim, but by such tame ejaculations as *Crumbs!*, *What the . . . ? OOOF!* and *AAARGH!* Indeed, perhaps the only 'creative' area of language use in the comic genre has been the melodramatic language of impact, which has produced multitudinous echoic formations such as *WHAM!*, *BLAM!*, *KERBLAM!*, *FOOSH!*, *KACHUNG!*, *VROOM!* and *CRRAAKK!* Orwell wrote of 'the extraordinary, artificial, repetitive style, quite different from anything else now existing in English literature' (1958, p. 119).

Xenophobic stereotypes predominate. 'In the *Gem* of 1939 Frenchmen are still Froggies and Italians are still Dagoes' (1958, p. 128). Orwell sets out the standard types:

FRENCHMAN: Excitable. Wears beard, gesticulates wildly.
SPANIARD, MEXICAN, etc.: Sinister, treacherous.
ARAB, AFGHAN, etc.: Sinister, treacherous.
CHINESE: Sinister, treacherous.
ITALIAN: Excitable. Grinds Barrel-organ or carries stiletto.
SWEDE, DANE, etc.: Kind-hearted, stupid.

NEGRO: Comic, very faithful.

(1958, p. 129)

By and large, these traditions continue, though script-writers are more circumspect about using insulting racist terms.

'Sex is completely taboo, especially in the form in which it actually arises in public schools,' Orwell observed. 'Religion is also taboo; in the whole thirty years' issue [of *Gem* and *Magnet*] the word "God" probably does not occur, except in "God Save the King"' (1958, p. 121). No longer. The major development of the past decade has been the growth of 'mature' or 'adult' comics, such as *Viz*, *Crisis*, *Brain Damage* and *Gas*. These have demolished most of the older taboos. While Johnny Fartpants is hardly an anarchic character, 'Paul Whicker the tall vicar' (also of *Viz*) has been described as 'a malevolent, hard-drinking cleric who abuses his Bible class, holds "Fuck the Pope" jumble sales and tries to bribe an investigating bishop ("Never mind the bullshit Whicker, I've been hearing some complaints about you")' (D. J. Taylor, *Spectator*, 26 May 1990, p. 22). 'Sinergy' [sic] (in *Crisis* no. 46 for 22 June 1990) depicts in slow motion a gruesome revenge taken by environmentalists against the 'monstrous greed of you and your fellow bankers who have destroyed the lungs of the world'. Interwoven in the plot are sexual politics with submerged racial tensions and some explicit sex leading to this tirade from a betrayed black woman: 'Bloody ugly bitch! Cow! Whore! How could he do it with such an empty-head, no brain slut? A bimbo . . . I can feel the violence coming on!' (end of episode). Dialogue in 'For a Few Troubles More' (set in Ireland, from the same issue) contains such gems as 'it was like hooer's piss', 'sod off, y'undead bastard!', 'Ah piss off, y'oul witch!', 'Ferfrigsake, mate! She's a face on her like a well skelped arse!' and a concluding euphemism, 'Oh fug'.

In all, the comic (like the novel) is no longer a genre but a highly diversified narrative form which combines realism and fantasy in potent combinations. Its linguistic diversity reflects the familiar division in register which is apparent in many aspects of literary culture.

Epigraph Sources

Chapter	Reference
1	(i) Beckett, *Waiting for Godot*, p. 91
	(ii) Santayana, *Interpretations of Poetry and Religion*, p. 148
	(iii) Plutarch, *The Rise and Fall of Athens*, p. 307
	(vi) Quoted by Kenneth Tynan, *The Sound of Two Hands Clapping*, p. 154
2	(i) Cited in Montagu, *The Anatomy of Swearing*, p. 8
	(ii) Plutarch, *The Rise and Fall of Athens*, p. 307
	(iii) *The Daily News*, 25 June, 1904
3	(i) *Piers Plowman*, C Text, Passus ix, 1. 46
	(ii) Cited in Owst, *Literature and the Pulpit in Medieval England* (1961), p. 417
4	(i) T. Wilson, *Logicke* (1551), I. b
	(ii) R. Pecock, *The repressor of over much blaming of the clergy* (1549), I, Introduction, p. 55 (note)
5	(i) Randle Cotgrave, *A Dictionary of French & English* (1611)
	(ii) *The Boke of the Governour*, I. xxvi
	(iii) *The Tempest*, I. ii. 363–5
	(iv) *Henry V*, II. iii. 53–4
	(v) *Romeo and Juliet*, II. ii. 109–12
6	(i) 'Heraclio Democritus', *Vision of Purgatory* (1680), p. 46
	(ii) Lewis Owen, *Speculum Jesuiticum, or the Jesuites looking glasse* (1629), p. 54
	(iii) Robert Brunne, *Chronicle* (*c*.1330), p. 320
	(iv) Sir T. Munro, *Life* (1799), vol. I, p. 221
	(v) Eric Partridge, *Words, Words, Words* (1933), p. 7

7 (i) *The Spectator*, no. 531, 8 November 1711
(ii) Sheridan, *The Rivals*, II. i
(iii) Boswell, *Life of Johnson*, p. 640
(iv) Dr F. J. Furnivall addressing the Delegates of the Oxford University Press on behalf of the Philological Society in 1878. Cited in Benzie (1983), p. 105
(v) Cited in Richard Ellmann, *The Life of Oscar Wilde*, p. 171

8 (i) H. L. Mencken, *The American Language*, p. 313
(ii) E. Goodheart, 'The Rhetoric of Violence', *The Nation*, 6 April, 1970, p. 399
(iii) H. W. Haygarth, *Bush Life in Australia* (1848)

9 (i) Shaw, *Pygmalion*, Act III
(ii) Kenneth Tynan, *The Sound of Two Hands Clapping*, p. 58
(iii) W. Charles Pilley in a review of *Women in Love* in *John Bull*, 17 September, 1921
(iv) Mervyn Griffiths-Jones, for the Prosecution during the *Chatterley* trial, 1960
(v) Lillian Beckwith, *Lightly Poached*

10 (i) *Early English Miscellany*, p. 54
(ii) Susan Sontag, 'The Third World of Women', *Partisan Review* 40, 2 (1973), p. 186
(iii) Gary Taylor, *Reinventing Shakespeare* (1990)
(iv) Rosalind Coward, *New Statesman & Society*, 9 June 1989, p. 42

11 (i) 'An ancient poet' (probably fictitious) cited by Swift in the Introduction to *Polite Conversation* (1738), p. 30
(ii) Swift, Introduction to *Polite Conversation* (1738), p. 30
(iii) H. C. Wyld, *A History of Modern Colloquial English*, p. 391
(iv) Mark Lawson, 'Banned Language', *The Listener*, 30 June 1988, p. 16
(v) Antonio Machado, *Juan de Mairena*, 1943
(vi) Aldous Huxley, *The Genius and the Goddess* (1955), p. 72

Bibliography

Allen, Irving Lewis, 1983: *The Language of Ethnic Conflict*. New York: Columbia UP.

Aman, Reinhold, 1987: *The Best of Maledicta*. Philadelphia: Running Press.

Anderson, George K., 1962: *The Literature of the Anglo-Saxons*. New York: Russell and Russell.

Atwood, Margaret, 1982: *Second Words*. Boston: Beacon Press.

Aubrey, John, 1972: *Aubrey's Brief Lives*. Ed. O. L. Dick. Harmondsworth: Penguin.

Awdeley, John, 1869: *The Fraternitye of Vacabondes*. London: *EETS* no. 9. [1560–1]

Bailey, Nathaniel, 1721: *An Universal Etymological Dictionary*. London.

—— 1730: *Dictionarium Britannicum: Or a more Complete Universal Etymological English Dictionary than any Extant*. London: T. Cox.

Barber, Charles L., 1964: *The Story of Language*. London: Pan.

Barltrop, Robert, and Jim Wolveridge, 1980: *The Muvver Tongue*. London and West Nyack: Journeyman Press.

Baugh, Albert C., 1951: *A History of the English Language*. London: Routledge and Kegan Paul.

Beckett, Samuel, 1959: *Waiting for Godot*. London: Faber.

Bede, 1960: *A History of the English Church and People*. Trans. Leo Shirley-Price. Harmondsworth: Penguin.

Bennett, H. S., 1952: *English Books and Readers, 1475 to 1557*. Cambridge: CUP.

Benzie, William, 1983: *Dr. F. J. Furnivall: Victorian Scholar Adventurer*. Norman, Oklahoma: Pilgrim Press.

Bloomfield, Morton W. and L. M. Newmark, 1963: *A Linguistic Introduction to the English Language*. New York: Knopf.

Boorstin, Daniel J., 1969: *The Americans*. Harmondsworth: Penguin.

Boswell, James, 1893: *Life of Johnson*. London: Macmillan. [1791].

—— 1950: *Boswell's London Journal, 1762–3*. Ed. Frederick A. Pottle. London: Heinemann.

Bowdler, Thomas, 1818: *The Family Shakespeare*. London: Longman, Rees, Orme, Brown, and Green.

Boycott, Rosie, 1982: *Batty, Bloomers and Boycott*. London: Hutchinson.

Brandford, Jean (ed.), 1987: *A Dictionary of South African English*. 3rd edition. Cape Town: OUP.

Bréal, Michel, 1900: *Semantics: Studies in the Science of Meaning*. Trans. Mrs Henry Cust. London: Heinemann.

Brinklow, Henry, 1874: *Complaynt of Roderick Mors* and *The Lamentacyon of a Christen Agaynst the Cytye of London*. London: *EETS* no. 22. [*c.*1542 and *c.*1545]

Burchfield, Robert, 1972: 'Four-letter words and the OED'. *TLS* 13 October, p. 1233.

—— 1989: *Unlocking the English Language*. London: Faber.

Carey, Peter, 1988: *Oscar and Lucinda*. London: Faber.

Caxton, William, 1967: *Caxton's Æsop*. Ed. R. T. Lenaghan. Harvard: Harvard UP.

Cawley, A. C. (ed.), 1958: *The Wakefield Pageants in the Townley Cycle*. Manchester: Manchester UP.

Chandos, John (ed.), 1971: *In God's Name: Examples of Preaching in England 1534–1662*. London: Hutchinson.

Chapman, Robert L. 1987: *New Dictionary of American Slang*. London: Macmillan.

Chaucer, Geoffrey, 1957: *The Works of Geoffrey Chaucer*. 2nd edition by F. N. Robinson. Boston: Houghton Mifflin.

Cleland, John, 1986: *Fanny Hill: Memoirs of a Woman of Pleasure*. Craighall: Ad Donker. [1749].

—— 1969: *Memoirs of an Oxford Scholar*. London: Sphere.

Collingwood, R. G., 1938: *The Principles of Art*. Oxford: OUP.

Coombes, H., 1973: *D. H. Lawrence: A Critical Anthology*. Harmondsworth: Penguin.

Cooper, Jilly, 1981: *Class*. New York: Knopf.

Danby, John F., 1959: *Shakespeare's Doctrine of Nature*. London: Faber.

Davie, Donald, 1952: *Purity of Diction in English Verse*. London: Routledge and Kegan Paul.

Defoe, Daniel, 1951: 'A Tilt at Profanity' (1712). In William L. Payne (ed.), *The Best of Defoe's REVIEW*. New York: Columbia UP.

Dillard, J. L., 1977: *American Talk*. New York: Vintage Books.

——1985: *Toward a Social History of American English*. Berlin: Mouton.

Draper, R. P., 1970: *D. H. Lawrence: The Critical Heritage*. London: Routledge and Kegan Paul.

Dunbar, William, 1932: *The Poems of William Dunbar*. Ed. W. Mackay Mackenzie. Edinburgh: The Porpoise Press.

—— 1979: *The Poems of William Dunbar*. Ed. James Kinsley. Oxford: OUP.

Egil's Saga, 1960: Trans. Gwyn Jones. Syracuse: Syracuse UP.

Einarsson, Stefán, 1957: *A History of Icelandic Literature*. New York: The Johns Hopkins Press.

Elliott, Ralph W. V., 1959: *Runes, an Introduction*. Manchester: Manchester UP.

——1974: *Chaucer's English*. London: André Deutsch.

Ellmann, Richard, 1988: *Oscar Wilde*. Harmondsworth: Penguin.

Elman, Robert, 1975: *Badmen of the West*. London: Hamlyn.
Enright, D. J. (ed.), 1986: *Fair of Speech*. Oxford: OUP.
Farmer, John S. and William E. Henley, 1890–1904: *Slang and its Analogues, past and present*. New York: Dutton. (Subsequently reissued as *A Dictionary of Slang*.)
Flexner, Stuart Berg, 1976: *I Hear America Talking*. New York: Van Nostrand Reinhold Co.
Florio, John, 1598: *A Worlde of Wordes*. London.
Franklyn, Julian, 1961: *A Dictionary of Rhyming Slang*. 2nd edition. London: Routledge and Kegan Paul.
Furnivall, Frederick J. (ed.), 1866: *Political, Religious and Love Poems*. London: *EETS* no. 15.
Gildersleeve, Virginia Cocheron, 1908: *Government Regulation of the Elizabethan Drama*. New York: Columbia UP.
Goffmann, Erving, 1981: *Forms of Talk*. Oxford: Basil Blackwell.
Gordon, R. K., 1954: *Anglo-Saxon Poetry*. Everyman's Library, London: Dent.
Gottfreid von Strassburg, 1960: *Tristan*. Trans. A. T. Hatto. Harmondsworth: Penguin.
Graves, Robert, 1929: *Goodbye to All That*. Harmondsworth: Penguin.
—— 1936: *The Future of Swearing and Improper Language*. London: Kegan Paul, Trench, Trubner. (Originally issued in 1927 as *Lars Porsena or The Future of Swearing*.)
—— 1972: *Difficult Questions, Easy Answers*. London: Cassell.
Green, Jonathon, 1984: *Newspeak*. London: Routledge and Kegan Paul.
—— 1984: *The Dictionary of Contemporary Slang*. London: Pan.
—— 1988: *The Slang Thesaurus*. Harmondsworth: Penguin.
Greene, Robert, 1591: *A Notable Discovery of Coosnage*. London.
Greer, Germaine, 1970: *The Female Eunuch*. New York: Bantam.
Grose, Francis, [1785]: *A Classical Dictionary of the Vulgar Tongue*. London. Ed. Eric Partridge. London: Routledge, 1931, repr. 1963.
Gurr, Andrew, 1980: *The Shakespearean Stage, 1574–1642*. Cambridge: CUP.
Harris, Frank, 1966: *My Life and Loves*. London: Corgi.
Harman, Thomas, 1869: *A Caveat or Warening for Commen Cursetors, vulgarely called Vagabones*. London: *EETS* no. 9. [1567]
Heimskringla, see Snorri Sturluson
Hibbert, Christopher, 1971: *The Personal History of Samuel Johnson*. London: Longman.
Hillerbrand, Hans J., 1964: *The Reformation in its Own Words*. London: SCM Press.
Hornadge, Bill, 1980: *The Australian Slanguage*. North Ryde, NSW: Cassell Australia.
Howard, Philip, 1977: *New Words for Old*. London: Hamish Hamilton.
—— 1984: *The State of the Language: English Observed*. London: Hamish Hamilton.

—— 1985: *A Word in your Ear*. Harmondsworth: Penguin.

Huggett, Richard, 1969: *The Truth about 'Pygmalion'*. London: Heinemann.

Hughes, Geoffrey, 1988: *Words in Time*. Oxford: Basil Blackwell.

Humphries, Barry, 1988: *The Complete Barry McKenzie*. London: Methuen.

Huxley, Aldous, 1955: *The Genius and the Goddess*. London: Chatto and Windus.

Jack, R. D. S. (ed.), 1988: *The History of Scottish Literature*. vol. I. Aberdeen: Aberdeen UP.

Jennings, Gary, 1965: *Personalities of Language*. New York: Crowell.

Jespersen, Otto, 1962: *Growth and Structure of the English Language*. 9th edition. Oxford: Basil Blackwell. [1905]

Johnson, Samuel, 1755: *A Dictionary of the English Language*. London: printed by W. Strahan.

Katz, Ephraim, 1979: *The Film Encyclopaedia*. New York: Crowell.

Kermode, Frank, 1973: *Lawrence*. London: Fontana/Collins.

King, Stephen, 1979: *The Long Walk*. London: New English Library.

Kinsley James (ed.) *see* under Dunbar

Krafft-Ebing, R., 1892: *Psychopathia Sexualis*. Trans. C. G. Chaddock. Philadelphia: F. A. Davis.

Kramarae, Cheris and Paula A. Treichler, 1985: *A Feminist Dictionary*. London: Pandora.

Labov, William, 1977: *Language in the Inner City*. Oxford: Basil Blackwell.

Lakoff, Robin, 1975: *Language and Woman's Place*. New York: Harper and Row.

Latham, Aaron, 1975: *Crazy Sundays*. London: Secker and Warburg.

Lawrence, D. H., 1950: *Selected Essays*. Harmondsworth: Penguin.

—— 1960: *Lady Chatterley's Lover*. Harmondsworth: Penguin. [1928]

Leith, Dick, 1983: *A Social History of English*. London: Routledge and Kegan Paul.

Lewis, C. S., 1960: *Studies in Words*. Cambridge: CUP.

Lindesay, Sir David, 1884: *Ane Satyre of the Thrie Estates*. London: *EETS* no. 37. [1602]

Lodge, David, 1989: *Nice Work*. London: Penguin.

Mackay Mackenzie (ed.) *see* under Dunbar

Malory, Sir Thomas, 1947: *The Works of Sir Thomas Malory*. Ed. Eugene Vinaver. Oxford: OUP. [1485].

Mayhew, Henry, 1983: *London's Underworld*. Ed. Peter Quennell. London: Bracken Books.

McLeod, A. L. (ed.), 1963: *The Pattern of Australian Culture*. Ithaca: Cornell UP.

McCrum, R. *et al.*, 1986: *The Story of English*. London: Faber/BBC.

McDonald, James, 1988: *A Dictionary of Obscenity, Taboo and Euphemism*. London: Sphere.

Mencken, H. L., 1936: *The American Language*. 4th edition. New York: Knopf [1919–36].

Michel, Dan, 1886: *Ayenbite of Inwit*. London: *EETS* no. 23. [*c*.1340].

Mirk, John, 1905: *Festial*. London: *EETS* no. 96. [*c*.1450].

Montagu, Ashley, 1973: *The Anatomy of Swearing*. London and New York: Macmillan and Collier.

Moore, Harry T. (ed.), 1955: *Sex, Literature and Censorship: Essays by D. H. Lawrence*. London: Heinemann.

Mort, Simon (ed.), 1986: *Longman Guardian Original Selection of New Words*. Harlow, Essex: Longman.

Morton, James, 1989: *Low Speak*. London: Angus and Robertson.

Moss, Norman, 1984: *The British/American Dictionary*. London: Hutchinson.

Murphy, John J., 1966: *The Book of Pidgin English*. Brisbane: Smith and Paterson.

Murray, Elisabeth K. M., 1977: *Caught in the Web of Words*. New Haven and London: Yale UP.

Neale, J. E., 1958: *Essays in Elizabethan History*. London: Jonathan Cape.

Neaman, Judith S. and Carole G. Silver, 1984: *A Dictionary of Euphemisms*. Hemel Hempstead: Unwin.

Nixon, Richard, 1974: 'Transcripts of Eight Recorded Presidential Conversations,' Hearings Before the Committee on the Judiciary, House of Representatives, 93rd Congress, 2nd Session, May–June, 1974.

Njal's Saga, 1960: Trans. Magnus Magnusson and Hermann Palsson. Harmondsworth: Penguin.

Orwell, George, 1958: 'Boys' Weeklies' (1939), in *George Orwell: Selected Writings*. Ed. G. Bott. London: Heinemann.

Owst, G. R., 1961: *Literature and Pulpit in Medieval England*. 2nd edition. Oxford: Basil Blackwell.

Page, R. I., 1973: *An Introduction to English Runes*. London: Methuen.

Paros, Lawrence, 1988: *The Erotic Tongue*. London: Arlington Books.

Parran, T., 1937: *Shadow on the Land – Syphilis*. New York: Reynal and Hitchcock.

Partridge, Eric, 1933: Words, Words, Words. London: Methuen.

—— 1960: *Slang*. 3rd edition. London: Routledge and Kegan Paul [1933–50].

—— 1963: *Swift's Polite Conversation*. London: André Deutsch. [1738].

—— 1968: *Shakespeare's Bawdy*. London: Routledge and Kegan Paul. [1947].

—— 1977: *Origins*. 3rd edition. London: Routledge and Kegan Paul [1958–66].

—— 1986: *A Dictionary of Historical Slang*. (Abridged by Jacqueline Simpson) Harmondsworth: Penguin [1937–61].

Pearsall, Ronald, 1969: *The Worm on the Bud: The World of Victorian Sexuality*. London: Weidenfeld and Nicolson.

Plato, 1951: *The Symposium*. Trans. Walter Hamilton. Harmondsworth: Penguin.

Plutarch, 1967: *The Rise and Fall of Athens*. London: The Folio Society.

Potter, Simeon, 1963: *Our Language*. Harmondsworth: Penguin.

Pyles, Thomas and J. Algeo, 1970: *An Introduction to English*. New York: Harcourt, Brace.

Rabelais, Francis, 1904: *Five Books of the Lives, Heroic Deeds and Sayings of Gargantua and his son Pantagruel*. Trans. Sir Thomas Urquhart (books I and II) and Peter Antony Motteux (books III–V). London: A. H. Bullen. (1653–94]

Rawson, Hugh, 1981: *A Dictionary of Euphemisms and Other Doubletalk*. London: MacDonald.

Robertson, D. W., Jr., 1963: *Preface to Chaucer*. Princeton: Princeton UP.

Rochester, *see* Wilmot

Rolph, C. H. (ed.), 1961: *The Trial of Lady Chatterley*. Harmondsworth: Penguin.

Ross, Alan S. C., 1973: *Don't Say It*. London: Hamish Hamilton.

Salgado, Gamini (ed.), 1972: *Cony-Catchers and Bawdy Baskets*. Harmondsworth: Penguin.

Salus, Peter H. and Paul B. Taylor, 1969: *The Elder Edda*. London: Faber.

Santayana, George, 1900: *Interpretations of Poetry and Religion*. New York: Scribners.

Shakespeare, William, n.d.: *The Works of William Shakespeare*. Ed. W. J. Craig. Oxford: OUP.

Shirley, Frances A., 1979: *Swearing and Perjury in Shakespeare's Plays*. London: Allen and Unwin.

Smollett, Tobias, 1771: *The Expedition of Humphry Clinker*. London: Routledge and Sons [1894].

Snorri Sturluson, 1932: *Heimskringla, or The Lives of the Norse Kings*. Ed. E. Monsen. Cambridge: W. Heffer and Sons.

Spender, Dale, 1980: *Man Made Language*. London: Routledge.

Storr, Anthony, 1964: *Sexual Deviation*. Harmondsworth: Penguin.

Strentz, Herbert, 1989: *News Reporters and News Sources*. Ames: Iowa State UP.

Swift, Jonathan, 1925: *The Prose Works of Jonathan Swift*. London: G. Bell.

—— 1963: *A Complete Collection of Genteel and Ingenious Conversation*. Ed. Eric Partridge. London: André Deutsch. [1738].

Tacitus, Cornelius, 1964: *Tacitus on Britain and Germany*. Trans. H. Mattingly. Harmondsworth: Penguin.

Tanner, Tony, 1965: *The Reign of Wonder*. Cambridge: CUP.

Thompson, Donald F., 1935: 'The Joking relationship and Organized Obscenity in North Queensland.' In *American Anthropologist*, N.S. 37, pp. 460–90.

Todd, Loreto, 1984: *Modern Englishes: Pidgins and Creoles*. Oxford: Basil Blackwell.

Tolkien, J. R. R., 1963: 'The Monsters and the Critics' (1936). In Lewis E. Nicholson (ed.), *An Anthology of Beowulf Criticism*. Notre Dame: University of Notre Dame Press.

Trollope, Anthony, 1983: *The Prime Minister*. Ed. J. McCormick. Oxford: OUP.

Trollope, Frances, 1927: *Domestic Manners of the Americans*. London: George Routledge. [1832].

Tynan, Kathleen, 1987: *The Life of Kenneth Tynan*. London: Weidenfeld and Nicolson.

Tynan, Kenneth, 1975: *The Sound of Two Hands Clapping*. London: Jonathan Cape.

Ullmann, Stephen, 1951: *Words and Their Use*. London: Frederick Muller.

—— 1962: *Semantics: An Introduction to the Science of Meaning*. Oxford: Basil Blackwell.

—— 1964: *Language and Style*. Oxford: Basil Blackwell.

Vico, Giambattista, 1948: *The New Science*. Trans. Thomas G. Bergin and M. H. Fish. Ithaca: Cornell UP.

Wilmot, John, Earl of Rochester, 1984: *Poems*. Ed. Keith Walker. Oxford: Basil Blackwell.

Woolf, Rosemary, 1968: *English Religious Lyric in the Middle Ages*. Oxford: OUP.

Wyld, Henry Cecil, 1936: *A History of Modern Colloquial English*. Third edition. Oxford: Basil Blackwell.

Subject Index

Word Index